Coming, Ready or Not!

This book is dedicated to the memory of my dear Uncles, "Our" Alf and "Violet's Alf", Ted, George, and Len – with respect, affection, and gratitude for all of life's chances.

"Belief in a myth will permit the faithful to discount reality." Dr.Heinz Redwood.

"The problems [which social scientists] try to answer arise only in so far as the conscious action of many men produce undesigned results, in so far as regularities are observed which are not the result of anybody's design. If social phenomena showed no order except in so far as they were consciously designed, there would indeed be no room for theoretical sciences of society...It is only in so far as some sort of order arises as a result of individual action but without being designed by any individual that a problem is raised which demands a theoretical explanation." Friedrich von Hayek.

"I praise God and ever shall, It is the sheep has paid for all." Anon.

"Man must choose whether to be rich in things or in the freedom to use them." Ivan Illich.

"The first step in the evolution of ethics is a sense of solidarity with other human beings." Albert Schweitzer.

"One of the main deformations in all thought about the past is the assumption that what did happen had to happen and that the attitude of men involved in an unresolved matter conforms with the judgement and perceptions of those wise after the event." Hugh Ross Williamson.

"There is someone who is cleverer than Voltaire, cleverer than Bonaparte, cleverer than any of the Directors, than any Minister in the past or in the future; and that person is everybody [tout le monde]. To engage, or at least to persist, in a struggle in which you may find everybody interested on the other side is a mistake, and nowadays all political mistakes are dangerous." Duff Cooper.

"Public policy, stripped to its basics, is a choice among value alternatives. What one person will vehemently contend is the correct policy and another will say is wrongheaded will not depend on empirical measurement, but on the persons' values, philosophy, and ideology." John Kasarda.

*"Acts of injustice done
Between the setting and the rising sun
In history lie like bones, each one."* W.H. Auden.

"It is the diligent hand and head alone that maketh rich – in self-culture, growth in wisdom, and in business." – Samuel Smiles.

"...buck rabbits won't dig. Not can't – won't." Richard Adams.

'Coming, Ready or Not!'
The Realities, the Politics, and the Future of the NHS.

Reflections on the potential of consumer power to renovate health care.

John Spiers

Professorial Research Fellow, The Global Policy Institute, London Metropolitan University.

Lately, Visiting Professor, School of Humanities and Social Studies, University of Glamorgan.

Formerly Member of the Board of the National Care Standards Commission, and of the executive of the National Association of Health Authorities and Trusts.

Also Chairman, Brighton Health Authority, Brighton Health Care NHS Trust, the South East Thames NHS Management College, and The Patients Association.

Previously a Senior Visiting Fellow and Head of Health Care Studies at the Institute of Economic Affairs, London.

Founding Chairman of Civitas, and a founding member of the Advisory Council of Reform.

With a foreword by Professor Philip Booth, Editorial & Programme Director, Institute of Economic Affairs, & Professor of Finance, Public Policy and Ethics, St. Mary's University, Twickenham.

EER
Edward Everett Root, Publishers. Brighton, 2016.

Edward Everett Root, Publishers, Co. Ltd.,
30 New Road, Brighton, Sussex, BN1 1BN, England.

edwardeverettroot@yahoo.co.uk

Public Policy Series, No.1.

© John Spiers, 2016.

John Spiers has asserted his right under the Copyright, Designs and Patents Act 1998 to be identified as the author of this work.

www.eerpublishing.com

All rights reserved. No part of this publication may be reproduced, stored in a retrieval system or transmitted, in any form or by any means, electronic, mechanical, photocopying, recording or otherwise, without the prior permission of the copyright owner.

Hardback ISBN: 978-1-911204-03-9
Paperback ISBN: 978-0-954-2075-19
eBook ISBN: 978-0-954-2075-95

Typeset by the author in Book Antiqua.
Designed by Pageset Limited, High Wycombe, Buckinghamshire.
Printed and bound by CPI Group (UK) Ltd, Croydon, Surrey.

Contents

The author ix

By the same author xi

Acknowledgements xiii

Foreword by Professor Philip Booth xv

Stop press on Cancer services xvii

Introduction xxi

PART ONE:

1. "Coming, ready or not!" The realities, the politics, and the future of the NHS 1
2. The Great Divide. What you believe if you are a centraliser and a statist. What you believe if you are a dynamist 25
3. Beware 'Choice'! 39
4. How to make the market? 53
5. Practising being practical 63
6. The moral approach of the radical right 65
7. Incentives, and the problem of knowledge 69
8. Berlin's Two Concepts of Order 87
9. The radical agenda now 89
10. No Master Plan 93
11. What's in the way of change? 101
12. Abolish the customer? Or, safe in *whose* hands? 111
13. Tell me, doctor, what *will* make choice real? 117

PART TWO:

14. 'Only half way to paradise'? Social enterprise initiatives: the opportunity, the challenge, and the deficits of individual empowerment 135
15. Money is not enough. Or, why Mr. Brown's approach cannot work 143
16. Inside-out. Or, the contradictions revealed by present policies 157

17. History as it might have been. And Might Still Be. Labour's opportunity for Health Care Reform 167

18. Illustrating Liberty. The cases of Miss B, & of MMR. 197

19. Is choice disempowering? 207

20. The 'My Daughter' test. Championing the patient 213

21. Uncurling the rope 219

22. Right Place, Right time. The relevance of NHS estate management to advancing the reforms. Or, How many beans make five? 227

PART THREE:

23. No More Soviet 'Akademogorok.' Or, Stop Taking the Medicine from Dr. Marx 235

24. Sidney Webb, 'self-deadness', & the NHS 245

25. Open Sesame! Derek Wanless and the *official* revelation of crisis in health care 261

26. Working practises in the medical profession. The *Health Service Journal/ Glaxo Debate, 23 May 1995* 271

AN ENTERTAINMENT [?]:

27. Whatever Can We Do With The Kids Today? The 'Heritage Hospital Experience.' A Bank Holiday treat 277

THE KEY MESSAGE:

28. Changing the rules, to achieve change 297

IN CONCLUSION:

29. Conclusion 305
30. Finale 319

The author

Professor John Spiers has had an unusual career. He took a First Class Honours degree in History at the University of Sussex. While a graduate student there he founded The Harvester Press, the scholarly book publishing firm. He has been innovative entrepreneur, company executive, author and an adviser to government. He built his firm from scratch, founding it at age 28. The firm won the Queen's Award for Export Achievement in 1986, being only the third publishing firm to have done so then. He has since held national appointments in healthcare, education and the arts, and he has played a leading part in healthcare studies in several national 'think-tanks', including the Institute of Economic Affairs, The Social Market Foundation, the Centre for Policy Studies, Reform, and he was the founding Chairman of Civitas (to which he gave its name) in 2000.

John is a well-known independent speaker and writer on healthcare, on which he has lectured in Britain, America, Asia, Australia, and in Europe. He is not a member of a political party. He was for a number of years a Visiting Senior Fellow at the Institute of Economic Affairs in Westminster, specialising in healthcare policy. He served there as Head of Healthcare Studies. He was also a member of Prime Minister John Major's Citizen's Charter Advisory Panel concerned with exploring measures of specific standards of service to consumers. He served as Chairman of Brighton Health Authority, Brighton Health Care Trust, the NHS South East Region Management Centre, and The Patients Association, whose re-launch he led in 1995. He is a Fellow of the Royal Society of Arts. He was joint Chairman of Arts for Health.

In 2001 he was a founder member of the Advisory Council of Reform, the national think-tank. He was Health Policy Adviser to The Social Market Foundation, and Chairman of The Health Policy Committee of The Centre for Policy Studies. He was an executive member of the National Association of Health Authorities and Trusts, and in 1999 was an Adjunct Scholar at The Cascade Policy Institute, Portland, Oregon studying American healthcare policy.

He is now a Professorial Research Fellow at The Global Policy Institute, London Metropolitan University. Between 1998 and 2013 John was a Visiting Professor at the University of Glamorgan, initially in the Business School and then in Humanities and Social Studies. He is a Senior Research Fellow in the Institute of English Studies, University of London, where has published books on English Literature and publishing history. He was recently appointed to the External Advisory Board of the new Centre for Book History at Bangor University. He is also a Visiting Fellow in the Ruskin Programme at the University of Lancaster, and has served as a Trustee of the Ruskin Foundation, responsible for John Ruskin's property, 'Brantwood', at Coniston Water.

He was appointed in 2001 to the Board of the new National Care Standards Commission, on which he served until 2004.

COMING, READY OR NOT!

John once toured The Royal Sussex County Hospital at Brighton in a wheelchair (and with a wheelchair-bound woman patient and her virtually blind husband) to dramatise what he called 'the invisible hospital'. This is the one which managers too often overlook but which is often the awkward and unwelcoming reality for patients. This tour promoted user-friendly access, although it made him unpopular with local consultants.

He appointed the first-ever Patient's Advocate in an NHS Hospital, in 1991. He gave the Patient's Advocate direct access to himself and to other executives. She successfully provided information as well as listening, acting as a messenger within the system, mediating in disputes and trying to solve problems – as well as seeking to prevent their recurrence. This became a model for the NHS. However, it also underlined the need for financial empowerment of the individual.

He also established the first Clinical Performance Improvement Unit in an NHS Hospital, in 1993. But he was criticised by consultants at Brighton for his comments on very poor UK cancer care.

By the same author

The Re-Discovery of George Gissing. [with Pierre Coustillas], London: National Book League, 1971.

The Underground and Alternative Press in Britain. Brighton: The Harvester Press, 1974.

'Things to Fix', An initiative using the best ideas of Brighton Health care staff to help patients, staff and the organisation. Brighton: Brighton Health Care NHS Trust; 1994 [with Pauline Sinkins].

The Invisible Hospital and the Secret Garden. An Insider's Commentary on the NHS Reforms. Oxford: Radcliffe Medical Press/London: Institute of Health Services Management, 1995.

An Innocent Elopement. Patients and Empowerment. [Lecture], London: The Patients Association, 1996.

Sense and Sensibility in Health Care. [co-author], edited by Marshall Marinker. London: British Medical Journal Publishing, 1996.

Who Owns Our Bodies? Making Moral Choices in Health Care. Oxford: Radcliffe Medical Press/Southampton: Institute for Health Policy Studies, 1997.

User Involvement in Health Care – What Next? London: Association of Charitable Foundations 4th Annual Lecture on Philanthropy, 1997.

Dilemmas in Modern Health Care. [editor], London: Social Market Foundation/Profile Books, 1997.

'If this is a question, is this an answer? Patients and empowerment: first principles, moral problems, and patient benefit.' In Tom Ling, editor, *Reforming Healthcare by Consent.* Oxford: Radcliffe Medical Press, 1999.

The Realities of Rationing. 'Priority setting' in the NHS. London: Institute of Economic Affairs, 1999.

Socialised Medicine in Great Britain: Lessons for the Oregon Plan. Address to the Cascade Policy Institute, Portland, Oregon, 1999.

'Safe in *whose* hands? Effective consumer power in health care.' In Edward Vaizey, editor, *The Blue Book On Health.* London: Politicos, 2002.

Patients, Power, and Responsibility, The First Principles of Consumer-driven Reform. Oxford: Radcliffe Medical Press in association with the Institute of Economic Affairs, 2003.

Who Decides Who Decides? Enabling choice, equity, access, improved performance and patient guaranteed care. Oxford: Radcliffe, In Association with The Institute of Economic Affairs, 2008.

Gissing and the City. Cultural Crisis and the Making of Books in Late Victorian England. [editor], Houndsmills, Hants.: Palgrave Macmillan, 2006.

The Culture of the Publishers' Series [editor], 2 vols. Houndsmills, Hants.: Palgrave Macmillan, 2011.

Serious about Series: American cheap libraries, British railway libraries, and some literary series of the 1890s. London, Institute of English Studies, 2007; second edition, Brighton, Edward Everett Root, 2015.

By Book or By Crook. The Secret History of a Victorian Publisher [R.E.King], in preparation.

The Publisher who Shaped the Future. George Routledge and British Publishing, in preparation.

Alfred John Root. Land of Promise! The Memoirs of an Edwardian North London Boy [editor], 3 vols., in preparation.

Acknowledgements

We each rely on one another in the journey of life for all the help we need. My many scholarly debts are acknowledged in my foot-notes. I am very grateful to my friend and colleague Professor Philip Booth for contributing his Foreword, and for all his encouragement and support for my work.

My greatest personal debts are to my family: to my Mother, Kate Spiers [*nee* Root], to My Grandmother, Kate Root [*nee* Warren], and to my Uncles Alfred John Root, Edward Everett Root, Alfred Hackett, George William Webber, and Leonard Warren – the dedicatees of this book. My wife Leigh has always encouraged my work, and renewed my self-belief in darker moments. I owe much, too, to my early inspirational teachers – particularly to the remarkable Mr. Morley Gayton, to the supportive and skilled Mr. T. D. Powell Davies, and to Phyllis Oliver. These first taught me the value of historical thought and its principles at Red Hill School, East Sutton.

I am also indebted to Mr. John Jones, Mr. Bob Payne, Mr. Lawrence Lowe, and Mr. Dipak Nandy. So, too, my thanks to my Headmaster, Mr. Otto L. Shaw JP, and to Mr. J. J. N. McGurk, the historian who taught me later at Catford. My teachers at the University of Sussex, including Professor Lord Asa Briggs, Professor Donald Winch, Dr. Stephen Yeo, Dr. Peter Burke, Professor E.P. Hennock, Professor L .D. Lerner, Dr. Cedric Watts and Dr. Geoff Walker, who were a truly remarkable group in those pioneering inter-disciplinary days. My later academic colleagues at the University of Glamorgan – especially Professor Michael Connolly and Professor Rod Dubrow-Marshall – have given me much support, whilst not necessarily agreeing with me.

Important supporters, friends, and influences on my work, as I have mentioned, have been Professor Philip Booth and the late Arthur Seldon at the Institute of Economic Affairs. My friends Roy Lilley, the late John Simmonds, the late Dr. William Pickering, and Professor David Marsland of Brunel University have helped me shape my ideas through their own work and in our discussions over more than 25 years. When I was the local NHS chairman at Brighton Mrs. Margaret Dann was always a wise and special supporter. My friend Professor Karol Sikora has been an inspiration for many years, and he kindly wrote a Foreword to one of my earlier books, *Patients, Power and Responsibility. The First Principles of Consumer-driven Reform*.

A great stimulus to keep going, and to continue to press for liberty, choice, self-responsibility and change, continues to be provided by the adherence to public-sector myths, the fog and muddle, the evasions and half-truths of official policies offered by each of the leading British political parties. Acceptance of the unreformed NHS (like the BBC) remains the default position of all leading political parties, despite the actual observable results. We are all the losers.

JS.

Foreword by Professor Philip Booth

When somebody in Britain is treated and cured of some ailment, they often praise the NHS. "Thank goodness for the NHS, they might say", as if, somehow, treatment and recovery would have been impossible without the NHS. This is strange because very few countries have healthcare systems that are completely financed and controlled by central government and yet, not only do people get treated for and recover from ailments in other countries, health provision tends to be better. For example, in Holland and Germany there is little central planning of health provision, yet nobody talks about waiting lists and the whole process of providing healthcare more or less circumvents politicians. But, the outcomes within such systems are better – much better.

This bizarre elevation of the status of the NHS, so that people tend to talk about health provision in the UK as if they would not get care if they lived elsewhere, tends to be replicated when people think about healthcare through time. Perhaps this was illustrated most vividly at the opening ceremony for the 2012 Olympic Games when "NHS" was flashed up in huge letters. Ironically, the hospital that was used to celebrate the NHS was founded well before the NHS was created. And there were dancing nurses in clean, smart uniforms that have been abolished by the NHS to give way to attire more suitable for completing paperwork and attending meetings.

In fact, healthcare was provided very effectively before the NHS. There were certainly gaps in provision, especially amongst the non-working population who were often not insured. But such gaps could have been filled using mechanisms more like those developed in the rest of Europe instead of creating a nationalised system that, sadly, does not deliver.

In other European healthcare systems, the patient has power and choice. In the UK, people cannot improve their health provision by choosing a different provider that better meets their needs. Instead, they have to work through the political process by exercising "voice". This leads to the needs and wants of politicians, providers and campaigners being met rather than the needs and wants of patients. In particular, the articulate triumph over the rest.

John Spiers, in this excellent book, demonstrates from his own practical experience how the NHS is failing and how it has been captured by its bureaucracy and producer interests. There is not necessarily a deliberate attempt by administrators, politicians and doctors to run the system for their own benefit, but a mechanism has been created whereby it is almost impossible for producer groups to discover and deliver the preferences of the people who use the service.

The author also brings out important moral objections to a completely state-funded and state-controlled health service. Essentially, the NHS removes from individuals the ability to make choices about some of the most intimate and important aspects of their lives. It should be possible for families to choose between a range of commercial, mutual, civil society and religious institutions when it comes to healthcare. They also ought to be able to make decisions about the kind of healthcare they receive – do they wish to have a provider who will provide excellent personal care during a terminal illness or a provider well known for treating patients with all the latest technology? Does a particular family wish to pay for access to invasive reproductive treatment or would they prefer a package that provides more natural forms of assistance with fertility? These are personal and, often, ethical decisions and the state has no right to take them on our behalf except in very particular circumstances.

Of course, there is a strong argument that the state should ensure that nobody should go without healthcare, but this does not mean that the state should finance and provide all healthcare.

Not everybody will accept all the arguments in this book. Indeed, I do not agree with the case that is made for euthanasia. I believe that choice in healthcare is essential for human dignity. Being able to make such choices is essential to what it means to be human. However, to take choices that end the possibility of all choice or to turn the providers of care into those who actively bring an end to life, has moral and practical consequences which I cannot accept.

Nevertheless, John Spiers' arguments in this book are compelling. Change will come to health provision in the UK whether or not producer interests are ready. Technology will transform care in the future in ways that may entirely bypass traditional providers. However, policy changes that put the patient in charge and ensure that providers respond to the patient rather than the other way round, are necessary if we are to get the most out of the coming revolution.

In a bean counting kind of way, the NHS is regarded as reasonably efficient by international standards. However, it is not serving those whom it is meant to serve by providing families with the care that they want in comfortable and humane circumstances. As such, it cannot be thought of as efficient by any reasonable economic metric. Certainly, according to the international studies, it fails when it comes to preventable deaths arising from treatable conditions.

As with all nationalised industries, the NHS provides us with less for a given amount of money. Healthcare is too important a service for this to be a tolerable situation any longer. The time has come to promote freedom of choice and the freedom of providers to respond to the needs of patients. John Spiers makes that case very well. It is now time for the politicians to respond.

Philip Booth BA PhD FIA FSS
Editorial and Programme Director, Institute of Economic Affairs,
& Professor of Finance, Public Policy and Ethics, St. Mary's University,
Twickenham

Stop press on Cancer services

There is much in this book about inadequate cancer services in the UK.

As we go to press, the *Daily Telegraph* reported (31 July, 2015) the wonder of a golf-ball sized artificial heart implanted for the first time, by a surgeon, Professor Stephen Schueler, at the Freeman Hospital, Newcastle-on-Tyne. *And* – nationally – that Britain is still experiencing very poor cancer care. Britain is eighth from bottom in league table comparisons of cancer survival in 35 Western countries, latest research from the OECD shows. We are on a par with Poland and Estonia.

The system here fails many, and for reasons which easily could be much better managed. The newspaper reported under the headline "Cancer patients only sent for tests after three visits to doctor." A quarter of cancer patients were dissatisfied with their care, and were losing faith in their doctor, said scientists from University College, London and the University of Cambridge. They studied data from 70,000 patients, and found that of the 60,000 people who were diagnosed by their GP, nearly 13,300 had been seen two or three times *before* they were referred for cancer tests. More than one in 10 felt that information had been deliberately withheld from them during their treatment.

On 5 September 2015 *The Times* reported under the headline "Outrage as NHS cuts funding for dozens of cancer drugs." The *Daily Telegraph* also reported the story. Thousands of cancer patients are to be denied life-extending drugs as the NHS's Cancer Drugs Fund (set-up by David Cameron in 2011) has too little money to meet demands. The Fund is to axe 25 treatments in England. This comes on top of cuts earlier this year, and is likely to halve the number of patients benefiting from the Fund. The Rare Cancers Foundation estimated that *another* 5,500 patients a year – with late-stage breast cancer, bowel cancer, and other diseases – will miss out on the treatments already affected by the cull last January. That removed 25 of 84 treatments. It has already affected treatments for 5,000 patients.

These are indeed sweeping restrictions, under budgetary pressures. And as other innovatory cancer drugs become available the situation can only worsen, unless the NHS shifts to a much broader funding basis. The drugs which will now not be funded include Kadcyla and Avastin for breast cancer, Revlimid and Immovid for myeloma, and Abraxane – the only cancer drug on the list for pancreatic cancer. They all work well for many patients. And, bizarrely, many remain available in Scotland and in Wales (which receive large tax-transfers from England). Negotiations continue between government and the pharmaceutical companies, who should be encouraged to continue to innovate.

Diagnosis is unsatisfactory in many cases in the UK, too. Here, patients themselves are in part to blame for not consulting earlier. Almost half of cancers in the UK are diagnosed at an advanced stage, when treatment is less likely to work.

COMING, READY OR NOT

On 5 August 2015 the *Daily Mail* reported that cancer survival rates in England lag well behind others in the West, despite millions being spent on diagnosis and treatment. Patients here are more likely to die of the six most common types of cancer than those in Australia, Canada, Sweden and Norway. In some cases survival rates are a third lower than the best performing countries. And even though there has been some improvement, researchers say that it will take years before government strategies can offer patients the best scans, drugs, and surgical procedures. This itself seems far too optimistic, unless the funding structure broadens, for at present the government cannot pay for drugs that work and can be available, so how will they afford the next generation of innovations?

The study reported in August 2015 was undertaken on behalf of Cancer Research UK by the London School of Hygiene and Tropical Medicine. See the full research report published in the *British Journal of Cancer*. [**British Journal of Cancer** online publication 30 June 2015; doi: 10.1038/bjc.2015.164.].

The researchers looked at cancer survival rates for six types of cancer, in England, Australia, Canada, Denmark, Norway and Sweden. The result are truly shocking. With the exception of Denmark, England's figures are the worst for all types. And especially so for lung-cancer where five-year survival rates are 12.7% in England, compared with 17.3% in Canada.

Only 20.7% of patients diagnosed with stomach cancer in England can expect to survive for five years, a third lower than the 27.9% rate in Australia. England lags more than a decade behind, the figures show. For ovarian cancer the five-year survival rate is 35.2% – lower than that achieved by the other nations except Denmark in 1999.

For breast-cancer five-year survival rates in England have improved, from 81.1% in 2004 to 84% in 2009. This reflects the major new emphasis on the condition, and new investment. But even then the five-year survival rate remains behind the 86.2% of both Australia and Sweden.

Why is all this so? The reasons include patients being unaware of symptoms. Misdiagnosis by GPs is also a factor. And some/many patients may not have been offered the most effective forms of surgery or the latest drugs. There is also much variation across the country.

In 2011 the government set aside a £200 million annual budget aiming to ensure that cancer patients were not denied drugs on cost grounds. This was a significant advance. But, consistently overspent, the fund rose to £340 million in January 2015. Before the September 2015 decision to limit access to more of the effective cancer drugs the Fund's costs were predicted to reach £410 million this year. And as more of us live longer, while other new drugs also arise from the work of researchers, what will the Fund need to be? How will the money be found? In addition, other unavoidable NHS costs also multiply. For example, what will be the cost of the planned changes to consultant contracts for weekend working in hospitals, to act on the 11,000 or so estimated by a new study in the *British Medical*

Journal (supported by a separate study by the Royal College of surgeons) as dying unnecessarily because of weekend failures in care? There is much to do to bring standards up to what is normal overseas. But other countries – with a broader funding approach – will also continue to improve services and access, too. Meanwhile, is the NHS to continue to be entirely tax-based, and with no specific economic incentives for individuals to act self-responsibility too, helping to reduce the need for care and the demand for it?

It is difficult for me to forebear to ask the following two questions: "What might be so very different now if the politicians and the doctors endorsed a much broader financial base for the NHS, observed why and how overseas countries organise funding, where patients do so much better? And if they also saw the likely developments ahead? If at Brighton and elsewhere, too, the senior consultants who rebelled in 1994 had also listened to me about the very serious shortfalls in cancer care in the UK in the 1990s, and given me backing to enlarge this debate about overseas examples when compared with the many avoidable deaths in the UK. That backing was much needed. We still have to confront the problems and the challenges today. Life is about improvement. We should act for radical changes in funding and in management.

JS, 7 September, 2015.

Introduction

I hope to persuade the reader that the best possible means by which to deliver what the NHS set out to do is to give every individual financial power by introducing a Health Savings Account, tax-based, and with incentives to top-up too. For the NHS desperately needs a much broader financial base. We must deliver choice, equity, access, improved performance and patient guaranteed care. We lack competiveness, in both purchasing and provision, yet this is essential to encourage innovation, and to lift all eyes and thus all boats.

These are all significant deficits at present. None of the other existing proposals for change address them.

I hope to persuade politicians to argue in vibrant language in favour of the liberal, adaptive, capitalist, free market, where we produce all of the wealth which pays for all services. And to protect competition so that we do genuinely address the deficits.

Here, as I have written previously, "Money talks, and Preference Walks."

And as Robert Burns wrote of money the purpose is:

> "Not for to hide it in a hedge,
> Nor for a train attendant,
> But for the glorious privilege,
> Of being independent."

First, doctors, nurses, and other health professionals. We need them to lead and to work for change.

We are fortunate that there are very many such who are outstanding, deeply committed, caring, and skilled. Many, too, are unusually able communicators. But they, like patients, suffer in an under-funded, over-pressured system – which (alas) their own Trade Union, the BMA has helped to create by its stubborn resistance to change. Neither they nor we can much longer stand the cracks and collapses of the present NHS state-monopoly and entirely tax-underfunded system.

When you are ill you want to see a doctor, not a manager. So we need to do much more to enable good health professionals to help us, and to have better lives themselves. Presently, work-pressures and morale are all problematic. Many doctors are retiring early, too, fleeing this hopeless and demoralising situation. This is a dangerous position, and one for which genuine radical change to funding, purchasing and provision is an essential and urgent next step.

My hope is that this book may make some contribution to encouraging politicians to address these issues frankly. And that they should make the clear argument, with eloquence and persistence, for the liberal free capitalist market, which does more for 'ordinary' people than any other social mechanism. But which remains a major deficit in our provision of good healthcare and of better education too. I offer an alternative to the received default position – surprisingly, still accepted by Conservatives as well as the left – that the NHS is the best approach to care. It remains unlike any system adopted anywhere else in the world. We need to ask why. Politicians need to lead opinion, to shift public perceptions, and to outline the genuine and deliverable benefits of alternatives. Health professionals, too, need to collaborate with these changes.

This book offers a number of entirely new studies concerned with releasing individual economic power in the hands of all consumers, and providing direct economic incentives for reform of the NHS. These new essays also give me the opportunity to print some earlier pieces, including some talks to medical professionals and to NHS managers.

All are concerned with the underlying principles and the actions necessary for successful change. They are vignettes about principles, problems, and policies. They deal with issues in *current* debate in 2015. And this, despite the earlier dates of some of these pieces, the issues remain astonishingly current, and either unaddressed or unresolved. Indeed, depressingly so.

Technology is the key to social change. Information can have an explosive impact. And it is the Internet, Facebook, Twitter, &c. which are changing public knowledge, and prompting much new questioning. Information is an entity in itself, a violently explosive force. People are reading and talking, and observing the NHS and the alternatives. This is giving politicians a push down what will be a long hard road. Hallelujah!

I had intended to publish all of these pieces earlier, but instead circulated dittoed copies to some friends and colleagues, in what I suppose might count as a first edition of sorts. I am still asked for copies of some of the earlier pieces and I take this opportunity to bring them together in this more permanent form.

I publish now even if a Conservative-Liberal Democratic Coalition government was elected in 2010, and even though a Conservative government succeeded this problematic coalition in 2015. Perhaps [?] some attempt at some revisionist NHS reform is in progress, albeit without passing individual financial control to the consumer. This, too, despite the incessant claims by politicians to pass power back to 'the people.' The basic principles of self-responsibility – and of direct economic incentives for changed personal behaviour – each remain fundamentally relevant. It is these foundations which would be the best direct incentive and guide to self-responsibility in the individual, and good access to reliable and effective specific and individualised or personalised services. All that I have written thus far remains relevant because none of the fundamentals have changed at all.

Above all, we need a smaller government which protects and directly encourages competition. Together with direct economic incentives to influence behaviours.

Overall, I make the cohesive argument that if we are to cope with the many

INTRODUCTION

pressures of an ageing population, rising costs and new expectations – and to take the many opportunities for personalised care from the genomic revolution, new drugs and new inter-active technologies – we need very large reforms. These inexorable pressures and demands on the creaking system are indeed all *Coming, Ready or Not!* For the pressures for change are ineluctable. As, indeed, are the opportunities. Successful reforms will necessarily depend on direct individual financial incentives, and on the NHS itself being prepared to change. On people accepting a shifting role, and on staff being granted *permission* to change. *Competition* will be crucial if we are to shift the stone.

The issues are cultural as much as political. Structures are cultural. A viable, evolving, market-based system is possible only if direct incentives and rewards are introduced to alter cultures, and only then if people willingly endorse change. All this necessarily includes major revisions to attitudes as well as to cultures, institutional structures and systems. That is, if services are indeed to respond to the personalised preferences of individual consumers. And if these services are to change for better individual outcomes, to enhance personal self-responsibility and to achieve greater productivity and cost effectiveness too.

All this will only really be meaningful if we do indeed link it to specific and individual economic incentives and levers by which it can be individually effective. If we wish to modernise the NHS and social care, to encourage much more self-responsibility, to financially empower individual 'choice', to broaden the financial base, and to benefit from competition, then there are specific policy recommendations which should form a new framework.

First, however, let me say something about the digital revolution, which is the greatest force driving the train which is indeed *Coming, Ready or Not!*

Technology is the greatest force for social change. And all our lives are now pivoting on it. New digital chronology is fundamental to networking, which is itself changing patient's wishes, knowledge, and expectations. In terms of networking, the future is of countless blogs, websites, discussion forums and *local* sources of online information together with *international* comparisons. These now include many sites which are generated by users, and the political demand for information from doctors and from the Royal Colleges will be unstoppable. As so it should be.

Computers – and robots – are going to continue to improve exponentially, and to do new and unprecedented things, not least the capture and exchange of unprecedented personal information. Digital information is exponential, and combinatorial. Computers will be on the side of the consumer of services. This is the modern drumbeat to which doctors must listen.

As we know, the key building blocks are already in place. And processing speeds, storage capacity, download speed and the range of complex tasks easily discharged will add exponentially to our opportunities. Rapid and accelerating digitization will continue to change everything. And we are only at the beginning. It will capture and create value. It will reveal and unfold new bounties and much more freedom of choice. All the digitised information is now being sent over networks, compared and contrasted by consumers, and used in purchasing and treatment decisions which they are taking for themselves.

In all our lives digital technology makes available massive bodies of relevant information, and results from the NHS and from doctors cannot be excluded.

We are at what technologists call an 'inflection point.' Digitization increases knowledge, understanding, and action. And people anywhere can access data, consider it, take advice, consider the problems, and make a personal decision about their own preferred solution.

Doctors should welcome all this, too. For IBM estimates that it would now take a human doctor up to 160 hours a week reading the literature just to keep up with new material. Only computers can now cover all the new medical information in many clinical journals, report a summary which is relevant to a particular specialist – as well as help a doctor match a patient's symptoms, medical history and test results with current knowledge. Together they can then formulate both a good diagnosis and a modern and individualised treatment plan.

Already, I read in Erik Brynjolfsson and Andrew McAfee, *The Second Machine Age. Work, Progress, and Prosperity in A Time of Brilliant Technologies* (New York and London, 2014) that the number of digital pages and images on the Web exceeds one trillion. And children with smartphones today have access to more information in real time via the mobile web than the President of the USA had 20 years ago! This information is available today for free, together with over 1 million apps on smartphones.

Last year users collectively spent 20 million hours EACH day just on Facebook – much of the time creating content for other users to consume. As we are told by Brynjolfsson and McAfee, that's ten times as many person-hours as it took to build the entire Panama Canal.

There are apparently 43,200 hours of new YouTube videos created every day. At the last estimate, which is probably seriously lower than the daily truth now. Google fields well over 100 billion queries a month. There are more than 250 million new photos uploaded every day on Facebook. There are hordes of user reviews on Amazon, TripAdvisor and Yelp. Facebook reached a billion users in 2012. The numbers must be vastly higher now. And electronic devices are deliberately designed so that users can add value for other users to access. They deliver huge amounts of data continuously. Why not about the results from all doctors and medical teams, adding this to our collective wealth? Will this not increase choice, and improve quality?

As Brynjolfsson and McAfee argue, *most of the digital gains are ahead of us!*

In the past 2 years the planet has added more computer power than it did in all previous history. Over the next 24 years, they say, the increase will likely be over a

INTRODUCTION

thousand-fold. They suggest that our generation is likely to experience two of the most amazing historical events: the creation of true machine intelligence, and the connection of all humans via a common digital network. This will transform the planet's economics. And so the bounty of new technologies is spreading everywhere.

How can – and why should – doctors hide their results? And limit global feedback? Or discourage and prevent information flows? It will surely be widely disseminated, newly focussed and precise, and the basis of individual decision-making about ourselves. This will be the best kind of unforced equality.

Digital models of learning and teaching are an essential opportunity. Such innovations will surely improve standards, require re-training where quality was inadequate, and oblige managements to re-examine decision-making authority, governance systems, recruitment, incentive systems, information flows, hiring and training and many other aspects of organisational processes. Quite right, too, for such changes can generate many productivity improvements and quality gains. And the second and third-best will have to get their acts together.

Digital oversight will ensure what we have not thus far been able to achieve with the NHS. It will reveal for all to see *relative* performance, and measured against *absolute* standards. This will impact on individual doctor and NHS Trust earnings. Standards will have a new and transparent importance. For patients will surely prefer to be treated by those with the best proven quality, even within the capacity constraints of the existing NHS.

The best performers, too, should be given the opportunity to expand their facilities – attracting willing individual revenues from Health Savings Accounts – while the less good performers will face harsh competition. And in a digital economy the poor performers, who kill people now, will no longer be able to hide behind consumer ignorance, geographical barriers, or incantatory professional obfuscations. Consumer ratings will chase them in public. Differences in quality, convenience, attitude and price will really matter, as they should.

With a few clicks, over 2 million books can now already be found and purchased on the net. But aren't your medical and clinical prospects as important? Why not information for free here about the results individual doctors and clinical teams achieve in the NHS? What if we had had this on Mid-Staffs? Or at Alder Hey? Or Morecombe Bay? Or St. Hilda's, near you? Dynamite indeed! Wikipedia, Facebook, YouTube, Twitter, Instagram, Pininterest, Craigslist, Pandora, Hulu, Linked-in, Whatsapp, Google – no doctor can turn back this tide. No Royal College can step aside. No politician can resist its imperatives.

There *is* no way backwards. And consumers will rapidly learn, in mutual exchange, which questions to ask and what counts as a useful answer. As Brynjolfsson and McAfee say, digital technologies can replicate valuable ideas, insights and innovations at very low cost – and people will increasingly ask why the information they want remains hidden by the politicians, by the Royal Colleges, by the GMC, and by the NHS.

COMING, READY OR NOT!

Digital information is good at disseminating how others have defined and measured value. Millions choose restaurants, hotels, airlines, cheaply, quickly, efficiently, using the net. Millions use structured comparison sites like FindTheBest.com and Gocompare.com. Why not on doctors? Consumers must be enabled to search for and compare doctors. This will definitely change substandard performances, too. The weaker will no longer be insulated by NHS bureaucracy, and by long waiting-lists or self-protective claques of doctors. The issue will be who can deliver the better service, and for less?

There must be better matches, greater timeliness, improved customer service and experience, and increased convenience for the service-user too. Then the incomes of NHS facilities can rise or fall *depending on how well they use the four key intangible assets: intellectual property and expertise, organisational processes and capital, user-generated information, and the human capital of their staffs and how work is organised more effectively.*

And so, in the NHS, the transformation that will be brought about by digital technology and personalised medicine is inevitable. And digital medicine can not only be profoundly beneficial to consumers. It can improve the lives of professionals, too. By doing a better job they can feel better about themselves, better about the world around them, better about their work. Managers, too, need it to co-ordinate increasingly complex processes in which specific, timely, intimate and individual patients are the real focus.

Digital information – and global health-trips, too, with people wishing to travel and to pay to go to better services overseas – will rapidly produce many new interactions. These will all change existing transactions and relationships. Including improving the personalisation of care, much more specific targeted drug treatments, a new precision of the execution of clinical tasks, adequate training, integrity and the much more consistent co-ordination of work, together with higher morale to motivate work and co-operation.

All this is a team process. And the sharing and networking of information helps people to know what and how they are doing, helps them to learn, encourages them to cooperate with fellow workers. It can lift morale, and the reliability and consistency of work too. Reliability and coherence and basic competence and conscientiousness in discharging routines – taking a history, studying test results, washing your hands! – are all essential. But too often lacking in the NHS – despite its grand promises, which have not been delivered.

A much fuller picture of what is going on here, and with networked comparisons, will help us all. It had better do so, as demands for healthcare continue to increase, and we do not have the resources to do it all well if we waste much of doing it badly, if many are under-employed, if a good number do not add value as defined by the customers.

Of course, doctors will try to 'game' the system, but we are already alert to that. In addition, some of the Godlike respect for doctors will ease. And this is no bad

INTRODUCTION

thing, even if faith in healing does have an effect. Doctors will certainly become less condescending, arrogant and sanctimonious. Again, no bad thing.

I expect we will find that there are a few really outstanding doctors, and many in the middle range. Of course, if patients join a mutual purchasing body –my proposal Patient Guaranteed Care Associations – then the managers there will know what the ratings mean, and be doing the purchasing on behalf of their financially-empowered members. They will also help patients to know and understand what they are doing. And try to ensure, too, that the problems which patients cause to themselves can be addressed with self-responsibility.

We will be told that people cannot handle the digital programmes and the machines. That old scare. Well, the new generations live by them. Children as young as two now use i-Pads, if parents are not watching! And the machines teach them, so that their skills grow. They are very soon very competent 'players.'

As the economist Tyler Cowen says, too, it is remarkable how the computer games industry, on line, has educated millions. The educational accomplishments and intellectual advances required are not trivial for game-players. As he says, "Many of those role-playing, time-extended, multiplayer games are forbiddingly hard or at least so it seems. They involve hundreds or thousands of people manipulating hundreds or thousands of virtual characters, not always human, spread across (virtual) geographic space and engaged in trade, battles, elections, and many other activities, all governed by complex rules within the game and governed by complex software at the level of player interface. And yet people learn those games nonetheless and often master them."

A prospective patient who wants to consult with an adviser? No problem. Easy-peasy. Genie, he/she already out of bottle.

We can expect that some appraisals of doctors will be brutally honest, and shake them up. New training, re-education, hard work, discipline, change will be enforced. Equally, doctors, no doubt, will rate patients too! And try to avoid the worst of them! We can also see that some doctors might decide to take on the worst patients, do what they can for them, and perhaps expect to be paid a premium for taking them on.

At all events, this is surely the end of the notorious The Secret Garden of doctor's lives. The end of them preventing us from learning about their practices, and their mal-practises too. And any failures to disclose will be damning. We will expect to see a slow refinement of practices, improvement in outcomes, and generational changes in attitudes, all well-geared for improving our lives.

Digitisation will thus be absolutely at the centre of medical practice. And in this new digital world of transparency, individual accountability and appraisals we are looking at a gradual process of radical but incremental, trial-and-error evolution which will change almost everything we do. As we go forward new machines, new man-cyber partnerships, new evidence will create other programmes and capabilities.

COMING, READY OR NOT!

We will at last clearly see how much value each player is contributing in goods and services. In partnership – men and machine, two blades of the scissors. I welcome this new era, which will be both different and better. It will take into the consumer's hands much that is currently held inappropriately in the hands of politicians. And Doctors *must* climb aboard.

As to state spending, it's certain that the biggest government budgets will remain health and social care, education and welfare. The elderly will increase in numbers, and in their demands. They vote, too. Medicine and care, one way and another, will take upwards of a fifth of the economic output. Indefinitely. We will all be a lot older, and there will be many more of us. We will be more conservative, too, but not less demanding. We can shift some of these inevitable health and elderly care costs, and we can each plan for ourselves now, if we are still young enough to afford it. But these costs cannot vanish. Indeed, they will go on rising both in absolute and in per capita terms.

And so if we are to pay for all this we need to help *businesses* to create wealth constantly. We need to ensure much more for the buck, too. Difficult choices will have to be made as well. We have to face either dilution of services, or enormous fiscal changes, or changes in eligibility, and much greater self-responsibility and life-style changes too. Probably all of these. Certainly, as a nation we need to waste less on poor services and on hugely wasteful unearned welfare, too. Those who have little or no income, little or no education and training, who have saved nothing, started no businesses, lived in debt, invested nothing, demanded all from the state, failed to get up in the morning or turn up for medical appointments – these will continue to burden public services.

It is neither possible nor wise to try to create a false and politically imposed equality. This is a political ideology which entirely falsifies realities. And the so-called 'deep State' has dug terrible pits into which we have all fallen.

But we are in a terrible fix here. And, frankly, I do not know what society can do now about these people at the lowest levels. More rationing, more delays, and less waste in consumption seems inevitable. Much more personal effort to be healthy is essential – and it is exercise, diet, self-care, self-motivation and conscientious attitudes – as well as demographic status and genetic inheritance – which makes the most difference anyway. These factors are the determinants of the greatest health outcomes. So much of poor health status is self-inflicted. And left-liberal demands for equality, imposed "social justice" and diversity do not tackle this issue. One thing is very clear: those who respond to the necessity of more self-control will be healthier, but those who do not respond will lose in many ways.

It does not seem very likely that the long-term welfarists will respond very much. Theirs is now a deeply embedded culture. And so to have any chance of sustaining these poorest at any decent level of living we need to achieve a high productivity, high income economy, for sustainable growth. And we do need to tackle self-responsibility and reduce unnecessary demand in the NHS where we

INTRODUCTION

can. Especially so if we cannot do much to discourage an entitlement culture because the politics (and the BBC!) won't allow us to curb it very much.

Everyone should be paying less tax. Everyone should be taking more personal responsibility. Everyone should be making their own self-responsible decisions, with much more of their own money. And with a conservative, flat-tax economy as the basis for a booming economy. We most definitely do not need politics to be the threat that it has become to successful businesses.

***

In my recent work, *Who Decides Who Decides? Enabling choice, equity, access, improved performance and patient guaranteed care,* I made the detailed case for a series of inter-linked policy changes.

Thus:

1. The tax-based funding of health, social care and long-term elderly care should be brought together.

2. Every person should hold a lifelong Health Savings Account. Ideally, this fund would be based entirely upon personal savings, as in Singapore. Every holder of an HSA would be encouraged to add to the initial tax-based investment, with tax incentives to do so. Non-taxpayers and other low-income groups would continue to receive support. Hypothecated funds from taxes would be paid into personalised accounts.

   However, a key feature of HSAs is that once your personal fund reaches a set level your required payments can reduce and possibly even cease. This provides a real incentive to be frugal with expenditure. In terms of social and elderly care funding, the HSA would end the discrimination typical of the NHS towards the elderly and other groups by ensuring *that everyone* had individual economic power. It would also be a means for encouraging ways to expand revenues via additional, voluntary co-payments. If the holder negotiated a bi-annual 'health plan' there could also be incentives for achieving specific objectives such as changing lifestyles. This would directly impact on preventive care, as we have seen with the development of the policies offered by Pruhealth.

3. Competitive purchasing organisations in localities should offer their services to individuals who would decide where to place their HSA. These would be mutual, cooperative, member-owned organisations – my Patient Guaranteed Care Associations.

4. Competing provider organisations should offer a pluralist response to competitive purchasing.

5. The management of existing monopoly institutions should be regularly contested. Notably, in A&E services and large district general hospitals, CCG's and teaching

hospitals where specialists are clustered and where doctor training is exclusively approved. These managements should be contestable on a periodic basis. It is not only politicians and policymakers who should be subject to challenge and recall. This is increasingly an issue as many more NHS Hospital Trusts and CCG's merge, apparently to avoid competition.

6. Rapidly audited information should be promptly published to empower comparisons. I have urged the establishment of an Independent Disclosure and Information Commission.

7. The proposed Independent Medical Inspectorate, long advocated by Dr. William G. Pickering, should be instituted immediately.

Informed and financially-empowered choice would then genuinely *be* personal choice by being backed in every individual case by money. It would be ineluctable, unavoidable and a permanent factor in a market. It would require both *competing* purchasers *and* competing providers to seek willing revenues from the actual users of services. Money would be mobile. The individual would express preferences both by joining a mutual, cooperative purchasing organisation (a PGCA) and by negotiating about specific service (and costs) with that organisation. Choice would not depend on a list of centrally directed priorities, which can be and, indeed, are being actively ignored by CCG's. Choice would be particular, specific, individual, powerful, and cumulative.

As my proposed Health Savings Accounts imply, we need to carefully re-examine a number of key structural issues focussed by individual financial empowerment. These include taxpayer subsidy, the administrative mechanisms, the role of insurance, the creative possibilities of tax relief and so on.

There are clearly some major steps that we should take. One key was most persuasively demonstrated by the Nobel prize-winning economist Kenneth Arrow (and as economist Tim Harford shows). This is to adjust the starting position. To give the poor the financial power and the free choice which they have been denied, with the introduction of Health Savings Accounts. Instead of interfering with markets we should equip those who have done least well from the NHS to gain the fullest benefits from them.

In brief, do not obstruct the evolution of the market, but set up the conditions for a genuine market with all its advantages. Enable organisations to innovate. They do this most when they are under the most intense competitive pressures. If not, many do not ever do so. To do these things:

- Empower the customer with both knowledge and information, the power to make comparisons, and money to make personal choices effective.

- Move from limited choice and the recent introduction of personal budgets in social care to a Health Savings Account for everyone.

INTRODUCTION

- Make purchasing locally competitive.

- Make individual funds mobile, to enable the purchasing tools to evolve effectively.

- Protect competition.

- Require a minimum level of catastrophic insurance.

- Measure and publish the patients' experience.

- Cease to subsidise providers.

- Ensure pluralist provision and end the predominance of monopoly providers and purchasers.

- Use direct incentives that will change structures, cultures, behaviours, purchasing and provision.

- Halt the drive towards a national tariff for all services. Let *local* negotiations agree prices, on every element of service costs including staff incomes. Competitive purchasing and provision is how to reduce costs and waste, and to encourage innovation.

- Substitute direct personal economic empowerment (and self-responsibility) for indirect politics.

We can then achieve the self-responsibility, the positive incentives for change, and the access to good services which the NHS has promised but which it has so signally failed to achieve. For there is no other way for the individual to be sure of access to a specific, timely, personal, and relevant service. Which voting does *not* deliver.

This approach will help us to meet the new challenges of care. Every modern society faces daunting dilemmas in care provision. Chronic disease *is* the greatest and most costly and demanding of all our healthcare burdens. It is an urgent necessity to introduce incentives and rewards to dramatically revolutionise self-care and preventive care. The entire system is challenged by chronic diseases – such as cancer, diabetes, Altzheimer's disease, AIDS, arthritis, and heart disease. The requirement of good care means helping patients to live with their condition (or conditions), and to self-manage so as to lead a full and active life for as long as they can.

Patients will have to accept greater responsibilities. But thus far, over half a century, the NHS has infantilized them. They now need control and information. Many have to change how they live, or the system will collapse. The necessity is for collaborative management. This calls for changed attitudes on the part of both the medical adviser and the patient. Prevention and long-term self-care should pivot on incentives and rewards.

The pressures of chronic care, of new demands and rising expectations, and the costs arising from a larger population that lives longer, and which expects the benefits of new technologies – all this asks fundamental questions about what to provide, how to provide it and how to pay for it.

We are not alone. We, and other nations, have tried tight central control. We have tinkered with aspects of 'managed [rationed] care' and 'quasi-markets' which were not real markets at all. We have recently begun to see some marginal choice in acute care, and more in social care. But without proper competition we will never meet these challenges *in the system as a whole*.

We are now, it seems, beginning to take individual choice seriously as the best means to make changes. This now needs to be *directly* linked to individual control over money, to make personal choices effective, and to encourage self-responsibility too.

But a structure set in place over more than 60 years cannot be replaced overnight. Yet we *do* need *much* bolder initiatives than have yet been proposed by any of the three major political parties. The pilots for personal and local social care budgets are much under-estimated. They genuinely make the unambiguous case for root-and-branch change in funding, individual empowerment, successful purchasing and pluralist provision. What we have learned from direct payments to the disabled and from personal budgets for elderly social care offers positive guidance. But they are not enough unless we spread them throughout all health and social care.

The inexorable axis on which the potentials for successful change turns is the fundamental choice between dynamism and statism. Dynamism is represented by individual financial-empowerment, and the impact of economic incentives on structures, cultures, on performance, on self-care, and on innovative adaptive change. Statism is represented by a centraliser ideology, by reliance on others ('why doesn't the *government* do something?') and by those 'experts' who claim to know our interests better than we can know them for ourselves. It is for each of us to take responsibility – *to do something ourselves* – and not to keep turning to government.

This book thus critiques and rejects the arguments of statist ideologies. And it turns aside, too, the arguments of those proto-Marxian "opinion formers" in many British academic institutions, in charities, and in tax-based public broadcasting, who over-influence public mis-understandings of the choices between care policies, and between ways of living our lives. These self-appointed "opinion formers" have misled us for so long on what the state can and should try to do in 'public services' – and on what we can do for ourselves.

Instead, we need to consistently set out a dynamist case for direct economic and information incentives for patient empowerment, self-responsibility, and professional rapprochement, for permission to local staff to change, and for self-responsible customer-driven reforms. This book offers the choice of dynamist rather than statist approaches to a future which is approaching rapidly, the fast train on the track, whether we are ready or not.

JS, Twyford, Sussex, 5 August 2015

PART ONE:

1. "Coming, ready or not!" The realities, the politics, and the future of the NHS.

"Nothing lies like the truth." Nelson de Mille.

*The issues remain unaltered, despite the lapse of time. Indeed, startling so. And so I reprint this talk, given as the Annual Lecture to The National Association of Primary Care Annual Conference at the International Conference Centre, Birmingham on 15 November 2001. There were a thousand doctors present. Over-ambitiously, I prepared much more than I could deliver in the time. I have taken this opportunity to print the text in its entirety.

The topic I have been given by the examiners asks me to address the present, future, and politics of the NHS. How to fund and guarantee the delivery of prompt access for all to appropriate quality care is clearly the question of the day. And the question is asked and influenced more by culture and politics than by any other factors.

I accepted your invitation even though I do not have the detailed knowledge and experience which you have in actually delivering care, in doing it day to day. And so I hesitate, with the words of Dickens' *A Christmas Carol* in my mind. Where he said "it is always the person not in the predicament who knows what ought to have been done in it, and would unquestionably have done it too…" And when I look at the complexity of what you do I have a sense that every day the more I know, the more I know the less I really know.

For me, this lecture, however, is a return to the perennial issues that engaged me at Brighton – to try to see services from the patients' point of view. To be concerned about access, quality, funding, responsiveness, behaviour, culture, patient voice, and the impact of political realities. Cash, capacity, choice, competition, and compassion – if you like. As I consider these dilemmas and continuities I am reminded of what the Australian marine biologist Julian Pepperell wrote: "May the fish that get away lure you back again." I have retained this commitment despite my experiences at Brighton. Indeed, this may be because, as W. S. Gilbert says in the wonderful recent film about the Savoy Operas, *Topsy-Turvy*, "There is something inherently disappointing about success."

This lecture is necessarily a rapid and rough ride over a large and bumpy field. And too cursory a look into some rather well-swept corners. But I will try to offer a framework for considering the culture and political nature of British health care, the daily realities that culture and politics shape, and how a genuine transformation can occur. I try to figure out why things mean what they mean – if you take my meaning.

I will address the following questions:

1. Can the NHS as presently structured *ever* deliver the promised equity, 'fairness', reliable individual access, choice, improved performance, and patient guaranteed care??

2. Must we go through the present cycle of increased investment but little cultural change to demonstrate to public and politicians that it cannot do so?

3. Will the Prime Minister himself insist that the next general election is about health-care, funded, purchased, and provided on a different basis – and if so, why?

4. Is higher taxation and either voluntary or compulsory health insurance inevitable and a necessary financial model, if we want to financially empower the individual so that we can actually deliver the founding ideas of the NHS?

5. How can patients become more self-responsible – and, indeed, professional lives become more liveable?

These questions get to the ground of all the dilemmas. Most fundamentally, how to make sufficient money happen, how to enable individual choice and provider competition to happen. So as to increase choice, control costs, improve quality and productivity, change the culture, and expose poor performance to scrutiny and direct incentive for improvement. And what that means in individual lives. These are cultural and moral questions. Each helps us to ask how we can attain an equitable, accessible, reliable and affordable system of care and a different way of seeing ourselves, too. With much more cash and more capacity, with more choice and competition, with better outcomes and higher life expectancy, and with higher morale and professionally satisfying work.

A system which encourages consumer choice and more accountability, both of professionals, providers and of consumers themselves. A system which requires patient self-responsibility, personal self-awareness, individual self-care and the responsibility to make cost-conscious, cost-effective – often difficult – choices. Balancing risk, with the individual making the inevitable and necessarily personal trade-offs. *Learning* as an adult. *Being* an adult.

If we want this we had better think seriously about how to structure an approach, what it is going to cost, and how it is going to be financed. Is this achievable only through higher taxation to match European levels of investment, and more direct payment through insurance or through other devices to increase private investment?

There are many different realities. Yours will depend on what you do, the pressures in your work, and how you view the world. I take it that for politicians the political realities in health care mostly concern votes, re-election, and surviving change. For them the issues are short-term. The realities for professionals are, of course, about treatments and results. But these lives too include the influence of politics on patient benefit, and professional satisfaction. The realities for the patient concern access – or its denial – diagnosis, choice, and outcome. They ought, too, to concern self-responsibility, self-care, life-style, and a proportionate view of what is possible. But there are few direct incentives encouraging and rewarding this. Too few appreciate that the best way to avoid the cure is to avoid the illness. And that the most appropriate rationing is probably to ration oneself. Without direct and personal economic incentives it is very difficult to get people to do what they envisage to be against their short-term interests.

However, the overwhelming common reality in our present system is that politics is more important than patients, doctors, or medical practice. And it is a particular political mind-set which insists – albeit with benign intentions – that "rational co-ordination" and more planning is pre-ordained and can correct the failings of a centralised structure. It is indeed this structure and its assumptions which disempowers everyone involved, including the politicians. And because there is no free market in health care, never think there is no market. There is. There is a political market. It follows the rules of universal suffrage. Votes are bought in it. And, it seems, that every attempt to change the nature of the NHS either makes much of it worse, or merely reinforces the systemic failures.

It is in the political structure where these tensions resonate. It is here, too, that interest groups block change if they can. It is here that politics itself blocks the path to more dynamist, more innovative, more creative solutions. Politics itself has institutionalised these difficulties. But I will suggest it will be the political imperatives of an electoral system which will now impel and compel change.

When he was Minister of Health the late J. Enoch Powell said that politicians are concerned with the general consequences of individual decisions, but doctors – indeed, all those associated with primary care – are concerned with the individual relationship with the patient, and with the consequences of general decisions made by politicians. These tensions persist. Rudolf Klein called them the tensions between "an absolutist ethic of treatment and a utilitarian approach to resource use."

b. The major constraint to change is cultural, and thus political. "The prison of awe."

The major constraint is cultural. This is, indeed, the crucial political reality. Max Weber said that man is an animal suspended in webs of significance he himself has spun. The iconographic status of the NHS makes prisoners of us all, ministers included. [1] For the cultural, practical, and political problems of British health care are a common inheritance. Perhaps the most important constraint on reality, present, and future is this "prison of awe." This mythical mirroring of realities. This credulous willingness to believe. The NHS a symbol of sanctity in a wild world. We are all prisoners of this occult status of the NHS. Or have been, until lately. Emotion, perhaps inevitably, is at the root of much of our difficulty. It is, curiously, because of this that the NHS is both fundamentally stable *and* constantly volatile. An NHS constantly changed but persistently the same. The British have been married to the NHS, as Venice to the sea. But, as Professor Nick Bosanquet has said, "the power of the ideal often swamps any objective assessment of the means." [2] Thus we have often confused an ideal – best feasible care – with an institution.

A fundamental example concerns the notion of public service. And the proper protection of "the public domain", in the interest of the well-being of all. Is it really true that public service can only be given by public sector organisations? And must we only choose between state monopoly and open markets? What do we mean by "public service"? We need to consider how private and voluntary means also regularly deliver public purposes. Public enterprise has shown it can serve the public interest. The Concordat is re-defining public service by realising that good service to the public – in harmony with 'public-service' values – is given by many organisations in the voluntary and in the independent sector. This has long been so. Long-term care. Acute care. Mental health care. The entire Hospice movement. Services delivered to high standards. We are now beginning to see more diversified provision and more from the private sector, whilst retaining the public service ethos by which the NHS has defined itself. And the clock has not struck thirteen.

To try to get the job of NHS reform and modernisation done within the old nationalised structure New Labour has very significantly increased spending. And it has shifted ground remarkably, too. The two-part Concordat, although still a very small part of all that the NHS does, is crucial psychologically and politically. [3] It is the first open-minded major bulletin of change for the strategic development of public-private relationships. The Concordat is one sign of the search to find politically-negotiable bridges to a changed system. So, too, in my view, is Mr. Alan Milburn's Fabian Society lecture, his comments concerning choice of GP and hospital treatment, more provider freedoms and incentives to improve performance, stressed when he appeared before the House of Commons Health Select Committee as it reviewed Department of Health expenditure. There was a significant shift in thinking since *The NHS Plan* was published. But there is a good long way still to go.

Fast-track surgery units and specialist centres such as orthopaedics; overseas buying; the NHS renting private care from the independent sector; foreign companies setting up units here – all these increase provision and flexibility. The search for real change is on. However, the problem of how to get more sustainable revenues remains, as does how to empower the individual. And these are the unavoidable issues. The great guns, if you like. How they come about and how they change power relations – and the controls exercised by politicians – is crucial, too. For cultural change is essential. And this can only be prompted in large part by empowering service users financially, jointly and individually, in mutual-aid organisations. And empowering those who give service to do so. Indeed, it is not only insufficient to increase revenues without such a change. For the changes in quality, provision, responsibility, and funding which we seek are, I believe, otherwise unavailable unless there is significant cultural change.

The NHS is wholly politicised. But it is not this government alone which has politicised health care. Nor is it this government alone which has micro-managed the system. Nor are Tory claims that they will reverse this at all credible, at least without very significant cultural changes. For the NHS is inherently political, endemically centralising, and necessarily limiting to patient information, patient choice, and user responsibility. Its financial structure, too, necessarily limits the funds available. Of course, any health care system is political in some senses. But not all are centralised, bureaucratic, or limiting culturally in quite the way that ours is. Ours has entrenched centralisation and bureaucracy, because it was built on political assumptions which rejected dynamic user-led evolution. We live in a system where government decides what it is appropriate for the individual to spend on health care.

It is these problems which make it so difficult to make the NHS a patient-focussed service. I know that your organisation had endorsed this aim. And, of course, those such as North Bradford PCT which have achieved much through empathy and imaginative management. But they press at, and designate by implication, the limits of a system in which the less well-served patient has no choice, exit, or individual financial clout. Patient choice without individual, self-responsible financial clout will, I suggest, remain a chimera. Much mental health care, too, as the Sainsbury Centre emphasised again last month, remains persistently tied to the medical model. Users and carers remain uninvolved in care planning.

But even if they were to be more involved Trusts would remain very controlling. Many CCG's do much to try to shift this. However, stronger CCG's as purchasers are not in themselves a sufficient change. For the user has to be able to choose between purchasers. It is not sufficient nor is it appropriate to give the power to "decision-makers", as the Conservative health spokesman Dr. Liam Fox has urged. Two reasons why. First, doctors and professionals should be the advisers. Not the decision-makers. Second, the service user should be the decision-maker. And individual revenues should have to be sought from willing consumers. Then behaviours and attitudes would necessarily change. And, as I will suggest, revenues would increase, as would individual self-responsibility.

As he reminded me, my friend Julian Amery once told Harold Macmillan that "Good jockeys ride difficult horses." The present effort at reform is revealing how difficult things actually are, and how hard it is to achieve change through politics. It is also revealing to the public and to the media that the old approach looks likely to be insufficient. For example, official figures released on 9 November showed an increase in NHS spending from £44.2 billion in 2000/1 to £48 billion this year. There was a sharp fall in waiting times, but no significant increase in the number of hospital patients treated. The impact on patient satisfaction (and on NHS productivity) is therefore probably small. However, an effort including major new investment in trying to make the present system work may be the only way for people to understand that it can never work. The only way they are going to stop believing in it.

Politicians wish to manage change, and to survive it. The evidence of little change despite much larger investment – though hurtful in the short-term in poll ratings – is, I think, a necessary prelude to a shift to a radical solution. It creates the opportunity for politicians to persuade themselves, one another, and the public at large. And to lead a different kind of debate.

Politicians, too, are prisoners of the system, and the history that systems create. They, like everyone else, need help in finding devices for effective change. Ministers set initiatives in place, willing the difference. They live in a universe where levers seem to be connected to live wires, but often aren't. Even someone like the present Secretary of State – Mr. Alan Milburn MP – who is certainly knowledgeable, committed and courageous. He has, for example, sought to tackle the hospital-driven culture and is negotiating for the performance data of individual doctors and clinical teams to be personalised. He doesn't think the problems are only about money. Indeed, he is challenging many assumptions, including his own. He has made it clear that we need a variety of ways to access quality care. And that the monolith is as problematic as the lack of money.

But the Secretary of State has, however, no alternative but to seek to micro-manage in a system without price, market, or user responsibility. Mrs. Thatcher's Secretaries of State were in the very same spot. And the so called "internal market" modestly offered cost-efficiencies but offered no choice or exit for unhappy patients, no individual financial control for informed patients, no dynamic entry for new providers, no sufficient demand-side shifts despite the relatively brief experiment with GP fundholding. Indeed, it gave markets a bad name without even trusting them.

This is, in part, because politics has limited NHS change to the supply-side. Mrs. Thatcher herself, with a General's eye for country, absolutely forbade discussion of financial re-structuring and demand-side change. When directly challenged to do something radical about the demand-side she told a private 'think tank' lunch (at the IEA in Westminster) in 1989, "Do you want me to *lose* the next election?" [4] And so the culture, the context, the inherited politics are often against politicians, against you, against us, against patient benefit.

A culture powerfully determines which initiatives might be acceptable. It is held to determine which initiatives might have a hope of achieving change. Politics disciplines and restricts the pressures that money otherwise alone exerts – on supply, on choice, on accountability, not least on the accountability and self-responsibility of the patient. Politics prevents any successful de-centralisation which could readily deliver choice by the individual. And patients meanwhile are shaped by a culture where they believe they cannot learn to acquire an effective voice nor efficient exit as a solution to individual supply-side difficulties. Until political realities change nothing fundamental will change.

What we might hope for instead of the centralised NHS is collective responsibility, collective action without collectivism. A cohesive but not a controlling society. Redemptive power without reductionism. One of the keys to shifting from collectivism to collective responsibility – for example, in a genuine insurance system like that of France – is to understand the misunderstanding about the nature of knowledge (indeed, the whole big and incorrigible philosophical problem of the possibility of knowing other minds) on which state monopoly relies.

For there is an important misunderstanding about the nature of knowledge which we should address. The centralised model of care assumes that planners can know what should happen. It does not recognise the severe limits to the possibility of gathering such knowledge about the individual (and often tacit) preferences of others – let alone limits on how this often tacit knowledge can be centralised or converted into policy. It relies on the idea that an expert can know someone else's good, or "needs" better than they can for themselves, in the determination of "need", its risk-benefit calculations, and judgements about values and indeed about individual moral choices. Thor Heyerdahl, in another exploratory context – in his *Green Was The Earth On The Seventh Day* – speaks of our having "invented a magic word, and with it we have camouflaged an ignorance...We [think we] eliminate an ignorance once we have a name for it." [5] We have done just this in the context of the NHS and state monopoly with our reliance on the word "expert", on the word "consultation", and often with the fashionable but mis-understood word "empowerment."

Michael Polanyi, in his *Personal Knowledge, Towards a Post-Critical Philosophy*, has urged the critical importance of tacit knowledge, which people only articulate within themselves when they face an important decision. And that tacit knowledge is one example of local knowledge, dispersed amongst individuals. [6] It is difficult for planners to gather and interpret this knowledge, which changes all the time. Indeed, it is difficult enough to capture and respond to *even* when there are price signals, as Marks & Spencer, IBM, Dunlop and others have shown in failing to gather, comprehend, codify and respond to changes.

And Friedrich Hayek, I think, is very persuasive when he tells us that you can never collect enough knowledge at the centre to guide all the independent actors in an economy on what to do about service, investment, production, and so on. *You need the 'discovery process' of the market. There is no central information-sharing substitute.*

It is not possible for planners to think up an alternative or 'optimal' plan since no-one knows what this would be. This problem of the state seeking a substitute for market incentives and guidance is in part revealed in the current tension between central government trying to get failing Trust management to do what they are told to do. Failure means more centralisation, not less. But this does not seem to shift very much of what matters. Indeed, the idea of performance funds distributed from the centre suffers from the same weaknesses. It is unconnected with the "reward" earned from a voluntary decision to buy from a provider in a competitive market. As Hayek said in his seminal 1945 lecture, 'The Use of Knowledge in Society', "The peculiar character of the problem of a rational economic order is determined precisely by the fact that the knowledge of the circumstances of which we must make use never exists in concentrated or integrated form but solely as the dispersed bits of incomplete and frequently contradictory knowledge which all the separate individuals possess...." [7]

This truth ultimately and fundamentally undermines all centralising systems. And I suggest that we are all constrained by the past, as well. By the difficulties that electoral politics itself puts in the way of politicians being enabled to move towards alternative methods of funding, provision, and purchasing. We are constrained especially by the intellectual and political basis on which the NHS was founded and structured. The notion that the state should centrally determine public expenditure decisions. We – as a "fair" nation – became prisoners, too, of one definition of equality. No-one can get more, so all will get less. We must all join hands and cross the finishing line joint-last, but together.

Here, the colourless grey decade of the 1940s is long gone, but its strong light makes deep shadows. The Secretary of State this past week rightly said, "The old NHS, like the coal board and British rail is gone...for me the NHS is not a structure but a set of values about treating people. That is a really, really profound change." Yes. But to *know* the errors of past ways, is not necessarily to know how to *escape* the consequences. For the political structure which set these ways in place itself hinders the ability of politicians to build majority support for change. Alan Milburn is, of course, surely right to say that "It is a fantastically liberating thought that you can get your health care irrespective of your ability to pay. But the practice on the ground has got to match the elevated nature of that principle." The NHS dream is embedded in a romantic and an idealising emotive tradition. But the NHS has consistently failed to meet the dream. And this spreading realisation is undermining its cultural and political legitimacy. We need other ways to deliver Alan Milburn's hopes.

There is a real sense in which people have voted themselves poor health care, by clinging to the idea that it can somehow be 'free.' There is now, of course, no escape from price, from affordability, from choice, from opportunity cost, and from self-responsibility. For professionals, escape from politics will be welcomed, I suppose. But there can be no escape for health-care professionals from external intervention. Performance management *is* inevitable. And appropriate. If not by the state, then by patient preferences expressed through mutual-aid purchasing co-operatives to which individuals voluntarily subscribe with their 'tax fund.' Nor can there be any escape for consumers from cost-conscious choices, from affordability, from self-responsibility, from the ethical and human responsibility (and opportunity) of learning to choose.

There is one over-riding cultural and political problem. This is that reform of a state monopoly system has so far been almost an impossible political task in a democracy. As we see from *The NHS Plan*, it takes a huge amount of time and effort to move the stone. It is difficult to make progress in the time frame the public will accept. The political and health-investment cycles do not coincide. To pose an alternative – such as French or German-style compulsory insurance – will take a great deal of courage and leadership. However, what is "politically possible" is never static. It can be changed by leadership, and it is changed by events. I will come on to suggest that we may be entering a situation where several new factors for change coincide, and that these will prompt a new national debate deliberately led by the Prime Minister, who will focus the next general election on health care. Indeed, for the government there may be no alternative. As Evelyn Waugh says in *Officers and Gentlemen*, "In the war of attrition which raged ceaselessly against the human spirit, anti-climax was a heavy weapon."

c. So what of the political future?

There is no doubt that there is very significant additional money being applied to the problems. Tony Blair, as Prime Minister, has made a huge personal commitment to reverse the decline of the NHS. And the Secretary of State has shot this golden arrow with all the power of his considerable elbow. But will it reach and travel far enough, swiftly enough, and strike deep enough? Will it increase revenues sufficiently, increase capacity swiftly enough, and bring us up closer to European levels of access, outcomes and longevity in a time frame which makes sense politically? Can it do so without individually-responsible, economically-empowered choice, and without top-up insurance options? Will the public believe the existing NHS National Plan is working to achieve its objectives? And can spending more on providing public services in the present structure, but more expensively, achieve the vitally necessary cultural change as well as much greater revenue and access? And if not, what then?

There is, of course, much improvement, but this is like the proverbial ice-berg. Much of it remains invisible to patients. A relatively small proportion of new funding goes into front-line services, although increases in salaries do have some impact on quality as this can improve motivation. However, as one writer in *The Guardian* said last week, "patients are not going to thank Labour for a service moving from the problematic to the merely adequate." They have to experience improvements personally, and at the level of political consciousness. Meanwhile, you can see modernisation of the NHS referenced everywhere in the NHS, save in the productivity statistics. Too much remains virtual. Patients live in the actual.

There is one governing rule. In politics, *perception is all*. And it is perception of what is happening – reflected in the polls, and in private focus groups, as well as in the political antenna of Ministers – which will decide what happens next, both to health care and to the government. Especially what happens in the three years before the next election, focussed as it must be on public services. Of course, at a general election people may vent their anger. But I would be amazed if Mr. Blair lets it get to that. Instead, I believe he will seek to move "ahead of history," to express with empathy the tacit understandings he feels and senses concerning the mood of national failure.

The public has had high expectations of the NHS. Certainly so, when compared with the potential of the NHS to deliver, or by comparison with what it is necessary to invest to achieve these expectations (and in a different institutional setting too). This is so even if British expectations are lower than those of Swiss, French, German, Australian, or American consumers, who subsist in a different cultural, political, and health-care climate. High British expectations have, however, been encouraged by a lack of realism amongst politicians and public. Prompted by half a century of paternalism. Misled by the notion that somehow government (or the tooth fairy) 'pays' for everything. Expectations were raised again by *The NHS Plan* and by the size of New Labour's overwhelming majority. These hopes are almost certainly much too high. [8]

The electoral and political risk is that grand delusions create great disillusion. For the public appears to be convinced that things continue to get worse. Public patience has turned first to puzzlement. And from puzzlement to an understanding that there must be a better way to secure genuine access to optimal service, in the main free at the point of delivery. People are no longer dazzled by the prospectus, and they are struck by its unreliability. Nothing enlivens a political leader like the prospect of electoral disaster. And there is no obvious solution to the problems of health care deliverable without political pain. So in an electoral democracy it comes down to judgement about political chances. A careful reading of John Rentoul's biography of the PM suggests that he has a deep commitment to equality in care, to a moral view of society, and to the idea that we should act together as a nation on health care. [9]

If I may borrow from Dickens' Mr.Jaggers, "Put the case" that the government's own private opinion polls and focus-groups urgently suggest that people will erupt in anger at the next election, remembering that the last was substantially about health and education. "Put the case" that people increasingly say the NHS doesn't work and something else must be tried. "Put the case" that this is particularly true of those who do vote – especially the 11 million pensioners, who are a third of the voting electorate – those in the suburbs, the A's and B's, those in the middle-ground who decide British elections, who have been the principal beneficiaries from the NHS, and who seem to be becoming much angrier about its deficits and denials.

There is already a mill-stream of stories of deficit and denial, themselves supplemented by the tools of the information technology revolution. Browning wrote (1887):

THE REALITIES, THE POLITICS AND THE FUTURE OF THE NHS

Which was it of the links
Snapt first, from out the chain which used to bind
Our earth to heaven...?

We cannot know which of the shocks and scandals, and which of the huge cultural shifts we see around us, have the most influence on opinion. Certainly, there is cumulative change from every fresh concussion. Do not under-estimate the impact that a long and assertive media campaign concerning the NHS and European comparisons will have on the national mood. Or in the run-up to the next election. Paxman running amock with his rasping sarcasm. James Naughtie, helping us all with his listening skills. And a positive commitment to change from all the newspapers and electronic media. Leading commentators like Melanie Phillips, Michael Gove, Peter Riddell, and Stephen Pollard already point us towards European models.

This week's *Sunday Times* leader insisted on an open market for patients and GPs. The editorial called for "the blast of competition." And the *Daily Mail* is constantly corrosive about the present situation. These help set the context. They are key drivers of change. We might note, too, that none of the key structural Thatcherite and Tebbit reforms of the wider economy in the 1980's enjoyed majority support before the event. All politically impossible – until achieved.

New clinical imperatives, too, will emphasise the gulf between the NHS and, for example, the French and German systems of funding and capacity. Cancer is a prime example. The government has made action on cancer a top priority. Professor Karol Sikora, Professor of Cancer Medicine at Hammersmith Hospitals Trust, however has recently said that the UK cannot afford new cancer treatments without changing funding mechanisms. New, more effective but more costly treatments are emerging. Ethical dilemmas worsen.

But people are not free to buy excluded drugs known to be effective, because of local funding policies. New drugs which inhibit cancer growth and affect the blood vessels around cancer sites will make the issue more pressing. If individuals owned their own fund – which they do under a compulsory insurance scheme as in France and Germany – they could provide for these drugs, as could MS patients seeking beta interferon, now denied by the British government's rationing body, NICE. It should be stressed that by insurance I do not mean the voluntary system of the USA, which leaves many without cover. Nor do I mean private insurance which selects out in a two-tier system. I mean cover for all. This necessarily means a compulsory system, probably including further incentives to add to funds.

The government has set unforgiving measures of success. There are vast electoral penalties for failure. What will New Labour do? Leave the boats tied to water-worn posts? Remain deaf to the nation? Fail to listen and to lead? Treat the problem of anger, as did the Tories under a grey moth like Major, merely as a request for more information and pump out press-releases, seeking to achieve the approved response? As did Major, cite the billions spent, whilst eyes glazed over in boredom, misunderstanding, or disbelief? Put in more hit teams? More sacked management, more merged hospitals, more targets, more close direction of professionals, and the long slow grind towards incremental change? While the gaps between ourselves and others overseas become more obvious, more publicised, more painful, less deniable? Will health-tourism or travel by Brits going overseas for prompt and decent care grow, too? The opportunities, quality and lower costs are emerging in Asia. In my judgement this is a significant new trend.

I do not believe New Labour under Mr. Blair is walking unprepared towards the guns of electoral defeat. But a new approach is essential. No.10 is surely carefully studying how to launch a national debate, as a prelude to further incremental changes towards a mixed funding structure. And why, No.10 surely asks, cede the initiative on European models to the Conservatives. Iain Duncan Smith's interest in European models may itself prove an important contribution to changing the context of debate, and to reaching towards a new knowledge and understanding of how matters might be re-arranged. Reports like the Audit Commission's on Hospital Accident & Emergency Department failures, though superficially damaging to government in fact can help government to build the case for systemic change. [10]

I suggest the Prime Minister will lead a different debate.

This looks counter-intuitive, perhaps. You might think that continuing difficulties will discourage that approach. That Ministers will insist it's all about to work. Time, faith, hope. But I think there is this other, positive, pragmatic and principled political choice, to deliberately focus the next general election on the challenge of encouraging the evolution of new institutions for better care that we face as a nation. That is, if we want to really deliver the values and ambitions of the NHS. The right thing to do and the right thing to do politically may coincide. This is about a politician responding to changing and often tacit public understandings, helping to articulate them and give them meaning. Tony Blair has shown he can do this. And it seems that there is a genuine public appetite for change. Indeed, an expectation of it at a time of unprecedented living standards. There looks to be a coincidence of factors driving us to this destination, and the presence of a national leader prepared actually to lead is an important factor.

In many senses, it depends on how you ask the public the question. If you ask, "Do you want to save the NHS in 24 hours?" you get one kind of answer, though it's changing. But if you ask – which no-one yet does – "Do you want us to give you a legally enforceable contract which guarantees you no waiting lists, modern drugs always available, choice of doctor and treatment, much better outcomes, much higher professional morale. But it will cost you what top quality costs – mostly in taxes. Do you want this?" I think you'll get a more favourable and useable answer. Of course, people will have to appreciate that taxes can rise, or they can pay by a deduction into their own individual fund. Paid from weekly or monthly income, with the employer paying the same or a proportionately higher or lower contribution. But in this way we could make the change in principle, and gradually push up to European investment levels, where there are no waiting lists, many more doctors and where OECD comparative evidence shows that treatments work better, so there's greater life expectancy. If we make this case, you might get another kind of answer. And that, I submit, will be the cluster of questions which can engage a national debate about choice, access, tax, insurance, outcomes and guarantees. It offers a route to getting solutions which are proven and known to work – even if inevitably this must take time, after decades of under-investment.

The questions you frame – and the answers you thus prompt – much influence your ability to achieve change. For the questions are themselves educative. Ideas matter. Leadership shapes the discussion. It changes the nature of the debate. There is an educational role of politics, in helping us to find practical answers to real problems and implementing solutions in government. This is that you are trying to provide people with words and ideas which fit their predicament better than the words and ideas which they are using at the moment.

Admirers of the incomparable Robin Williams, and of Walt Whitman – all honorary members and admirers of the Dead Poets Society – will cry "Carpe diem, o Captain, my Captain." And as a French writer said, "History begins at ground level with footsteps." For this is about leadership. And whatever your political views – and anxieties about leadership itself – no one doubts that Tony Blair can provide this. He changed the name – and perhaps the nature – of an entire political party. He led the way, almost alone, on Kosovo. He has offered courageous leadership in response to the terrorist attack on America. He did so over Clause 4 and the shift from wholesale nationalisation, over changed trade union relations with the old Labour Party, over the closed shop. And over the struggle against Militant, and over One Man One Vote. All vital in their ideological significance to re-educate an entire political party.

I do not under-estimate something which Tony Blair shares with few others – certainly there is something of Churchill and of F. D. Roosevelt in his make-up, in the magical capacity to transform situations, his freedom from fear of the future, his empathy, premonition and welcome for the coming wave he can ride, his faith in his ability to mould it and succeed. His ability, too, apparently to be able to negotiate what can be negotiated across traditional frontiers, and to appreciate what can and cannot be finessed.

We could soon see the largest and the latest if not the last major act of modernisation this country has yet seen. That is, the re-launch of the NHS and the re-modelling of health care led by a Prime Minister and a Secretary of State committed to the genuine delivery of equality of access. The approach will be reassuring, and in the conversational tone. The approach will be in what Mr. Blair's biographer John Rentoul calls his "Bipartisan Reasonableness." To build coalitions, to persuade people that this is how to put their principles into practice. This is Mr. Blair's special skill. As is his ability to sense and be in touch with people who are not in politics. There are several vital elements if a real debate, and the prospect of real change in funding, is to be achieved. It will take delicate skills, determined commitment, careful planning, the right timing – and luck. Mr. Blair has given ample proof that he is gifted with all of these. More than Napoleon's Generals, and perhaps more even than William The Conqueror, neither of whom ultimately ruled a willing and peaceful people.

The pivotal device will I think be incentives for savings to supplement compulsory social insurance, even if this begins as a small percentage of personal income or an additional modest cost for the employer. The key device for change will be a Health Care Savings Account (or it could be called a Medical Savings Account, as championed by the Adam Smith Institute, or a Stakeholder Health Account). The individual would almost certainly have to accept a mix of compulsion to insure – but taxes do that – and an incentive could be offered (tax deductions) for further individual payments. Then they would voluntarily subscribe to an insurer which would purchase care on their behalf. The basic contract would be community-rated. It would not exclude the risky. It would deliver 'all needed care', as defined by clinicians. There would be incentives to invest above the minimum. An excess – as in a Medical Savings Account – and a no-claims bonus, accruing into pension or long-term care cover. Catastrophe-cover, too. Cash payments for minor items. Perhaps we should not stand on the tip-toes of expectation. Certainly, the task of change may take two generations. Yet this is itself an argument for making a constructive start now.

In addition there will be an emphasis on re-distribution, especially in providing better care for the low-paid. The system, too, might be weighted in favour of disadvantaged families, including the working poor, by additional credits or tax transfers. This would keep Gordon Brown on board. Contemporary trade union experience of mutuality and of independent health care will be part of the appeal Mr. Blair makes to the Labour Party itself. There is, too, already a proven willingness to pay, and for others a frustration at not being able to pay. Self-pay and acute self-funding is rising, too. In 1992 this was at the 12% level in terms of the income of an average independent hospital. It is now 20% in some locations, 40% in others. In excess of 200,000 people now pay privately each year, without medical insurance, for acute surgical procedures. A willingness to invest in alternative therapies and medicines is already well noted. Some 3.5 million trade unionists have cash benefits, or are members of cash benefit funds.

Mr. Blair will, I think, underline the need to recognise the merits of a coalition of charities, churches, public and private sectors – voluntary and not-for-profit organisations – and the extra capacity they could supply if revenues were provided. He will, too, continue to encourage investment and development in the independent sector, which has shown it is capable of managing investment well. The long-term care story underlines this. So, too, does the hospice movement, itself entirely the result of charitable endeavour.

There are now 430,000 health and care beds in the independent sector. Some 150 million bed-nights are offered in long-term care each year. There are more than 200 independent hospitals, with more than 11,000 beds. There are some 5,000 private and voluntary nursing homes. There are 1 million surgical procedures a year undertaken in the independent sector, more than 400,000 out-patient appointments a year, and more than a third of all medium-secure mental health care is located there. The total value of the independent sector healthcare provision is more than £17 billion.

Some 25% of the membership of the Royal College of Nursing is employed in the independent sector. In addition to the more usually referenced providers we should add to the independent sector summation the independent provision of fitness centres, health food enterprises, the manufacture and provision of complementary medicine and alternative therapies. There is, indeed, an immense individual reliance on independent provision – and often a preference for it, and a proven willingness to pay for it where it exists. [11]

Language will matter, as will the atmospherics of the discussion. The solution has got to be clear, and able to be described in simple but vibrant language. Solutions, indeed are not deliverable if a politician cannot describe them succinctly. As Mr. Blair has said, "Strip down a policy or opinion to one clear line before the media does it for you. Think in headlines." Mr. Blair recognises that to control the debate he must control the language of that debate.

The key areas for change are funding – both in its levels and in its control – and self-responsibility. These are not the only issues. But both are very basic. This is a pivotal reality. For you cannot get good health care on the cheap. And the individual has a job to do, too, to be and to live healthy.

If you want access, and quality, if you want quality time with a doctor, it is also a principle reality that it costs money. But a recent estimate said that to reach EU spending levels a VAT rate of 27%, or a tax rise of 2p. in the £ would be necessary here. This year the UK health spend will be £49.5 billion. To match the current Eurozone average spend we would require to spend many billions more. [12] Of the 13 EU countries we have the 13th lowest level of private spend. But extra money alone will not make the cultural changes concerning empowerment that we want to see (and which I have been advocating since 1991 when I was first Chairman at Brighton). Reflecting on foreign investment levels, it is indeed, remarkable how much is done in the UK with so relatively little. But we cannot remain a low tax, low spend health care system. We need considerable extra funding, and consent will be necessary.

d). The politics comes down to two things.

First, which financial mechanisms can most effectively deliver purchasing and provision to achieve the founding values of solidarity, equity, access, and can best ensure that everyone can get timely access to appropriate and even basic treatment. But within a dynamic, evolving, system of individual responsibility, empowerment, and choice.

Second, which new funding mechanisms can credibly be introduced, given that the politics are embedded in our inherited culture, which itself restricts the room for political manoeuvre. It's important to remind ourselves that without price any increase in funding uncovers new unmet demand, which stretches the gap once more. So one question is, where do you place price in a system? At the point of entry into a health plan for the future, by compulsory insurance, or at the point of use? We shall have to face this, for price is the only known effective mechanism for matching demand with supply. And the only known mechanism for setting prices and distributing scarce resources efficiently is a market efficiently distributing scarce resources. This, however, does not mean payment for critical illness interventions at the time of use, though it cannot exclude – save in dream-land – pre-payment, either by taxation or by insurance.

The majority of developed countries have social insurance schemes which guarantee access for all. They combine this with some kind of price mechanism which permits choice to influence the flow of funds. They pay more, but they get more. They are expected to exercise personal responsibility. Voluntary and not-for-profit provision predominates. Tax and insurance collected is specifically guaranteed as health expenditure. There is an important link between behaviour and consequences. In France and in Germany, for example, standards seem higher. There is equality of access. Everyone is covered. Treatment is prompt. Costs are generally lower than ours. There is solidarity, cohesion, differentiation, and ethical competition. Britain, however, is unusual in its dependence on public provision. [13]

You may ask, but why is compulsory insurance different from income-tax, and why is it better? There is a clear answer. It is this: because the individual owns the fund and it is directly spent on personally chosen care. We need the benefits of individuals being linked to "their fund", as the French have shown. This is more directly achieved by identifying individual funds with individual contracts for care. We need genuine social insurance, to raise sufficient money and to accomplish these psychological and cultural gains – and we need mutual purchasing where a PGCA would have both economic and cultural clout. For this will re-connect behaviour, life-style, and health care outcomes, which is crucial. And then people can get all needed care on a community-rated basis, where they want it, when they want it, how they want it.

Can politicised health care decided upon at an election do this for you? No, it cannot. For health care is a uniquely personal, intimate, separable, time-sensitive service, specific to the wants of the individual. It is not secured either by voting, by "consultation", or by third-party payment. It is not secured by holding the system to account at an election, particularly when there has been no choice between party policies. One set of rascals replacing another set does not do it. Having a say in how a system is run is different from having a say about a personal service supplied when you want it. Having a choice to move your account to a preferred provider is more powerful than an occasional vote, which is itself lost in the big bundle of election questions and answers.

A compulsory payment into social insurance is a more effective way to create the hypothecated health tax the left has asked for years without number, and it has these other cultural benefits too. It directly links extra spending and personal services. And it could also have has an equity element – as in the Singapore system – for saving into long-term care costs.

If we move to a European-style system, the tax-take for health care will not go down. Beware the politician who says otherwise. He is either naïve or porkifying. And, as P. J. O'Rourke tells us, "A politician who claims he's going to cut the size of government is saying he's going to creep up on himself and steal his own wallet." [14]

Of course, there is no European-system as such. Denmark, for example, has many of the same problems we encounter, from a socialised system. And France and Germany, too, have their problems, in controlling costs. But even with a more restricted supply they will remain immensely ahead of us on capacity, investment, many outcomes, and longevity. I would swap their problems for ours any day. For they have the incentives of self-responsibility built into the structure, and this gives them effective ways to resolve difficulties. In France and Germany there is a legally enforceable contract for service between the user and the provider. Each has solved the problem of how to get more money into the system. And how to ensure you get more performance from it, too. European insurance systems, by the by, are not open-market in their tone. They are generally run by left of centre coalition governments. They are not Thatcherite projects at all. And, with regard to access and equity, private insurance in Europe does not buy anyone *clinically* superior service. This is another important moral issue, and the position on this in Britain remains exceedingly uncomfortable in a two-tier system.

Operations in France are available much more quickly. But – the world turns but does not change – Franco-German rivalry remains. There is a German story about the French system. They say in Germany, "Do you know you have to wait *a whole week* in France for a hip replacement. You pay all that insurance. And they can't even run their health service properly!" In fact, you can wait as much as two weeks for a hip or knee replacement in France. In reality, seriously ill people in France do well. It's the hypochondriacs and people demanding anti-biotics for colds who end up out of pocket. One Danish municipal Mayor has come up with a novel way to reduce costs. He sends senior citizens to the sun. Farum, a town about 9 miles NW of Copenhagen, gives its older people annual holidays to improve their well-being. They fly in groups to Spain, where they spend their time making friends and talking about their ailments. They are said to stay in touch with one another when they get back, and spend more time comparing medical notes with one another and avoid a trip to a GP. Danish Mayors face re-election every four years.

Why should people go for compulsory insurance or higher taxation, or both? Tough one. It is a matter of emphasis whether you insist on the risks or the opportunities. There is no conflict concerning ends. And it will, I think, depend on several things. First, there is a generational change, with new technology connecting people up to how it's possible to live, and how others live. This is changing expectations, which cannot be fulfilled by a system depending on taxation alone. Second, people are beginning to appreciate that where a fund is owned by an individual it can be directly used by them to buy care. Third, more and more people are experiencing care *outside* the NHS, including through the Concordat and soon from being sent to Europe by the NHS itself for an operation. By Christmas some 60,000 operations will have been purchased in the independent sector by the NHS via the Concordat this year. This is changing what patients, and those they talk to, want for the future. Fourth, the Prime Minister's leadership can – and, I believe will – change the entire framework of the argument, and open the door to a change which the British will accept, even reluctantly, as unavoidable and right. He has left it late. But…

e. The challenge for *you*r organisation!

My own view of the future is that Primary Care Trusts might evolve as mutual-aid organisations, either as care-delivery organisations, or as competing insurers and purchasers of care, offering differing care packages at different levels of investment. Including a national Guaranteed Health Care Package available to all regardless of ability to pay – and paid for by tax transfers to the poor. This indeed can appeal to the history of Labour itself, although this history is now cast in shadow. Unfortunately, the history of mutual-aid has mainly been written by its enemies, with the noticeable and honourable exception of one or two scholars, notably Frank Prochaska and David Green. [15]

People have latterly submitted to the tempting promise of the warmth [sic] of the all-absorbing authority of the state and given up reconstructing society on the old basis of mutual aid and support. But the revival of a network of institutions of voluntary mutual support – purchasing through insurance companies, professional associations, trade unions, voluntary bodies, families, churches – is essential if voluntary, mutual, and charitable resources are to be heightened and legitimised on a much larger scale. Another Brightonian, Prince Kropotkin, in his *Mutual Aid*, emphasises "the constructive genius of the masses in their mutual-aid institutions." That is, mutual support without depriving the individual of initiative and whilst also fortifying self-jurisdiction. [16]

This is not to push government entirely aside. Indeed, the rule of government remains important. It is, indeed, a vital part of the solution. But its limits and ambitions must be clear, and controlled. Government must ensure law and order, the protection of competition, of property and of the rights of the individual. And it must make the framework of agreed rules – particularly to guarantee to everyone a high standard of care, and also to prevent the elimination of competition.

The guarantee of access for all is essential to public confidence. The guarantee of competition is essential for the maintenance of the conditions for dynamic and organic evolution. Within such a framework of rules NHS hospitals could become local charitable and self-governing institutions, earning revenues from willing purchasers. They would agree contracts for access, quality as well as quantity, price, and outcome. Government would withdraw to the essential rampart of controlling the framework of rules. It seems likely that the NHS facilities would continue for some time to play the most significant role, for that is where the capital, equipment and skills are significantly located. The public health function – for example, a strategy to deal with infectious diseases and of vaccination – would be maintained.

I hope that this lecture will not be merely a note in a bottle, swept away by the waves, with the slim wish of the shipwrecked sailor that it may someday fetch up on a distant if welcoming shore. So I would like to propose to you that your organisation sets up a new fast-reporting Commission to inform and lead the debate. [17]

You know that you learn the real questions about managing – and surviving – change when you actually try to get the job done. With financing and with quality, we have got to discover the practical links between policy and practice, which is the hard bit to achieve. You can offer unique leadership. Uniquely, you have the trust of the public. There is a massive opportunity for leadership, in taking us all to a practical, pragmatic, politically-aware vision of funding and access. There are important issues concerning the transition to a new system. These should be addressed by your National Association: principals, numbers, time-frame, detail. What is current experience of access, cost control, subsidy, capacity, outcomes in Germany and France, for example? How does this relate to what we want to achieve?

We need a serious study: we need sustained hard thinking about detail to give coherence to policy. You cannot snatch policy from the ether. It's not a back of an envelope job. The most successful policy changes follow a longer period of serious study. We need a genuine and a rigorous enquiry into every aspect: authoritative, thorough, patient, practical, current, pragmatic, and non-party. This needs to explore a coherent plan to lay out the ground, to clarify the key issues, to address the benefits and the problems, in a renovated system which can be made real for people, in detail on the ground as well as in the mind's eye. This will help set the context and increase the choices for patients, as for politicians. It is important, too, that a serious study led by you would make a start for change with a large number of professionals owning the change, committed to it, leading opinion about it.

Of course, I imply a framework of principle, too. And one which itself and its implementation is a living issue – with individual leverage for choice and change. We need a compass by which we make both an intellectual case and by which we develop the detail. For the compass I suggest there is no substitute for applying to contemporary problems the idea that liberty is an end, not merely a means. Of course, this is to make both a moral and a practical case, both for better health care, for scepticism concerning bureaucratic solutions to diverse individual and social problems, and concerning taxation and too encroaching a state.

As one politician – Enoch Powell – admitted, "politicians do not cause the dawn to come, though, like the birds in the morning, they may think that they do." And Hayek is right, too. [18] It is ideas that change the world. And it is the transmitters of ideas who filter which views and opinions are to reach us, how facts and ideas are presented to us. It is these opinion formers – organisations like your own – who change the context of politics. We must have the courage of our convictions. For an inclusive, appropriate care system. We are not there yet. But we may be closer. However, we should recall John Ruskin's words from his *Modern Painters*. He said, "It seems to me that the simplest and most necessary truths are always the last believed."

NOTES.

1. Politicians in France and Germany, too, struggle with the problems of efficiencies, capacity, scarcity, cost, savings, and the electoral consequences. However, they do so from a cultural basis which rejects rationing, waiting lists, denial of quality treatment, and discrimination between patients irrespective of medical condition. See Redwood, *ibid.*, passim. On some current difficulties see Robert Graham, "French public health workers nurse wholesale grievances," *Financial Times*, 22 January 2002.

2. Nicholas Bosanquet, *A Successful National Health Service* (London, Adam Smith Institute, 1999).

3. Department of Health, *For The Benefit of Patients. A Concordat with the Private and Voluntary Health Care Provider Sectors* (London, Department of Health, November 2000). Department of Health, *Building Capacity and Partnership in Care. An Agreement between the statutory and the independent social care, health care and housing sectors* (London, Department of Health, October 2001). The think-tank Reform has made the point that the number of patients treated through this agreement "remains a tiny fraction of the total workload of the NHS", which is an annual total of 5 million operations. The budget for purchasing private operations is less than 0.1% of the NHS budget. Reform, *Briefing note,* 11 December 2001. Dr. David Green has made the point that the private sector is being used by Whitehall only as a sub-contractor, with the NHS continuing as a centrally-planned bureaucracy. In his account "The private sector and internal contestability are nothing more than the management tools of central managers to incentivise local managers." This is what Green calls cherry-picking management techniques from capitalism, without liberating producers to explore new and better ways of serving patients. D. Green, "Public is better than private", *The Guardian*, 6 July 2001.

4. Private information, from the most senior source.

5. Thor Heyerdahl, *Green Was The Earth On The Seventh Day* (1996; London, Abacus edition, 1998).

6. Michael Polanyi, *Personal Knowledge. Towards A Post-Critical Philosophy* (Chicago, University of Chicago Press, 1962).

7, F. A. Hayek, *Individualism and Economic Order* (Chicago, Chicago University Press, 1948); *The Constitution of Liberty* (Chicago, Chicago University Press, 1960), *Studies in Philosophy, Politics and Economics* (London, Rout ledge, 1967), and *New Studies in Politics, Economics and the History of Ideas* (London, Rout ledge, 1978).

8. Department of Health, *The NHS Plan: A Plan for Investment, a Plan for Reform*, Cm.4818 (London, HMSO Stationery Office, 2000).

9. John Rentoul, *Tony Blair, Prime Minister* (London, Little, Brown, 2001. See also Andrew Rawnsley, *Servants of The People. The Inside Story of New Labour* (London, Hamish Hamilton, 2000). Mr. Blair makes it clear that he did too little, too late, and could and should have been much more radical in his approach to the NHS. He regrets it now, but too late. However, other politicians have not learnt the lesson? This latter note added 31 July 2015.

10. The recent report from the National Audit Office alleging that nine NHS Trust managements had fiddled their waiting lists is another example which I believe will encourage support for change. It exemplifies, too, both how managements in quasi-monopolies inevitably are incentivised to function, what it is they make their priority, and that increased central control is an ineffective way to give managers incentives to serve consumers. Instead, they serve politicians. National Audit Office, *Inappropriate Adjustments to Waiting Lists*, London, NAO, 19 December 2001. Wonderful language from the School of Sir Humphrey Appleby, too. "Inappropriate adjustments"! See also Nigel Hawkes and David Charter, "Hospitals 'betray trust;' by fiddling waiting lists", *The Times*, 19 December 2001.

11. I am grateful to my friend Barry Hassell, Chief Executive of The Independent Healthcare Association, for these figures. It should be noted that most private hospitals are small, relatively low-tech, with no emergency admissions, and when problems arise patients are often transferred into NHS emergency facilities. See also Frank Dobson, "The last thing the NHS needs is another dose of the private sector", *The Independent*, 28 January 2002.

12. One estimate suggests that additional spend is of the order of an extra £45 billion a year by 2005/6. The equivalent, the 'Reform' campaign estimated, of 15p on the basic rate of tax. This may or may not deliver the required improvements. Certainly, since Labour came into government spending has been increased by a third in real terms, with only marginal increases in productivity, and with no judgement possible on quality. To match the future spend by, say, 2005/6, it has been estimated that we will need to go as high as 10.7% of GDP, which implies a much bigger tax rise – with its potential, too, for further weakening economic performance and reducing GDP. See David Smith, "So how do you want to pay for it?" *Sunday Times*, News review, 2 December 2001; David Smith and Rosie Waterhouse, "New Labour's quack cure for the NHS", *Sunday Times*, News review, 9 December 2001; David Smith and Eben Black, "Families pay £207 a month for the NHS", *Sunday Times*, News review, 9 December 2001. Government has based its plans on an EU average spend on healthcare of 8%.

Some analysts believe this to be an under-estimate of the current EU average. And it will not in any case be at that level by 2006 because of upward trends in spending in all EU countries. Projections suggest an EU average in 2006 of around 9.1%. To reach this the UK would require a real annual increase in healthcare spending of 7.7-8.7%, or significantly higher than the 5% real annual growth in the government's calculations. To reach a 9% target researchers have suggested that healthcare expenditure would need to increase by a total of £29.2 billion over five years. This implies tax increases of 10p. on the basic rate of income tax, or a gradual increase of VAT to 27%, or reductions in other already hard-pressed public spending areas.

Sustained economic growth would contribute some of the necessary funds, but it hardly looks capable of contributing it all. And higher taxes would in themselves depress productive economic activity. Even if much higher investment levels are attained, these may not be sufficient, given the decades of under-investment in British healthcare. See J.Appleby and S.Boyle, "Blair's billions. Where will he find the money for the NHS?", *British Medical Journal*, 3120, 2000, pp.865-867; A. Towse and J. Sussex, "Getting UK Healthcare Expenditure up to the European Mean. What Does That Mean?", *British Medical Journal*, 320, 2001, pp.64-642; Heather Gage, "NHS Malaise: diagnosis and treatment options", *Economic Affairs*, Vol.21, No.4, December 2001, pp.9-13. The Institute of Fiscal Studies warned in January 2002 that tax may have to rise by as much as £7 billion to maintain growth in public spending in health and education, while permitting Mr. Brown to go ahead with planned tax credits and maintain the existing safety margin in public finances. See Gary Duncan and Philip Webster, "Blair warns of tax rises to improve NHS", *The Times*, 21 February 2002.

13. Germany has a social insurance system established by Prince Bismarck in 1883 on a national basis. Care is funded by a blend of statutory health insurance, taxation, and private insurance, with additional co-payments. German health-care insurance is employment-based. Some 90% of Germans are covered by compulsory health insurance, which is paid for by employers and employees. The balance of civil servants (who have a separate scheme) and high-income individuals have identical access, although the latter pay into their own private systems. Unemployed people and those on benefit are covered by the state. Hospital provision is diverse, and there is choice of doctor and of hospital. Some 51% of beds are in the public sector, another 30% are provided by private, not-for-profit organisations, and the balance are in private, profit-making institutions. Germany has twice as many doctors and three times as many beds per head of population as in Britain, which offers the spare capacity necessary to choice, and to efficient competition. All classes of people have the government guarantee of access to good care. Outcomes and user-satisfaction are much better than in the UK.

France has a system structured on a compromise between egalitarianism and classical liberalism, insisting that all have equal access to good care whilst ensuring that choice and competition are maintained. The basis of funding is compulsory social insurance, which covers 99% of the population. This compulsory insurance pays for half of total health expenditure, and about a quarter of costs are covered by out-of-pocket payments. Private insurance and voluntary mutual funds covers the rest. Again, there is much more choice, and a similar guarantee of access for all. There are virtually no waiting lists (except for transplants). French hospitals are public, private not-for-profit, and private for-profit. The private sector offers about a third of all beds. There are twice as many doctors and beds per head of population as in the UK. The Government closely regulates the system.

For the earlier history see the indispensable E. P. Hennock. *The origin of the welfare state in England and Germany, 1850–1914: social policies compared* (Cambridge, Cambridge University Press, 2007).

See OECD Electronic Publications, Paris, *OECD Health Data 1998: A Comparative Analysis of 29 Countries,* and *OECD Health Data 2001: A Comparative Analysis of 30 Countries* (10th edition); David Marsland, *Welfare or Welfare State Contradictions and Dilemmas in Social Policy* (London, Macmillan Press, 1996); *Seeds of Bankruptcy* (London, Claridge, 1988);

"Methodological inadequacies in British Social Science", in S. Cang (ed.), *Feschrift for Elliott Jaques* (Washington, D.C., Cason-Hall, 1992); "Not Cancelled – Postponed: A Revolution in Healthcare", *Health Business Summary*, Vol.13, pp. 4-9, 1994; "Public Service Plus: The Role of the Independent Sector in Health Care", *Health Summary*, Vol.13, pp.8-132, 1996.

E. Jabubowski, *Health Care Systems in the EU, A Comparative Study. European Parliament Working Paper*, SACO 101/revised. Brussels, European Parliament, 1998; World Health Organisation, *World Health Report 2000* (Geneva, WHO, 2000); R. Freeman, *The Politics of Health in Europe* (Manchester, Manchester University Press, 2000), 'European Policy Research Unit Series'; David Smith, "So how do you want to pay for it?", *Sunday Times*, news review, 2 December 2001; Reform, *Briefing note*, 11 December 2001 (Reform, London 2001); Karol Sikora, "New ideas needed to revive the NHS", letter, *The Times*, 20 February 2002.

David G. Green and Benedict Irvine, *Health Care in France and Germany: Lessons for the UK* (London, Civitas, December 2001) contains interesting material comparing the British, French and German systems, and reports interviews with French and German patients. This material was published in December 2001, after this lecture was delivered. But see also letter from Hilary Bramley, an NHS-trained nurse who has worked in the French health service, "NHS care row", *The Independent*, 25 January 2002.

14. P. J. O'Rourke, *Eat The Rich. A Treatise on Economics* (1998; London, Picador edition, 2000).

15. John Jewkes and Sylvia Jewkes, *The Genesis of the British National Health Service* (Oxford, Blackwell, 1961); Frank Prochashka, *The Voluntary Impulse, Philanthropy in Modern Britain* (London, Faber & Faber, 1988); *Philanthropy and the Hospitals of London, The King's Fund, 1897-1900* (Oxford, Clarendon Press, 1992), and *Royal Bounty* (London, Yale University Press, 1995). See also D. G. Green, *Working-Class Patients and the Medical Establishment* (London, Maurice Temple Smith, 1995); the magisterial Bentley B. Gilbert, *The Evolution of National Insurance in Great Britain, The Origins of the Welfare State* (London, Michael Joseph, 1966); Helen Bosanquet, *Social Work in London, 1869-1912* (London, John Murray, 1914; new edition, introduction by C. S. Yeo, Brighton, The Harvester Press, 1973); Robert Whelan with Berendina Smedley, *Helping the Poor. Friendly visiting, dole charities, and dole queues* (London, Civitas, 2001). See also, John Vincent. *Disraeli* (Oxford, Oxford University Press, 1990), especially pp.115-116.

16. There is good contemporary evidence, too, that when local communities take voluntary work seriously, local energies and aspirations can be harnessed, and that this can produce startling results when compared with the failures of big bureaucracies. The voluntary sector now engages 3 million people, accounting for £12 billion of services. See the account of the sector, and of specific initiatives in Tower Hamlets, East London, given by Brian Appleyard, "Will this be Britain's can-do revolution?", *Sunday Times*, news review, 3 February 2002.

17. Regretfully, I was not sufficiently persuasive. Nothing was done. Note added 31 July, 2015.

18. F. A. Hayek, *Individualism and Economic Order* (Chicago, Chicago University Press, 1948); *The Constitution of Liberty* (Chicago, Chicago University Press, 1960), *Studies in Philosophy, Politics and Economics* (London, Routledge, 1967), and *New Studies in Politics, Economics and the History of Ideas* (London, Routledge, 1978) and Robert Shepherd, *Enoch Powell, A Biography* (London, Hutchinson, 1996).

2. The Great Divide.

What you believe if you are a centraliser and a statist.

What you believe if you are a dynamist.

[Those] "thousands of immortal creatures condemned without alternative or choice, to tread, not what our great poet calls 'the primrose path to the everlasting bonfire', but one of jagged flints and stones, laid down by brutal ignorance..." Charles Dickens.

Before we consider future policy we should set out what represents 'The Great Divide.' This characterises the fundamental nature of the entire debate.

This divide is between the centraliser, and the dynamist. Between those who believe that hierarchical control administered by 'experts' should rule. That an ideology could and should construct a comprehensive and sufficient set of answers for all of us on to how to live our lives. And the alternative is offered by those who vest their faith in adaptive, trial-and-error evolution. It is a choice between knowing best and listening best, between having no individual responsibility and for the individual to shoulder this.

This choice offers very different views of the potentials of governments, of individuals, and of the nature of knowledge and ethics which guides policy and services – as well as guiding the individual living their own life. The choice is both instrumental and moral. It distinguishes between the language of 'self-improvement' and the rhetoric of positively-directed human perfectibility.

What does the centraliser believe? That we do not know our own individual interests best, but that 'experts' do know these. That they, on behalf of the state, should be in control – either from Whitehall, from a quango, or from local government. There must be a blueprint for all change, which they understand and manage. If you think thus, you usually believe in 'a system', rather than in the individual.

You also usually maintain a deep faith in 'planning' – despite the global shift away from greater government intervention and higher state spending, despite the collapse of the Soviet Union in 1989 and the Russian empire in Eastern Europe, despite the convergence of most societies on a common model of economic and social/political organisation based on liberal democracy and lightly regulated capitalism, despite the evidence of centrally planned economies such as North Korea and Zimbabwe, despite the results of the European Union's Common Agricultural Policy, despite the experiences of 'corporatist' Britain between 1945 and Mrs. Thatcher's first election in 1979, despite the insensitivities of local government (which would not be changed by a new agenda of 'localism'), despite public hostility to newly-planned health-service 'reconfiguration' in the first decade of the 21st century. It's despite a lot! We should carefully consider the foundations of this thinking which, however, still seeks to engineer ideologically preferred outcomes in the major public services of education and healthcare.

What, by contrast, does the dynamist believe? That knowledge is best gathered by free markets. Indeed, that this is the only way that such specific, individual and changing knowledge – much of it often tacit – can be expressed and gathered. That the responsibility of the individual is the greater source of personal and social and moral benefit. That the individual should be in control. That there must be no master-plan, but instead adaptive discovery. Similarly, we should examine this way of seeing, feeling, and acting. And that a liberal capitalist market economy (effectively, a hybrid democratic welfare capitalism) is the context for creating wealth, generating surpluses, paying for necessary social welfare, and which despite its flaws, has no alternative economic system waiting in the wings. This is the great divide. [1]

The first surprise is that such a chapter should still be useful, or even need to be attempted. However, in an era of New Labour Managerialism, Brownite Spenthrifting, and Compassionate Conservatism, this is the unfortunate necessity. The ideas in favour of hierarchy and of giantism still offered by the centraliser should have vanished with the decades of cruel experience and horrific knowledge of the Soviet Union under compulsory communism. We should be much more suspicious of the idea that the state is the essential architect of measures to provide all key services, and that the state must work hard at redistributing wealth.

It is extraordinary that these ideas persist, given the evidence in the wider economy in favour of market-based management rather than of central control. But they do so persist, notably in academic life in Britain, within the NHS, and in some leading charities and think-tanks which are taken seriously by the media and the public. These are viewed as "independent", which is to overlook their ideological frame of mind. There is, indeed, strikingly often a surprising lack of a plural perspective in analysis, research and the "objective" academic evaluation of alternatives. Thus, much commentary on health policy formulation is single-sided. What counts as evidence, what is legitimate as a frame of view, is too narrowly based.

There are honourable and outstanding exceptions, notably the late Dr. Arthur Seldon, the late Lord Harris of High Cross, Professor Philip Booth, Professor David Marsland, Professor Nicholas Bosanquet, Dr. David Green, and Dr. Heinz Redwood, most of whom are commentators associated with the Institute of Economic Affairs. Professor Julian Le Grand (a left-winger) and Mr. Roy Lilley are two noted independent commentators. But too often, however, 'the usual suspects' cite 'the usual suspects', and ignore those arguments with which they disagree, rather than confronting them and arguing back. It is not even that they have carefully considered the arguments in favour of markets, or against giant hierarchical organisation. They have often not even thought about them. They are still captivated by the notion that the acquisition and disposal of goods and services by the beneficent state will bring justice, if not prosperity, to all. Meanwhile, outside the NHS (and the attendant welfare and poverty 'industry') life styles and standards have dramatically improved, beyond the expectations of anyone who looked forward in 1945.

The development, evaluation and implementation of health care in the UK is, alas, too often contested from one chief point of view, that of the statist. This offers a political concern for fairness, equity, and solidarity. But it is rooted in socialist theory without reference to actual socialist practice. The different ways to achieve fairness, equity and social solidarity are singularly overlooked. This is not pragmatic. It is political. Indeed, the Department of Health does not need to control the debate (though it often does so by drip-fed, short-term contracts to think tanks and academic departments, and by pressure on 'independent' commissions, and by strategic staff transfers). It is a frame of mind which controls the debate. Those living within this frame of mind predominate in a number of leading think-tanks and University centres of health studies, as sources of commentary. Key figures from the Department of Health move in and out of some of these, with no apparent change to their intellectual or professional luggage, profile, or cultural role. One recent Permanent Secretary of the Department of Health became Chairman of the left-leaning advocate of the NHS, the King's Fund.

This cultural luggage includes the idea that the principles of health care funding, purchasing, and delivery are obvious. Here Robert Nozick offers us fair warning: "One persistent strand in utopian thinking…is the feeling that there is some set of principles obvious enough to be accepted by all men of good will, precise enough to give unambiguous guidance in particular situations, clear enough so that all will realise its dictates, and complete enough to cover all problems which actually will arise. Since I do not assume that there are such principles, I do not assume that the political realm will wither away. The messiness of the details of a political apparatus and the details of how *it* is to be controlled and limited do not fit easily into one's hope for a sleek, utopian scheme." [2] The NHS – as did the Soviet Union – represents this utopian temptation.

It was my own experience visiting behind the Iron Curtain (the USSR, and China) on official trade missions in 1980 and 1981 that the most pro-Western people in the world were the ordinary Soviet and Chinese citizens. But in the UK the most centralising (and often *sotto voce* pro-Marxist) people seem to be many of those "experts" who organise or endorse the bureaucratic allocation of rationed goods, whose scarcity is the deliberate and direct result of state monopoly policy. As Sir Alfred Sherman said in 2005, "there are probably still more Marxists in Oxford than in Moscow and more class warriors on the Clyde than the Neva, even if their faith has declined, while 'tax and spend' retains its inherent public appeal." [3]

It is thus important to seek some understanding of what centralisers believe, in identifying, assessing, and combating the impact of these ideas on British health care. And to spot where they are coming from, and what their statements imply. For they speak unto millions every day. They do so, within the old structure of docility and gratitude which has characterised the NHS for most of its 60 years. They speak, too, to a picture of society, of disease, and of opportunity which looks backwards to the twilight of the 1940s, rather than outwards to the actual picture individuals form and face today. They shadow a socialism which has comprehensively failed, but of which many still dream. We should be catching *them* in the wrong every day, as we seek a different kind of change.

Sixty-five years soon pass. The way we live now is much altered from the 1940s. There continue to be wholesale changes in society, in our relationships with ourselves, with others, and with government. To name but a few chief points: the new inter-active global information technology, rapid generational change, affordability and choice, the levelling up of standards in almost every respect (achieved by markets), the new balance between acute and chronic disease, much longer life expectations, the rise in individual expectations of personal responsibility, the fall of old ideas of experts disciplining passive recipients of services. But even despite these global social and cultural trends – and even if most of us have moved away from the idea of using state institutions (as in 1945) to transform society *en masse* – the approach to user power (and thus, to information and to access to financial clout) remains paternalist.

And the approach to politics (and to health care reform) remains set in the idea that before the individual can matter he or she must be integrated into a group, be "involved" in a consultative exercise, or be part of a political mechanism. To matter *as an individual* in health care is, it seems, illegitimate. This is an extraordinary situation. Indeed, the approach to improving health care remains one of assuming that the only way an individual could or should seek to improve health care is by being politically active. However, we should take a peep at the past, which as William Faulkner said, is neither dead nor past. Indeed, its frozen attitudes are all around us.

Let us ask:

<u>a) What you usually believe if you are a centraliser, a statist (and/or a 'communitarian'):</u>

1. **That order requires political design.** That is, that solutions require an overarching plan. That there is a rationality which is different than that offered by the market, but that it can only be interpreted on our behalf, developed and managed by experts, and by a powerful professional class. This, by contrast with the notion that you should offer people a choice of bridges to their own self-determined futures in a diverse web of relationships of their own choosing. And within an adaptive, creative, evolving society of surprises and innovations.

   The centraliser believes that there is one best way, one model of social perfection. And that bureaucracy, politicians, and professionals – the powerful and the wise (in what Milton Friedman called the 'iron triangle'- which excludes the fourth party, or service-user from decision-making) – can know what this is.

   This is the rationalist delusion that social engineering can perfect life and create a new kind of person, free of the inevitable burdens of individuality and choice. It is a survival of a pre-Darwinian need for ancient, universal authority, what Walter Pater called a search for the "beauty of holiness" and the "elegance of sanctity". Lenin was a leading member of the crew with this view.

The economist Joseph Schumpeter wrote of the "gale of creative destruction." This, by contrast, with the calamitous consequences of Marxism-Leninism, the most evolved vanguard "expert" view expressed both by Gosplan, by the camps in Siberia, and by the "cultural revolution" in which many millions were put to death.

2. **That it is government that makes communities.** And so, through "top-sight" – the bird's eye-view – 'experts' can see not only the big picture but all the individual details critical in individual lives, tastes, preferences and values, and that policy thus can be constructed – both in the interests of the individual, the local and national community. This assumes that our individual preferences, our values and interest, are deducible by others. That diverse information amongst millions can be so gathered – and by experts rather than by price and markets. That communities are made by government, rather than by voluntary action and association. This approach depends on the notion that each of us has an unproblematic, inner nature from which our "needs" can be deduced, and, indeed, known in advance. This concept has had many totalitarian children, marching under the banners of "historical inevitability" and of the Webbian "expert" knowing best.

The concept of "needs" stands there still – it is the nuts and bolts of things, the breath and sight of reality in NHS approaches to the renovation of centralism. But contrast "needs" with "wants" which only the individual can express for themselves in making moral and voluntary but self-responsible choices, free of determinism and close supervision by "experts."

The consequences of "needs analysis" can indeed be grim, for individuals and for the general society. For patients are not units of a plan, but individuals. A community is a voluntary association. But patients who need innovative treatments which are costly are often a prime target for rationing in the plan.

3. **That there are knowable individual "needs" and specific outcomes which politics can and should achieve and which can somehow be captured in advance and then set into 'policy.'** That is, that not only can experts decide (or "assess"!) our "needs", but that they can decide on what should be acceptable quality to the diverse individuals, or how high quality can and should be, and on the priority listing of who should be treated first, and who last or not at all. Here "need" is an imprecise concept, open to subjective interpretations and political, ethical, and administrative judgements, and where the emotions of the "decision-maker" are not necessarily those of the patient, explicit or tacit.

The language of "needs" – to which the majority of NHS managers cling keenly

– is part of the armoury of centralised rationing and bureaucratic control. The moral problems are many, if we accept the idea that "needs" can be decided on our behalf by the centraliser. Who is in most serious "need"? Which patient is of most value to society? Is a child a higher priority than an adult? Is the patient who has waited longest to be treated next? Is outcome (or the capacity to benefit most) to decide priority? It may seem so. But who judges that, and how? Who pre-judges it? On what basis? Age? Gender? Colour? Origins? Class? Previous costs? We can see how dangerous this is.

Who meets which criteria of some quality and life-adjusted ratio devised by health economists? The use of the word "needs" raises the challenge of whether we want such judgements made about ourselves by others, if indeed, they can be made on anything but an arbitrary basis at all. What is the evidence for decisions? What are the "facts"? The problem is very significant in areas of genuine shortage, such as renal care where there are too few organs available for transplants. "Needs" contradicts the self-responsibility implied by the word "wants." Its partner in this burglary of the patients' rights is ageism. [4] Its frame of mind is refluxed in the advocacy of the virtues of rationing by academics and administrators, despite the evidence to the contrary from almost all OECD members.

As the historian and cultural commentator Shirley Robin Letwin wrote: "The NHS was designed to satisfy 'needs' rather than 'wants.' 'Needs' are given by nature, and only experts, doctors and social scientists can know how to satisfy them. Therefore, the patient is to be seen not as a consumer, deciding what he wants, but as a passive recipient of whatever the all-knowing powers on high decide that he ought to have. Therefore consumer sovereignty would defeat the purpose of a national health service …[the organisation] aimed to treat passive bundles of 'needs' rather than independent consumers with a will to choose what they wanted and a right to complain about how their wants were being satisfied." [5] We should beware, too, of what one commentator has warned of concerning the "results of prejudice, preference, professional blindness, failure of moral nerve, and conditioning, which parade as the grand and obvious discoveries of objective scientific method." [6]

4. **That "decision-makers" can have all the relevant information about individuals, their values, life-styles, and preferences concerning treatments, practitioners, side-effects, individual trade-offs, outcomes, and what they can and would prefer to live with.** That decision-makers can know – how? through "consultation"? through voting? – what is usually tacit information embedded in the lives of individuals, expressed in their relationships and habits, and which they may not articulate even to themselves. Not, that is, until they face a health crisis of their own and ask a doctor and ask themselves what might be done? This belief of "decision-makers" (the phrase is proclaimed from above as a respected and legitimate category – but are we not all decision-makers, or shouldn't we be?) assumes that human values and preferences can be derived from some general theory of understanding about human nature, and what all want. Indeed, that we

all want the same things, and that these are not in conflict. Isaiah Berlin has shown us that this is not the case.

5. **That government should decide what it is appropriate for the individual to spend on health-care, where and how it should be "allocated" or "targeted."** This is usually in the interests of a political objective such as an imposed and artificial "equality." Indeed, the assertion here is that optimal outcomes and values are technical questions. However, it is a political decision to determine the size of the health care and social care budget, or what we can "afford" – as recent huge increases in NHS expenditure demonstrate. A budget is an administrative vehicle for controlling expenditure. As Heinz Redwood has pointed out, the fact that expenditure is tightly controlled is unrelated to what is or is not affordable. And, as I have argued, it is the individual who should make this decision for themselves. [7] It is difficult to resist the idea that if government must decide then this is a totalitarian view, even if founded in benign intention and expressed in seemingly supportive and emotive language.

6. **That it is legitimate to use political power to deny choice, limit experimentation, over-ride competition, suppress competitive processes and local knowledge.** This, in the interests of political objectives such as harmonisation, consistency (which the NHS does not – indeed, cannot – deliver in practice), to short-circuit the feedback of the market, and control the pace and nature of progress. This misunderstands that knowledge is inherently dispersed. It can only be captured by individual purchasing decisions, and by price. The alternative idea sets out a contempt for ordinary human beings, indoctrinating them to abandon – indeed, not even to attempt to develop – faith in their own judgement. It deters learning to choose. It denies the nature of knowledge. It debases the fundamentals of individual moral sovereignty and responsibility (for themselves, for their choices, for their actions, and for consequences), of private judgement about private things, and the very nature of what it is to be a human being who must face both him/her self and the challenges of the world.

7. **That to be good the future must be finite, predictable, "safe"; that change is scary.** Thus, a good future must be the product of detailed, technocratic blueprints or a return to an idealised, stable past. This contradicts much of what we know of the real world.

8. **That political activism can and should secure improved individual services acceptable to all.** This, via "consultation", user "involvement", citizen's juries, and participation in planning processes. The assumption here is that such processes do indeed inevitably empower service-users, and so the results are thought to confirm the assumption. There is little or no doubt in 'knowing' minds. And this despite the gulf between a minority consultative "jury" and the large number of (rationally) non-participating present and future patients.

9. **That it is reasonable to meet the demand for more consumer influence over**

services by shifting power from the centre to local government, and that this actually diminishes central control. Statists argue this case even though regional and local government are centres of power much more like central government than they are like smaller, self-governing, member-owned, mutual, co-operative and democratic institutions. Devolution seems likely to be permission to implement locally what has been decided nationally. This is so whether devolution happens under a Labour or a Conservative administration. This is qualitatively different from decision-making by individuals, enjoying self-responsible liberty.

As John Marenbon has written: "The concentration in regional and local authorities is as much centralisation as the concentration of power nationally – and more so when, because of the closeness of the governed to their governors the freedoms of individuals and small, intermediate institutions are all the more limited." [8] Individuals, small groupings, voluntary associations, local mutual-aid efforts, personal moral responsibility and the institutions of freedom are all under-mined by the intrusion of government – whether central, regional, *or* local – in territory which should be the responsibility of the individual.

10. **That the purpose of government is to find a common ground on which everyone can agree.** This is the statist emphasis, rather than government setting out deliberately to respect the diversity of different possible conceptions of a good life, of what is reasonable, of what an individual may prefer, of what may evolve unexpectedly over time.

<u>b) Let us ask what do you usually believe if you are a dynamist?</u>

Look at the mirror of the future. Or at the opposite of the above.

- **That the unique existence of individuals must be taken with the utmost seriousness, and that they are not resources for others.** Each individual has their *own* life to lead.

- **That there are principles of an open system which are applicable to *all* situations, and that these are as applicable to health and social care as to any other area in life.** For in health and social care the wider social gains we seek can only be achieved in an open system. Thus, the gains we see elsewhere in life – from fluidity, variety, ingenuity, risk-taking and experiment, unexpected innovation, competition, adaptation, learning, risk-assessment by the individual, improvement, evolution and the diversity and subtlety generated in spontaneously emerging order – are not otherwise achievable. It is also this extension of capabilities which is so much wanted, and can offer individuals so much in health and social care. Fundamental here is incentive, pluralist competition, the disciplines of the open market, and individual choice and self-responsibility.

- **That the spontaneous co-ordination of the actions of many people** itself generates order. And one which is more flexible and more open to evolution than imposed hierarchical order.

- **That we should support a structure which enables dynamism to function.** And thus we should limit universal rule-making by government to broad and lasting principles. That is, to an active role – protecting choice and competition, making and watching over some fundamental rules. And serving as an umbrella beneath which individuals can follow their preferences, express themselves, test alternatives for themselves. This, by contrast to the centralising planner who looks to a pre-ordained map by which to govern each foreseeable situation, and thus to retain control. For the planner wants detailed rules which apply to everyone: for example, government will decide what is spent on health care, where, and for whom.

- The alternative is to allow genuinely democratic, member-owned organisations and structures to evolve, to seek to deliver an agreed 'good' such as appropriate – and probably, targeted rather than wastefully universal – health cover for all. This within a general framework of enabling rules maintained by government. As in France, for example, this would especially protect choice and competition. And it would require government to set standards for training and registration, for quality and safety, for public health measures, for transparency of financing and of contract, for comprehensive coverage of the population, and for relationships between insurers and providers.

- **That government should recognise and respect the diversity of different possible conceptions of a good life, of what is reasonable, of what an individual may prefer.** Here, the protection of competition as a key role.

- **That the future is inviting, not intimidating.** That progress instead comes not from a central blueprint, but from an evolutionary, decentralised, unpredictable process which ultimately raises all boats.

- **That one cannot determine in advance how people will make personal trade-offs, how express their different values, beliefs, preferences, complexities.** That tacit knowledge cannot be known in advance, or gathered into 'policy.' That you cannot determine in advance which people will come up with the best ideas. Instead, individual values must be enabled to be expressed, and all ideas must be enabled to be tried out to see how they will work.

- **That free choice and competition alone enables this to happen.** And that it alone can gather knowledge from individuals and release sufficient and new resources, prompt new and varied provision, and check deficits, denials, and excesses much less easily adjusted by government, managers and bureaucrats in the absence of open markets.

- **That there is a direct link between direct incentive, personal investment and the provision of preferred, personal, intimate, separable benefits in health care.** Without this recognition there will remain too little political support for governments to raise sufficient funds for care, from a mix of tax-based (mandatory) and personal, voluntary (optional) extra spending.

- **That markets are the only way to gather the scattered information to solve the 'information (or knowledge) problem.'** This information is relayed through prices to interested parties, not least to the dispersed consumer of services. For prices reflect a multitude of individual preferences and allow us to benefit from the knowledge permanently and widely dispersed (and constantly changing) – which lies beyond the reach or ken even of centres of invention and science.

- **That the central planner gets the nature of knowledge wrong.** The planner believes that the knowledge of what a patient would prefer can be gathered – by general elections, or by "consultation" and the "participatory democracy" of citizen's juries – which seek to second-guess the values and preferences of others. Yet the planner cannot make decisions without the necessary but dispersed and often unarticulated tacit knowledge of present and future patients. Planners, instead, must substitute their own judgement and hypotheticals for the dispersed knowledge only conveyable through freely-set and competitive prices and market processes. It is no surprise that 'voice' without the possibility of 'exit' to a preferred alternative is notably ineffective.

- **That "community" matters, but that it is reliant on the notion of voluntary behaviour.** That is, we join communities voluntarily. Indeed, it is a mark of civilisation to protect that idea. This means individuals being able to choose from diverse communities. Essential here are the ideas of choice, and of voluntary action, of collective action without collectivism. As Robert Nozick wrote: "If the [diverse] ideas must actually be tried out, there must be many communities trying out different patterns. The filtering process, the process of eliminating communities that our framework involves is very simple: people try out living in various communities, and they leave or slightly modify the ones they don't like (find defective). Some communities will be abandoned, others will struggle along, others will split, others will flourish, gain members and be duplicated elsewhere. Each community must win and hold the voluntary adherence of its members. No pattern is *imposed* on everyone, and the result will be one pattern (if any) only if everyone voluntarily chooses to live in accordance with that pattern of community." [9]

- **That "legitimacy" and "responsibility" greatly matter, as well as "community."** That "legitimacy" for an entity is only achieved by the voluntary adherence of individuals – for example, by voluntarily joining a mutual-aid organisation to purchase care on one's behalf. Indeed, the idea of "Responsibility" is of little meaning unless we ask "Responsible for what?" For ourselves and our behaviour? This necessarily displaces a single, static model by the differing rules (or, if you like, options for services) of diverse communities. An example of a diverse community might be a mutual-aid organisation buying health-care for voluntary subscribers, which must compete for adherents. As such organisations succeed the more legitimacy they enjoy, the more local knowledge they incorporate and reflect in their work. Indeed, these gains are driven by devices that allow the expression of our individual knowledge. And to individual and thus collective benefit.

- **That the individual must be allowed an understanding of their own lives.** This necessarily implies individual control and learning.

Both the statist and the dynamist believe in a central organising intellectual principle. Yet how different these are, in nature, in working, and in their consequences. For the statist the principle is an imposed unity of sameness. For the dynamist the commitment is to an open-ended process, not a specific outcome, one which encourages diversity, evolves through trial and error, and offers what the important cultural commentator Virginia Postrel calls "a rich ecology of human choices."

The argument on the side of the dynamist is that unconscious and spontaneous evolution can generate better – that is, both more effective and more legitimate – solutions than social engineering produces, has produced, and is likely to produce. To that extent the dynamists are the party of life. They are open-minded about solutions which emerge from the interaction of all the individuals concerned. They do not under-estimate the intelligence of ordinary people. Nor their capacity to learn to choose. They do not insist that they are brighter (the Americans say "smarter") than the millions of people who vote with their money in the daily referendum of the market-place. They do not insist that people need not trouble themselves about anything that matters in health care, for a providential state and providential "experts" will think for them about what is good for them, as perpetual parents.

Instead, dynamists believe that ordinary human agents can be trusted – indeed, must be trusted – to know what is best for themselves. And we live in a better society and enjoy better individual lives if we each take ultimate responsibility for our own choices. So this is about freedom and moral witness.

Dynamists believe that compulsion should be avoided. But in health care some compulsion may be an unavoidable key to the door which leads to greater investment, greater capacity, higher morale, an improved environment, more diverse provision, the funding to support it, and the prompt to creativity and responsiveness in services. You probably don't much like compulsion through insurance and the requirement to join a mutual-purchaser. But there may no other way, as young people think they will live forever. And we do require to broaden the financial base of health purchasing and provision if we are to take up all the new opportunities which new cancer drugs, for example, offer to us. This remains a philosophical and a practical conundrum, and a source of great discomfort to dynamists.

Price – and the recognition of cost, by consumers – are essential elements. What you believe about price and value matters. You may believe a thing is worth what people will give for it, and that it isn't worth anything else. Or you may believe people value what they get for nothing, or at least without appreciating true cost. However, price is unavoidable. More than that, it is to be welcomed. For we know of no other device for sorting out choices, distributing scarce resources cost-effectively and efficiently. Other than markets we know of no other device for establishing prices, or for distributing resources efficiently. There is, also, alas, no escape from affordability.

It is difficult to resist the thought that the ideas of centralisers reflect a common fear amongst the privileged classes at the end of the 19th century, carried over into the 20th and now into the 21st century. That English society might still one day fall victim to the undisciplined, uneducated, and uncultured "mob", and that the chaos of the French Revolution might still occur on British soil. For many in the 19th century, Carlyle's *History of the French Revolution* (1847) was a familiar text, and a warning that social upheavals were inevitable if reforms were ignored. But intellectuals still fear to educate the working-classes.

The Paris Commune of 1870 had reminded people of the potential of chaos. At Tennyson's funeral Edmund Gosse had written of "the unparalleled masses of the curious", outside on the Westminster pavements. The danger of the crowd, the fear of a rising tide of chaos, seems still to be part of the mental machinery of the planner, and a source of determined resistance to financially-empowered democracy. So, too, the denial of the sharing of forbidden knowledge together with the fear from above of the dire consequences of too much knowledge in the hands of those below, the uncomprehending public. This idea – rampant in modernist literature, but also in the daily conversations of many in the NHS – co-exists with the offer of knowledgeable leadership from above, on our behalf, in a skein of imposed "positive liberty." Like it or not.

Choice, for and by "the common reader"? Alfred Wallace, Darwin's great contemporary, said that "plants live where they can." But animals have to a great extent the power of choice. And we alone have free-will. We should hold tight to this liberty, and try to secure all of its benefits. We should decline the temptation to believe that the state alone can represent the bonds of union between people or be the only proper initiator of further development. If we do so we will join the legion of those who reject what Michael Ignatieff dismissed as "the radiant tomorrow", which has usually only to be achieved by totalitarian means. We instead prefer to rely on responsible scepticism concerning authority, and in faith in ourselves.

We should recover Tennyson's refrain from *In Memoriam* (1850):

> *"There lives more faith in honest doubt,*
> *Believe me, than in half the creeds."*

Or, from the great insider-outsider Joseph Conrad, with the idea in *Nostromo* (1904) that "Action is consolatory. Only in the conduct of our action can we find the sense of mastery over the Fates."

We do not want our life-choices placed in the hands of "experts", planners, and politicians – if we can help it (which we can if we decide so to do!).

The critic Kevin Jackson says that Ruskin's most famous maxim is that the highest of all mortal powers is the power of sight. As Ruskin wrote, "The greatest thing a human soul ever does in this world is to see something, and tell what it saw in a plain way. Hundreds of people can talk for one who can think, but thousands can think for one who can see. To see clearly is poetry, prophecy and religion, all in one." [10]

This is *the* difference between the centraliser and the dynamist.

I am not alone in these views. Professor David Marsland – a great dynamist – writes that prejudice in principle against markets and in favour of monopoly state provision of health care has negatively shaped British sociological analysis of welfare in general and health care in particular since 1945. [11]

As he shows, sociologists tend, with few exceptions to underplay to the point of active denigration the potentially positive role of markets, competition, enterprise, and incentives. They over-estimate the scope for effective central planning. They lay greater emphasis on generalised principles of presumed social justice than on the particularities of individual consumers' wants and satisfactions. The King's Fund and its commentaries is a leading UK example. Such statists also under-estimate the scale and significance of costs and down-play their importance in rational policy development. They sympathise with the concerns of trade unions and professional associations, at the cost of different kinds of managerial efficiency, consumer satisfaction, and of individuals learning to choose. They presume on some general trend of history towards increased state control and away from active participation by private, independent, and voluntary producers and suppliers of goods and services.

By contrast, Professor David Marsland is intellectually and methodologically rigorous. His work is pure gold. It contains much material relevant to the subject matter of these present essays, notably on un-asked questions, un-researched problems, and un-toward assumptions. As I have suggested, too, Virginia Postrel's work – *The Future and Its Enemies. The Growing Conflict over Creativity and Progress* – is the essential companion in considering the statist and the dynamist and their two world views.

NOTES.

1. I am especially indebted to Virginia Postrel's important work, *The Future and Its Enemies, The Growing Conflict over Creativity, Enterprise, and Progress* (New York, The Free Press, 1998). I have drawn extensively on her arguments and insights. This brilliant book should be on the desk of every health service manager. But I would be surprised if there is even *one* copy on *any* desk *anywhere* in the NHS. In addition, a number of books in recent management literature and in 'transaction-cost economics' do much to remove any faith we might retain in hierarchy, in large hierarchical organisations and in how these function in the real world. See Jeffrey Nielsen's *The Myth of Leadership. Creating Leaderless Organisations* (Mountain View, CA.., Davies-Black, 2004), and Kenneth Cloke and Joan Goldsmith, *The End of Management and the Rise of Organisational Democracy* (New York, Jossey Bass Wiley, 2002).

Professor Oliver Williamson (of the University of California at Berkeley) compared the costs of doing things in the marketplace and of doing these within public bodies. The results showed that the costs of doing things within hierarchical organisations can be very big. Chris Dillow has discussed this evidence and argued that one reason for the failures within large organisations is communication failure. "Subordinates have lots of reasons not to tell bosses the truth. They don't want to burden 'busy' people with detail, or rock the boat, or be the victim of 'shoot the messenger' syndrome. The upshot of this was famously described by the late Kenneth Boulding: 'The larger and more authoritarian the organisation, the better the chance that its top decision-makers will be operating in purely imaginary worlds.' See Chris Dillow, *The End of Politics. New Labour and The Folly of Managerialism* (London, Harriman House, 2007) and his article 'We put up with terrible, inept government. Why?', *The Times*, 30 May 2007, p.19.

2. Robert Nozick, *Anarchy, State, and Utopia* (Oxford, Basil Blackwell, 1974), p.330.

3. Alfred Sherman, *Paradoxes of Power. Reflections on the Thatcher Interlude* (Exeter, Imprint Academic, 2005), p.20.

4. David Millward, "Doctors 'are still writing off patients aged 60 and over'", *Daily Telegraph*, 19 January 2002.

5. Shirley Robin Letwin, *The Anatomy of Thatcherism* (London, Fontana, 1992).

6. L. D. Willard, "Needs and Medicine", *J.Med.Phil.*, 7,3, pp.259-73.

7. Heinz Redwood, *Why Ration Health Care? An international study of the United Kingdom, France, Germany and public sector health care in the USA* (London, Civitas, 2000). See also my *The Realities of Rationing* (London, Institute of Economic Affairs, 1999).

8. John Marenbon, The Dominance of Centrism and the Politics of Certainty (London, Politea, 1997), p.9.

9. Nozick, *ibid.*, p.316.

10. John Ruskin, cited in Kevin Jackson, *A Ruskin Alphabet* (Tonbridge, Worple Press, 2000).

11. David Marsland, "Progressing Health and Healthcare", in R. E. Krausz and G. Tulea (eds.), *Starting the Twenty-first Century: Sociological Reflections and Challenges* (New Brunswick and London, Transaction Publishers, 2001).

3. Beware 'Choice'!

"Every one of them wore chains like Marley's Ghost; some few (they might be guilty governments) were linked together; none were free." Charles Dickens.

You want 'choice'? Well, consider: there is no greater reality check than a cheque. We need to keep this clearly in mind as we consider how to make choice real, individual, and effective.

'Choice' in public services is now a key offer from all three main political parties. As an attitude, however, it is inadequate. Even as an aspirational – even, an inspirational – policy it falls short. That is, unless we seriously consider how can it be made to work, instrumentally, for every individual. And how can it increase 'equity – for more assured access, greater safety and good outcomes – for all. This last matters, for without confirmed equity in tune with the British notion of 'fairness' the necessary changes to improve health care will remain politically problematic. Certainly, the necessity to sell genuine choice seems to discourage politicians from adopting that other necessary quality, "courage." They fear being led into that electorally hazardous territory about which Jim Hacker's advisers warned him. How else to explain a decade of silence from H.M. Loyal Opposition, which has not even opened the debate on how to make *individual* choice effective? Yet no debate can be won until it begins. [1]

Labour in power has hardly done better. Gordon's billions, thrown at education and healthcare, have not adequately improved quality, patient safety or productivity. [2] The long-standing failures to achieve equity by the NHS remain as indelible as ever. The poor, the ethnic, women, the disabled, the unlucky, the mentally ill – all these are still persistently identified as the victims of discrimination within the NHS, and of deficits in equity.

Too often, the alternative to facing cash and choice has been substitute and standstill policies which buy three apples for two pence, and sell two apples for three pence. The NHS system still lacks direct economic incentives for change. In schools, too, there have been too few incentives for teachers to adopt approaches which enable Janet and John to learn to read. [3] Opinion polls suggest that the voters are frustrated, angry, and disappointed. Popular commentators (such as the *Sunday Times* first leader writer in November 2007) have suggested that "There has been waste on an epic scale as public sector managers have gorged on the current of cash. Improvements in public services did occur, but they were hardly value for money, when compared with the tens of billions of pounds poured in…" And: "In Labour's ever larger public sector tent, reward is linked only tenuously to performance and is often given even in circumstances of failure." [4]

'Choice' is seen by politicians as the antidote to these deficits. 'Choice' is the fashionable new mantra. It is the new 'cry.' 'Choice' is the new 'big idea.' 'Choice' is the new participatory slogan. It may even be the oxygen that can revive opposition parties. But is it a genuine credential for change in health-care provision, or merely cosmetic? What can 'choice' mean for the individual seeking a personal, timely, and separable service? And how is effective 'choice' in health care (and in education) to be achieved?

Disraeli said that "We govern men with words." But we need to de-mystify the word 'choice' and to be clear what it can and cannot mean. If it stands alone it means little.

The short answer to making choice real in every life is to give people back their own money, and to give the poor tax-credits so that they stand in the same purchasing position as the middle-classes.

In addition, I suggest, this is the only way in which two major objectives can be achieved: professionals can be re-motivated, and equity (of access, safety and outcome) can be achieved. Neither objective has been satisfactorily attained in the NHS. Indeed, both professional morale and equity seem now to be worse than ever. The British traditionally seek fairness. Choice is the route by which the disempowered can be empowered, and the many groups disadvantaged by the NHS can at last secure leverage, equity, and better health care.

So I begin this discussion with a serious health warning. *Beware.* Beware. Beware the word "choice." It is now the small change of the politics of 'ins and outs', of bids for votes. It is becoming 'the centre ground', where British general elections – we are told by pundits – are usually won. But it has no effective meaning unless directly linked to money and to incentives. The Prime Minister said, in his Queen's Speech on BBC2 TV broadcast on 6 November 2007: "You are the patient. You are in charge." I quote verbatim. But what can this possibly mean, if the individual does not control the money? It means nothing. It has no operational or instrumental meaning. It is merely rhetoric.

And so those politicians who speak loosely of 'choice' now have to move from aspiration to effective instruments for change. There is a clear basis for doing so. In addition, the greatest political risk would seem to be to take no risks, and to misunderstand the mood of the times in the search for safe sanctuary.

Four points which are the pivot of all I will say on choice and healthcare.

1. Care is for every individual a uniquely personal, intimate, timely and personal experience. This is one of the fundamentals of why choice matters. There is a key distinction between being able individually to command such *a personal service* and seeking to discipline *a system*. Even if you think you can do so in an occasional, diffuse election about a bundle of competing policies. Even if you think you can reliably secure what has been promised once the election is over.

2. Choice concerns the nature of society and what we think of the potentials of

individuals and also of governments. As F.A. Hayek said, learning to choose is both a moral issue and a necessary quality of becoming an adult. It is indeed intrinsically virtuous, and not merely instrumental. But there is no virtue without the instruments to make it real for the isolated and scattered individual.

3. Genuine choice for all is *only* possible if a series of linked conditions co-exist. These are: individual control over tax-based funds; competing (including independent) provision and capacity; information and advice; and regulation to protect competition, both from monopoly and from political interference.

4. The evidence shows that people do want choice, as we will see in a moment.

As I have said – it bears repetition – the short answer to delivering uniquely personal care, to do so in a moral framework, and to make choice real is to give people back their own money, and by giving the poor tax-credits. For choice to be an instrument rather than an aspiration we need real and specific levers and incentives which work. As the economist Steven Landsburg famously said, "People respond to incentives. The rest is commentary." [5]

First, the individual must have control over a personal tax-based individual healthcare fund. I have urged Patient Fund-holding – the individual with a tax-based fund (or a tax-transfer if poor) which they take to a mutual, co-operative purchaser, the Patient Guaranteed Care Association. In my recent books, *Patients, Power and Responsibility* and then *Who Decides Who Decides?* I set out the details of how this would work, and of how to 'get it done.'

As I have urged earlier, there *is* no greater reality check than a cheque. Choice, if it is to be an effective incentive, must offer to bring more funds to the good provider, less to the bad. Otherwise, the provider incentives are to side-step any extra and un-funded work. It is the individual and not the politicised pressure-group that should commit the individual funds, via the mutual purchasing association which attracts mobile money. Too many people demanding your service but with no new funds is hopeless. No one wanting your service is a real incentive. Choice must bring the direct incentive for providers to seek willing revenues. Choice must make a certainty of cash ebb for declining service. Choice must be individual, not collective. This, too, will then reveal poor quality and under-performance

Financially-empowered choice requires integrated social design. This must encourage freedom for local, adaptive autonomous evolution, including professional and clinical freedoms within a market context. Indeed, professional performance can only be enabled in such an environment. For good professional performance is directly linked to adaptive change.

Professionals can be managed in three ways: by targets (which they dislike), by themselves (a privilege which is no longer acceptable), or by an evolving market. The keys to that are financial empowerment and incentive *both* for individual choice *and* for professional development. We can both conserve *and* improve, in a framework not only of law but of moral compliance in a system with a sense of equal justice. Choice, indeed, is conciliatory.

We can hardly hope to make significant progress, however, if we think we can do so by not changing anything very much. We are not 18th century Whigs. Leadership and timing are everything in politics too. Leadership includes the ability to sense and act on the need for change. Politically, the necessity is to measure change to the needs of the times. So far as professionals in medicine are concerned, choice should be seen both as conciliatory and necessary, by both professionals and politicians. Practical measures and real instruments for choice are needed, based on careful analysis and on public persuasions. Root-and-branch systemic changes can, indeed, be made while strengthening the character of professional life.

This need not be dangerous ground. Instead, it can be the field for a more harmonious society. Doctors matter – and individual, financially-empowered choice can strengthen the professional rather than weaken their position. Choice can actually empower professionals and managers in the necessity of adaptive behaviour in a proper market as they develop new ways to help patients. This is the only alternative to de-motivating central targets. An age of transition, of course. But everyone ever born has lived in an 'age of transition.' Here we are not unusual. The required and systemic architectural change can be achieved, brick by brick, by and with professionals. These can be based on practical measures rooted in careful analysis. But let's get on with it. As Richard Donkin recently wrote, "If your ship has been wrecked and you have taken to a life raft, your world is the raft and the sea, and you had better get used to it. Survivors very quickly begin to model and map their real environment instead of one that may have been more comfortable and familiar…." [6] Or, as Lawrence Gonzalez has said, it's important to discover the first rule of life: "Be here now." [7]

All very well, you may say. But no one wants choice, do they? And they can't make it work, can they? And they aren't informed, or informable, are they? And when they have choice, they don't use it, do they? And if they do use it, they decide what "we", the managers who know their interests better than they know themselves would have done anyway, don't they? So why all the fuss?

Well, some *evidence*, if you please.

I call to the stand Professor Julian Le Grand, Richard Titmuss Professor of Social Policy at the London School of Economics and formerly Mr. Blair's senior policy adviser at No.10. Julian and I have known one another for 50 years. We were students together at the University of Sussex in the mid-1960s, and Julian is no right-wing radical. But his recent book, *The Other Invisible Hand*, summarises important evidence. [8] I draw on the evidence which he discusses. He shows that recent British Social Attitudes Survey, Audit Commission, and YouGov and Ipsos MORI polling evidence suggests that people want choice. And that the less well-off, usually without choices in their lives, wanted *more* choice in health and education. There were, indeed, larger majorities in favour of choice among the less well off than among the middle classes (who have it anyway, via their cheque books). NHS pilots evaluated by the Picker Institute showed, too, not only that people take up choices when they exist, but that the poor and disadvantaged want *more* choices than the middle-classes.

The clinical evidence, unsurprisingly, shows that choice is good for you. A sense of control has a powerful effect on the ability to respond to treatment and on speed of recovery. The clinical evidence shows, too, that people with the same condition make very different choices with regard to preferred treatments, likely experiences and outcomes, and the consequences with which they choose to be able to live. Given choices people often make surprising decisions. Decisions that planners may not make for us. Decisions we might not make for ourselves. But which they prefer for themselves. Deciding between what Isaiah Berlin called "incommensurables", or difficult choices each of which has inevitable consequences and side-effects. [9]

In addition, effective choice can be more socially inclusive and be designed to give greater funds and power to the presently disadvantaged. Choice has thus both an intrinsic and an instrumental value. It is about a better society and about better, more effective services for individuals. It can, too, deliver those eternal British verities of fairness and of services free at the point of use.

We all want high quality, efficiently managed, responsive and accountable local services, delivered equitably. We also want continuous, cost-effective, adaptive innovation – and autonomous incentives to go further.

Crucially, we want incentives for improvements. As Professor Le Grand says, too, we want these *embedded within* any system. Unavoidably embedded. For the challenge is to design a system of *effective* choice with many *personal* and *public* benefits. One, too, which can lift professional morale by encouraging more autonomous, adaptive behaviour locally. The alternatives of centralised targets, hierarchical decision-making, and market mimicry without individual empowerment – citizen's juries and the rest – are unconvincing. The waves may ebb and flow, but there is no doubt about the direction of the tide.

Dostoyevsky once said that "The formula that two and two makes five is not without its attractions." But we should be suspicious of the many governmental substitutes for choice, including politicised localisation. Real choice relies on markets, the guarantee of competition, prices, and having alternative or surplus capacity. Markets use the particular to realise the universal. Uniquely, they gather dispersed knowledge for focussed change. As our own post-war history in Britain shows us, markets and markets alone can give the poorest all the fundamental choices enjoyed by the middle-class. So the challenge is to empower the individual with cash and cash transfers in a market – to enable individuals to select appropriate treatments and outcomes, and to enable organisations to achieve greater productivity, cost savings and adaptive change.

However – markets, prices, and alternative or surplus capacity have been forbidden words in Whitehall healthcare debate. And so in public services there has been much market mimicry, posing as choice.

Thus we have had:

- Proposals for greater accountability by having directly elected local health boards, but with no necessity for providers to respond to individual financially-empowered choice.

- Much recent talk of focussing on local priorities.

- More provider freedoms but with no demand-side change.

- NHS staff running consultation events about the configuration of services, and setting this agenda – which is very different from an individual being able to secure a preferred service when wanted.

- Offering *a say*, even *a greater say* as a proxy for individual, financially-empowered choice. Thus, involvement as citizens but not as financially-empowered consumers.

- The continued delivery of NHS-designated 'needs', not consumer discovered 'wants.'

- Choices as posed by managers, and as set against their standards.

- A patient's forum representative on every NHS Trust – 600 new voices amongst 60 million.

- Necessarily unrepresentative citizen's juries.

- Eventual, diffused, generalised electoral accountability, but which secures no individual choice when an actual service is wanted.

- Master-plans and centralised controls and targets which do not encourage adaptive discovery.

And so, to repeat, the two vital correctives to the imbalances of power which ordinary people experience as patients are, first, that the individual must have control over a personal, mobile, tax-based individual healthcare fund. And, second, that this should be spent by taking the fund to one of a number of competing and not state-owned but membership-controlled, co-operative, mutual purchasers of care. It cannot be spent on lottery tickets.

The argument, demonstrated in every other walk of life, is that cash compels. 'Conversations' at the pay-desk with consumers in a real market concerns what they want, and are ready to pay for when services are priced. Here, cash provides security and opportunity. Cash gives the individual help in the most directly useful way. It empowers the specific individual. It is directed at securing a specific service. Decisions about spending cash involve, too, individual responsibility and personal judgements about relative value and value for money. Opportunity costs. A system of patient fund-holding based on taxation and on tax-transfers would bring all into one market for one service. It could be combined, too, with direct incentives to help people to help themselves, by topping up if they wish.

Cash makes explicit the cost borne by the taxpayer. It would require providers, too, to seek willing revenues from consumers who had the control over mobile patient fund holding. With cost-consciousness and prices, cash operates the market. It puts the premium on patient satisfaction. It changes attitudes behaviours, and environments. It makes every detail count. It affects how people are heard, whose voice matters, how people are listened to, how what they try to say matters as well as the words that they actually use.

Crucially, too, cash empowers *the silent* as well as the vocal. It empowers anyone wanting to get on with their lives, and not to be consumed by political and health-care activism in a beggar-my-neighbour system where vocal groups shift resources from the less vocal. In the existing NHS my gained renal care is your lost cancer drug. Cash, in patient fund-holding, would empower the poor, the ethnic, women, the disabled, the unlucky, the mentally ill, all those persistently identified as the victims of discrimination within the NHS. Too often, the alternative to facing cash and choice has been stand-still policies which buy three apples for two pence, and sell two apples for three pence.

Paradoxically, it is for politicians to free us from politics – both national *and* local. It is for a political leader, with persuasive language and a convincing narrative, with courage and determination – and with a sense of timing as well as of equal justice – to ride that wave. That is, if they wish to lead an effective government with a clear sense of direction. Someone capable of true leadership, and of a broad vision. It is for a political leader to set politics aside. It is for a political leader of intellectual and moral certainty to respond to the changed background and the potentials for change. It is for a political leader to offer long-term thinking, and instruments for change. It is for a political leader to recognise the moral and the practical issues, to press intelligence forward. And, to offer strong leadership and a clear sense of direction – operating against powerful interests (but whose own true interests they do not see) for the benefit of the people as a whole and for the newly financially-empowered individual.

Labour could appeal to its own older traditions of mutuality. The Liberal Democrats could go back to similar attitudes. Or the Conservatives could look again at Disraeli, as 'one nation' Conservatives sometimes do. It was Disraeli who encouraged the Conservative Party to take a mass line, and to un-couple the supposed links between freedom and progressivism, freedom and collectivism, as Professor John Vincent has shown. [10] And the need now, in this context, is for a successor of convinced and practical certitude. Conservatism (small or large 'c') and modernity can be happily reconciled. But for this we need extraordinary leadership, so that power passes into the hands of the individual as a consumer.

Douglas Hurd's superb new biography of Peel points the way, even on the model of a managerialist like the mill-owner's son. As Lord Hurd says of Peel: "He stopped calculating a balance. He convinced himself that the idea with which he had sympathised for twenty years must be given full and dramatic expression in the repeal of the Corn Laws. The political risks had not disappeared, but to Peel in his new state of mind at the end of 1845 they could no longer be decisive." [11]

As with food, so with healthcare – the requirement is to move beyond tactics to a prolonged period of public education, combining analysis with necessary repetition, spreading understanding, exposing the realities of the present system and the alternatives. In 1997 I urged leading Conservatives, new to opposition, to do this. Alas, they did not. Now, however, the politician who offers genuine instruments to make individual choice real will offer a policy that will define a party.

Disraeli, in his novel *Coningsby*, wrote: "Brains every day become more precious than blood. You must give men new ideas, you must teach them new words, you must modify their manners, you must change their laws, you must root out prejudices, subvert convictions, if you wish to be great." Here, there is the necessary guidance for a consistent message, persuasively emphasised, repeated until it becomes familiar, friendly and understood. As Hurd says, "Politicians in general are divided between those who by nature complicate and those who simplify." He cites, too, the founding statement of purpose printed by *The Economist* in September 1843 (and still printed in the paper): "to take part in a severe contest between intelligence which presses forward, and an unworthy timid ignorance obstructing our progress." [12]

The simple argument concerning choice is demonstrated in every other walk of life. This is that cash compels. It puts the premium on patient satisfaction. It changes attitudes behaviours, and environments. It makes every detail count. It affects how people are heard, whose voice matters, how people are listened to, how what they try to say matters as well as the words that they actually use. In the search for equity, too, cash in patient fund-holding would empower the poor, the ethnic, women, the elderly, the disabled, the unlucky, the mentally ill, all those persistently identified as the victims of discrimination within the NHS.

We might note, *en passant*, that you are not empowered if your own income is taken away from you, and given to someone else – a GP for example – to spend on your behalf. That does not empower you.

The necessary prelude is for politicians to set out a clear statement of values, to refer all NHS events to these, to lead opinion and understanding. Then radical change to empower choice can gather greater support and understanding *between* general elections. Politically, the task is to continue to re-shape tacit assumptions about what can count as conventionally reasonable, sane, politically deliverable, commonsense realities – especially showing that individual choice can be empowered and effective. The moral as well as the instrumental challenge is to achieve much, including self-responsibility in civil association, based upon arguments carrying both intellectual and moral certainties.

It is not as if we are driving with no maps. We are not without positive recent British experience. We have had the great success of the revolution in eye care in the High Street. As I show in *Patients, Power and Responsibility*, this has placed everyone in one market. We already have direct payments for social services, too, where payments are controlled by service users. IF, that, is they know about the option. IF they are offered the option. IF staff agree with the policy. IF they are interested in it. Big IFS. But I am advised by a senior NHS regional manager that there is still only about 10% take-up. Staff, in assessing patients, do not have time (or the interest and commitment?) to talk about direct payments, and very many service users know nothing of the option. We can and should do something serious about this situation by making it work for all. We should extend direct payments incrementally to other services too, and benefit from the incentives these give service users. To mental health care, to 'total' cancer services, to palliative and respite care, to maternity services, to long-term care – and soon excluding nothing.

Choice then asks us to decide who, what, when and how. And to distinguish clearly who is doing the choosing. Indeed, the issue is, crucially, *who decides who decides*.

Succinctly, in summary:

- Choice, Competition, and Capacity are a trinity.
- Preference and Price are twins.
- Money talks and preference walks.
- 'Choice' without instrumental definition is an abstraction without any meaning.
- Indeed, it can mean anything or it can mean nothing.

'Choice' in local voting may change one candidate for another, one board member for another. But it does not guarantee an individual a personal, timely service. There is no test of the moral and individual utility of 'choice' save the individual economic empowerment of the present and the future patient. Otherwise, 'choice' is unverifiable and of no value as a touchstone of policy. Unlinked to the financial empowerment of the individual it is a mere word, capable of serving any interest or emotion in general but not capable of serving any patient in particular.

As a test of policy, 'choice' alone is neither radical nor conservative. By itself the word is, indeed, bad politics. It is bad psychology. And it is bad economics. It is not useful. It is divorced from meaning. It is an abstraction – like 'power', 'pain', or 'pleasure' – to which any meaning may be annexed, as you wish. Standing alone, 'choice' is false to the debate, and from its falsity other dangerous falsehoods unfold. It, too, leaves the 'two nations' structure of the NHS undisturbed, and here the articulate middle-classes still do much the best. Here, indeed, we have a 21st century version of what Walter Bagehot called the "elegant facade" of English institutions. These disguised social, economic, and class realities. The failure to give real financial meaning to 'choice' leaves such an essentially elitist system undisturbed. 'Choice', therefore, should not be only a general, even a polemical, instrument of government, but a specific instrument of the individual.

In summary, financially-empowered choice can deliver equity, motivate professionals, support the evolution of adaptive discovery and of new methods, and encourage more self-care and (linked to insurance and an 'excess') discourage some demand. But if and only if the individual has control over money. Then, every-one a winner. William Dean Howells, in his book entitled *A Hazard of New Fortunes* in 1890 suggested that the solvent of life in a new metropolis seemed to bring about the "deeply underlying nobody" in everyone. This is our objective, if we are to have 'choice' neat – and neither shaken nor stirred by politics.

You may still insist upon locally-elected boards as the answer. It may be that we should believe that planners can forecast in advance what the individual will want, and when, and in what quantity and quality, and at what price. It may be that planners are best at deciding between "incommensurables", or those difficult choices which we may each face concerning outcomes, consequences, side-effects, and intimate trade-offs. It may be that the community and not the individual should decide what treatments and outcomes each individual might cope with best, or prefer, live with or refuse. It may be that it is from bureaucratic decisions – even better informed bureaucratic decisions on the basis of your 'greater say' – that creative, adaptive innovation and evolving benefits have arisen in society. It may be that the ordinary citizen's psyche is infinitely malleable, and the individual perfectible. It may be that a better society arises if the individual is immersed in a bureaucratic collectivity.

It may be that individual fulfilment is of necessity communal as well as separable. It may be that we are all better if policies are generally formulated far away from us in our busy lives, and that we should not expect control. Instead, we may only occasionally and somehow "influence" these issues (and if we wish to be a politicised activist) with "a greater say." It may be that personal autonomy should indeed be politicised by a consultative process. It may be that to get better healthcare we all need to become political activists, to take part in consultations, to sit on citizen's juries and go to meetings, rather than concentrate on living our lives, doing our jobs, sharing with our families, making commitments to our own hobbies and interests, and securing good healthcare when the time comes. [13]

However, Geoff Mulgan offers an excellent summary of the proper gloss on such claims: "The simple fact is that our ability to exercise control is strictly limited by time. Most people intuitively understand this, and happily leave jobs to others. One of the virtues of complex societies is that we do not actually need to understand how a VCR works or how municipal rubbish collection is organized. We do not control every aspect of life because if we did there would be no time for work, love and play. The fully democratised society in which we had to take part in all decisions is for many a vision of hell, an endless branch or committee meeting writ horribly large. Because most people limit the time they devote to participating in democratic structures, control always threatens to fall on to self-appointed cliques, who effectively disenfranchise those unable or unwilling to participate. As a result, democratic structures that demand intensive participation often prove unstable. This has been the experience of many collectives and co-operatives, where the principled commitment to full participation in decisions results in ever more time being spent in meetings, and, in the worst cases, a sense that people are interfering in each other's work." [14]

The creative alternative is for financially empowered individuals acting in markets, the coexistence of representative and direct democracy for all classes, and light regulation of a pluralist structure in which government protects competition. Of course, it may be, indeed, that in a necessarily beggar-my-neighbour service such as the NHS (which no other nation, by the by, has ever copied), we should then be content that an active, aggressive, patient lobby or a distant bureaucratic "expert" will inevitably shift resources to where the wheel squeaks loudest. Perhaps we *are* better-off if we think that the alternative to empowering the person who knows where the individual shoe pinches is to empower the noisy, the well-organised, the obsessive and the strident. All this may be so. You may believe these collectivist things. But, as the Duke of Wellington responded – when a man who met him said "Mr. Smith, I believe." – *"If you will believe that you will believe anything."*

NOTES.

1. Alas, the Conservative Party wasted its years in opposition (and since?) when it could and should have been persistently making the case for a liberal capitalist democratic market society. It could then have come into power with a supportive and informed public giving it backing against the very powerful vested-interests wholly opposed to reform. There was no serious thought given as to how to do so, nor of how to make 'choice' mean something real and to financially empower the individual patient. Note added 29 July, 2015.

2. The Conservative leader David Cameron told his party conference on 3 October 2007 that top-down targets must be scrapped, and professionals trusted, while emphasising outcomes. "What we have got to do is make the NHS and doctors answerable to the patients and not the politicians." *But how?* See Francis Elliott, '"Unscripted" Cameron delivers a textbook speech to the faithful', *The Times*, 4 October 2007, pp.6-9.

3. As to the similar situation in schools, a review by the University of Cambridge reported in November 2007 that the £500 million spent on attempting to raise the standard of English

in primary school has had almost no impact on reading skills. National testing in schools appears not to have driven up standards, and the current system could also be giving up to a third of children wrong grades. This Cambridge Primary Review was the biggest inquiry into primary education for decades. Alexandra Frean, '£500 m literacy drive is a flop, say experts', *The Times*, 2 November 2007, p.33.

4. There are many examples of work that could be cited. One recent one is that of the Royal College of Physicians, which issued what *The Times* called "a damning report" on "inadequate and unacceptable" care for patients with fractured bones. Nearly one third of operations for the 75,000 hip fractures a year were delayed beyond the 48-hour target, even though delays increase the risk of death. After surgery for the most severe fragility fractures, less than half of patients were on the appropriate osteoporosis treatment. David Rose, 'Doctors say care for falls unacceptable', *The Times*, 7 November 2007, p.7. See also Patrick Sawer, 'Patients are losing faith in NHS system', *Sunday Telegraph*, 4 November 2007, p.16. See also www.patients-association.org.uk for details of the survey reported here.

Frank Field MP, in a recent summary article, suggested that large numbers can neither read nor write, despite a doubling of the educational budget since 1997. One in three primary school pupils moving to secondary schools fail to achieve the minimum skills in English, Maths and Science. Only half of pupils at age 16 gain a minimum leaving standard of 5 GCSE passes at A* to CV, including English and Maths. The GCSE, of course, was a dilution of the old GCE, which it replaced. Some 206,000 eligible young people aged 16 to 18 are neither in education, employment or training. Frank Field, 'The kids have a neet solution', *Sunday Times*, 11 November 2007, p.6, news review; 'Slim down the fat cats', *Sunday Times*, 11 November 2007, p.20, comment. Also, Maurice Chittenden, 'Quango fat cats reap the price of failure – even more money', *Sunday Times*, 11 November 2007, pp.12-13, news.

5. See Steven E. Landsburg, *The Armchair Economist. Economics and Everyday Life* (New York, Simon & Schuster, 1995).

6. Richard Donkin, 'A survivor's guide to life, the universe and work', *Financial Times*, 9 August 2007, p.9.

7. Laurence Gonzales, *Deep Survival. Who Lives. Who Dies and Why* (London, W.W.Norton, 2007).

8. Julian Le Grand, *The Other Invisible Hand. Delivering Public Services Through Choice and Competition* (Princeton and Oxford, Princeton University Press, 2007). See also his 'Markets, Equality and Welfare' in J. Le Grand and S. Estrin (eds.), *Market Socialism* (Oxford, Oxford University Press, 1989), and *Motivation, Agency and Public Policy. Of Knights and Knaves, Pawns and Queens* (Oxford, Oxford University Press, 2003). See also J. Appleby, A. Alvarez-Rosete, 'Public Response to NHS Reform', in *The British Social Attitudes Survey*, 22nd *Report* (London, Sage, 2005). For a deeply depressing alternative statement of the most old labour ideological antediluvian attitudes possible, see A. Pollock, *NHS plc: the Privatisation of Our Health Care* (London, Verso, 2005).

9. Isaiah Berlin, *Two concepts of liberty: An inaugural lecture delivered before the University of Oxford on 31 October 1958* (Oxford, Clarendon Press, 1963).

10. John Vincent. *Disraeli* (Oxford, Oxford University Press, 1990), p.22. There are here more vital insights in a short book than in many lorry-loads of academic monographs. A permanent work which is a masterpiece by the finest historian of his generation. Like

Joseph Chamberlain and J. Enoch Powell, Disraeli saw no necessary co-relation between the working-classes and socialism, nor between public services and an over powerful centralising state.

11. Douglas Hurd, *Sir Robert Peel, a Biography* (London, Weidenfeld & Nicolson, 2007), a work of high-grade historical understanding and great political perception, which is, however, hardly a surprise. His view of Peel offers a less aloof, less tactically-inept figure when compared with the man described in Robert Blake, *The Conservative Party from Peel to Thatcher* (London, Fontana, 1985).

12. Hurd, *Peel*, *ibid*.

13. Citizen's juries cost a lot of money, with no discernible value arising from them. NHS 'Jurors' were paid £869,930 this year [2007]. See Matthew Parris, 'Gobble, gobble! Another turkey from, Farmer Brown', *The Times*, 8 November 2007, p.19.

14. Mulgan, *Politics in An Antipolitical Age*, pp.128-9. The Militant Tendency sought to take over The Labour Party in the 1960s and 1970s on the basis of an obsessive commitment to attending every meeting, and boring everyone else until 'Militants' were a majority still remaining at the end of meetings could pass their resolutions. We have seen the revival in 2015 with the carefully orchestrated campaign to elect Jeremy Corbyn MP as Leader of The Labour Party, I add on 31 July 2015.

4. How to make the market?

"If we proceed without a thorough knowledge and accurate comprehension of the nature, extent, and magnitude of the difficulties we have to encounter, or if we unwisely direct our efforts towards an object, in which we cannot hope for success, we shall not only exhaust our strength in fruitless exertions and remain at as great a distance as ever from the summit of our wishes, but we shall be perpetually crushed by the recoil of this rock of Sisyphus." Thomas Robert Malthus.

In my Introduction I listed the key steps:

- Empower the customer with both knowledge and information, the power to make comparisons, and money to make personal choices effective.

- Move from limited choice and the recent introduction of personal budgets in social care to a Health Savings Account for everyone.

- Make purchasing and as much provision as possible locally competitive.

- Make individual funds mobile, to enable the purchasing tools to evolve effectively.

- Protect competition, both in purchasing and in provision.

- Require a minimum level of individual catastrophic insurance. And encourage top-ups of health funds by tax-incentives.

- Measure and publish the patients' experience.

- Cease to subsidise providers.

- Ensure pluralist provision and end the predominance of monopoly providers and purchasers.

- Use direct individual economic incentives that will prompt changes in structures, cultures, behaviours, purchasing, and provision.

- Halt the drive towards a national tariff for all services. Let local negotiations agree prices, on every element of service costs including staff incomes. Use competitive purchasing and provision to reduce costs and waste while improving clinical quality.

- Substitute individual financial empowerment for politics.

1. How to go forward?

My analysis is an act of optimism about change concerning the behaviour both of individuals and of organisations.

To achieve good health care for all we need free, competitive, pluralist, trial-and-error, suck-it-and-see markets. The discipline of competitive choice in a market is at the root of this. So, too, is the information function which is best served by competitive offers of provision.

The complicated challenge of providing appropriate modern health care is most effectively and efficiently delivered in a regulated market-place. My concern is how to help make this position politically persuasive in practical terms. And how to make it credible to those who have growing doubts about the present NHS but who have otherwise rejected market institutions in health care, on ideological and statist grounds or from mis-founded anxieties about 'market failure.'

A key question is, 'how will the market be made?' We can see the answer to this question clearly. Effective competition is essential, with organizations seeking willing revenues. It will be regulated by government, rooted in a core guarantee of good care which is available for all in a legally enforceable contract. It is important to free up both demand and supply. Elements essential to the market are greater capacity (which Mr. Alan Milburn, when Secretary of State, started to address seriously and creatively); good public information, and empowered individual choice from the mobility of personal tax-based funds.

Here, too, the necessary skills must be developed both by the existing NHS and by voluntary and charitable endeavours if patients are to be advised and supported to enable them to make choices and to benefit from changes. The experience of introducing direct payments for social care is encouraging for it has produced advisory support too. This has been of a high-grade, and easily accessible. We should explore much further the potential for change from a market approach which exists in every other area which have apparently been off-limits in discussion of markets – notably in Accident and Emergency services, where half of all hospital work is done. In all this, self-responsibility should be directly linked to incentive, and to price.

To turn self-responsible market solutions into realities in health care we need to take Matthew Arnold's words seriously, when he urged us "to see the object" – in our case, the NHS – "as it really is." To help us to do so we need to clarify what choice really means. Choice is the individual expressing a costed-preference when financially empowered to do so, thus testing out specific adaptations against competition. This basic point is best seen in a social context, when our economic institutions rely on offering it. And in providing adaptive answers which subsequently receive support or are amended by other innovations. Choice relies on the first principles of a culture of freedom – including experiment, dynamism, property rights, and economically-empowered self-knowledge and self-responsibility.

Of course, these are necessarily moral, social and practical questions rather than being merely instrumental ones. They are by no means restricted to the economic questions of financial motivation and of self-regarding (but socially productive) self-interest. A free market economic model is critical, but insufficient by itself. For the fish swims in a sea of values, emotions, and the social structures within which markets function. These co-exist in that difficult territory where law, preference, norms and values, attitudes to risk and to other challenges, behaviours, expectations, concepts of justice and of consent, of 'fairness' and of self-responsibility overlap and interact. These are all questions where culture, personal and public morality coincide.

Many people now realise that the NHS is much less effective – in terms of access to services and their outcome – than they had hoped or believed. The question is, what to do about it? How to make sense of the NHS debate? And how to build legitimacy for politically-persuasive change – persuading voters of the merits of voluntary exchange as a substitute for State monopoly and direction. And to carry with us some large numbers at least amongst the fearful, the doubting, and the ideologically opposed?

Choice is the talisman to enable us to find a way through all this. For when people have genuine choice the system has the responsibility to find out where best care is given, and what it is – thus facing the comparative realities of cost, opportunity, and the necessary conditions for success which the evidence implies. Here, it seems that the keys are direct incentives; effective consumer power; the introduction of constant and effective feedback and adaptive adjustment from dispersed knowledge and consumer action. This is only achievable from the expression of changing relative prices, competition, and market mechanisms promoting continued experimentation in a Hayeckian process of discovery.

So direct market incentives are the key to sharpening the understanding of opportunity and of individual service in an alternative approach to good care for all. Otherwise:

- why should any provider try harder?

- why innovate if it doesn't pay?

- why do, if doers are unvalued?

- why worry, if consumers cannot exit?

- why consider revenues, if they come allocated from above?

- why be concerned with results and examples if no benefits or outcomes are noticed?

- why strive if one man's increase is another's diminution in a beggar-my-neighbour structure?

- why work harder, if it just brings more work and no rewards?

- why try to achieve improved performance and better outcomes, if process not performance is valued and rewarded?

- why do more work when there are no additional funds coming in?

So direct incentives, price and markets are the necessary spur to change and improve. They are the key to the transformation of British health services – and much more trustworthy and effective than inspection, regulation, and politicised targets. The functioning of markets is, too, essential to the individual staff member earning individual self-esteem, to ambition and enterprise, to a necessary spirit of endeavour, to the prompting of imagining and the actions of doing.

'Price' is, however, a forbidden word. Don't dare mention it at The King's Fund, or in Richmond House, or at Leeds! Or even in the Conservative Party? But we do need to carefully consider price if we are to make progress. For it alone efficiently co-ordinates supply and demand. A market makes for homogeneous and improving prices. It reduces the costs of transactions. It prompts the marriage of knowledge, means, and opportunity. Both incentive and price in markets generate change from below. And they provoke a necessary sense of pace, enterprise, and the revenues it generates. Each is essential to the measurement of performance, to empowered choice, to suitable investment, to necessary individual reward, and to heightened individual and social expectations, and to their fulfilment. So, too, to the necessary bonding of a nation, in which social purposes and individual aspirations are combined (or reconciled), with one people in one market for one service.

We see this already in the recent revolution in the optical market in the UK, freed of the disadvantages of central control. And so, too, we can attain the necessary restoration and repair in the wider NHS – for greater access, for a wider financial base, for improved standards, changed attitudes, flexibility and versatility, greater initiative, autonomy, and market responsiveness. And we can end the indifference we so often meet, and give support for local initiatives, and do something to remove the resistance to investment in technological changes too. We need to see the abandonment of hierarchical controls and the costly but unhelpful state apparatus of multiplying targets, costly over-inspection and over-regulation – all of which itself undermines effective teamwork, corrodes staff morale and diminishes the potential for an informed and capable workforce. We should end a structure in which producers have been more important than consumers, in which new techniques are distrusted, and in which both the individual and co-possibilities are marginalized

The fundamental device which will sharpen change and prompt energy, ingenuity and enterprise is the delegation of financial power to the individual. The mobility of an individual healthcare fund – the power of exit – should be constituted as Patient Fund Holding. This step – the bird that flies to signal land – is essential, since the self-responsible individual (patient, and staff) can empowered. This step, too, depends on securing by contract a legally enforceable core guarantee of good care. This will encourage the self-responsibility of every party and agent, whilst dissolving structures which obscure the necessary realities of the market.

In one sense only are these essentially *practical* matters, rather than matters suitable for ideological framing. For they are truly moral questions – as well as being concerned both with dynamic processes, and the evolution of comparative advantage by providers. They involve expectations, notably that we expect things *to happen* rather than welcoming a comfortable static position. The object is to make the most of our economic, social and cultural means. The yield will be a positive sum-game; all will benefit. That is if what one is seeking to maximise is popular and ready access to a preferred personal, intimate, separable and timely service to achieve individually welcomed outcomes. Clearly, policy is constrained by politics. And since no one likes to lose place or advantage there will be the necessity to negotiate honourable exits and new opportunities, together with re-training and adaptation. At the heart of my proposals is the notion that no empowerment is as effective as self-empowerment.

The presence of more competition and of innovations in marketing are essential if we are to see *striving* as well as learning organisations, and if secure access to reliable care is to be available for all. Scarce resources must, of course, go to the most efficient producers (or, in economic terms, to the profitable employment) rather than to those who use power to sustain the *status quo* and continue to subtract 'political rents' as a prime objective. And, as the distinguished economic historian David Landes says, "That is the point of innovation and initiative: they are not there until they are there." [1] People make the difference: people who choose the services, people who deliver them. It is people who will offer continuous improvement, and who will be rewarded for achievement, in a non-adversarial collaborative venture between willing purchasers and determined providers who have to seek voluntary revenues.

We cannot allow the solutions to yesterday's problems (they did not prove to be solutions at all!) to hinder social purpose in addressing tomorrow's challenges. We need to focus on prospects ahead. And, perhaps paradoxically to some, we can go forwards by looking backwards – or go east by sailing west. Indeed, we do not lack landmarks in an open sea. We can re-endorse voluntarism, co-operation, mutuality, and self-responsibility. We can do so provided this is based on individual economic empowerment, and not merely on a vague 'community' empowerment by 'mutuality' – whatever this flappingly loose term means, if anything, in Prime Minister jargon. For this latter idea – if it is one – seems to be a key without a matching lock. Leadership matters, too, if we are to evolve social and political institutions which enable us to master the problems and encourage dynamist solutions, achieve a more open market which will be a stimulus to rationality, efficiency, and improvement.

Beneficial changes will be based on incentive and invitation to effort. But they are not inevitable. *Change will not make itself.* The obvious will not necessarily come about. We each have to take responsibility for making changes happen: to evolve new institutions which are creative and adaptable; to share knowledge; to advance the competent and remove (or re-train) the inept; to recognise merit and to reward it; to enhance opportunity and applaud initiative; to depend on both competition and emulation; to respect enterprise, to make a priority of performance. Here, it is essential to identify and to endorse the first principles of liberty, the rights of property, and of personal liberty and autonomy. Basic to the structure are the rights of contract, and the guarantee of competition and choice.

This is government's role, to guarantee competition, reliable individual access, quality and cost-effective outcomes through suitably managed markets. If we do not make these explicit and implicit commitments we will certainly find ourselves in a world of higher volume activity (but not necessarily higher productivity), greater state investment (but not necessarily improved value), many more rivets and targets (but no more autonomy), more talk of empowerment (but no more effective choice), more decentralisation (but with no greater leverage for quality as determined by individual and specific consumer preferences).

As Hugh Ross Williamson puts this: "One of the main deformations in all thought about the past is the assumption that what did happen had to happen and that the attitude of men involved in an unresolved matter conforms with the judgement and perceptions of those wise after the event." [2]

If we want cultural change, we will have to help make it happen. This means facing up to the many cultural impediments, and opposed forces who seek to prevent tomorrow, and who do not easily address the poor consequences of their own faiths as we see in the debate – for example – on the proposed Foundation Hospitals.

We should rely on the Scottish sage for guidance. Adam Smith told us: "The natural effort of every individual to better his own condition, when suffered to exert itself with freedom and security, is so powerful a principle, that it is alone, and without any assistance, not only capable of carrying on the society to wealth and prosperity, but of surmounting a hundred impertinent obstructions with which the folly of human laws too often encumbers its operations; though the effect of these obstructions is always more or less either to encroach upon its freedom, or to diminish insecurity." [3]

However, we do not merely want new policies polished and on parade. Speculation is insufficient, and it is difficult for it to command confidence. We need a viable marriage of understanding and of practical actions. What I call 'Getting it done.' We need a real breakthrough, led by a Conservative who puts the case eloquently and constantly for a liberal, capitalist free market, in which much better healthcare and education can be reliably provided. Fundamental questions must be asked and practical solutions evolved as answers which are themselves politically persuasive. Otherwise, well-funded, well-organized institutionalised vested interests – professional guilds presenting themselves in the guise of the national interest – will continue to predominate, to the disadvantage of the scattered consumer. And to that of the Conservative Party if it fails to make the case for a liberal, open, consumer market economy as the basis of all of our freedoms, and the producer of the wealth by which to aid the poor.

Describing the cumbersome, wasteful, often degrading inefficiencies of the incentive-innocent NHS is the easy bit. But what to do about it? That's the harder bit. We should, I suggest, focus on those economic devices which achieve equality of opportunity, of access, and of individual choices about preferred individual outcomes. This does not offer a conflict between an appropriate process and a suitable individual outcome in care. For it offers everyone economic empowerment, access to advice and advocacy (via my Patient Guaranteed Care Association, or mutual-purchasing – and bargaining – organization). Such a body would counterbalance many difficulties of asymmetric information. And, too, offer the collaborative ability – by assessing market signals, medical knowledge and information on professional performance – to determine and achieve wherever practically and medically possible a preferred personal outcome.

Changes to how services are provided – for example, in the home rather than in hospital – are much more likely to happen if the political power of hospitals is counter-balanced by the purchasing strength of co-operative purchasing. The autonomy of the individual and more autonomous local organisation would both be beneficial. So, too, would the explicit audit and accountability at the heart of successful change.

The NHS regularly talks of the importance of 'local ownership.' Whatever *that* means. And of NHS professionals "working with local communities." Whatever *that* means. However, the genuine development of the Patient Guaranteed Care Association as a democratically-controlled, member-owned purchaser of services with willing revenues, tax-based, from voluntary members would make local controls real. Facilities such as day-care centres and crèches would be supported in this purchasing model, and service-users encouraged to initiate and own them. The legitimacy of the structure would be enhanced, and it would necessarily be more flexible and more responsive to the consumer. Much more so than in vague political chitter-chatter about "community ownership."

Different social and economic institutions of course imply alternative intellectual, practical, cultural, social and cultural costs. This is both a general and a personal question. As we consider the performance of the NHS – when compared with leading OECD countries – the opportunity costs of the central monopoly approach to funding, purchasing and provision have clearly been significant – both by comparison with other external systems (notably Switzerland) and by contrast with what might have been if we had taken a social insurance approach in 1948. [4]

Yet many people feel unable to change what we have. Or they wish to do so but do not see how to do so. They are hardly helped by current political debate. Or by Whig history, in which until very recently every shadow of the pre-history of care before the NHS has been darkened, with the NHS presented as the inevitable line of 'progress.' Much of this 'history' depends on propaganda, historical ignorance, myth, and guess-work. And even now – in despite of all the documentary and comparative evidence of the comparatively poor NHS performance when considered alongside the OECD countries – at Whitehall the cause of market liberalism is today receiving surprisingly little support from those who would be expected to be its friends. We have yet to see if the proposed NHS Passport (from the Conservatives) or the proposed Foundation Hospitals (from Labour) at the heart of the government's second term reforms of the NHS will empower the individual. It seems very unlikely.

The sceptical case remains powerful until disproved. Few Conservatives – who might be expected to argue for free, competitive markets and consumer choice effected by decentralising economic power to the individual – do so with any persuasive power or deep-rooted conviction. Michael Howard, when Shadow Chancellor of the Exchequer, has recently come closest to analysing the challenges from a market perspective, with his references to the Austrian school and competition. And with his commentary on the powerlessness of the consumer and the need for "patients to be given the power of the consumer."

Howard has recently spoken of his Party's proposal for a Patients Passport when "patients would be allowed the option of moving between any NHS provider and would be allowed to take some or all of NHS funding with them." But even he talks of "users of public services, and professionals who work in them, being given a greater say" – which is not the same thing at all as being able to command a personal, intimate, separable and necessarily timely service, with the individual holding cash in a voucher for the full cost of treatment. We still await from any politician detailed policy proposals about incentives and the direct financial empowerment of the service user across the whole NHS territory. [5]

To enable these proposals to be politically persuasive it is important both to achieve the legitimate interests and adhere to the appropriate values of society, and it is to the empowerment of the individual to which we can properly look. For each supports and reinforces the other – in Joseph Cropsey's words "to make freedom possible and to make of freedom a form of virtue." [6]

Nobel economics laureate Professor Amartya Sen has recently said, too, that "Even though the idea of freedom is sometimes formulated independently of values, preferences and reasons, freedom cannot be fully appraised without some idea of what a person prefers and has reasons to prefer. Thus, there is a basic use of rational assessment in appraising freedom, and in this sense. Freedom must depend on reasoned assessment of having different options." [7]

NOTES.

1. David S. Landes, *The Wealth and Poverty of Nations. Why Some Are So Rich And Some Are So Poor* (London, Little Brown, 1998), p.447.

2. Adam Smith, *Inquiry into The Nature and Causes of The Wealth of Nations* (1776), Book Iv, chapter 5: 'Digression on the Corn Trade'.

3. Hugh Ross Williamson, *Historical Enigmas* (New York, St. Martin's Press, 1974), p.272.

4. *OECD Electronic Publications*, Paris, *OECD Health Data 1998: A Comparative Analysis of 29 Countries*, and in *OECD Health Data 2001: A Comparative Analysis of 30 Countries* (Paris, OECD, 10th edition).

5. Michael Howard, 'Reform of the public services: The boundary between the private and public sectors", speech to Centre for Policy Studies, London, 24 March 2003, CPS transcript. And M. Howard, Speech to *the Guardian* Public Services Summit, 3 February, 2005. See conservative-speeches.sayit.mysociety.org/speech/600456. However, as party leader from November 2003 to December 2005 he did not do it!

6. Joseph Cropsey, *Polity and Economy. An Interpretation of the Principles of Adam Smith* (The Hague, 1976), cited in Gertrude Himmelfarb, *The Idea of Poverty. England in the Early Industrial Age* (New York, Alfred A. Knopf, 1984),

7. Amartya Sen, *Rationality and Freedom* (Cambridge, Mass., Harvard University Press, 2002), p.5.

5. Practising being practical

"We put too much faith in systems, and look too little to men." Benjamin Disraeli.

In my recent detailed study, *Patients, Power and Responsibility*, I set out in more detail a practical approach to change which will, I believe, achieve social solidarity, equality of access, higher quality, greater capacity, improved professional pay and morale, and enhanced funding with individual insurance 'top-ups.' The poor will be empowered by cash transferred from taxes, and thus be supported by the middle class and the rich, in accessing good quality care. The argument reflects the propositions put forward by Hayek and the Austrian economics school, and which I explore further in this present essay. [1]

The main points of my practical proposals are:

1. Individual responsibility is the key to good health care and personal health status. To achieve both patient empowerment and individual self-responsibility (for own care; for consequences of behaviour; for choice) every patient will be given control over a personal fund of cash, in voucher-form.

2. Every adult will become a Patient Fund Holder, with this tax-based Health Savings Account credit to pay for health and social care.

3. Government will set out a 'core' package of care which this will pay for: Patient Guaranteed Care, or 'Pretty Good Care.'

4. This core package will be legally enforceable – unlike the existing system where patients have no legal leverage to ensure timely and appropriate access.

5. Every adult will buy compulsory social insurance with their individual tax-based fund: Patient Guaranteed Care Insurance.

6. They will take the insurance to a Patient Guaranteed Care Association – a competing, mutual, co-operative purchaser of care, organised regionally and nationally, and led by professionals. PGCAs could also be insurers. Let the market decide.

7. 'Catastrophic care' and children will be covered by a special tax-based fund within the core-care package.

8. Every patient will have a bi-annual 'health MOT' – with direct financial and other incentives to take seriously exercise, non-smoking, reduced alcohol & drug consumption. Incentives to be relevant to individual concerns: e.g., if a

football supporter, tickets to Premiership or Championship games; if rugby, to Twickenham; if tennis, to Wimbledon; if music or opera, to Glastonbury, to 'heavy metal' gigs or folk festivals, to Glyndebourne, etc.; if a traveller, air-miles or hotel vouchers.

9. Government's role will be to protect choice and competition, and to ensure economic incentives are enabled to work – for without these no progress is likely.

10. To ensure the system has political legitimacy and change is politically persuasive, a new approach must achieve social solidarity, equality of access, higher quality, greater capacity, improved professional pay and morale, and enhanced funding with individual insurance 'top-ups.'

11. Key to it all is the discipline of pluralist market competition (price, incentive, etc.), and self-responsibility which bites. Money talks, and preference walks.

12. The poor, who have done less well from the NHS, will then be in the position enjoyed by the middle-class – getting more from the state for their money, and being on equal terms to those with money. There will be one people in one market for one service – as now exemplified by the recent, successful optical revolution in the British high street.

Instead, Labour seeks to over-spend its way to security. Inevitably, there will be service improvements because more money means more capacity. But the fundamentals – notably the denial of individual choice, and its substitution by 'expert' planners – remain. Without direct incentives, choice, and the discipline of pluralist competition we shall never attain European levels of quality care.

NOTE.

1. See Friedrich von Hayek, *Individualism and Economic Order* (Chicago, Chicago University Press, 1948) ; *The Constitution of Liberty* (Chicago, Chicago University Press, 1960), *Studies in Philosophy, Politics and Economics* (London, Routledge, 1967), and *New Studies in Politics, Economics and the History of Ideas* (London, Routledge, 1978)

6. The moral approach by the radical right.

"Who's in the next room? – who?" Thomas Hardy.

Radical right reformers are often tagged by a slack media and an ideological left as being immoral, uncaring, uncompassionate. But what can be *more moral* than wanting to ensure that everyone has access to a personal, timely, individualised service when they want it?

We do indeed stand amidst the largest of subjects: truth and justice, hope and disparity, reality and illusion, morality and meaning, and how to live our once-only lives. And all in a complex, problematic, challenging, adult, modern world. In considering these questions I suggest that the over-riding moral point is that freedom is not merely a means, *but an end in itself.*

The instrumental (or practical) argument is that there is large scope for improving UK healthcare by market processes. The moral argument is that we *are* indeed one another's neighbours. The cultural argument is that radical reform based in free markets does not lead us to chaos and anarchy, nor to mere economism and rampant selfishness. Indeed, as Dr. Mark Pennington has stressed – echoing Friedrich von Hayek – markets uniquely offer "a realm of voluntary planning characterised by private property and freedom of contract."This is more adaptive, more sensitive and more successful than bureaucratic, centralist planning. [1]

This approach does not produce jungle nihilism and the atomised, de-socialised individual. Instead, it generates spontaneous, positive, individually and collaboratively negotiated order. This arises from the action of better incentives which encourage self-responsibility and adaptive flexibility in provision and in individual self-responsibility. There is the debate.

Hayek's argument is that spontaneous order, liberty and better outcomes are inter-linked. In terms of social solidarity. And the results are wholly positive. Individual empowerment and the expression of costed preferences is the key. *Learning to choose*, and thus the evolution and the elevation of understanding is one result – and one which is not otherwise attainable.

The economic empowerment of the individual will thus encourage self-responsible decisions when individuals consider costs and benefits. Mutuality will be one direct result. Mutual, co-operative action will re-emerge when individuals voluntarily join a purchasing organization [PGCA] in un-coerced collaborative action. The poor will then be active players, empowered in a market, supported by tax-transfers and by advisory services. They will thus do much better in terms of health status and care than under the NHS in terms of mortality, morbidity, and self-image. Diversity and differentiation will increasingly make preferences count. All this can be attained where it has not been obtained by collective (but unrepresentative) democracy and the deliberations of planners.

This is collective action, without collectivism. It is solidarity without solecism. It is equality of access, without us all being asked to join hands together to finish the race joint last.

So we need to explore these many questions which are still in the way. Notably, how to persuade the many – including NHS staff – of the merits of markets.

Then we need to reconcile ideas – that were once unimaginable save amongst free market pioneers – with the idealism of the NHS. This idealism has itself, however, created as many problems as it solved. Its coercive interventionism has proved to be at best ambiguous in effect, and at worst counter-productive, notably for the poor. It has, too, permitted vested interests to identify the private interests of a part as the general interest of the whole society.

These errors are both a failure of morality and of practice. They remain a standing reproach to the NHS, and to the moral society. None have arisen through the raw release of economic appetites in the market. Instead, the contrary is the fact. This situation has come about through the *exclusion* of the poor from effective, well managed markets in which they could have been financially empowered to join co-operative organisations buying care on their behalf. Direct incentive has been an absentee.

Instead, the state has been coercive in practice, without achieving the objectives that were promised – and which liberals (such as Dr. D. S. Lees) in the 1940s said could not be delivered in this way. [2]

We need now to look again at how the moral commitment to the poor can best be discharged. And how, too, as Adam Smith argued, the poor can be – as much as the rich – free, responsible, moral agents sharing a common human and moral nature.

We need, too, an adult discussion of all the risks as well as all the opportunities associated with freedom. [3]

The moral and instrumental arguments in fact coincide. For healthcare should not be exempted from the *benefits* of a liberal market order. And a shift to a market-based approach can be shown to be both politically persuasive, and legitimate.

This is a vital task of Conservative political leadership. It chimes with Robert Nozick's argument that the role of the 'inspirational State' is to allow the processes of learning in a moral and a cultural structure which creates the opportunities for civilised existence on a theoretical, a practical, and an experimental basis.

THE MORAL APPROACH BY THE RADICAL RIGHT

The key to this is dynamic market evolution, in which peaceful voluntary exchange expresses and empowers values and preferences. [4] For the market economy is not just a device for maximum efficiency and financial soundness, although it is that too. It is a moral approach to the expression of individual commitments, where each of us finds that the expression of our values and wishes builds both into successful services and into the context of a society of liberty.

Several different kinds of 'content' arise from this context. First, in terms of the expression of a plurality of values where the consequence is decisions on what to produce, how to produce it and what to value. Second, producers and consumers educate the wants *of each other*. Niche markets, creativity, serviced to those with a choice, majorities acting on minority learning, understanding how to do better – all these are amongst the results. Opportunity-cost is essential to showing how much people value things. This means considering price much more carefully. I discuss this in more detail in my books, *Patients, Power and Responsibility*, and *Who Decides Who Decides?*

Thus, on moral and on practical grounds – including the interests of social solidarity and better healthcare for all – I urge that government should support and reinforce a market-led approach of relative prices – which uniquely transmit crucial messages and guidance – and protect competition. Governments, indeed, should cease to suppress and supplant it. Thus and only thus can we escape the damaging institutions of the NHS, which lack the necessary information, feedback, and incentives to serve the consumer.

NOTES.

1. Mark Pennington, *Liberating the Land. The Case for Private Land-scale Planning* (London, Institute of Economic Affairs/Profile Books, 2002), p.97.

2. D. S. Lees, *Health Through Choice. An Economic Study of the British National Service* (London, Institute of Economic Affairs, 1961). I am grateful to Lord Ralph Harris of High Cross for pointing me to this important and far-sighted analysis.

3. It is interesting to note that Tom Paine, he of *The Rights of Man* (1791-2) an icon of the left in many respects (admired, for example, by the dangerously influential E.P.Thompson), can be credited with deriving what we now call the voucher system – for he advocated payments to parents to be spent on schools of their choice! See Gertrude Himmelfarb, *The Idea of Poverty. England in the Early Industrial Age* (New York, Alfred A. Knopf, 1984), p.92.

4. Robert Nozick, *Anarchy, State and Utopia* (New York, Basic Books, 1974).

7. Incentives, and the 'problem of knowledge.'

"What is now proved was once only imagined." William Blake.

As we have seen, the challenge of 'the problem of knowledge' is fundamental. It is how to gather sufficient, current, appropriate, and highly detailed information which is necessarily hugely dispersed. And to do so constantly, in a permanent programme of revision and re-gathering, which is in fact what happens in all successful commercial enterprise. This challenge – which has necessarily been beyond the capacities of the NHS and of state education – shows that prices and direct personal and organizational economic incentives are essential if choice, competition, investment and responsiveness are to exist. For only in priced markets can we gather the necessary information, so that we can provide what people want (and are willing to fund).

Meanwhile, the NHS planner struggles to discover many things. Who wants what? Where? When? At what level of quality? For which preferred outcomes? How much do they want it, by comparison with the alternatives? What are their personal trade-offs? How are we to discover this? What is to be produced and provided? And at which levels of price and quality? With how much differentiation? With which features, standard and optional? Accessed, how? Who is to get what? When? This is the difficulty of who knows, and who decides, and how? Who makes the rules? Who audits who? There are future, unborn patients too. Who will want what, and how will they view it, at some time in the future?

Consultation about plans and the shape of services in the future hardly excites the normal individual nor gathers the knowledge that people have. We need to recognise the nature of this often tacit 'knowledge.' For this itself limits what officials can accomplish. The nature of dispersed knowledge is that the individual does not necessarily know that they have it, or require to consider it until a personal crisis beckons and brings them up short. Then – seeking a survival strategy for cancer for example – the individual poses questions that matter to *them*, when taking advice. Notably and usually, what are the choices, what are the alternative treatments, what are the outcomes, and who says so? What do other patients like me say, who does a good job, what are my chances, what must I do, can I get access to the help I want?

The individual does not at this point ask to be permitted to plan future services. Nor has s/he often wished to do so in advance. Most of us have been too busy, just getting on with living our lives. But when faced with an illness, we mostly want action NOW. The equity that matters then concerns access to quality care which the individual deems suitable to their coping strategy in crisis. It is *at this point* that differentiation matters to the individual, whereas central systems seek to treat everyone the same.

In addition, the wish to enable local, *tacit knowledge* to be expressed by people with personal values and preferences which vary widely, should not be conflated with the idea that this objective can be delivered by more local decision-making in advance by officials. Hayek shows that this is not possible. The scattered knowledge of millions of individuals and their likely preferences in the future cannot be known or "revealed" to expert interpreters by "improved consultation," nor expressed in policy and in setting "priorities." The opportunity exists for each party in the doctor-patient partnership to "instruct 'the eye of understanding.'" But usually only at the moment of necessity.

Further, ask again "what is health"? It is not an objective 'norm', or a static standard, or something easily determined by a regulator. It is, in an important sense, defined by the life specific people want to lead. The disabled show us this clearly, when they accept and cope with disadvantages which those of us without these would find forbidding and perhaps unsustainable. My own Mother was seriously disabled at birth. And I saw how determinedly she coped, never accepting disablement, even though her legs were in irons into her teens. She made it clear that different people will set themselves different goals, make different risk-assessments, seek different trade-offs and coping strategies, concern themselves with different standards and definitions of appropriate outcomes, and live life *through* disablement rather than be suppressed by it. Health and human purposes are two sides of one leaf. And they are a matter of individual choice.

The classic statement is, of course, Hayek's in his article "The Use of Knowledge in Society" (1945): "The peculiar character of the problem of a rational economic order is determined precisely by the fact that the knowledge of the circumstances of which we must make use never exists in concentrated or integrated form but solely as the dispersed bits of incomplete and frequently contradictory knowledge which all the separate individuals possess...There is beyond question a body of very important but unorganised knowledge which cannot possibly be called scientific in the sense of knowledge of general rules: the knowledge of the particular circumstances of time and place...To know of and put to use a machine not fully employed, or somebody's skill which could be better utilised, or to be aware of a surplus stock which can be drawn upon during an interruption of supplies, is socially quite as useful as the knowledge of better alternative techniques." [1]

These are all reasons why a dynamist approach – and the signals and summary that price represents – are so helpful, so efficient, so empowering at the moment when the individual wishes to make a decision, and which brings this tacit and personal knowledge into focus. Then, too, this decision becomes part of articulated local knowledge as a body of knowledge which influences what is provided for others to choose from as well as for the individual seeking to command a specific service. And thus local knowledge is itself dynamic, evolving, adjusting to the information that services offer – and the newly minted decision of the newly diagnosed individual itself may contribute to further innovations.

The key point is that just as the centre cannot gather the necessary knowledge for centralised decision-making so, too, local knowledge cannot be snatched up in a net, focussed in one place, and seen as a static 'fact.' Local knowledge is necessarily detailed, constantly changing whilst encapsulating critical details of significance to individuals, the subject and the object of circumstance. And price expresses this knowledge of changes in local conditions. However, the individual not only responds to price signals, but creates innovations by their own imagination and efforts, too. Our rich heritage of charitable endeavour shows this with historic power.

We see in every shop in every day of our lives – indeed, in every area of our lives bar 'public services' and state monopolies – that direct incentives answer these questions. They do so by gathering *and* distributing information. They prompt conscious action by service-users and buyers, staff and management based upon the news this gives to them. This is essential to the consumer, to the provider, and to their actual and potential competitors. When a consumer makes a choice in the market-place the incentives are to get good information *before* making a purchase, for the consequences will be borne by the individual concerned.

All these conscious actions arise from otherwise deliberate individual and un-random actions which merge into a whole which is not itself consciously directed or forecast, and which, indeed health care planners have found it impossible to replicate. This is the often tacit information which even the individual may not have discerned from themselves. For example, few think what they would do about their hip until they are told that the pain they experience at 80 years of age may be helped by a hip replacement. Or what would each of us do if diagnosed with a cancer?

Without price and incentives we cannot solve the problems of allocation and investment with which 'experts' in the NHS wrestle with. They cannot discover by politics what people prefer, for the nature of knowledge is such that it is so dispersed (and, intrinsically tacit) that it is impossible to know individual preferences in advance and how each person will respond when faced with scarcity, price, risk, and alternatives – which they express when relating to relative prices, examining what they are prepared to pay for, and how to allocate resources. This information is beyond the reach or capacity of 'experts' seeking to formulate policy in the name of 'public welfare.'

The centralised system – allegedly 'scientific' and 'objective' but in fact much influenced by vested interests and the interests of planners themselves as a professional group – thus wrestles (helplessly} with this 'problem of knowledge.' But competitive, pluralist markets succeed in the co-ordination of services and support the necessary context for their evolution. They allow too for different people to be motivated by different incentives, and at different times of their lives. No one incentive will work for all, or necessarily for any one individual at all times. And in the NHS, negative incentives focus professionals on politicised targets, short-term decisions and political benefits, and vested interests. Thus, fiddled figures and the rest.

Planners simply do not have any way to gather the information or to encapsulate it into 'policy' which will co-ordinate what the market does unconsciously. The emulative behaviour which arises when improvements emerge is itself a crucial part of the value. New investments and ideas create not only new opportunities but new knowledge itself – and focus individual values on their own knowledge and expectations. Competitive, pluralist markets focus individual behaviour and preference. The successful are emulated. This often happens unexpectedly. For example, no-one designed the Internet, or the existing mix of modern computer products, or the diversity of modern book publishing, or the mix of foods you can go out and buy.

The price-system is, too, the mechanism by which relative decisions are made, and by means of which the dispersed information is focussed. This itself is a necessarily relative decision. It is applicable to healthcare, where 'government failure' is both inevitable and endemic, given the true nature of the problem of knowledge. If we want providers to respond to consumers, if we want consumers to be self-responsible, if we want to free up the relationship between mandatory and optional extra funding, we need to rely on pluralist, disciplined markets.

In plural markets with financially empowered consumers all boats rise. Nothing stands still. No-one has the capacity to stop the race. This, a truth that IBM, Dunlop Tyres, Pan Am, Marks & Spencer and any number of 'established' and 'secure' businesses have discovered. Not all remain with us today. The unexpected evolution of the consumer-driven internet is the most striking contemporary example, itself evolving beyond national boundaries and easy jurisdiction.

It is evident that values and knowledge are significantly subjective, and information is diffused, uncertain, and often unknown. The act of choice itself often helps *create* the necessary knowledge, both from within the individual and by selection from without. *Individual interpretation* is an essential element, notably concerning a choice of alternative outcomes. This knowledge grows and changes over time, both for the consumer and the producer. They are influenced by multiple factors, including opportunity, entrepreneurship, and innovation.

We often discover when we want when we go looking, and find what we did not know we wanted. We evaluate services and our own preferences as we explore the options. The market offers us the means to test a variety of choices in a permanent process of re-discovery. Both consumer and provider test out possibilities, in a pluralist competitive market-place where no-one knows what will work best and be supported most until it is tried out in practice. This Hayeckian process of re-discovery is not encapsulated in 'needs-led' analysis.

This is a crucial point and one that is constantly stressed by many publications from the Institute of Economic Affairs, in every area of activity. For example, by Dr. Mark Pennington in his study, *Liberating the Land. The Case for Private Landscale Planning.* [2]

Here, I believe the problems of land-use planning and of healthcare planning are fundamentally identical. Each lack relative resource-prices and thus the information necessary to determine which of all possible combinations of resource uses should be adopted, in order to generate the highest value from the available inputs. Prices can only be determined by open competition, in which market participants are open to challenge.

As Dr. Pennington – who emphasises the role of the market as a form of decentralised social planning – says, "From a Hayeckian perspective, planners (democratically elected or otherwise) can never perceive and respond to as many instances of dis-coordination as can individuals who have the freedom to exchange property titles in the market. Where production possibilities and consumer preferences are in a state of constant flux, planners simply do not have the appropriate 'social welfare function' to guide their decisions." [3] For so-called rationalist planners – buttressed by the unpriced 'market mimicry' of citizen's juries; focus groups; patient advisory services, and other 'citizenship' devices linked into regulatory processes which are all substitutes for genuine markets. These cannot gather appropriate information or manage the inevitable and permanent uncertainties in decision-making, which only markets can address. Nor, in view of its impossibility, should they seek to do so.

In reality, dispersed knowledge is brought together in differing circumstances by differing consumers and producers. The situation is constantly in flux. This may be alarming to the ideological statist or the centralising 'expert', but it is both a fact of life and an essential characteristic of adaptive, evolving, efficient systems. This uncertainty is dynamic. It constantly changes. It is unknowable in advance. It is the result of individual choices, constantly made and re-made. It cannot be gathered and distilled by centralising systems or even by decentralised 'consultation' It is diffused through society – subjective, and not even consciously held in the consumer's mind until it is necessary for an individual to address a specific question, such as what do I want?

As Mark Pennington notes, "If a world of objectively given knowledge existed, then there would be no scope for individual choice, for people would have no option but to respond to the objective stimuli before them. Similarly, where preferences are assumed to be known and constant, the role of consumer is reduced to that of an automaton. If objective knowledge of relative resource scarcities and consumer preferences could be made available in 'scientific' form then it would indeed be possible to dispense with the market in favour of central planning and to have the allocation of resources supervised by government officials employing the techniques of social cost/benefit analysis." [4]

And, as Pennington points out, a world of perfect foresight cannot exist under *any* institutional setting. So, "the key question for political economy is to ascertain which institutions are best suited to operate in an uncertain world where the assumptions that underlie the rationalist model cannot exist in reality. The task of the political economists, therefore, is *not* to highlight the failure of social and economic institutions to attain a state of perfect co-ordination, but to provide explanations for the degree of co-ordination that we *do actually see.*" [5]

This position is the dynamist, democratic consequence of the mix of many market elements in many millions of lives. And this is subjectively subject to incentive, price/quality comparisons, and personal values and assessments of risks and benefits. The subjective expression of a huge number of personal variables is unknowable in advance. Politicised public consultation in sparsely attended meetings where vested interests predominate are no substitute. Nor can the dispersed knowledge which markets capture and express be gathered by the many devices of 'market mimicry' (substituting for direct incentive and feedback from competitive markets) which are offered as an alternative. I analyse this 'market mimicry' further in my book *Patients, Power and Responsibility. The first principles of consumer-driven reform*. I show that the job cannot be done without a market process, offering choice, competition, price comparison and the gathering of preferences which are constantly changing. Strategic planning, too, needs to be nimble, in response to market trends and opportunities. It *needs* the information which only markets can provide.

The notion of a 'common good' postulates something which others judge on our behalf – and which may be neither common nor good. It is insisted upon by 'experts' in terms of 'Progress' and the 'pattern of history', which they interpret on our behalf, usually politically. The alternative is freedom for rational self-determination, or freedom from coercion by others. Here, the common good – which is otherwise difficult to define, and who is to do so? – is helpfully stated as the freedom of an individual to exercise choices. This, by contrast with our rights being subsumed in some notion of the common good defined by others ('The Party'; Sidney Webb; 'the expert' planners; the Commission).

This analysis focuses us on the contrast between being enabled (ineffectually?) – by occasional (but necessarily conflicting) voting, by 'consultation' to have *a say* (or a greater say) – or being able individually to command a necessarily personal, intimate, separable, and timely service.

Many never, ever vote for a winning candidate or a winning policy. And even if they do, this does not guarantee a specific service to an individual. The difference between being able occasionally to seek to discipline *a system* and between being able to access a desired specific service is axiomatic. This is I suggest a choice between being governed by a beggar-my-neighbour agglomeration of policy yielding to unrepresentative pressure groups – as in a democratic system, whose accountability is often illusory – or by qualitative choices made by individuals in trial-and-error adaptive processes (of the kinds detailed by Virginia Postrel's important Hayeckian book, *The Future and Its Enemies*). These inform the market. [6]

INCENTIVES, AND THE PROBLEM OF 'KNOWLEDGE'

This discussion concerns the nature of knowledge (and its knowability), of motivation and behaviour, of risk and its assessment, and the potential of social solidarity and of collective action without collectiv*ism*. We have to look at issues concerning public and private goods, and the context in which these are produced. Here, mere economism will not do as a tool of analysis. We have to consider social and economic institutions, within which we explore the nature of ourselves and of our lives and potentials. We can see then that decentralisation, diversity, discipline, decision-making by individuals and thus differentiation lifts all. And that control, command, conformity, and cash-limits have the opposite effect. In the NHS expectations arise, and are then "satisfied", often after a long queue which itself seems to breach the moral contract the tax-payer thought he had with the State. In a dynamist approach, however, everyone has the opportunity not only to get 'the best', but also to discover for themselves what that comprises.

The revolution in the UK optics market – which I study at length in *Patients, Power and Responsibility* – is a persuasive and local example of how economies really change. There, as in all markets, reputation, review and reward are directly linked to costed choices and results (in NHS terms 'outcomes') reported by individuals to one another, informally and formally. Failure finds its certain and swift feedback; success its switched resources, from losing organisation to winning provider. We have to find ways to help change many of the minds of the more than a million employed in the NHS who need to appreciate the benefits of dynamism, both for themselves and for patients. We need to do so making the convincing case – from many contemporary examples which everyone can see and know, and which can genuinely apply to health and social care, too. A walk down any High Street would be a good start.

To go forward we must envisage persuasive institutional alternatives to de-centralise power to the individual, and not merely to local quangos. The key is to encourage direct and appropriate incentives for change – both by purchasers, providers, and patients themselves, in greater self-responsibility. Each of these three elements, indeed, offers scope for reform from within – at the individual and the community level. This however, can only work if each of these possible partners has to consider an incentive structure which requires them to weigh costs and benefits, and to be clearly accountable for their own decisions. If these elements can be set in place then, however imperfect, markets are much more likely to achieve access to high quality healthcare for all and on a consistent basis of improvement than the alternative of state planning, a restricted funding base, uncompetitive purchasing and uncompetitive provision. And, indeed, more likely than the devices and masques of 'market mimicry' we see tried, and which are innocent of the financially-empowered consumer.

We need, too, to remove negative incentives such as targeting volume which is easily measured – and embracing positive incentives – which impact on outcomes, which are harder (but not impossible) to measure and audit. Ask the patient after 6 months, can you walk with the new hip, without pain?

Negative incentives impact on behaviours already: for example, managers fiddle the figures on waiting times, to please political target-makers. Doctors are pressed to deal with lumps and bumps which have been 18 months on the waiting list, and time runs out for dealing with life-threatening cancers. Morale falls; early retirements rise. None of this targeting and central 'needs' analysis necessarily or sufficiently improves services or outcomes.

Changed incentives *can* do much to change behaviour (or process) and culture in which behaviour is embedded. Otherwise (as in opinion poll results urging higher taxation to pay for the NHS) a preference without a cost is merely an irresponsible demand. Cash or the voucher (Patient Fund Holding) is the necessary economic vehicle and the measure, with price explicit even if this is not charged at the moment of service. Without price we do not have a way of making decisions amongst the many demands and the multiple possible combinations of how we might use resources.

There was much early talk of empowerment by the new Blair government from 1997. [7] Mr. Alan Milburn, as Secretary of State for Health, directly addressed the inequalities which have continued to arise from the functioning of the NHS. [20] However, under Mr. Brown as Prime Minister in 2007 we quickly slid backwards, away from individual empowerment back to Citizen's Juries. This is one of the several approaches which I call 'market mimicry' – and which are set out in full in my bigger books. These cannot achieve empowerment of the consumer. The one action which will have the most direct impact is to give the individual a personal healthcare fund. And thus control over resources which will impact on the actions, incomes and future of local managers and healthcare professionals. Then, we shall see "Action Stations!" Similarly, the individual patient will have to appraise costs and benefits, and to consider risk, a choice of provision, and possible alternative outcomes. Then we shall see more self-care, more self-responsibility, more consideration of the cost and consequences of individual behaviour.

The necessary radical shift is to equip all patients as consumers with both money and information. And to empower each of us to call on tacit knowledge and information from within themselves, which (as Michael Polanyi argued) only the individual can do. This itself is an important part of the self-definition we each need to resolve for ourselves in securing appropriate care, itself more likely in a plural and competitive market. Unlike the traditional Irishman at the roadside, we do need to get from here to there. [8]

The device with the greatest potential to take us forward in these terms is crispy notes. We should delegate the money to buy the services to the people whose own interests are most directly involved in the decisions about their care. Only money and a priced system provides the necessary direct incentive for each individual to weigh and consider competing alternatives, and to call upon explicit and tacit knowledge and advice in doing so. Only when consumers have a real incentive to consider costs and benefits will we achieve self-responsibility, and its many associated benefits. Similarly, direct incentives will impact on provider and purchaser performance. And, too, as I show in this book, they can even do so on A&E services, which have been thought to be beyond the reach of competitive improvement – due to regional monopoly, specialists clustering together, large-scale capital costs, and Royal College control over training and validation.

The scope is significant, and we have reached the time to act. Direct cash payment for consumers to purchase some social services is a major shift. [9] But was not, by 2007, having much more than a ten per cent take-up. Since then the opportunity to extend it more widely to the whole NHS has been entirely squandered. When making assessments staff do not have time or interest in it and they do not often advise clients about the option. However, in terms of both equity and service improvements we should keep in clear view that money is "the least immutable of all class distinctions." [10] Individual economic empowerment can make the greatest differences, and more certainly so than politics, consultation, or "having *a say*." We need to cease, too, to think of "the poor" *en masse*, as a collective working class, and permit each person to emerge in all their possible variety and individuality, individual character and social ethos.

At present, staff have no direct incentives – save for political targeting and regulation. This, however, too often delivers processes but it does not necessarily improve performance. This is not to say that much good work is not done, for clearly this is the case. Even projects like the Expert Patients Programme make *some* contribution to understanding and to self-management and self-support. But they are still relatively marginal, and they are small-scale. There is, too, the element of patients being trained to see the problems of the system. Some 20,000 patients will have been involved in this particular pilot by 2004. [11] What we need instead are clear incentives for choice and competition for funds. With everyone involved required to consider costs, user preference and satisfaction, and the competing alternatives other providers can offer. Meanwhile, it is politicians who set up the processes and the regulatory framework which substitutes for pluralist competition and its disciplines.

Barriers to change.

It is not, even so, easy to achieve change. After 65 years of the NHS it would be surprising if it was. We do however need to find ways to open up to a wider receptivity to new ideas – to move people from what Michel Foucault calls "the stark impossibility of thinking *that*" to another system of thought. [12]

This is not an easy task, for there is an intransigence of imagination even now. And especially so as people who believe in central controls have characteristically defended this approach in terms of superior expertise and the greater good. These are anti-democratic affirmations that they would be shocked to see deployed by others for other purposes. But they do so to justify cultural power used for political purposes – notably politicised equality.

And, as Lionel Trilling noted, "It is often true that the success of a social or cultural enterprise compromises the virtues that claimed our loyalty in its heroic, hopeless beginning but there is a kind of vulgarity in the easy assumption that this is so always and necessarily." Trilling quotes D. H. Lawrence, too, on the importance of learning from experience: "The world doesn't fear a new idea. It can pigeonhole any idea. But it can't pigeonhole a new experience." And it is the experience of successful markets which can do much to change cultures, attitudes, and expectations. [13]

We know that many people react to innovation with anxiety and resistance. Frank J. Sulloway has pointed out that even today Darwin's theory of evolution, however compelling the evidence, is still resisted. Anomalies are often only ever recognised long after the fact. We find it easier to assimilate anomalous new facts into existing cognitive structures, than to accommodate these structures to anomalous findings. It took more than a century for Copernicus's claim that the Earth revolves around the Sun to be accepted. Alfred Wegener's theory of continental drift was not accepted for 50 years. Paradigm shifts are very difficult to accomplish. [14] As Thomas Kuhn's *The Structure of Scientific Revolutions* tells us, strongly held beliefs can preclude the observation of the most obvious of phenomena. [15]

Debate is made more difficult, too, because opposing sides usually offer *one* moral universe in which only *their* moral concepts apply. Commisario Brunetti notes in Donna Leon's recent novel *Wilful Behaviour*: "I'm afraid it costs people too much to abandon what they believe...If you give your loyalty and, I suppose, your love to ideas like that then it's impossible to admit what madness they are." [16] Ideas, once established, have the longevity of myth. Emanuel Litvinoff once noted, too, "And doesn't the Talmud say truth is heavy so people don't like to carry it?" [17] Few old dogs learn new paradigms. Psychological defences can be stouter than castle walls. We may, indeed, need to rely instead on generational change. As Max Planck remarked, "A new scientific truth does not triumph by convincing its opponents and making them see the light, but rather because its opponents eventually die, and as a new generation grows up that is familiar with it." [18]

Guidance on this journey can be taken from many sources. For example, from the economic historian David S. Landes: "I am reminded that superstition and magic are not dead...No doubt, because weak mortals that we are, we look for comfort where it is to be found. Even scientists and technicians are vulnerable, for science and reason are tough companions. Nonetheless, illusions, delusions, and faith are excluded in principle and practice from inquiry and discovery." [19]

And as Landes says, the ultimate advantage and beneficence of scientific knowledge and technological capability is today under attack, even in the Academy. "The reasons for this reaction, often couched in preferences for feeling over knowing, range from disappointment at Paradise Unfound to fear and resentment by laymen of unknowable knowledge." [20] He points out the directions in which the world is *not* going – notably those routes advocated by

INCENTIVES, AND THE PROBLEM OF 'KNOWLEDGE'

Marxian Socialists and Communists, and nostalgics for a mythic stateless society. Each, perhaps, represent mistaken good intentions. However, "Reason will triumph because reason pays. More is better, and in choosing goals, material achievement is the best argument." [21]

The re-assurance offered by a legally enforceable core guarantee of prompt access to quality care for all – Patient Guaranteed Care – is, I suggest, an essential part of the process of people 'learning by doing.' That is, shifting their own ground through experience, and understanding that there are better ways in liberal markets.

One of the keys to health is in our own hands: the way we each live our lives. This is necessarily the subject of personal responsibility. We need to examine how direct incentives can be encouraged and supported. The costs of not doing this are very considerable. As Derek Wanless showed in his first report, of 2002, *Securing Our Future*, a high-level of individual engagement could deliver savings of up to £30 billion by 2020 – or half of the existing NHS budget. For each £100 spent on encouraging self-care some £150 of benefits could be returned. Between 60 – 75% of healthcare costs are now associated with people with chronic conditions – many of them entirely preventable. Co-ordination and integration of care services is another necessary but too often undelivered element, but on which a free competitive market of direct and personalised incentives could impact. In addition, a sense of self-worth, of control over one's life, of being able to shape and express personal preferences – and of being individually financially-empowered to do so – is a crucial element in individual well-being. [22]

To educate and to persuade – as well as to give ourselves guidance for the future – we must set out first principles and governing axioms – of good health care, of social solidarity, and of a society of liberty. Then we can set out practical solutions in harmony with principle. These principles must be the basis by which we should regulate activity, test proposals, and subject institutions to criticism and reform. And to refer every day every NHS event, explaining why things as they are and how they could be different. This educational opportunity is not yet being taken by the leading political parties.

I take the first principles to be:

- the rule of law.

- a social order which arises from spontaneous evolution and market decentralisation rather than from central direction (always provided the individual is empowered economically).

- respect for private property rights, and private decision making.

- the central value of voluntary exchange, in which individuals co-operate with others to satisfy wants.

- respect for the individual and reliance on self-responsibility, individual action and mutual-aid, whilst valuing the differences between people.

- the ultimate protection of the consumer through choice and competition.

- social solidarity, but not ideologically enforced and artificial equality.

- compassion and concern for others, and the protection of the poor.

These are the protections of welfare, justice and truth which constitute the major elements and context within which we can have self-responsible liberty.

Second, I seek to refer the daily events of the NHS to these first principles, to explain the meaning they encapsulate, and the alternative approach we could seek to deliver.

Third, I urge specific devices which would change things for us all, in social solidarity. Devices which genuinely enable us all to benefit from market mechanisms in a society of liberty and of self-responsibility. These need to capture and articulate the emotive force which has been associated with the NHS. Language matters, as does leadership. For this will be a society where we see and appreciate what Adam Smith called "sympathy," and which shows that informed self-interest enables each individual to come to a consciousness of themselves.

It is important to evolve an analysis which clarifies the benefits of these devices, and which persuades the doubters, not least by showing how a different approach would actually work in detail. Self-reliance is a critical element, especially to the poor, as Henry Mayhew well understood long ago now: "There is but one way of benefiting the poor, viz. by developing their powers of self-reliance, and certainly not by treating them like children." [36] The challenge is to enable the individual and the provider to benefit from an approach which makes a market, which recognises property rights and choice in a pluralist competitive framework, and which enables these levers to raise standards and improve value for money. All this whilst seeking to satisfy and retain support from patients and the public.

I urge:

- a *legally enforceable* core guarantee of prompt access to quality care for all – I call it Patient Guaranteed Care – or Pretty Good Care.

- effective consumer power from individual financial leverage: individual economic empowerment by tax-based Patient Fund Holding in a Health Savings Account, with tax transfers to the poor. This is a specific mechanism which will guarantee choice to the individual, instead of merely generalising 'choice' in elections, planning or 'consultation' –

themselves processes dominated by interest groups, and the interests of politicians and bureaucracies as shown in 'public choice' analysis by James Buchanan, Gordon Tullock, Douglass North, Arthur Seldon and others. [23]

- we should each hold social insurance, using our HSA – I see no alternative to compulsion here.

- provision should be made competitive, and control localised through my proposed Patient Guaranteed Care Associations to ensure responsiveness to market-based incentives.

All this is intended to achieve social solidarity, as well as service improvement. We will each take this insurance to a PGCA. These co-operative, mutual purchasing organisations will compete for individual subscriptions from Patient Fund Holders. These will be private bodies, open to the public. They will be owned by and accountable to their subscribing members. They will facilitate competition, experimentation, adaptive change – and offer the Patient Fund Holder different 'communities', different approaches, different packages of care specific to varied preferences.

This innovative institution is essential to facilitating consumer choice in a competitive environment, as well as to promoting the discovery process of future wants and the subjective expression of preferences.

These organisations, too, will free us from class-based privilege and politicised 'consultation' – which favours the organised, middle-class without addressing or solving the magnitude of the challenge of discovering knowledge from 60 million-plus minds. Much more certainly, too, the poor will be empowered through tax transfers, bringing them into an effective market as if they were middle-class players, with full access to advice from the PGCA.

The PGCA will be headed by expert clinical and managerial leadership. It will purchase a negotiated package of the core services and discover other niche opportunities on behalf of voluntary members.

For these will be local, regional, mutual, member-owned, democratic voluntary proprietary communities. Their success, and the value of their assets, will be directly tied to consumer support.

This is to urge the recovery of working-class mutuality, of voluntary co-operation, of self-association in institutions that stand between the state and the individual. Each provider and each purchaser will offer an appropriate bundle of services – the core package and others – in an experimental, adaptive process where each will discover the most wanted mix of services necessary to retain patient support and voluntary membership so as to maintain a competitive advantage.

Unlike existing NHS institutions – hospitals, Primary Care Trusts, &c. – each will be subject to processes of competitive entry through which the most appropriate services and systems will be discovered. The financial survival of each will be directly tied to their success in achieving this. Over every shoulder will be the possibility of another organiser offering differing arrangements at different prices to attract voluntary membership. The whole will facilitate market-exchange in the community, through a community, and between communities. Overall, the incentive for all parties will be to amplify the benefits both of competition and co-operation. This is the process described by the economist Ludwig von Mises, involving us all in an on-going process of "competing in co-operation and co-operating in competition." [24]

There will thus be:

- direct incentives for personal responsibility, and for individual understanding and responsibility for the consequences of personal behaviour.

- a minimal supervisory role for the State, based on belief in an open market and including the responsibility to maintain the value of the Patient Fund Holding credit and tax-transfers to the poor.

- a much reduced emphasis on bio-medicalisation of every aspect of our lives, with greater self-reliance.

All these devices need to be both adaptive and efficient. This requires the protection of competition, and a focus on outcomes. This can only arise from the protection of individually empowered choice and sustained competition. *Learning to choose*, as Hayek, urged, is fundamental to self-responsibility and to the evolution of the system. So, too, is a direct personal link between behaviour, costs, and consequences.

These commitments require:

- the maximum degree of freedom for the individual consistent with one person's freedom not interfering with another's.

- the maximum dispersal of power compatible with a democracy.

- resistance to functions being assigned to government which can be performed more effectively in competitive markets.

- the State both as active facilitator and umpire – in a government of laws, not men, required to protect competition and choice, and thus to enforce those contracts voluntarily entered into by private parties – by patients and their co-operative purchasers. Government will supervise a framework of rules limited to supporting first principles, and the courts will settle disputes on a case-law basis.

And:

- otherwise, scepticism about the claims of government when it wishes to limit freedom, on our behalf and in our interest.

- the avoidance of coercion being substituted for voluntary action where possible.,

- respect for the individual and reliance on individual action.

- social solidarity: healthcare for all as a pillar of a society of liberty, and an approach which reinforces these foundations.

- open-ness and accountability.

- an evolutionary, incremental system responding to consumer's wishes.

- direct incentives.

- no detailed master-plan.

We could recognise that the actions of individuals comprise both rational and irrational acts. We all of us have many motives. And thus the legitimacy (and politically persuasive) of reform proposals must stand many tests if support is to be built and sustained. The British test of 'fairness' – which cannot be the same as the insistence on politicised equality (however elusively measured) – is, I suggest, fundamental in the debate. My answer is to offer Patient Guaranteed Care – legally enforceable by contract. Ensuring access to all of the core package of 'Pretty Good Care.'

I suggest that people will support change more readily (and with a better conscience) if it is clear that the poor will have equal access, and that extra income does not enable the rich to secure better clinical care, save for optional extras. I suggest that this is the landscape of if, and only if. And that voluntary mutual co-operative purchasing organisations – PGCAs – will undertake the technical assessments on behalf of the individual consumer, who will not need to become a specialist or a permanent activist, which the emphasis on citizenship often requires.

Here too, evocative language matters. It is, as Blair appreciated, a vital aspect of leadership.

Notably, in the selection of the questions to ask.

Not 'How can we save the NHS in 24 hours?'

But...

- 'How can we ensure that the poor do much better?

- How can we optimise the individual opportunity of access?

- How assist individuals to define and achieve their own preferred outcomes and make choices?

- How match cost and choice?

- And – for academics! – how manage a risk-pool, and cope with moral hazard, adverse selection, and free-riders? How balance wants and competing choices – both between and within individual lives?

- How legitimise the distribution of services in a situation of inevitable scarcity?

- How improve funding and re-balance mandatory and optional spending?

- How link self-responsibility, self-care, price and demand?

- And what to do when, as Isaiah Berlin warns us, many objectives are necessarily in conflict, and thus "incommensurable"?

None of us can ever have it all, nor necessarily agree on what "all" comprises. Here, direct economic incentives are crucial, as I have suggested, both in asking and in answering such questions.

NOTES.

1. F. von Hayek, *Studies in Philosophy, Politics and Economics* (London, Routledge, 1967).

2. See Mark Pennington, *Liberating the Land. The Case for Private Land-scale Planning* (London, Institute of Economic Affairs/Profile Books, 2002).

3. Pennington, *op. cit.*, pp.37-8.

4. Pennington, *ibid.*, p.36.

5. Pennington, *ibid.*, pp.36-7.

6. Virginia Postrel, *The Future and Its Enemies, The Growing Conflict over Creativity, Enterprise, and Progress* (New York, The Free Press, 1998).

7. See Arthur Seldon, *Capitalism* (Oxford, Basil Blackwell, 1990) – his masterpiece. The IEA has recently published *Capitalism: A Condensed Version* (London, IEA, 2007), with

introductions by John Blundell and Philip Booth. See also James Buchanan, *The Limits of Liberty* (Chicago, University of Chicago Press, 1975); James Buchanan and Gordon Tullock, *The Calculus of Consent* (Ann Arbor, University of Michigan Press, 1962); Douglass North, *Structure and Change in Economic History* (New York, W. W. Norton, 1981), and *Understanding the Process of Economic Change* (London, Institute of Economic Affairs, 1999). Also the discussion in the Introduction to my *Patients, Power and Responsibility. The first principles of consumer-driven reform* (Oxford, Radical Medical Press, 2003), with a Foreword by Professor Karol Sikora.

8. "Health Secretary announces new plans to improve health in poorest areas", Department of Health Press Release, 20 January 2001.

9. See, Michael Polanyi, *Personal Knowledge. Towards a Post-Critical Philosophy* (New York, Harper Torchbooks, Academy Library, 1964 edition), and his *The Logic of Liberty* (Chicago, University of Chicago Press, 1951).

10. Gertrude Himmelfarb, *The Idea of Poverty. England in the Early Industrial Age* (New York, Alfred A. Knopf, 1984), p.480.

11. See full discussion in my *Patients Power and Responsibility*, chapter 13, 'Cash on the nail.'

12. Sean Dodson, "Supporting self-care", *NHS Magazine*, May 2003, pp.22-3.

13. Michel Foucault, *The Order of Things. An Archaeology of The Human Sciences* (New York, Vintage Books, 1970), p xv.

14. Lionel Trilling, *Beyond Culture. Essays on Literature and Learning* (London, Secker & Warburg, 1966), p. xv, p. xviii.

15. Frank J. Sulloway, *Born to Rebel. Birth Order, Family Dynamics, and Creative Lives* (New York, David McKay, 1996).

16. Thomas S..Kuhn, *The Structure of Scientific Revolutions* (Chicago, Chicago University Press, 1962).

17. Donna Leon, *Wilful Behaviour* (London, William Heinemann, 2002), p.211.

18. Emanuel Litvinoff, *Journey Through a Small Planet* (London, Michael Joseph, 1972), p.18.

19. Max Planck, cited, Paul Streitz, *Oxford* (Darien, CT, Oxford Institute Press, 2001), p.23.

20. David S. Landes, *The Wealth and Poverty of Nations. Why Some Are So Rich And Some Are So Poor* (London, Little Brown, 1998), p.512.

21. Landes, *op. cit.* p.513.

22. Landes, *ibid.*, p.515.

23. Wanless Report, *Securing Our Future Health. Taking a long-term view. Reviewing the trends affecting the health service* (London, Health Trends Team, H. M. Treasury, April 2002).

8. Berlin's Two concepts of Order.

"It is certain that there is an immense amount of remediable misery among us; that in addition to the poverty, disease and degradation, which are the consequences of causes beyond human control, there is a vast, probably a very much larger, quantity of misery which is the result of individual ignorance, or misconduct, and of faulty social arrangements." T. H. Huxley.

Overall, I suggest that what is at stake in these debates is two different ways of thinking about life, as posed by Isaiah Berlin's *Two Concepts of Order*. This extends my earlier discussion of the 'problem of knowledge.' [1]

First, dynamism – or the spontaneous order generated in a self-organising and self-coordinating "system" (or approach) which arises from the adaptive market. Its evolution is the consequence of many individual decisions which create complex, creative, and previously unforecast consequences. To achieve this innovative society it is not necessary for each contributor to be part of a politicised consultative process. People can just make their own wishes known, and the dynamist pattern emerges. This solves the 'informational problem' (which government/planners/'experts' otherwise cannot do) and it generates constant feedback and adjustment by bringing buyers and suppliers together at agreed prices, levels of quality, and availability. This is not chaotic – and no one wants to live amidst chaos. The spontaneity, or adaptive evolution, of competitive markets, indeed, can and has achieved much more in both volume and value than we can otherwise attain. The noted post-1945 exceptions have all been in so-called 'public services', including the NHS, education, and the BBC.

The order that arises from competitive markets is neither chaotic nor need it be threatening. And so we must explain the case to those who fear change. Notably, that the co-ordination and the opportunity that spontaneous order offers is not otherwise attainable in the NHS. The NHS has to cease being an exception. For creative Darwinian evolution is the essence of the economy everywhere and on every day.

Paul Samuelson, one of the most famous and widely read and influential 20th century economists, made the point clearly: "[There is] convincing proof that a competitive system of markets and prices…is not a system of chaos and anarchy. There is in it a certain order and orderliness. It Works. Without [centralised] intelligence. It solves some of the most complex problems imaginable, involving thousands of unknown variables and relations. Nobody designed it. Like Topsy, it just growed." [2]

Second, there is statism – or central control, hierarchy, allocative (and artificially imposed) scarcity and state monopoly in funding, purchasing, and provision. We can and should show, too, that any 'market failure' is self-correcting, rapidly corrected, and adaptive – unlike 'government failure' which is often very slow or even politically impossible to correct in a structure of stasis, of central control, of hierarchy, of allocative (and artificially imposed) scarcity, and of state monopoly in funding, purchasing and provision.

Here, I suggest that the NHS was not a good idea that went wrong, but a bad idea.

This is so, first, because it contravenes the first principles of access and liberty.

Second, because it contradicts economic realities.

Third, because it misunderstands human psychology and mis-states the true nature and source of knowledge.

Fourth, because it contradicts the sources and prompts of individual behaviour, values and preferences in an open society.

Thus, in Hayekian terms it could never have succeeded. And it cannot do so now at any level of public expenditure that the Labour and trade union leaderships wish to set. This is not to say that extra spending does not generate new capacity and achieve service improvements – but not necessarily higher productivity. But this does not solve the problem of planners that they cannot know individual preferences or empower choice, in the absence of market prices.

NOTES.

1.. Isaiah Berlin, *Two concepts of liberty: An inaugural lecture delivered before the University of Oxford on 31 October 1958* (Oxford, Clarendon Press, 1963); Isaiah Berlin, *Four Essays on Liberty* (London, Oxford University Press, 1969).

2. Cited, A. Kemp, "The mixed US system" in *Monopoly or Choice in Health Services?* (London, Institute of Economic Affairs, 1964), p.48.

9. The radical agenda now.

"Without will and freedom there can be no virtue and vice." Gertrude Himmelfarb.

How can this radical agenda become politically feasible? We can be optimistic. Many changes – social, cultural, demographic, scientific, financial and – especially – technical are coming to a head at the same time. As I outlined in my Introduction to this book, new technologies are changing *everything*. And this has hardly started.

There is a shift in what Gertrude Himmelfarb called the "moral imagination." [1] And we are seeing the revival of a focus on the real intermediate territory of democratic mutuality, a territory between the individual and the State. One in which individuals can successfully act in solidarity and also pursue their own private interests. There is a sea-change in attitudes to what was once said to be the best health service in the world. Results are more explicit. Knowledge of what happens overseas is spreading. And the questions of 'Why?' and 'Why not?' are becoming insistent.

As public scandals, failures in service, and very serious errors in management multiply many people now see that other approaches overseas do significantly better. There is a generational change, too, supported evermore by the new information paradigm from the web.

However, we must inevitably initially rely on politics to remove politicians from the command and controlling micro-management of services. But politicians will only take their hands away from electrified wires. And if the Blair/Brown/Cameron 'Big Spend' does not achieve services comparable to the best abroad they will surely and inevitably retreat from the present structure in the interests of electoral security? My fictional chapter 17, below, on Mr. Blair's Great Health Consultation, examines this question.

Key 'rent-seekers' – the BMA, Royal Colleges, &c. – will also, I suggest, see that they can derive advantages from change. Life will just be better. Working conditions, pay, morale, can all improve. Self-responsible patients may prove less frivolous, if not less demanding. Costs will become visible. Healthcare professionals can form the leadership of the local purchasing and providing communities which I have proposed. Hospitals freed from Whitehall mini-management can venture forth with innovation relevant to their localities. Political interference and incessant targeting will only decline if both purchasing and provision become truly competitive, and open to the decisions of local people self-organized in co-operatives. This can be a great relief to professionals, to other staff, and to patients.

Indeed, to many now the mediating ideas of welfare and the NHS seem as much obstruction as opportunity. Certainly, we can no longer take the Whig view of the NHS as the origin, evolution, and development of appropriate health care services. But we still need to tackle these ideas seriously and to debate them. Ideology needs to be unpacked, confronted, and considered.

We need, particularly, in conceptualising the real problems of the denial of self-responsibility by the individual – the overwhelming threat of obesity, diabetes, heart and cancer diseases – to clarify how to introduce direct economic incentives for self-responsibility. And to synthesise the wish for universal care and the operation both of free market instruments in practice and as basic categories of thought which guide adaptive, evolutionary change. We need to do so without compromising the integrity and the complexity of the evidence and its meanings. We need to explore how we can encourage a shift from a deep and often unthinking rejection of market mechanisms – an inherited background within the public sector – to seeing the world differently. For, urgently one conception does need to give way to another, integrating both morality and action.

A dynamist approach needs to serve as a believable explanation of their experience, sensibility and consciousness for every party – for current patients and potential patients, for professionals, for all staff, and for politicians. Each participant, too, in John Wesley's terms, must be endowed *with their own worth*. Notably, we need to address how *the formal rights to care* – which have too often been insubstantial, denied or diluted – can become a *genuine* economic and social right, guaranteed and *enforceable by law*.

And thus we do need to ask a different order of questions than those asked by welfarism and by increased "consultation" with "experts." These questions require a different treatment, eliciting from agreed information different meanings. These meanings can be creatively structured by ideas, values, attitudes, images and perceptions about autonomy, liberty, social solidarity and self-responsibility – with one *shared fundamental* being the moral wish to equip the poor to achieve good care. Presently, they are at the very back of the queue.

In the short-term no doubt the BMA, RCN, Unison and others will oppose any changes. But political leadership – in its own interests, and possibly in ours too? – can marshal media and public opinion to begin the processes of change which will rapidly reveal their benefits. A radical programme built round first principles, and restructuring individual incentives, will change the picture. We need a conservative Party which believes in markets, and constantly makes the case.

The questions that we have then to address in improving the persuasiveness of the case, are several.

They include:

- how can we offer alternatives which are seen to have legitimacy, and which chime with such British values as 'fairness' and the idea that the weak, the poor, the unlucky must be protected by the strong?

- what are the keys to building *political* support for market-led changes?

- how can we encourage greater understanding of the benefits of adaptive markets, and of the concomitant economic institutions of choice, competition, price and investment forward – and their relevance to successful health and social care in social solidarity for all?

- how can we persuade people to accept and adopt arguments which are diametrically opposed to the many socialist and centralising ideas which have guided their well-paid professional careers?

- how can we introduce market mechanisms whilst avoiding the known risks of adverse selection (or refusal of cover for the chronically sick: answer, government compels), moral hazard (or carelessness when insured: answer, incentive to share consequences, and limit conditional benefits), free riding ("I won't pay"; answer: just put up with some of it, but prosecute the worst offenders).

- how can we avoid monopoly behaviour, and stimulate the essential element of disciplined competition (and where competing firms should always be themselves disciplined by competition)?

- how can we ensure – socially insure! – that unexpected risks do not ruin lives by big medical bills (and persuade people that they won't?). A requirement for individuals to cover themselves with 'catastrophe' insurance, with the poor covered by tax-transfers?

- how do we achieve genuine social solidarity and voluntary, mutual co-operation (which is different from *politicised* compulsory equality), enabling us all to have reliable access to care?

- to what extent is coercive compulsion unavoidable – this, despite Robert Nozick's and Milton Friedman's warnings – if all are to be socially insured?

- how can we re-build those mutual, cooperative intermediate institutions which stand between the individual and the State, as they key to deciding who is to decide what to spend on health and social care, and how are we to decide? what are we to 'produce', and how much of it? at what levels of quality? by which mechanisms? how are we to distribute the costs? where is our information (or knowledge) to come from – the expert, or the market? on what basis of legitimacy and consent? (Pass by, for the briefest of historical moments, the consequences of the genomic revolution for access to services).

- what is government's role to be, helping to foster and co-ordinate the structure of self-responsibility, mutuality, and competitive choice, whilst disciplining standards?

- *are people a priori* capable or incapable of choice?

There are market solutions to all of these questions. Key to acceptance of this is the idea that the rich must expect to pay for the poor, via redistributive taxes (which is not to endorse the wider claim that all incomes should be redistributed, or that differences between incomes are illegitimate). We require a successful economy to fund care, and high taxation is a disincentive and a burden to competitiveness. Yet I doubt, too, that cost pressures will allow lower taxation as we consider how best to fund healthcare, even if we encourage supplementary private insurance and even if we achieve the available gains in productivity.

NOTE.

1. G. Himmelfarb, *The Idea of Poverty. England in the Early Industrial Age* (New York, Alfred A. Knopf, 1984), p.19.

10. No Master Plan.

Mediocra Firma – Francis Bacon's family motto.

None of this implies a master-plan, or another all encompassing epochal explanation of all things under the sun.

It concerns *an approach.*

For, in taking a market approach we should not try to implement some pre-designed, micro-managed blueprinted Market Master Plan. Instead, we need an openly adaptive *approach.*

Here, I have sought to set out first principles which will enable us to benefit in terms of better health and social care by free markets embedded within moral and social assumptions (such as a culture of equality of access to care). And where we respect and rely on property rights, incentive, price, pluralism, and adaptive innovation via competition in provision and in purchasing, with individual financially-enabled choice.

All this asks for a structure of institutions enabled and also inevitably supervised by government. Most importantly, however, the processes of market development (and of the evolution of productivity) are unending, innovative, and necessarily responsive to consumers. It is not, however, subject to predestined planning of the kind that centralisers prefer. My mentors here are Hayek and Michael Oakeshott. [1]

One crucial difference between the present structures and the market alternative is obvious, although it is much resisted in present health care debates. This is that in centralised systems no one is ever allowed to get out of step, since this is said to threaten everyone who otherwise will not get the same care. If "the same care" is bad, or unreliable, or unproven, or unexamined, or unavailable, this is not much of a gain. The consequence of this universalist, politicised approach is too often that many get poor care, in the struggle to prevent anyone doing better than anyone else. Markets by contrast, enable us all to benefit when someone does something new, different, better. And when we can emulate this, just as someone else tries to devise a further better advance. These offers of new services, of new ways of doing things, are, of course, then contested and tested in the market place when consumers have free choices. Compare and contrast with the NHS, where even good innovations can take decades to be adopted by conservatively-minded professionals.

There need to be effective market disciplines for these gains to be possible. And there needs to be the overall *social discipline* of protecting choice, competition, and the benefits of pluralism. This, indeed, is a fundamental first principle. To that extent it is *imperfect competition*, or the continuing freedom to try new things, which we must protect. Rivalry and reputation are the protectors of the consumer, and in dynamic ways denied to the system by centralism, monopoly provision, and 'expert' consultation. And it is this rivalry which solves the problem of knowledge – of how to know what people prefer, amongst costed-alternatives. It is this necessarily dispersed (and often unconscious) knowledge of consumer preferences (most frequently, *qualitative* preferences) which centralising planners cannot gather, discover, or encapsulate or summarise in 'policy', as Hayek, Polanyi, Postrel and others have shown. Yet by its absence much innovative development is lost, as is much good individual service and outcome.

This free market approach is not to say that there should not be discipline. Indeed, markets are *the* efficient discipline. And we do not seek a market red in tooth and claw. Nor one in which government has no role. It has a key supervisory, active role. Notably, in protecting competition, and supporting individuals in challenging for legal rights.

Clearly, self-discipline is crucial for the health status of each patient, too. This, I suggest, is more likely in a market where true costs are revealed and where these have to be considered by each individual. And with a Health Savings Account, an excess on each insurance policy would deter frivolity. In addition, regulation by government is a key role. It must make the rules and overlook the framework rather than merely acting as a distant, neutral umpire. The adaptiveness of the health and social care market will need some guidance. This asks for a blend of supervised spontaneity. For example, there are strategic issues. Government will have to decide on what is included in the 'core' package of Patient Guaranteed Care, and then to canvass popular support. There will be much special-interest lobbying to referee. And it must protect medical standards in training and in practice, support and encourage appropriate research. Explicit audit – and thus, accountability – is essential. And the most explicit audit is open competition.

The issue here is what to regulate, how, by whom, and with which results. The test should be performance not process. Alas, my own personal experience as a National Commissioner suggests that regulation (and targeting) can much too easily be focussed on process and not on outcome, or on the appropriate appraisal of performance and consequences, unless we are very alert. This can disable services, demotivate staff, undermine management – and threaten the careers of politicians. In response I stress the key role of competitive purchasing, and of the protection of competition, rather than of provider reform (or who owns the provision of services) alone.

There remains the continuing difficulty, too, of how to ensure that self-regulating professionals actually regulate their own. This is the problem of "our gang." Here the role of external audit is crucial. Here, I explore and endorse the pioneering, independent work done by Dr. William G. Pickering on his proposed Independent Medical Inspectorate. [2] This is a necessary, urgent, relatively inexpensive, cost-effective and beneficial reform, and it should be taken with the utmost seriousness.

This is not to say that markets and regulation are mutually exclusive. I am pragmatic (Nozick, forgive!) about regulation, and suggest that they can be mutual and integral. Certainly, they must continue to evolve in a social context which necessarily changes. For example, consider the recent – if still very limited – changes that have begun to arise as a consequence of the scandals of Dr. Harold Shipman, the Bristol baby enquiry, and the disgraced gynecologist Dr. Rodney Ledward. And the changes being wrought in terms of the inter-connectedness of patients by the internet. These are seen to prompt suppliers to explore new opportunities for services including their bespoke-tailoring, location, co-ordination, integration and inter-connectedness. And they influence their price, environment, and so on.

None of this implies that there should not be co-operation. Indeed, my proposals for mutual (and mutually-supportive) co-operative purchasing by member-owned organisations to which we voluntarily take our taxed-based healthcare fund relies on effective co-operation. Here, the possibility of individual exit and of the mobility of a personal fund (Patient Fund Holding) is fundamental.

All this, too, is necessarily embedded in the social values, notably, in British terms, of what we perceive to be 'fair.' And my arguments concern the most effective way to fund, purchase and deliver care in the context of these perennial 'values.' To do so, I suggest, we will need to change much of the culture of healthcare as it prevails in the UK today. This necessary culture change is so huge that it can only be achieved by very direct economic incentives, choice, and effective competition. Competition, too, which is maintained and maintainable. So, too, we must respect and understand the necessity of profit, or surpluses for future investment. I urge that we need to grow up in considering this idea. The issue is not that we do not want profit (or surpluses, or a 'social dividend.') This is essential for investment forward, as well as an audit of successful and valued activity. The question is, how are the surpluses to be used. Profits are a means to our ends. They are necessary to improve services, to innovate, or to lower prices, for consumers. And purchasers which encourage this point of view will find better providers and happier subscribers. They will help differentiate information, services, and satisfactions.

Keats's *Poems of 1817* takes for its epigraph two lines from Edmund Spencer which are intended to point up the political overtones of the volume [3]:

> *"What more felicity can fall to creature*
> *Than to enjoy delight with liberty?"*

Here, to conclude, William Baskerville in Umberto Eco's *The Name of The Rose* says "Books are not made to be believed, but to be subjected to inquiry. When we consider a book, we mustn't ask ourselves what it says but what it means." [4] And this is the attitude I urge, too, both to the proclaimed text of its 'public-sector' theory and to the daily NHS events of its practice. So, too, when we consider structures, values and systems, and when we make conjectures about health care, public and private sector actions, and personal responsibilities.

I have sought to unpack and understand first principles by which we can be guided and which can educate us about the meaning of events, and the potential for change. That is, to discover and understand the meaning of cultural situations, which are always elaborate disputations about moral issues. I ask questions about our images of personal being, what we want or do not want to happen to us, our self-definition and self-affirmation. This inquiry is based in a lively belief in social and personal possibilities and in the personal nature of cultural achievement. It offers, too, an awareness of what each person can do towards the renovation of a culture, in exercising personal choices. These enquiries depend on the power of rationality, on judging by reason and on observing 'facts' in a critical spirit. For we each have to find a way for ourselves to discriminate, interpreting what Matthew Arnold called the "vast multitude of facts."

Wittgenstein said of one of his works that "This book will perhaps be understood only by those who have themselves already thought the thoughts which are expressed in it – or similar thoughts." [5]

Certainly, free market thinkers have countenanced these ideas and over a long period. But I hope to reach out to those who have wrestled with the problems – of the NHS, of public sector reform and institutional replacement – but have not countenanced these solutions. And not only to explore more knowledge – for example, of what is going on day by day in the NHS – but to make sense of it, both theoretically and in practical terms. Inevitably, I prefer some meanings and marginalize others. This is based in many years of observing actual practice. It is essential, since the NHS has simultaneously constituted both an ideal – best care for all, in a cohesive society – and an organised fantasy in actual practice. That fantasy has comprised many errors, including something for nothing, government as good at doing things, and exertion without incentive.

This attempt to dissolve fantasy and to offer the fulfilment of realities evolved in markets is of course itself recognised as an *ideologica*l labour. For it is a commentary not only on how things are, but on how I believe they could and should be. And how they might have been for 65 years past. It concerns, too, the nature of knowledge, and the presumptions of what can be known by experts about autonomous individuals. It is important for good health care and for a society of autonomous choices and of personal accounting that we each reach towards our own tacit and formal knowledge and our own answers in a society of co-possibilities. One where each of us can be autonomous in perception and judgement, in self-definition and self-criticism, in making private judgements of reality, in fathoming our own unique human experience as best we may – and for ourselves in self-responsibility.

Of course, there are those that prefer to be at the command of coercive wills, and who find autonomy uncomfortable. But this itself is a choice – the refusal to be left alone to look at our own dangers in our own ways. And there are those, too, like one of the past Dukes of Cambridge, who said on his retirement from the Army after a career in which he had opposed all reforms: "Gentlemen, there have been great changes in my time, great changes. But I can say this. Every change has been made at the right time, and the right time is when you cannot help it." [6] Those words could be inscribed over many famous pressure-group portals.

I rely, however, on the proposition that politically persuasive reforms *can* be achieved if we start with a guarantee of legally enforceable good care by legally-enforceable contracts. And that we ask how to create the market which can achieve this. For the future does not come about of itself. Much of it at least is the *result* of choices and actions in the present. The fullness, freedom and potency of life depends upon it. For actions must be based in consciously made moral judgements. And this possibility in free-will depends on states of mind – such as freedom, self-definition, self-esteem, and mutual service and co-operation in critical intelligence about social life. This is why we need a true awareness, a clear estimate of our situation with our healthcare, and the ability to discriminate choices about alternative approaches.

I offer what I hope is an open work, and one which relates Interest to Duty. An Open Work – Eco says it with initial capitals – is about an open market. [7] By an open work I mean one which encourages the individual to find a meaning which works for them. Hopefully, a meaning which will endorse incentive, choice, competition, and better outcomes in an adaptive, evolutionary market framework. This is what Eco calls the responsible collaboration between writer and reader. [8]

Eco says that authors do not really matter, only texts. And "the author should die once he has finished writing. So as not to trouble the path of the text." [9] This seems a rather extreme post-modernist position. And, indeed, fortunately not one to which he has himself paid obeisance. But the text is the thing, and he is right to say that it will produce its own effects, with each reader interpreting it according to their intentions and their own ideas and commitments – what Eco calls their social treasury of knowledge. Eco says a text is a device conceived in order to produce its Model Reader!" [10]

And in this case of mine to produce, I would say, the paradigm changes (or the preferred meaning and interpretation) to achieve the model politician who assists the model consumer, and the model market. The first, a hands-off creature; the second an economically empowered individual; the third an adaptive, evolving, dynamist approach to economic, social, and public life. We need acts of critical energy to carry these forward. But we need, too, to keep in mind Francis Bacon's family motto, *Mediocra Firma* – moderate things endure. And thus it is necessary to achieve balance, and to carry people with us by showing that *their* arguments lead to *our* conclusions. Moderation in language and a moderate approach is I suggest essential to the legitimacy and persuasiveness of the free-market case in the British context.

I hope these arguments will help to change the approach taken by the reader and influence the appraisal of the political market in engaging with the questions of healthcare reform, from a free-market perspective. Then we can now go beyond describing the defects of public monopoly and of government failure. These are well known, as is the idea that they are much more difficult to correct than market failures. We need to address government failure in healthcare. Here, we need a transformation first of vision and then of practical actions. I offer a structure to help us make the difficult transactions between the present and the future. And for each of us to ask, faced with a care choice, *what is true for me?*

The pragmatist philosopher William James captured this sense of how people might come to change old ideas for new: "The individual has a stock of old opinions already, but he meets a new experience that puts them to a strain...The result is an inward trouble to which his mind till then has been a stranger, and from which he seeks to escape by modifying his previous mass of opinions. He saves as much of it as he can, for in this matter of belief we are all extreme conservatives. So he tries to change first this opinion, and then that (for they resist change very variously), until at last some new idea comes up which he can graft upon the ancient stock with a minimum of disturbance of the latter, some idea that mediates between the stock and the new experience and runs them into one another most felicitously and expediently." [11] In these terms we need a willing suspension of the willing suspension of belief in the realities concealed by state monopoly institutions.

No book is an island. Every text should change its reader. No text offers completion. It is an exploratory construction and a hypothesis, in an adaptive process of intertwined interpretations, codes, new possibilities and changed attitudes to old and new ideas for both writer and reader to produce individualised meaning. Each has continuing conjectures amongst an often contradictory plurality of choices.

We could consider, too, as the subtle commentator on Eco, Gary Radford, says that the beginning of a text is made only fully meaningful in the context of its end. And thus, "As you, the reader, move through this text for the first time, the contexts for interpretation constantly grow and change. It is entirely possible that this context will shift, develop, and evolve in ways that you, the reader, do not predict. In order to derive the complete meaning of this text, you will have to read it twice; the first time to acquire the full content of the textual topics and the second to read it *within* the frames of those textual topics." [12]

As Radford himself says, I will see you again back at the beginning!

Together I hope, we will now abandon 'The Vanguard Party', which has misunderstood our history and our prospects in free markets, and so place 'the planning expert' in a more appropriate quarter – in the past. It is notable that Isaac Babel, an oppressed and ultimately purged Russian writer, satirically told the first Soviet Writer's Congress in 1934 that the Party gives us everything, and that we are deprived of only one right, the right to write badly. "Comrades", he said, "let us not fool ourselves: this is a very important right, and to take it away from us is no small thing." [13]

We need the freedoms to try, to get it wrong, and to try again. We need adaptive, evolutionary approaches. No Master Plan. Energy, autonomy, ambiguity, and the power of art – all are necessary elements in discovering the epiphany of valuable new surprises which will be true to external realities without being indifferent to our "meanings" or our personal "values."

The economic historian David Landes perhaps offers the key point in a succinct final line of his own: "We must cultivate a sceptical faith, avoid dogma, listen and watch well, try to clarify and define ends, the better to choose means." [14]

And J. P. Donleavy's *A Singular Man*, presented as a playscript, has a wonderful summary capturing every author's hopes: "Curtain, Tears, Applause, Royalties." [15]

NOTES.

1. See Friedrich von Hayek, *Individualism and Economic Order* (Chicago, Chicago University Press, 1948) ; *The Constitution of Liberty* (Chicago, Chicago University Press, 1960), *Studies in Philosophy, Politics and Economics* (London, Routledge, 1967), and *New Studies in Politics, Economics and the History of Ideas* (London, Routledge, 1978). See, amongst other works, Michael Oakeshott, *Rationalism in Politics and Other Essays* (London, Methuen; New York, Barnes & Noble, 1962), new expanded edition edited by Timothy Fuller (Indianapolis, Ind., Liberty Press 1991). Also J. Norman (ed.), *The Achievement of Michael Oakeshott* (London, Gerald Duckworth, 1993). For Virginia Postrel, see *The Future and Its Enemies, The Growing Conflict over Creativity, Enterprise, and Progress* (New York, The Free Press, 1998), and *The Substance of Style: How the Rise of Aesthetic Value Is Remaking Commerce, Culture, and Consciousness* (New York, HarperCollins, 2003). John Kay, *The Truth About Markets. Their Genius, their Limits, their Follies* (London, Allen Lane, 2003) is a powerful guide to this discussion, and I have gratefully drawn on his ideas and arguments.

2. Dr. William G. Pickering, "An Independent Medical Inspectorate", in David Gladstone, *Regulating Doctors* (London, Institute for the Study of Civil Society, 2000) – a trail-blazing study which should be the basis of much needed new reforms. Dr. Pickering's work is brilliant and of exceptional importance. See also chapter 20, "Incentives to change – in whose interest?" in my *Patients, Power and Responsibility*. Edward Everett Root, Publishers, are soon to issue Dr. Pickering's book, *This Will Only Hurt a Little. Achieving Patient Benefit and the Reform of Clinical Practice.*

3. See Lionel Trilling, *Beyond Culture. Essays on Literature and Learning* (London, Secker & Warburg, 1966), p.82.

4. Umberto Eco, *The Name of The Rose* (New York, Harcourt Brace Jovanovich, 1893), trans.William Weaver, p.316.

5. Ludwig Wittgenstein, cited in Daniel Kolak, *Wittgenstein's Tractatus* (Mountain View, Calif., Mayfield Publishing) p. xxxi; reference from Gary P.Radford, *On Eco* (Toronto, Thomson Wadsworth, 2003) p.1.

6. Trilling, *op .cit.*, p.217.

7. Umberto Eco, *Interpretation and Over interpretation* (Harvard, Mass., Harvard University Press, 1992), p.140.

8. Umberto Eco, *A Theory of Semantics* (Bloomington, Indiana, Indiana University Press, 1976), p.276.

9. Umberto Eco, *Postscript to The Name of The Rose* (New York, Harcourt Brace Jovanovich), p 7. , trans. William Weaver.

10. Umberto Eco, *Interpretation and Over interpretation, op. cit.*, p.64.

11. William James, *Pragmatism and The Meaning of Truth* (Cambridge, Mass., Harvard University Press, 1975), pp. 34-5.

12. Radford, *op. cit.*, p.33.

13. Trilling, *op .cit.*, p.122.

14. Landes, *op. cit.*, p.524.

15. The closing line of J. P. Donleavy's play, *A Singular Man* (London, The Bodley Head, 1965).

11. What's in the way of change?

"[Policy] madness, which has been defined as doing the same thing over and over and expecting different results." Richard Pipes.

To achieve real change which lasts we have to persuade those who don't want it, who do not want to be told to do it, or who fear it. It is important to identify what is in the way of change as well as what it is that is driving change – most notably, new technologies and new opportunities. And to understand where and why unavoidable conflicts lie in wait. For we will not advance unless we ask why there are red lights telling us to stop, how they work, and how they might go to green. There are many accumulated cultural, psychological, and political difficulties which obstruct radical change. These include questions which are both positive and negative.

For example, it is positive that we hold onto the commitment that all should be covered by health care. It is negative that leading politicians of all parties continue to insist on declaring the result of the game before a ball is kicked. Even so, there are many economic, cultural and psychological factors ineluctably driving reform. These are more powerful than any politician. They are the Tsunami that will change healthcare. We need to be aware of these factors as we consider the potential to re-appraise and renovate health care. They concern morality and values, as well as psychological, practical and political concerns. They include many things we want hold onto, as well, such as 'Enduring Values':

Enduring Values:

- The moral and essential commitment that no one should be deterred from receiving services, and no one denied help on the basis of having no money.

- Respect for the idea (in the main of being treated free at the point of service.

- Thus, social solidarity and the moral commitment to the idea that the poor, the unlucky, and the disadvantaged must have access to quality health care no less than that enjoyed by the vocal and socially competent middle-class.

Psychological, cultural, and practical barriers to change:

- The surviving (if declining) belief in the myth of the NHS as the best in the world.

- Resistance within the civil service to extensive, rapid, cultural change.

- Fear of losing Nanny: it may be bad, but we don't want something worse. The preference for a known evil over an untried good.

- Middle-class anxiety about the uncertainties of employment in a technological age, and the comfort of public services as a safety net.

The delusion of "free" services:

- Anxiety about future costs, lack of comprehensive cover, fear of being in the gutter and unable to get an ambulance without a Blue-Cross Card – the popular idea of American difficulties with voluntary insurance and the lack of a universal system. [1]

- Concern about what happens in the case of catastrophic illnesses, if we move to an insurance system

- The problem of those with pre-existing conditions and adverse selection of patients by an insurance-based system: would they be covered?

- The medicalised model of health care, which situates "health" in the physical and organisational structures of the NHS, and in the status of doctors, particularly hospital specialists.

- The notion that individual health is a collective rather than an individual responsibility. That health is what government should be doing. For example, the government must "do something" about obesity. This is a different idea from the idea that government should ensure that everyone has access to good health care, whilst taking responsibility too for their own lives and life-styles.

- The congenitally bureaucratic and hierarchical 'controlling' and number-crunching mind-set of the public-sector; byzantine procedures; lack of accountability, opposition to competition and individual choice amongst many staff members. [2]

- The prevalence of the word "need", which bureaucrats define, as they allocate resources and ration services. Need, allocation, and rationing are the trio of controlling ideas in the NHS. The word "need" is used in place of "want", which is a matter of self-responsible personal preference, in a cost-conscious decision (but which does not inevitably depend on the ability to pay at the time of service).

- Medical staffing shortages, and the lack of spare capacity to permit contracts to be shifted and thus to facilitate choice.

The closed mind of the centraliser, guided by political objectives:

- The political and managerial dominance of unmanaged and high-status hospital consultants.

The culture of the politically-correct:

- Producer dominance and professional vested-interests. "Secrecy, protectionism, paternalism, lack of accountability, and plain out-of-touch backwardness of the medical profession." [3]

Supplier-induced demand:

- Low staff-morale, and resistance to further change in what has been a constant revolution over a decade.

Local provincialism: the 'not-made-here, so it won't work' syndrome:

- Insistence, contrary to OECD evidence, on the efficiency and effectiveness, and of the "fairness" of the NHS.

- Relative public ignorance of overseas systems and lack of awareness of relevant information on results.

- Insufficient robust and comparative evidence on outcomes and reports of the experiences of service-users in different systems of funding, purchasing, and provision.

- Absence of explicit price, and thus (for health economists and politicians) no objective way to decide the "right" level of funding. Similarly, in this structure, no subjective way for individuals to make this relative decision for themselves.

Political barriers to change:

- Political bids for power by promising to spend more on the state monopoly system, and to "modernise" the existing structures.

- The strong position of 'old Labour' ideas, especially amongst 'public service' Trade Union leadership, and in the braking role of people like Mr. David Hinchliffe MP (when he was Chairman, of the House of Commons Health Select Committee), former Secretary of State for Health Frank Dobson, MP, Clive Soley, MP (when he was Chairman, Parliamentary Labour Party), and others including leading health care commentators (who are often opposed in principle to considering alternatives to state monopoly). [4]

- *A priori* dismissal by *The NHS Plan* (and by the Wanless report, *a la* G. Brown) of alternative funding approaches, without the evidence being properly appraised.

- The unmeasurable and insidious effects of cost-containment on quality – for example, limits on doctor's time with a patient, with possible untoward results such as failure to diagnose a problem.

- Failure of Margaret Thatcher's "internal market", which conducted the controversy on the wrong ground and so gave markets a bad name without giving them an opportunity to earn a good name in health care.

- Subsequent Conservative leadership failure to educate itself, and thus to encourage changes in public opinion, during the Major and Hague years 1990-2001 and incessantly since. [5]

- Cultural and political influence of quasi-Marxist ideas, which have helped create a situation where we are not informed consumers of health care.

- Influence of the honours system, co-opting leaders of independent charities, some user-groups, and potential dissident voices ("No CBE's in putting that view to Ministers, old chum", as a senior civil servant once said to me privately at the Department of Health in 1994).

- Political party insistence on tax and spend policies.

- Conservative misunderstandings of the challenge and responsibility of leadership from first-principles and of the paramount importance of undertaking public-education about pluralist, disciplined competitive consumerist markets in a meritocratic society.

Drivers for change:

- The digital revolution and information technology of the world-wide web, and associated products; globalisation; IT out-sourcing including tele-medicine; robotics; new imaging; and nano-technology, which will have to be funded.

- Notwithstanding the above, recognition of the benefits of disciplined, open, pluralist markets as against large-scale, top-down dysfunctional systems which are inflexible, not adaptable, do not innovate sufficiently, and cannot gather the necessary knowledge on which to act.

WHAT'S IN THE WAY OF CHANGE?

- Pharmaceutical, technical, and mechanical innovations, offering new opportunities for service to users. Thus, previously untreatable conditions can be subject to therapies; terminal illnesses become treatable; and more palliative treatments can be offered to long-term or chronically sick patients.

- Population change as the proportion of elderly and very elderly people is rising. This increasingly elderly population is having an impact on inflating health expenditures, as the elderly (who generally vote) demand higher-quality services on a longer-term, chronic-care basis. Now there are more than 10 million Britons over 75 than there were 50 years ago.

- The genomic revolution, and genetic predictions about the likelihood of future illnesses in currently healthy people, which will generate new preventative treatments (with attendant insurance difficulties?).

- Reduction of national income due to ageing and a smaller number of economically-active in the population.

- The rising costs of health and social care.

- The faster rate of NHS inflation.

- The impact of life-style changes, many of which are generating health difficulties for the individual.

- The wider impact of taxation for public sector investment on national economic performance.

- Reducing national income as elderly increase as proportion of the population.

- Public realisation that individuals have to sell assets to fund their own long-term care.

- Public expectations which the system cannot satisfy – and in an unpriced service will never satisfy.

- The Maastricht rules limiting the deficit financing of state welfare.

- The European Working Time Directive on doctor's hours.

- The requirements of international competition which promote concern about levels of taxation and competitiveness which is essential if we are to afford public services.

- European-wide rationalisation on tax, health care spending, and entitlements.

- A changed role for the British Treasury in becoming the chief department for creating and directing domestic policy, shaping welfare reform, tax, and wider health policy.

- Individual recognition of the imperative to provide for own long-term care as state funding unlikely ever to be sufficient.

- Greater calls on family members to do more to support and aid elderly relations.

- An increasingly 'consumerist' society, with informed, discerning and demanding service-users, some of whom know more about their condition than their medical adviser.

- Cultural insistence on open-ness, individual audit and accountability.

- Continued rise of standards visible in every other area of life in services not provided as 'public services' but suppled in open, competitive markets.

- Consumer expectations of increasingly sophisticated treatments and of more favourable outcomes (arising from emphasis on increasing effectiveness of treatments, and of evidence-based clinical practise) encouraging more people to seek medical interventions.

- Decline of deference to professionals.

- Individual expectation of being treated as a consumer, not a supplicant.

- Growing insistence on more information and choice.

- A generational change among the realistic young, whose voting power may oblige government to radically change the structure of health and social care.

- More aggressive insistence on services once a user is actually in the health-care system.

- Last-chance syndrome: in extreme old age people may be prepared to try anything to sustain life.

- Inability of existing economy to sustain existing system without financial reforms.

WHAT'S IN THE WAY OF CHANGE?

- Economically insupportable imbalance between public and private funding and too low total spend.

- Explicit limitations of a monopoly structure on efficiency and effectiveness.

- Failures in universal coverage; denials of service; dilution of service; unreliable quality; unnecessary pain and early deaths; personal desperation at poor treatment and lack of redress.

- Media impact of more individuals such as Mrs. Rose Addis, in making large numbers think hard about the basis of funding and provision of care, many of whom will eventually require loving daily care, close attention and costly nursing. [6]

- Huge geographical and thus arbitrary variations in access, equity, and quality more visible.

- Ageing and inadequate NHS capital stocks: poor environment.

- Major difficulties visible in A&E departments.

- Growing and visible gap between UK results and those of other systems.

- Increasingly obvious ageism and other biases in access and in service delivery.

- Inter-active technology informing service-users.

- Rejection of paternalism, and present insistence on explaining why things must be the way that they are.

- Option to move towards a new blend of public and private funding, and of co-payment and supplementary insurance (which would include primary care, preventive care, ongoing treatment for chronic conditions, accident and emergency care &c.).

- Cultural and clinical pressures to shift away from hospital care (where consultants throw the political weight) towards other treatments and settings, including greater use of pharmaceuticals, home and community care, with less emphasis on physicians and more on other health professionals.

- Supplier-induced utilisation, as physicians use their discretion – including "defensive" medical practice.

- Potential impact of insurance on increased utilisation.

- Continuing NHS catalogue of difficulties, deficits, and denials.

- An open and intense media focus, in which we are at last asking the harder questions.

- Impossibility of creating a consumer-led society without priced services and an informed market, with competing insurers, purchasers, and providers.

- Necessity of self-jurisdiction and self-responsible understanding of procedures and equipment in self-administration in domiciliary settings.

- Fundamental importance of self-responsibility in self-care and prevention of illness in determining health status and life-chances, and which requires direct incentives that work.

- Distrust of Labour Party motives concerning health care by public, which may support further reforms on a more radical basis than if led by the Conservative Party.

- Politicians driven by embarrassment, by electoral arithmetic, and by the wish to make a success of their lives.

- Influence of well-known 'media doctors', like Lord Winston, criticising the NHS and stating that the unacceptable is "normal", adding "the terrifying thing is that we accept it." [7]

- The influence and leadership of Mr. Tony Blair as Prime Minister, Mr. Alan Milburn as Secretary of State for Health, and Professor Michael Barber as head of the PM's Delivery Unit – each of whom who moved towards a different order of transformation of health and social care, and one or more of whom may return to the limelight if Mr. Brown should lose the General Election of 2009/10, if indeed he survives as Labour leader to fight it. [8]

- This long list prompts optimism. I suggest that the balance is significantly on the side of radical change.

NOTES.

1. See Kieran Walshe, "'Don't try this at home': health policy lessons for the NHS from the United States", *Economic Affairs*, Vol.212, No.4, December 2001, pp.28-32; M. Moran, *Governing the Health Care State. A Comparative Study of the United Kingdom, the United States, and Germany* (Manchester, Manchester University Press, 1999); H .T. O. Davies and M. N.

Marshall, "UK and US healthcare systems divided by more than a common language," *The Lancet*, 355, 336, 2000. But see also an early and still vibrant and relevant corrective by Arthur Kemp, "The Mixed U. S. System", in *Monopoly or Choice in Health Services?* (London, Institute of Economic Affairs, 1964).

2. See analysis by Minette Marrin," Cruelty and neglecting the state sector wilderness," *Sunday Times*, news focus, 27 January 2002; also, Marjorie Wallace, "Fear and anger in the A&E", *Daily Mail*, 25 January 2002.

3. "Over 50 years the profession [has] showed extraordinary passivity in monitoring standards. Only the most extreme 'Spanish practices' and wayward clinicians were spotted and referred on to the General Medical Council." Jennifer Dixon, "Transforming the NHS: what chance for the new government?" *Economic Affairs*, Vol.21, No.4, December 2001, pp.4-8.

4. Tash Shifrin, "Milburn's 'redefinition stirs rebellion," *Health Service Journal*, 24 January 2002; Frank Dobson, "The last thing the NHS needs is another dose of the private sector", *The Independent*, 28 January 2002.

5."No opposition has ever been put under less pressure on policy questions. Lack of pressure did not encourage hard thinking." Bruce Anderson, "Mr. Blair has no real agenda for public service reform", *The Independent*, 4 February 2002.

6. The case of Mrs. Rose Addis was a *cause celebre*. She was a 94-year-old Grandmother who endured 72-hours of very stressful difficulties in A&E. See *The Guardian*, 25 January, 2002; *The Daily Telegraph*, 27 January 2002.

7. Lord Winston, *New Statesman*, 12 January 2000.

8. Mr. Milburn undertook a significant journey, in changing his views and pressing forward major new reform ideas. "Milburn unveils his vision for a competitive future", *Health Service Journal*, 25 October 2001; Nicholas Timmins and Rosemary Bennett, "Private input 'could create new model for hospitals', *Financial Times*, 16 January 2002; Nicholas Timmins, "Extravagant vision may yield change only at the margins", *Financial Times*, 16 January 2002; leader, "Heading back to the future", *Financial Times*, 16 January 2002; Eben Black, "Blair takes on unions over service reform," *Sunday Times*, news review, 3 February 2002; David Charter, "Reformer Blair raises ghost of militant," *The Times*, 4 February 2002; Melissa Kite, "Unions mock Blair attack on 'wreckers'", *The Times*, 5 February 2002; Ben Russell, "Labour's radical plans for NHS ignore 'wreckers'", *The Independent*, 7 February 2002; Ben Russell, "Labour plans to overturn principle of free NHS", *The Independent*, 7 February 2002; David Charter, "Labour's new NHS vision," *The Times*, February 7, 2002; David Charter and Nigel Hawkes, "Milburn headhunts entrepreneurs to run failing hospitals", *The Times*, 11 February 2002; Nigel Hawkes, "Milburn replaces chiefs of failing health trusts", *The Times*, 12 February 2002; Ben Russell, "Troubleshooters to be sent into ailing hospitals," *The Independent*, 12 February 2002.

12. Abolish the customer? Or, safe in *whose* hands?

"In Soviet times, I knew, maps were often falsified or full of blanks." Colin Thubron.

* *An earlier and briefer version of this chapter was published in Edward Vaizey (ed.),* The Blue Health Book *(London, Politicos, March 2002), as 'Safe in whose hands? Effective consumer power in health care.'*

We should ask 'what are the tests of whether a user-led service is reality, or rhetoric?'

a). Abolish the customer!

In 1948 the NHS abolished the individual customer. Its endemic and intractable problems were thus set in place with its foundation stones. Here I offer some tests which we can apply to see if users of services are genuinely empowered by new policies offered by government. I have argued that only individual empowerment and control over a personal health care fund will provide the direct incentives to resolve the systemic snags of the NHS. These concern culture, cash, capacity, and outcomes. Consumer empowerment, I suggest, can uniquely broaden the funding base, enhance access, and improve outcomes. Empowerment is, too, the essential axis on which civil society and mutual-aid in health care can be renovated.

These are cultural questions. Each helps us ask how we can attain an equitable, accessible, reliable and affordable system of care and a different way of seeing ourselves, too. With much more cash and more capacity, with more choice and competition, with better outcomes and higher life expectancy, and with higher morale and professionally satisfying work too. Consumer choice concerns a broader accountability than that of professionals and providers. It concerns the accountability of consumers themselves. It calls for patient self-responsibility, personal self-awareness, individual self-care and the responsibility to make cost-conscious, cost-effective and often difficult choices, balancing risk and benefit. Learning as an adult. *Being* an adult.

It is a choice between paternalism and preference. As Colin Thubron has said, "A traveller needs to believe in the significance of where he is, and therefore in his own meaning." [1] But NHS service-users have had little or no influence on what happens to them in health care. This is the case despite the fact that they have seen their individual power over their lives grow in almost every other area of existence. Money talks, and preference walks. We have relied on markets in every area save for those which matter most: health and education. The system is constructed, instead, so that "experts" can know and provide for our "needs."

The NHS has substituted collective*ism* for collective (voluntary) action. In the bureaucratised state monopoly system individuals have had no individual economic power by which to signal their wishes, wants, and preferences. Instead, various "expert agents" – Ministers of the Crown, Civil Servants, GP's, Health Authorities, Primary Care Trusts, CCG's and "representative" bodies – have decided on their "needs," and on their behalf. They have assumed it is possible to second-guess the wishes of others. If this approach was applied to our food or to our shelter we would be outraged. Yet these are more fundamental even than our health.

In post-war Britain much credit is due to the tides of progress in liberal capitalist society. These have improved living standards, diet, housing, leisure, travel, and the quality of life. The poor and the disadvantaged have been aided and able to function in markets, to their own and the general advantage. Yet in health care the poor have done least well, with no bargaining power transferring signals about preferences and willingness to pay (as a Patient Fund Holder, from a medical savings account, funded by general taxation). But in the NHS these key externals have been suppressed. Competition, user autonomy, the transparency of information, and the permanent need of providers to enthusiastically satisfy consumers in order to win support, markets, and revenues, if they are to survive – all suppressed. Yet almost everyone has a capacity for autonomy.

Since self-responsible choice and competition were constrained the NHS was wholly politicised from day one. Voting and "consultation" has proved no substitute for choice and competition. Indeed, the key point at the heart of this debate is that the option of being enabled to *discipline* a system by an occasional vote or a sporadic consultation, is not the same as an individual being able to *command* a personal service when, where, and from whom they want it. And this is a fundamental deficit, for, of all aspects of our humanity, our health care is intimate, personal, specific, differentiated, and reliant on timely and appropriate services.

The general electoral accountability of replacing one set of rascals with another does not secure a personal service to the individual, whatever other satisfactions it may deliver. Nor is a specific service open to criticism through politics in the influential way experienced when a provider loses revenues because of customer dissatisfactions. The philosopher Jeremy Shearmur has reminded us of the importance of correcting our theories "rather than suffering the consequences of action on the basis of false theories: of allowing our theories to die in our stead." [3]

In the contrast between voting and the voucher, or between consultation and command, we have seen the fundamental distinction between "needs" and "wants."And that the concept of "needs" contradicts the self-responsibility implied by the word "wants." It's partners in this burglary of the patients' rights are both ageism and a gender-biased service. [5] Its frame of mind is refluxed in the advocacy of the virtues of allocative rationing by many academics and administrators opposed to individual empowerment and committed to health care for "populations." This, too, despite the evidence to the contrary from almost all OECD members and from an important recent study of Kaiser Permanente in America. [6] There is a vital point here, too, about the nature of modern care and the necessity of empowerment. Without patient empowerment, confident self-knowledge, more self-care and personal responsibility, the advantageous shift from institutional to domiciliary settings cannot be achieved. We need to endorse the principles of empowerment, whichever financially-empowering device is chosen to effect these changes. [7]

The non-market approach asks for us all to be health activists. Service-users do not exist as players unless they join organised groups, and even then they are merely voices without vouchers. Will Anderson and Steve Gillam have observed that there has been the difficulty "of enabling a massive state institution, supported by a powerful professional class, to treat its users as consumers, that is, to provide services which are responsive to users' needs [sic] and interests." [15] This implies that only something as powerful as money in the hands of consumers can make the change. And if individuals controlled their own fund, would reform of the NHS take 10 years?

b). What it would mean for a user-led service to become real rather than rhetorical.

How large is the gap between what we see around us now and what would be necessary for services to be user-led? The tests that rhetoric was converted into reality would include:

- That users control the agenda, through the cumulative and adaptive power of individual financial decision-making. Each consumer would be in charge of a mobile and personal health care fund with which they voluntarily subscribe to a registered insurer and to an approved purchaser which acts on their behalf. Thus, service users (banded together in mutual-aid organisations) would control budgetary allocation and directly influence the ability of providers to secure revenue flows. Consumers would have an open choice between competing insurers and providers, and thus between competing doctors, including GPs, and other services, including alternative therapies.

- That there is price-conscious choice between competing insurers, competing purchasers, and competing providers. Individuals would have the right to review plans at statutory intervals (annually, or every two years) and move if they wish. This will ensure consumer bargaining power and the incentive to satisfy wants.

- That there is meaningful choice, so that consumers can actually access services they wish to have, and incentives to encourage potential providers to come into the market to offer these to willing consumers.

- That consumers will be free to top-up their individual fund provided through taxation with supplementary insurance, and to negotiate a policy excess which would encourage out-of-pocket payment for small items, and discourage waste. There would be incentives and opportunities to invest above the minimum. And a no-claims bonus could accrue into pension or elderly-care cover. This would be part of the 'guaranteed care package' which government ensures is available to all. Any individual may choose to spend as much more of their own resources on health and social care as they wish. For example, on effective cancer drugs available in continental Europe but denied to patients by the NHS.

- That users are expected to predominate in decision-making about their own care, with legally-enforceable contracts for services between consumer, insurer, purchaser, and provider.

- That there are no barriers to information, including performance data on individual practitioners and individual centres of service.

- That information is made available in such a form and with such promptness that it can become personal knowledge, and is thus available for personal choices and for leverage.

That services encourage and equip people (by publishing relevant information) to ask the hard questions, which will make up provider deficits, rather than suppress information which conceal deficits in services.

- That the narrative experiences of users ("like me") are easily shared between users before they accept treatment – a therapy, a drug, an operation, care from a named individual, in a specific institution. This could include competing High-Street advice centres, some developed from NHS Direct, including support and access to patient groups on the net.

- That users' own expectations of their roles change, as they assume that it is reasonable, normal, legitimate, proper to ask for what they want and are ready to pay for, instead of being pre-occupied with guilt.

- That users themselves decide how much power they are to have, rather than professionals, managers, and politicians deciding how much power to grant them. Here, self-esteem would be strengthened as people feel more in control of their lives, as they are treated as a person and not merely as a "case."

- That people expect to take responsibility for themselves and their families. Thus, choices are rooted in self-jurisdiction, self-responsibility, and a personal assessment of risk, cost-effectiveness, and outcome (responsibly advised by competing advisory services) so that the individual can decide with which situation and outcomes they can live with and cope.

- That surprise, discovery, and learning to choose is welcomed in a framework where government sets the rules but otherwise limits its own role to setting standards, registering medical training, validation and inspection, tax-funding in a diverse funding system, public health initiatives, &c. Government would withdraw to the essential rampart of controlling the framework of rules.

- That front-line staff have the power to make a difference, and that we realise that money is not the only thing which achieves change. Attitudes, behaviour, communication make a considerable difference to service-users.

- That as a consequence of these changes creative management, morale, recruitment and retention would improve, as would the rewards for good services. Individual empowerment thus would empower many relationships for constructive change. When things go wrong there should also be effective redress.

When considered from the perspective of such a list, we see, how far we are from individual self-responsibility and from the personalised, consumer-led service to which the Secretary of State has referred. And we see, too, how much unjustified cultural (as well as empirical) propaganda there is about the benefits of a near-monopoly of funding, purchasing and provision by the state. This trio of near-monopolies is rooted in deep cultural error. It is one, which service users themselves have learned to accept and endorse. One which we all need to correct and improve in our own lives, as together we seek genuine justice and equity in a society of true liberty.

For all these things to be real and at the heart of a consumer-led service – indeed, its very axis – we need to see massive cultural shifts in expectations, attitudes, language, and behaviours, by politicians, professionals, and patients too. Indeed, many of these could come about without any extra money, if people changed their attitudes and really got themselves organised. But more money is necessary to prompt new provision, and direct incentives will assure cultural change. When considered from the perspective of such a list, we see, how far we are from individual self-responsibility and from the personalised, consumer-led service which the Secretary of State has set as an objective. Few, if any, believe the modern answers to its difficulties are more politics. Or, in Evelyn Waugh's words, "that in bumpf lay salvation." [5]

And the answer to the question, "Safe in *whose* hands?" Charles Darwin once said we are "all netted together." Social solidarity matters. But we have our own futures in our own hands. As economist Dennis Lees put it, "The major aim of the liberal is to leave the ethical problem for the individual to wrestle with." [6] If we seek a 'big idea', there is no substitute for an old one. However, we do better to seek the accumulated value and inter-actions of many ideas, adaptively accumulating change.

NOTES.

1. Colin Thubron, *In Siberia* (London, Chatto & Windus, 1999).

2. Jeremy Shearmur, "Popper and Classical Liberalism", *Economic Affairs*, Vol.21, No.4, December 2001, pp.37-40.

3. Shirley Robin Letwin, *The Anatomy of Thatcherism* (London, Fontana, 1992), pp.204-5. Examples of this dominant needs-mentality are as common as blackberries. It is regarded as normal, and as invisible as the air we breathe. The language is so pervasive as to be unnoticed, its assumptions so apparently unproblematic as to seem inevitable. But this is not so. See, as an example of assumptions presented as God-given, Jennifer Dixon, "Transforming the NHS: what chance for the government?", *Economic Affairs*, Vol.21, No.4, December 2001, pp.4-8.

4. Richard G. A. Feachem, Neelam K. Sekhri, and Karen L. White, "Getting more for their dollar: a comparison of the NHS with California's Kaiser Permanente", *BMJ*, 2002: 324, 19 January 2002, pp.135-43; A. C .Enthoven, "Commentary: Competition made them do it", *BMJ*, 2002: 324, 19 January 2002, p.143.

5. Evelyn Waugh, *Officers and Gentlemen* (Boston, Little Brown, Back Bay Books edition, 2000), p.272.

6. D .S. Lees, *Health Through Choice. An Economic Study of the British National Service* (London, Institute of Economic Affairs, 1961). I owe this reference to Lord Ralph Harris of High Cross.

13. Tell me, doctor, what *will* make choice real?

"Not to mention that most terrible drug – ourselves – which we take in solitude." Walter Benjamin.

Form may indeed often follow function. But *genuine choice* requires many things in addition to a structure of financially-empowered leverage. This context will not be fashioned by 'reason' alone. Or necessarily by 'a higher view', greater light, or special technical or 'expert' insight. It most concerns relationships, with ourselves and with others.

The primary care locale and the home is where most patients – unless taken in an ambulance to A&E – must first reflect and discover the necessity to consider alternatives. There are many necessary conditions for success, to establish genuinely empowered choice for the individual..

First, it asks for a doctor who is *interested in choice* and tries to make it a reality for the patient.

Second, it entails an understanding of the arts of conversation – by both doctor and patient.

Third, it requires education for understanding – both amongst doctors and patients.

Fourth, it calls on scarce time for these discussions to happen routinely.

Fifth, it necessitates much greater capacity to provide the foregoing.

Sixth, it implies a cultural shift to a wider cultural readiness by the individual to consider risk as it relates to the individual as well as to 'populations.'

Seventh, Isaiah Berlin's point, the appreciation (which is more than just understanding) that all choices contain their own costs, are often necessarily contradictory, and that there is no objectively "right" answer. We often have to choose between one 'good' alternative and another, and not necessarily between the good and the bad.

All these factors, if successfully appreciated, depend on a non-hierarchical, non-directive, non-assertive perspective – by both patient and adviser. They are weighted towards *l'esprit de finesse*. And, overall, we should keep in mind that "the only expert on what it is to be myself is me." Or, in Timothy Fuller's statement "we are in ourselves what we are for ourselves." [1]

As Lee Auspitz said, "Conversation requires entering obliquely into the world of others." [2] In a conversation, no one voice can seek to dominate the others, as in a disputation. The successful doctor will have an uncanny gift for this. It is not about holding forth, or knowing best. It is about 'listening best, not 'knowing best.'' It is about hearing intuitively 'the spaces in between.' It is about translating and interpreting, seeking meanings. (The Greek, *dialektike*). It emphasises hearing the fullest experience of the patient, insofar as we can experience anything of the interior life of another. It asks for the doctor to admit the patient's values and perspectives into the discussion. In addition to technical ability, as Emanuel Litvinoff noted in his memoir of East End Jewish life, "One listens not with the head – with the *neshumah*, the soul." [3]

As I suggested earlier, this means hearing more than the words said. Hearing the unsaid, pausing for the spaces between the words, the space between things. Being aware of the silent anxieties, nurturing the expression of tensions, respecting the patient's world. For here the doctor can empower the individual to act upon their insights in terms which will work within the context of their own life situation. This is made more difficult if one or other brings to the discussion a fixed agenda, and a specific destination to be reached whatever the conversation may suggest. But it is difficult for many doctors to consider that they might be but one voice among many that speak to and for the patient – including those 'voices' from the patient's culture, experience, folk-lore, family 'prejudice', and 'ignorance' (which itself can be a label for other people's sincere beliefs).

Yet each, the doctor and the patient, must be able to acknowledge one another, whilst each retains their integrity. This approach can bring into the picture the full character and limits of each voice. It emphasises that "we become what we learn and choose to make of ourselves; our birthright is to find a voice of our own." It reduces the claims of the 'absolute voice', of the pre-ordained pattern, of the expert. As Auspitz says (of philosophy), "It may put its remarks affirmatively or critically, with ardour or resignation, in an appreciative or dyspeptic tone, but it always has the same kind of thing to say: that each voice is less than complete, that its truth to itself, its authenticity, emerges from a specific context, and that there can be discerned in each voice 'languages' that are at once the common heritage of humanity and open to the individual modulations of a given speaker." [4]

Dr. David Misselbrook's exceptional book emphasises this concern. He seeks to understand the world of the patient, and admits to the conversation those concerns that are conveyed explicitly and those which lie behind the words and gestures, and may be either tacit, unconscious or semi-explicit in the patient's gesture and tone. This approach is fundamental to appreciating what the patient may mean by "health." The encounter is not one of scored recitative, more of an improvised dance in which each responds to the moves of the other. This was a personal quality which Auspitz noted in Oakeshott: "A clairvoyance in anticipating the direction of an interlocutor's thought [enabling] him to enter the flow with gravity or humour, a nod or a monologue, as the rhythm of the talk required." [5].

Affection and mutual-respect, too, loyalty and mutuality, are part of a fruitful connection. And, for both, teaching is learning, conversation is creativity, discourse is discovery – if there is the time. The conversation includes the conveying of information from both doctor and patient. And to share different senses of how to interpret and use it. If the doctor is to be understood and respected, if the patient is to be respected and understood, each must understand and respect the other as well as him/herself. And, just as a doctor must to some extent be a judge of character, so, too, must the patient have self-knowledge of their own character and being.

Then there is the question of how do we measure customer's preferences for quality (which is inevitably linked to cost and price)? The NHS does not provide the necessary devices (comparative prices; cost; competing provision; choice) nor the time, capacity, or education. The NHS fears increased and educated demand, which would smash its rationing structures. And, worse, the wider culture does not provide the education or the appreciation of the costs of choices. The NHS disconnects cost and price, and thus suppresses opportunity cost. However, in addition to an increasingly sophisticated understanding of how to measure benefit – of which Misselbrook is a leader – there is now a large body of research which suggests that treatments should take full account of the patient's perspective of values, treatment, and outcome.

Misselbrook's own study offers this perspective on therapeutic medical grounds. It shows that clinical trials and similar forms of evaluative study should incorporate the patient's perspective on these issues. Thus, it is crucial to give consumers the lead role in determining acceptable measures of outcomes. And, as Andrew Garratt and colleagues recently stated (reporting on quality of life measurement), "For complete assessment of the benefits of an intervention it is essential to provide evidence of the impact on the patient in terms of health status and health related quality of life. These terms refer to experiences of illness such as pain, fatigue, and disability and also to broader aspects of the individual's physical, emotional, and social well-being." [6] These, too, are issues concerning capacity and the personal probability of benefit. Or, of what counts to a patient as a benefit or a loss.

Clinical decisions should thus include these several dimensions of choice: assessing the patient's clinical and physical circumstances, to establish the problem and possible treatments; research evidence on efficacy, effectiveness and efficiency of options; likely consequences; patient preferences; and a clinical recommendation which the patient will be free to accept or decline. For, as Haynes, Devereaux and Guyatt said, "evidence does not make decisions, people do." But these authors also suggest that "providing evidence to patients in a way that allows them to make an informed choice is challenging and in many cases beyond our current knowledge of doctor-patient communication – very much a problem awaiting the generation of new evidence." [7]

However, many doctors recognise the argument that successful therapeutic relationships depend on each party sharing and respecting the knowledge of the other. For example, Kenneth J.Mukamal told the *BMJ:* "Every surgical procedure has associated risks and benefits; we should quantify them to the greatest degree possible and then work with our patients to match their beliefs and preferences with those risks and benefits." [8] And Peter D.White wrote that "As doctors we should present the rational and practical choices to our patients so they can use both the power of that knowledge as well as their own intuitions to decide what is best for them and their families." [9]

It can be no surprise that some doctors often fail to understand patients' preferences. It is, however, more surprising that many apparently do not integrate reliable new, peer-reviewed research findings into their own daily practice – and over lengthy periods of many years, sometimes of more than a decade, in some cases *much* longer! This, indeed, has been the conservatism of the profession since Galen. [10]

Misselbrook, politely, states that "The explanation for this is seen in terms of the personal and social processes within the profession. The quality of the evidence base for the treatment a patient receives will therefore depend upon the personality characteristics of the doctor, whether they tend to be an innovator or a laggard. We cannot therefore claim that we consistently use evidence for the benefit of patients. Its use is contaminated by the maintenance of our own medical culture." Further, "One has only to read the journals of the medical defence societies to see that complications still cause loss and suffering." [11]

In addition, no-one knows how big this problem has become, in part because iatrogenic problems may be difficult to define, in part because they are often not adequately recorded. Or not recorded at all? Perhaps not even noticed by some doctors? And no government has made any moves to create the Independent Medical Inspectorate which Dr. William Pickering has proposed, over many years now. This makes analysis problematic and invalidates many audits. [12] Further – and as a substitute for both individual choice and professional discretion – clinical guidelines and protocols proliferate, "irrespective of the paucity of evidence that they improve any important outcome measures." [13]

Not every doctor, of course, is on side for every kind of change. Some doctors object to the concept of the patient as a consumer, whilst others suggest that each successive round of NHS reform has restricted their own freedom to negotiate directly with the patient. [14] They view the idea of the patient as consumer as hostile, confrontational, combative language, and as describing an inappropriate change in the patient's role. [15]

Certainly, some of the most influential hospital consultants took this hostile view when I was Chairman of Brighton Health Authority and then of the Brighton

NHS Hospitals Trust in 1991-94. Some studies of general practice suggest, too, that the ambition of shared decision-making is making relatively little impact. [16] And competing demands and intense time pressures ensure that in areas where significant efforts to accomplish a situation of informed choices – such as in maternity care – these choices are quite consciously and deliberately still denied to people. Here, "right" and "wrong" choices remain the operative notions, with "choices" deliberately framed to guide patients to do one thing rather than another. This disables the chances of informed choices being made by consumers.

For example, hierarchical power structures result in some obstetricians defining the norms of clinical practice, and hence which choices were possible. Midwives, too, were reported to have rarely discussed the contents or the leaflets on *Informed Choice* – an NHS flagship policy – or distinguished them from other literature related to pregnancy. They made wrong assumptions about women's ability and willingness to use the information, and women were "bullied" into accepting interventions. This, in one of the most sacred and unique situations in every life. Researchers concluded that evidence-based leaflets are unlikely to promote informed choice unless they are introduced as part of a wider strategy that addresses power imbalances. But how is the midwife to stand up to the consultant? The compelling power of the external purchaser is the better bet.

It has been the case for some years that evidence-based practice has been offered as the answer to many problems. And that patient partnership was said to be the way to enable genuine choices. But some senior doctors are reluctant still to change their practice and to accept the legitimacy of subjective views expressed by patients or the legitimacy of quality of life research. And here in maternity care we have a situation where new literature specifically and deliberately designed to promote choices, which is evidence-based and has been the subject of trials, has failed. [17] Why? The missing link is money in individual hands, by which the pregnant woman could choose between providers who do what the literature promises and those – including some intransigent obstetricians – who do not do it, do not allow it, do not intend to allow it, and know they are disallowing user choice. The evidence is very explicit and incontrovertible.

The 10 research-based leaflets were the result of the *Changing Childbirth* report [18] – a celebrated landmark – and were developed by the Midwives Information and Resource Service, to support consumer choice. Randomised controlled trials verified their effectiveness. It was staff attitudes and organisational culture which got in the way – exactly the kinds of issues which the PGCA would seek to influence on behalf of its subscribers. My proposed mutual Patient Guaranteed Care Association [The PGCA] would have something to say if providers continued to manipulate women to comply with rather than choose how they want to give birth. Recent observations of ante-natal consultations and interviews with pregnant women and Mothers revealed that professionals often did not even discuss the widely publicised and distributed government leaflet *Informed Choice*.

The choices available were limited, too, by power hierarchies and by staff fearful of their superiors, by technology, and by fear of litigation. A quarter of those pregnant women surveyed were not given the leaflet at all. [19] A competing PGCA would not accept such a position on behalf of its subscribers, nor would the disconnection between satisfaction and payment remain for long.

One of the most exceptional contributions to current debates has been Misselbrook's book. He has shown that medicine cannot claim a privileged scientific position, "with doctors as experts possessed of some refined form of truth." [20] For example, there is a twenty-fold variation in referral rates between different GPs. [21] Much of this cannot be accounted for by any known variables. But two meta-analyses based on the same evidence reached opposite conclusions, underlining "the ultimate subjectivity of medicine. [22] However, tried and tested methods turn out to be harmful – for example, with treating back pain, which affects up to 39% of adults. The science base is often poor. [23] Bio-medicine, too, has no common method of measuring health status – and those used are neither coherent nor mutually compatible. [24] There is, too, a long latent period between fundamental discoveries and their diffusion and use in medicine.

Despite these doubts and difficulties there remains much determined clinical resistance to change. In addition, some advances have come very late in the day. [25] Misselbrook is clearly right to state – and my observations and experience especially of older hospital consultants confirm it – that "If our understanding of the world is no longer monolithic but is seen as relativistic and subject to change, then biomedicine perhaps must become more humble in its claims. It can no longer claim to have a monopoly on the definition of "health." It cannot even claim to be the sole or sovereign source of medical fact. The biomedical model is just that – a model, not an absolute truth. There are other models available. Biomedicine has great strengths, but also limitations. Medicine's methods must be examined for their effectiveness, but medicine must also be more open to public scrutiny of its aims. Experts cannot set these aims in isolation – they are a legitimate subject for debate and influence." [26]

Foucault described how doctors modify the patient's story, fitting it into a biomedical paradigm, and filtering out non-biomedical material. He called this "the doctor's gaze", in which doctors systematically look for particular bits of a story and filter out the rest. This is to view reality on only one level. It ignores the social context of medical problems. Misselbrook cites the study by Jewson, "The disappearance of the sick man from medical cosmology", stating that "The patient as a whole person is no longer the focus of medical attention. We have transferred our gaze firstly to organic lesions, secondly to biochemical and physiological disease processes. The patient has changed from being an equal participant in a local transaction to being a passive spectator of treatment administered by a powerful and controlling professional class." [27]

Tuckett spoke of the consultation between a doctor and a patient as a "meeting of experts", in which each make an equal contribution. [28] We do not know how many doctors truly believe this. But we do know from research in 1989 (or just yesterday, in terms of *social* change in medicine) that doctors interrupt a patient's flow of speech after an average of 18 seconds. [29]

In addition, the terms of the consultation are set by many factors, including the over-arching culture, which has empowered the professional and maintained the dis-empowerment of the lay-person. It is in good part why the middle-class (privileged with cultural power: right parents; right school; good University; professional status; social networks; money; accent; residence; networks; expectation of being heard) do best from the NHS. It takes a lot to effect a satisfactory relationship with professionals. A relationship of trust will always be tense, partial, and much of it cast in the terms of the professionals. But these cultural patterns of clout make a big difference to how the individual is treated, and flourishes.

As Misselbrook says, "There is always an inequality of power. The patient needs the medics, and the relationship proceeds on the medic's terms." They got there first, ranged the furniture, set the terms of discussion. The anxieties, self-doubts, concern about misunderstandings, negative emotions, guilt, self-blame, sense of failure, apprehension, regret, inability to describe symptoms precisely – all these tip the balance towards the model, language, expectations, and power of the professionals. [30]

Doctors and patients offer different mental models, different languages, and live in different worlds. Each offers complications and simplifications. Somehow, these models have to re-connect, with mutual benefit, without damage from either model. One, the biomedical model, may offer technical solutions, but the technical solution may be only part of the solution to the patient. This may be relatively unimportant to the patient, who brings to the negotiation personal concerns that may not be amenable to technical solutions within the bio-medical model alone. The other offers the patient's world of illness, where the outcome must be seen, experienced, and judged. Here, "every option, every outcome will have different meanings and different values for different patients." [31]

We all have very different belief systems, values, subjective commitments and judgements to which we refer possibilities. Illness may threaten self-image, relationships, social function, comfort, earning ability, future goals, expected life-span; the hope of being able to live to see your own Grand-children grow up: "To assume we know the significance of a diagnosis to an individual patient is just as daft as assuming we can guess the diagnosis as they walk through the door. We make a diagnosis mainly by talking to the patient. We can try to understand the patient's world by the same method, but we have to work at it." [32]

All these difficulties concern issues of meaning and of fundamental value. Of what counts as "knowledge." Of what is heard when we "listen." And of the ways in which language shuts out meanings, how it reflects (and deflects) value judgements made about people and situations, how it establishes stylised routines and forms of presentation, as well as how it might open up eyes and ears to meanings. Misselbrook discusses these questions in terms of "a prime area of border warfare: the doctor's world of disease versus the patient's world of illness." [33]

Illness, and diagnosis, are made to fit the system; the bits of the problem presented by patients are selected out to enable this to happen. However, "narrative-based medicine" is now being offered, to enable the patient's experience to be expressed, to support empathy between doctor and patient, to enable both to understand the meaning of illness for the patient. This encourages a patient-centred agenda, but it takes individual development, time, and a major shift in mentalities. [34] It would be a major commitment by a PGCA – as by a good GP – to help patients evaluate treatments, from their own perspective. And they would be helped to balance this against any perceived negative effects – concerning any fears they may have, any history, the costs, the negative side-effects, the fear of stigma from illness, and any other specific factors in their lives. This would take time, and money.

Many doctors now say that there is no question but that they are "now genuinely sensitised to the merits of patient-centredness in our consultations." These words (suggesting that the incompleteness of the biomedical model is now complemented with the patient's narrative) are from the Foreword by Dr. Roger Neighbour to Misselbrook's book. But the picture remains mixed. And we have no clarity about what "patient-centred" means. The doctor may mean the bio-medical model being sensitised to the patient. The patient may mean something quite different. Does "patient-centred" mean seeing the whole person, valuing and recognising the importance of the patient's culture (including irrational ideas), ultimately enabling patient preference to prevail, whatever the legal choices made? Or does it mean the doctor adjusting the biomedical model slightly, in some half-way stage of some kind, but where ultimately the doctor rigs the result, by framing questions, by not mentioning alternatives, or by doing what they would have done anyway if guided by the bio-medical model?

We still hear the language of "non-compliance" and of "inappropriate referral" (to A&E, for example, when there is no GP office open when a patient gets home from work). This language overlooks that patients often have a rationale for their own actions which makes sense to them even if it seems perverse to a doctor. Conrad, too, suggested that non-compliance is itself one fundamental way in which a patient can re-exert control over their own life, instead of letting an illness control them. [35] However, doctors holding onto a bio-medical model of illness were found to believe that patients were not competent to take an active role in consultation. They were less likely, too, to approve of patient access to records. [36]

A&E staff classified patients depending on whether they regarded their claim to the 'sick role' as legitimate or not. [37] There is much evidence that a patient-centred consultation style is far from the norm, and that doctors still seek ways to increase the probability of patients doing as they are told. [38] To achieve real change here still requires a fundamental re-think by doctors, rather than just bolting on "patient-centred care" as a theoretical extra.

Ultimately, the question is who defines what benefits patients? The individual's fears and concerns for the future are fundamental to the quality of care, and we should be discovering these, and informing policy and practice by the discovery, the narratives, and the insights. For the service-user should be the one who defines what benefits them. Theirs is "the locus of reality" by which the success of care is measured. It is crucial to understand the reality (of the service-user, of the patient), and to pursue outcomes that benefit them. As Misselbrook says, "benefits...have to exist in the patient's world of life experience, not just in our [doctors'] world of biomedical measurements. Especially not just in our world of intermediate medical outcomes." [39]

What patients bring is a model – articulated or not – by which they may have the means to understand what is happening to them, within their own framework of ideas. Patients tend to come to see a doctor when their own explanatory framework is failing to enable them to manage a problem successfully. But this does not mean that this framework must be abandoned. For lay coping mechanisms are a crucial area of self-definition and of self-responsibility. Patients, too, have their own health beliefs – from traditional family sources, background and education, social networks, media, the net. These are rational to them, even if medically 'incorrect.' These lay models enable people to cope effectively with many health problems, perhaps as many as almost 80% of them. [40]

Misselbrook says that it is futile for doctors to seek to overwrite patients' own health models and belief systems. Instead, there should be an accommodation between the lay health world and the doctors' world, since the patient's explanatory framework of meaning is a reference point for their coping mechanisms. [41] This is to argue for a recognition of the expertise of the patient, however inexpertly put in terms of the language of the doctor, and for its scope and content to be fully integrated into the consultation. A dynamist model will support and encourage this approach, through the contractual process of the PGCA with providers. And it will be important to support and motivate doctors. The PGCA will shape the services they provide, but they will themselves be managed by those with medical training as well as by professional managers who are not doctors.

To this extent the role of doctors will be re-professionalised, although there will always be closer accountability than in the days of near-total autonomy in "the secret garden" of the 1990's. The factors which patients value most will be necessarily at the forefront, since they will voluntarily subscribe to the PGCA. Thus such criteria identified by Haig Smith and Armstrong will be much valued, particularly in the general practice setting. [42] These were that: doctor listens; the doctor sorts out problems; usually the same doctor; with an appointment within 2 days; with staff friendly. In the best GP practices, too, we might add that tests are promptly done at surgery, and carefully examined too; where staff know me; with waiting time less than 20 minutes; a small practice; with nurses on the premises; with the entire 'tone' of the practice and staff attitudes set by the docs in charge.

Government's own criteria were different. They mostly concerned screening, training, and the environment. Not all of the concerns which were of greatest priority to patients lend themselves easily to measurement. But it is the hard-to-measure qualities of empathy (and the easy to measure factor of time given to the patient), which the PGCA will need to assess by systematically collecting and auditing patient's reports. This information will influence service planning, priority setting, and investment. The government's managerial model, which takes its priorities from bio-medicine, will have to shift to admit the dynamist doctor-patient relationship within the PGCA. This is to move to services for people, rather than for populations. We know that this helps. When the judgements of clinicians on which domains of health care (assessed in the short form questionnaire, S-F 36) would be most important to patients are compared – with the opinions of patients themselves, it was found in one well-known study that they disagreed. For example, on the treatment of multiple sclerosis.

As Rothwell and colleagues reported, "Patients with multiple sclerosis, and possibly those with other chronic diseases, are less concerned than their clinicians about physical disability in their illness. Clinical trials in multiple sclerosis should assess the effect of treatment on the other elements of health status that patients consider important, which are also affected by the disease process, are more closely related to overall health related quality of life, and may well be adversely affected by side effects of treatment." [43]

This study showed that patients can accurately assess their own physical disability, but that it may not – to them – always be the most important determinant of overall health related quality of life. Doctors and patients differed in their assessments of what was of most importance. My own knowledge of my Mother's life and that of one of her brother's, both of whom lived successfully with a serious disability, confirms this. Neither ever accepted the sick role, which absolves us from responsibility, nor did they accept its official sanction. Each remained problem solvers for themselves, holding on to recognition and self-respect, and when faced with a choice of working for low-pay or being socially sanctioned as disabled and therefore supported both sought to remain independent. They defined their own behaviour and their place in the world. This attitude is what we should seek to endorse if we possibly can do so.

Some kinds of certainty are dangerous, of course. A self-reflective doctor who knows the value of doubt, and who (for example) has read Ivan Illich and considered his ideas is more attractive as a person and probably more use as a doctor. As Richard Smith, editor of the *BMJ*, said, "When sick I want to be cared for by doctors who every day doubt the value and the wisdom of what they do." [44]

Misselbrook offers the ideal of understanding and attitudes that one would want from a GP: "Becoming a patient is a frightening experience. Being a patient requires a high level of mental and emotional activity that may be invisible to doctors unless we recognise the language of the patient's world. We all experience life as a narrative. As doctors we face a choice. Do we conquer the patient's narrative, forcing it to labour for the project of medicine. Or do we accept a role as the patient's assistant, seeking to help the patient to create their life, helping them with the imperfections and difficulties posed by pathology along the way?" [45]

Yet some doctors still continue to insist on the superiority of medical training and its "expertise." Some, indeed, are reported as taking strong exception to the implication that ultimately the patient must decide – even in 'power sharing.' They point to "destructive forces in the doctor-patient relationship." For example, some doctors apparently take the view that the job is technical, and that the doctor's gaze should be restricted in the search for relevant evidence. One told the *BMJ*: "It is absurd to say that there is no truth defined by experts, that patients are equals, or allow patients to define conditions and treatment. Although criticism of medical hubris is important, this is a denial of the nature of medicine. Clinical effectiveness depends on understanding the patient's beliefs and expectations. Patients are, however, not equals, and their beliefs do not have the ontological status of medical knowledge."

Because of envy, and a realisation of inequalities, "It can be difficult to tolerate powerlessness, ignorance, dependence, needing help, and being helped. For doctors it is difficult having their attempts to help being spoiled by the patient." Clearly, in a town like Brighton, with surviving sink-estates like that of the notoriously rough council estate of Moulescoomb, it might be tempting to write that: "Often patients come demanding investigations, referrals, or treatments. Acquiescence leads to further demands and feelings of desperation in the doctor. Attendant is the risk of unnecessary, harmful interventions just to do something." [46]

However, this is a version of the "patients are thick" view of medicine, rather than the disposition of the reflective gardener or the enquiring botanist. It excludes the art of entering into another person's thoughts. Its results impact from many years of patient dis-empowerment and disconnection from self-responsibility. It overstates the importance of the technical part of knowledge and under-states the expertise of the patient on their own world and values. It rather surprisingly pins its faith in the rationality and the efficiency of modern medical practice, in its consistency and predictability. This, despite documented iatrogenic damage caused by medical interventions in many locales, and in spite of much that is done with little supporting evidence, or much that is not done despite good evidence. For example, prescribing drugs with little supporting evidence, not prescribing drugs that have good supporting evidence, and not changing prescribing habits despite the evidence – all characteristics of British medical culture. [47]

This cultural interface is the opposite view to that which highlights that the patients' values and beliefs should be valued, that these contribute much to health benefit, that they offer attempts by patients at explanation of cause and effect, and that they bring the potential of constraints on demand from self-diagnosis and self-treatment of minor complaints.

The more fortunate patient will find that the over-arching issue here is not one of compliance, but of concordance, which is the means towards adult relationships between patients and doctors, in which they discover together a problem-solving mechanism which integrates group norms, health beliefs, evidence, and symptom analysis.

This is what Misselbrook calls "the locus of control" of the individual – where self-interests, cultural norms, and appropriate action are focussed. This is a considerable, individual and a cultural challenge. It requires much new role play and amended perceptions on the part of both doctor and patient. It is, however, morally and socially cohesive. Concordance, too, will only be real if the outcome of discussion is permitted to differ from that of the compliance model. As Misselbrook puts this: "It is not a sneaky way of getting patients to do what we want. It is a way of negotiating two different but valid perspectives, accepting that the patient makes the ultimate treatment decision." [48].

Many doctors resist still the idea that society, too, has a right to define their role. And some appeal behind the palisade of paternalism, which many patients still ask them to construct. Patients who wish this should be entitled to exercise such a choice. Many, indeed, prefer (or have been taught to prefer) a doctor-directed style, treating the doctor like a bank, drawing out the knowledge from them as the moment arises. Faith in the doctor and in the "prison of awe" has therapeutic value, and it has been particularly noticeable amongst the elderly. [49]

However, it has been shown that it is practicable to involve patients in decision-making, and that it is especially beneficial to do so early rather than late. When choices are made real it is no surprise that some choose to take part and some prefer not to do so. But the act by the doctor of seeking to negotiate can itself build common ground, and it can introduce new ideas which can accommodate the patient's own objectives.

The key role is to help the patient understand the nature and consequences of choices, without rigging the result and without deploring the choice a patient makes when informed. [50] The answer would seem to lie in extending choice, with the informed and autonomous patient much more aware of alternatives and consequences, with proper prices to discipline opportunity, in a culture which improves education for self-responsibility. This will include direct incentives to care for oneself and to ration demand for one-self. And incentives and support for those doctors who seek to work with a broader understanding of human values, who seek to blend scientific evidence and social and psychological understandings, in a shifted gaze which encompasses the truth that the patient is the one living the specific life under review.

For all this to be possible we require more time for consultation, more staff, more money. But it is not merely transactional, or a matter of economics. It concerns those relationships, expectations, and beliefs which can truly be expressed in the faith to enable others to make decisions for themselves. This in itself can be painful, both for the adviser, the patient, and the relative or carer. I have seen this myself recently in the life of my own Uncle, who has been much more like a Father to me, since I did not know my own Father. Taken ill with pneumonia at almost 89 years of age, he did not want to take anti-biotics to clear infection since they affect his eyes. He is only very partially sighted – one eye has failed and the other has a prism inserted, which gives partial sight. He struggled in hospital, and wanted to come home. He rejected the sick role, and its sanctions, and re-asserted his own priorities and his own model of his life. He wants to live his own life, in terms of his values and beliefs. His locus of control is within himself. He has strong coping mechanisms, and a powerful sense of personal autonomy. He *expects* to deal with problems in life when they arise. Without it he would have faded long ago. He does not look to others to take responsibility for him.

And it is this self-reliance and determination which has enabled him to cope with blindness, lung cancer, and many deprivations – including (aged 18 months, and blind from measles already by then) losing his Father in the First World War. This left his Mother with almost no money, and no career training. With four young children, two of them seriously disabled. He wants to live his remaining time with all the insistence, energy (and bloody-mindedness) which has characterised his first 89 years – and which have enabled him to cope with extraordinary disadvantages. He wants to re-assert a sense of control, of actively coping with his illness, its consequences, and his other accumulated medical difficulties. He may or may not take further medication. He may or may not accept social care help – he rejected this when it was offered to him in hospital, just as he has always said he rejects a very aggressive resuscitation regime when he comes to the end of his life.

His course will be stressful for him, and for his close relatives. But as he sees it, it is his life which he wishes to live in his own terms if at all possible. And, with many challenges, he has never accepted that his life should be medicalised or defined as a medical problem *in itself*, even when discreet "fixes" have been necessary for specific difficulties. When he says that he would not wish to delay death if it involved "hi-tech wiring, or junior doctors jumping on my chest", or complex revival techniques we must lovingly stand aside. When he says "when my time comes, give me a pill – that'll do" we re-consider the arguments for voluntary euthanasia. When he says that the end of life should be compatible with how his life has been lived, we must support whatever decision he makes. It is, of course, anguishing and difficult for those who love him to stand back. It is tempting to try to control his situation, and to make him do things "for his own good." It is easy to wish to help by pressing drugs upon him, and to nag about diet. But his best interests, in his view, are defined by himself. And it is important for his dignity, his value as a human being, for his self-expression and self-control, to support him in his wishes.

We can see that it is often uncomfortable to respect another person's health beliefs and to truly respect their autonomy. But if we believe that each of us is an expert in our own lives we must do so. Even if one "knows" that by co-operating with a specific care regime he may live longer, and be fitter. But the decisions are not ours to make. For the question is, "whose outcome?" And it is his which is uniquely valid, in his own consciousness and within the structure of his drives and beliefs about his condition and his potentials. It is no good arguing for this perspective and then backing away when it comes home to those closest to us. We need to respect the individual, and to build a structure in which we in our turn will be respected. [50]

GP's tell many tales of how odd patients can be. In August 2002 an elderly woman I know in Bournemouth told me that her husband was in hospital with a serious chest infection, due to "that virus that boys get, so that they can't pass exams – the ones girls don't get, which is why they are all passing the exams better." Patients bring extraordinary ideas with them, and these are very real to them. How we consider the sources of such notions, their power, and how to work within their framework to nudge towards greater understandings is a major challenge. How we answer such questions for ourselves both reflect and influence the nature of our entire society. And of our capacities to live within it – including our self-discipline, our responsibility for the consequences of our actions, and an appreciation that life is *a* risk, and that death ultimately is not an option.

As Misselbrook has said, "The challenge of patient-centred practice is not a box we can tick and leave behind. The need to be patient-centred has been well stated, but what this means is still largely uncharted. Constructing patient-centred medicine first entails deconstructing the world of medicine and the world of the patient in order to redefine the relationship between them." [51]

Here, liberty is not license. And by no means are all patients nice human beings. There are plenty of pigs outside sties. Similarly promise is not necessarily performance. A decision may or may not be a solution. But we need a clear structure of first principles to guide us, in both asking and answering these perplexing moral and ethical questions. Trade-offs are inevitable, and they should be as informed as possible. Professional guidance and support is an important element. But, in the end, we are necessarily alone with ourselves. This book asks what the first principles are, both in structuring fair, equitable, just, health care – and in asking how to make first principles real in the actual living of our daily lives.

The answers I offer make choice and self-responsibility central to the argument. But how are these objectives to be made real? Here the message is that consumer choice and self-responsibility is only possible with consumer payment as it is in private medicine and can be in a system funded by taxes such as the NHS. Consumer choice and self-responsibility can both be achieved *for* all and *by* all, as one people, in one market, with one service. This, too, is to place great value on the daily lives, attitudes, and values of "ordinary" individuals, families, and communities – rather than to emphasise pre-eminently 'high' culture, professionalism divorced from the trade-offs to be made by the patient, politics, and the exercise of power. [52]

NOTES.

1. As will be obvious, I am hugely and especially indebted for the work in this chapter to the superb book by David Misselbrook, *Thinking About Patients* (Newbury, Berks., Petroc Press, 2001). It was an education in itself. See, for individual reference, *op. cit.*, p.58; T.Fuller, in J.Norman (ed.), *The Achievement of Michael Oakeshott* (London, G.Duckworth,1993), p.75. The echo is from Michael Polanyi's Personal *Knowledge,Towards a Post-Critical* Philosophy (Chicago, University of Chicago Press, 1958).

2. Auspitz, in Norman (ed.), *op. cit.*, p.5.

3. Emanuel Litvinoff, *Journey Through A Small Planet* (London, Michael Joseph, 1972), p.36.

4. Auspitz, *ibid.*, p.9.

5. Auspitz, *ibid.*, p.5.

6. A. Garratt, L .Schmidt, A. Mackintosh, R. Fitzpatrick, "Quality of life measurement: bibliographic study of patient assessed health outcome measures", *BMJ* (324), 2002, pp.1417-22.

7. R .B. Haynes, P. J. Devereaux, G .H. Guyatt, "Physicians' and patients' choices in evidence based practice", *BMJ* (324), 2002, p.1350.

8. K. J. Mukamal, "Authors assume that they understand more than their patients do", *BMJ* (324), letter, 2002, p.1585. See Misselbrook, *op. cit.*, and *BMJ* issue 13 April 2002, in which these and other views on medicalisation of society are examined in a series of special articles.

9. P. D. White, "Power sharing is not a takeover bid", *BMJ* (324), letter, 2002, p.1214.

10. E. Antman et al, "A comparison of the results of meta-analysis of randomised controlled trials and recommendations of clinical experts", *JAMA* (268) 1992, pp.240-8; A .Haines, R. Jones, "Implementing findings of research", *BMJ* (308), 1994, pp.1488-92; D. Armstrong et al, "A study of general practitioners' reasons for changing their prescribing behaviour", *BMJ* (312), 1996, pp.949-52; J. Cockburn, S.Pit, "Prescribing behaviour in clinical practice: patients' expectations and doctors' perceptions of patients' expectations", *BMJ* (315), 1997, pp.520-3.

11. Misselbrook, *op. cit.*, p.20.

12. J. Geraci et al, "International Classification of Diseases, 9th revision, Clinical modification codes in discharge reports are poor measures of complication occurrence in medical patients," *Medical Care* (36), 1997, pp.589-602. I owe this, and several of the above references, to Misselbrook, *ibid.*

13. Misselbrook, *ibid.*, p.26, and references he cites.

14. Misselbrook takes this latter view, *ibid.*, p.27.

15. D. H. Bevan, "Regarding sick people as consumers changes their role", *BMJ* (324), letter,

2002, p.1453. Others suggest that "excessive accountability" seriously damages doctor morale. See I. Taylor, "At least some of the unhappiness is due to excessive accountability", *BMJ* (324), 2002, p.1453; D.P. Gray, "Deprofessionalising doctors?", *BMJ* (324), 2002, pp.627-8.

16. G. Makoul, P. Arnston, and T. Schofield, "Health promotion in primary care: physician-patient communication and decision-making about prescription medications", *Soc.Sci.Med*, 2000 (50), pp.829-40; F. A .Stevenson, C. A. Barry, N. Britten, N. Barber, C. P. Bradley, "Doctor-patient communication about drugs: the evidence for shared decision making," *Soc. Sci. Med*, 2000 (50), pp. 829-40.

17. M .F. Muldoon, S. D. Barger, J. D .Flory, S. B. Manuck, "What are quality of life measurements measuring?", *BMJ* (316), 1998, pp.542-5.

18. Dept. of Health, *Changing childbirth. Report of the expert maternity group.* (London, HMSO, 1993).

19. H. Stapleton, M. Kirkham, G. Thomas , "Qualitative study of evidence based leaflets in maternity care", *BMJ* (324), 2002, pp.639-643; A. O'Cathain, S. J. Walters, J. P. Nicholl, K. J. Thomas, M. Kirkham, "Use of evidence based leaflets to promote informed choice in maternity care: randomised controlled trial in everyday practice", *BMJ* (324), 2002, pp.643-645.

20. Misselbrook, *ibid.*, p.15.

21. A. Moore, M. Roland, "How much variation in referral rates among general practitioners is due to chance?", *BMJ* (298), 1989, pp.500-2.

22. M Lindbaek, P. Hjortahl, "How do two meta-analyses of similar data reach opposite conclusions?", *BMJ* (318), letter, 1999, pp.873-4; T. Fahey, N. Stocks, T. Thomas, "Quantitative systematic review of randomised controlled trials comparing antibiotic with placebo for acute cough in adults", *BMJ* (316), 1998, pp.906-10; L. Becker et al, "Antibiotics for acute bronchitis (Cochrane review), in *Cochrane Collaboration, Cochrane Library,* issue 1, Oxford: Update Software, 1999).

23. G. Waddell, G. Feder, M. Lewis, "Systematic reviews of bed rest and advice to stay active for back pain," *British Journal of General Practice* 1997 (47), pp.647-52.

24. C. van Weel, "Of patients and their illnesses," *European Journal of General Practice,"* 1998 (4), pp.3-5.

25. Misselbrook, *ibid.*, p.10.

26. Misselbrook, *ibid.*, p.16.

27. Misselbrook, *ibid.*, p.24; N. Jewson, "The disappearance of the sick man from medical cosmology, 1770-1870", *Sociology* (10), 1976, pp.225-44.

28. D. Tuckett, M. Boulton, C. Olson, A. Williams, *Meetings Between Experts* (London, Tavistock, 1985).

29. F. Frankle, H .Beckman, "Evaluating the patient's primary problem(s)", in M. Stuart, D. Roter

(eds.), *Communicating With Medical Patients* (Newbury Park, Sage, 1989), pp.86-98.

30. Misselbrook, *ibid.*, p.81.

31. Misselbrook, *ibid.*, p.83.

32. Misselbrook, *ibid.*, p.84.

33. Misselbrook, *ibid.*, p.35.

34. T. Greenhalgh, B. Hurwitz (eds.), *Narrative based medicine* (London, BMJ Books, 1998).

35. P .Conrad, "The meaning of medications: another look at compliance", *Social Science and Medicine* (20), 1985, pp.29-37.

36. N. Britten, "Hospital consultants' views of their patients", *Sociology of Health and Illness* (132), 1991, pp.83-97.

37. R. Jeffery, "Normal rubbish: deviant patients in casualty departments." *Sociology of Health and Illness* (132), 1979, pp.90-107.

38. S. Eggly et al, "An assessment of residents' competence in the delivery of bad news to patients", *Academic Medicine* (72), 1997, pp.397-9; S. Joos et al, "Patients' desires and satisfaction in general medical clinics", *Public Health Reports* (108) 1993, pp.751-9; B .Hulka et al, "Practice characteristics and quality of primary medical care: the doctor-patient relationship," *Med.Care* (13), 1975, pp.808-20; P. Ley, "Improving patients' understanding, recall, satisfaction and compliance" in A. Brooke (ed.), *Health Psychology* (London, Chapman & Hall, 1989); R. Haynes, "Improving patient compliance: An Empirical Review," in R. Stuart (ed.), *Adherence, Compliance and Generalisation in Behavioural Medicine* (New York, Brunner/Mazel, 1982). See also references in Misselbrook, *ibid.*, pp.186-7.

39. Misselbrook, *ibid.*, p.41.

40. J. Fry, *A New Approach to Medicine* (Lancaster, MTP Press, 1978).

41. Misselbrook, *ibid.*, p.44.

42. C. Haigh Smith, D. Armstrong, "Comparison of criteria derived by government and patients for evaluating general practitioner services," *BMJ* (299), 1989, pp.494-6.

43. P .M. Rothwell, Z. McDowell, C. K. Wong, P. J. Dorman, "Doctors and patients don't agree: cross sectional study of patients' and doctors' perceptions and assessments of disability in multiple sclerosis," *BMJ* (314), 1999, p.1580.

44. R. Smith, re-review of Ivan Illich's *Limits to Medicine. Medical Nemesis: The Expropriation of Health*, in *BMJ* (324), 2002, p.923.

45. Misselbrook, *ibid.*, p.89.

46. D. McQueen, "Patients are not doctors' equals", *BMJ* (324), 2002, p.1214; see also, for a much subtler treatment of these issues, Misselbrook, ibid., and several pieces by Dr. William G. Pickering: "Medical omniscience", *BMJ* (317) 1998, pp.19-26; "Does medical

treatment mean patient benefit?", *Lancet*,(347) 1996, pp.379-80; "A nation of people called patients", *Journal of Medical Ethics* (17) 1991, pp.91-2; "Patient satisfaction: an imperfect measurement of quality medicine?", *Journal of Medical Ethics* (.19) 1993, pp.121-22.

47. Le Fanu, *op. cit*; Misselbrook, *ibid*.

48. Misselbrook, *op. cit.*, p.180.

49. R. Savage, D. Armstrong, "Effect of a general practitioner's consulting style on patient's satisfaction: a controlled study", *BMJ* (301), 1990, pp.968-70; B. McKinstry, "Do patients wish to be involved in decision-making in the consultation? A cross sectional survey with video vignettes", *BMJ* (321), 2000, pp.867-71; R. Baker, "Characteristics of practices, general practitioners and patients related to patients' satisfaction with consultations", *British J. of General Practice* (46) 1996, pp.601-5.

50. J. Protheroe et al, "The impact of patients' preferences on the treatment of atrial fibrillation: observational study of patient-based decision analysis", *BMJ* (320), 2000, pp.1380-4.

51 This includes the need for legislation on voluntary euthanasia, putting patient's wishes first, and with strict safeguards to protect the vulnerable. I include this discussion with Mr. Root's express permission. See also A. J. Root, "Surviving the Slump", *Hackney History*, 2002, and his forthcoming memoirs: A .J. Root, *Land of Promise.. The Memoirs of An Edwardian North London Boy. Or, It's A Long Way From Shipway Terrace!*, in preparation.

52. Misselbrook, *ibid.*, p.4.

PART TWO:
14. 'Only half way to paradise'?

Social enterprise initiatives: the opportunity, the challenge, and the deficits of individual empowerment.

"We must, for the most part, choose how to act as individuals on the basis of moral beliefs which are merely fairly grounded, but when we make these choices we are <u>exercising</u> our freedom, whereas when governments choose, they are diminishing freedom." – John Marenbon.

This paper was given as the invited Keynote Address to the Inaugural meeting of the London Social Economy Task Force Health & Social Care Group at the City of London, Guildhall on 26 September 2006.

Social Enterprise – the new answer to health care deficits? *Maybe*. I am grateful to the Task Force for this opportunity to consider this and other related questions. 'Social Enterprise' is the new 'buzz word.' My chief point today is that I am interested by social enterprise initiatives. *BUT*.

First, the welcome. Some Social Enterprise initiatives are de-centralised and local, and seem to offer some new opportunities to individuals for improved outcomes and for greater choice. They claim to encapsulate and express democratic, mutual principles. I will consider, in a moment, the basis of this claim. Social enterprise organisations are evidently politically persuasive, seen as legitimate, and perhaps can build some local consent. However, they focus almost entirely on supply-side changes.

The 'third sector' is important. Many social enterprise organisations are said to be 'grounded in their local communities.' BUT do they really empower individuals as the users of services so that they can unrelentingly command a personal, intimate, timely and specific service? How many of those supposed to benefit from these schemes are involved in the original formulation of them, take part in their implementation and direction, really feel that they 'own' them, and vote to control their evolution? If not, what next?

There are now new social enterprises in health care by new public or private suppliers – such as the out-of-hours GP service Local Care Direct in Yorkshire [an out-of-hours provider], or Sandwell Community Caring Trust [a charity which runs residential and respite care], or the Kath Locke Centre in Manchester [the first NHS primary care facility to be run as a social enterprise]. The Secretary of State for Health has drawn attention to these as examples. But they do not, however, address the key issues of mutuality and empowerment. And they do not alter the demand-side deficits. [1] These are fundamental concerns.

I suggest that genuine mutuality, consent, legitimacy, and the individual empowerment of individual service-users will come only from demand-side change. Meanwhile, without financially-empowered consumers or service users, we should ask some basic questions which some social enterprise initiatives suggest they have answered. Thus: are social enterprise initiatives legitimate in the local community? Allison Ogden Newton (Chief Executive of Social Enterprise, London) mentioned this concern just now. They are said to have 'common ownership.' What does 'common ownership' mean, how is it expressed (and commanded), and by whom? By staff, or service-users, or both? If staff only, how does this ensure an individual can be certain of a service when they want it? If staff only, whither 'mutuality'? Allison mentioned 'consultation' as a unique selling point for social enterprises. But I query how 'consultation' enables an individual to command a specific, individual, necessarily timely, personal service. And the issue, too, surely, is not the education *of* service-users by managers, but the education *of* managers by service-users.

This points up the dilemma of why and how do social enterprise initiatives empower the individual in new ways, if at all? And what can 'mutuality' mean if people do not join voluntarily, and thus become the voting members of the enterprise, employing (and having the capacity to change) its managers and leaders? It is surely wholly inadequate for the 'member' of the social enterprise initiative only to be the staff – as in those which form the common model. This is not mutuality, as the service-users are excluded from mutual control. And so we should ask whether such deficits suggest that social enterprise initiatives are becoming the latest, polished version of market mimicry, of seeking to retain old NHS mentalities, and a further stage in the refusal to return economic purchasing power to the individual?

We need to look hard at what is the basis of these social enterprise structures. And at their large claims to emphasise the true basis of social solidarity, equity, individual opportunity and self-responsibility, fairness and mutuality. Are these just another label for hierarchical organisation, which seeks to keep power and control in the same professional and bureaucratic hands as before – albeit, for honourable reasons? Or can they encourage adaptive, local, evolutionary change to release the wishes of individual service-users as the commanding imperative? And thus replace structures of hierarchy and control by experts who claim to know our own interests better than we know them for ourselves. *For here, the ultimate issue is who decides who decides.*

I suggest that social enterprise organisations reveal the continued social deficit in terms of voice and choice. They do not empower the individual, unless you believe in the model of 'agency' and of experts always knowing in advance what people want, people who they have never met and who do not usually want to spend their lives in 'healthcare activism' and lobbying.

Thus the BUT. Which – the good news! – is itself an opportunity.

Social enterprises *can* indeed open the door to genuine changes which can at last deliver voice and choice as well as strategic and social objectives too. IF.... For there is an opportunity here for you to reveal, to lead, and to inform these debates about these demand-side deficits. To help achieve genuine mutuality, deep-rooted community allegiance, individual empowerment and self-responsibility. You can thus help to deliver both service-change and social solidarity. Equality of access. Higher quality. Greater capacity. And improved professional pay and morale – which also matters.

The alternative is discouraging. Indeed, I think that if social enterprises focus on process, on relatively unambitious structures, and on the short-term they will rapidly be left behind by the changes which I believe are inevitable after the next General Election, which will focus on better European experiences, and on individual financial empowerment and self-responsibility. A key issue will be who are the purchasers to be, and how are they to be organised? They will, I think grow from Primary Care Trusts, but with individuals in control as mutual and willing members, choosing between commissioners and the packages of care they offer to buy with the member's funds they can attract. Those funds will be mobile, which they are not now.

In my recent book, *Patients, Power and Responsibility*, I suggested that money talks and preference walks. Cash would command care for the silent and the non-activist especially and in a unique way – as the middle classes know, for they operate both the NHS and a morally unacceptable dual market. I want every individual to be able to command timely access.

Fundamentally, I believe that the poor and voiceless, who have done least well from the NHS and social services, can only be empowered by being enabled to join mutual, local, social enterprise organisations which have to seek willing revenues, instead of relying on money from above. These need to purchase care by attracting the willing revenues offered by every individual holding a savings cash-credit, and who willingly joins as a voting member. This is not the same as the current social enterprise model of 'mutuality.' Nor would service-users be privatised shareholders receiving cash-dividends, since any surplus or profits are not to be distributed as money given back to members but as improvements in services, including cost improvements. The poor would thus, at last, be on an equal basis, supported by tax-transfers from the middle-class and the rich. These could even be loaded in their favour, as Professor Julian Le Grand has suggested – so that the poor can both access good quality care and make up some present deficits.

When I was chairman of a leading academic book publishing group for 20 years I always chuckled to hear that there are three kinds of books: newly announced, previously announced, and perennially announced. The problem of voice and choice is perennially announced. Social enterprise 'consultation' has a history. Thus far the many acts of market mimicry, market avoidance, and other attempts at achieving both choice and voice, have not achieved individual empowerment.

We have had:

- incessant government targets.
- modernisation bodies.
- 'accountable' (sic) Foundation Trusts.
- 'a say' for users, even 'a greater say,' for the individual.
- 'an expression of preferences.'
- 'more involvement.'
- Local authority scrutiny committees.
- surveys, but with no cost to the individual attached.
- Citizen's Juries.
- Patient Forums.
- Planning Consultations.
- Devices of market mimicry like the internal market.
- Organisations said to be 'owned' by patients – but as tax-payers in the way I and 60 million others owned British Rail, but could not influence it, and where the notion of ownership was meaningless as it carried no power.

The experience and the deficits of all these substitutes for individual empowerment reveal three key and fundamental points concerning individual empowerment:

1. Health and social care is necessarily and uniquely individual, personal, separable and timely. Planning, consultation, and local agencies do not enable or empower individual command over specific services. Nor does voting, or being 'consulted.'

2. Most people do not want to be health-care activists. They want a service when they want it. And they want to have a local organisation which can ensure that they get appropriate care and on time. Thus far, they do not have this.

3. There is a vital distinction, between seeking to discipline a system by occasional voting and consultation – having "a say", or having "a greater

say" – and being able to secure a necessary, individual, personal, intimate, separable and timely service.

How to resolve these issues?

We can evolve a regulated market structure in which not-for-profit social enterprise organisations in pluralist competition are encouraged by incentives and disciplined market choices, IF individuals can move between them and take their NHS fund with them if they are dis-satisfied.

Such an organisation could help build genuine voice and choice (and, by the by, individual self-responsibility for own individual health care too).

If we truly want individual choice, empowerment and self-responsibility, as we should in a democracy, we must recognise that only the wearer of the shoe knows where it pinches. And that the wearer should choose (and, if they wish, change) the shoe or the shoe-supplier.

My proposed structure – extending the impetus of social enterprise – offers a new approach to a legally-guaranteed core package of care for all. This turns on purchasing and delivering a guaranteed care package, confirmed in law from government. I set this out in practical detail in my recent detailed book. And then the essential economic empowerment of the individual to achieve access to it, as one people, one service, in one market. Individual responsibility, too, is the key to good health care and personal health status.

The individual patient fund will be mobile, but only to be spent with a mutual social enterprise organization, which competes with others like them for the willing funds. These would be competing, mutual, co-operative purchasers of care, organised regionally and nationally, and led by professionals and managers. They would bring together willing members, buy on their behalf, and be accountable to them as a member-voting body.

Government's activist role will be to ensure that incentives, choice and competition works, and to require strategic and community objectives are met. There will be one people in one market for one service – as now exemplified by the recent, successful optical revolution in the British high street. Again, see the chapter in my *Patients, Power and Responsibility*.

Let me focus here on just one example of current social enterprise practice which points up the problems of present structures. My family are from Hackney and Shoreditch. I am very interested in the organisation of the East London Integrated Care (ELIC) organisation. As the recent King's Fund report on [Social Enterprise and Community-Based care*: is there a future for mutually owned organisations in community and primary care?*] shows – but, note, without demur of any kind, and without noticing any of the difficulties – this is an organisation shaped by clinicians. Fair enough in many respects, if service-users could move between such competing organisations. But it is only professionals who are defined as members. Service-users are not members. It is controlled by a Council of 10 professionals and one representative of what is called patient interests – from amongst the massive number of diverse patient concerns. Who decides who decides? And even if there were 101 such user representatives it would still be a beggar-my-neighbour competition for scarce resources.

Most people are busy living their lives. Rationally, they do not think about healthcare until they have a problem. They do not take part in planning or in consultations. Most do not discover the treatment choices, their preferences and values, what outcomes they could best live with, their own inner feelings, until the situation arises. Who can represent them, in advance?

What does such a structure as the ELIC one described by the King's Fund say about the exclusion of service-users from mutual membership? *One* patient representative? And if I am a Parkinson's disease sufferer, how does an orthopaedic patient (for example) represent me? If I am a Somali-speaking Mother of five, probably not even registered with the NHS (as many in East London) how am I represented? Or if I am a mental health patient? Or if I am a diabetic, how does an activist cancer-patient who is very successful in obtaining new drugs – perhaps by going to court – 'represent' me? In a beggar-my-neighbour situation (such as in the NHS), the effective 'representative' shifts funds to one area of the NHS, but away from another. And who knows my wishes? Who can empower me? How?

How might we go a lot further than the present structure of social enterprises?

I have urged that genuine mutuality requires the individual to join with others similarly to be financially empowered with tax-funds in a democracy, to control their own health and social care funds, necessarily carefully regulated by government.

Crucially, the individual health and social care fund must be mobile. The individual could then take their tax-fund to a competing, mutual, democratic social enterprise organisation which has to seek willing members and willing revenues. Mutual organisations could bid not for aggregated NHS block contracts, but for the funds of individual willing members, and then buy services from alternative suppliers with these funds.

How to get there? We can take 'next steps' by building on the existing provision of direct social care payments under the control of the disabled and those purchasing social services formerly delivered without patient control by local authorities. This change, too, has generated successful advisory and support bodies to help people make informed decisions. Many people thought by some to be least likely to make competent decisions are doing so every day. We can build a new kind of mutual organisation on the basis of these experiences. [2]

Finally, may I urge that these are moral issues, and not merely instrumental questions. My approach relies on the notion that as social beings we premise our days – after all, the scarcest things in the world – on the assumption that we have free will and thus self-responsibility. This is a moral debate in which we can each be held responsible for consequences. One where we are expected to make choices for ourselves and be expected to associate ourselves with the results.

I am a Visiting Fellow at the IEA. And so please excuse me if I conclude with F. A. Hayek, which you will perhaps expect. Hayek has always been the messenger from the future. He tells us that we learn by choosing, as responsible, democratic adults. And that informed rather than market mimicry – offers "a realm of voluntary planning characterised by private property and freedom of contract." That is the challenge which social enterprises must face. This is an adaptive, evolutionary process of discovery. I believe it is positive, and purposeful. Yours is an opportunity and a challenge. The monolith *is* adrift. Service-users *can* re-shape new models, in genuine mutuality. Yours *can* be a key voice for voice, choice, and improved outcomes, which service-users do much to determine. IF....

And these issues will not go away. [4]

NOTES.

1. Patricia Hewitt, Secretary of State for Health, *Social Enterprise in primary and community care* (London, Social Enterprise Coalition, 2006). Another is the South East London Doctors Cooperative, a non-profit making limited company owned, managed and financed by 460 GP members, providing out of hours services for some 90,000 patients in Lambeth, Southwark and Lewisham. Jeremy Davies, 'After Eden, things look rosy in the social enterprise garden', *Health Service Journal*, 15 February 2007, pp.14-15. This article lists 25 social enterprise 'pathfinders'. See also Alan Milburn, 'Putting the voluntary Sector Centre Stage', speech to National Council of Voluntary Organisations, 12 November 2003; 'The Voluntary Sector – a Partner in Reform', speech to Association of Chief Executives of Voluntary Organisations', 30 November 2004; 'Social enterprise – a Partner in Reform', speech to Social Enterprise Coalition, 25 January 2005.

2. King's Fund, *Social Enterprise and Community-Based care: is there a future for mutually owned organisations in community and primary care?* (London, King's Fund, 2006).

3. See my detailed chapter 11, 'Cash on the nail', in *Patients, Power and Responsibility*, pp.97-107 for a detailed discussion of direct payments. Also, C. Glendinning, S. Halliwell, S. Jacobs, K. Rummery and J. Tryer, 'Bridging the Gap. Using Direct Payments to Purchase Integrated Care', *Health and Social Care in the Community*, 8, pp.192-200, 2000; F. Hasler, *Clarifying the Evidence on Direct Payments into Practice* (London, National Centre for Independent Living, 2003); Joseph Rowntree Foundation, *Making Direct Payments Work for Older People* (York, Joseph Rowntree Foundation, 2004); J. Leece and J. Bornat (eds.), *Developments in Direct Payments* (Bristol, The Policy Press, 2006); private communication with senior NHS manager, October 2007.

4. The government has estimated that there are at least 55,000 social enterprises in the UK, accounting for 5% of all businesses with employees, and with a combined turnover of £27b

a year, or 1% of GDP. They are astonishingly diverse. They include many businesses trading with a social purpose – of which perhaps the best known is *The Big Issue*. Others include care homes, housing associations, various different kinds of co-operatives, leisure and fair trade businesses. Some are also Community Interest Companies, under the 2004 legislation. Of these, however, relatively few are concerned with health and social care. We still need, however, to put some fundamental questions to them, notably about individual choice and empowerment. Government continues to invest in social enterprise. In January 2007 the Department of Health announced a £73m fund to be given to 'start-up' social enterprises in health and social care over the following four years. In August 2007 twenty-four were given £1.4m of national funding between them to deliver community health and social care services.

The DoH has a Social Enterprise Unit to encourage not-for-profit firms to provide services. But who do they directly empower? In July 2007 Linda Marks (Senior Research Fellow) and Professor David Hunter (Professor of Health Policy and Management), both of Durham University's Centre for Public Policy, published the first academic research on social enterprise bodies. This was commissioned by the trade union Unison. Its conclusions were that those working in the health service were becoming unaccountable and bureaucratic, as they moved away from their community focus and community roots. However, the report did not favour competition. Unsurprisingly, it blamed it. Thus: "Collaboration and sharing of good practice could prove difficult in an increasingly commercial and contractual environment." Linda Marks and David Hunter, *Social Enterprises in Primary Care. Changing Patterns of Ownership and Accountability. A Briefing Document* (London, Unison Positively Public Unit, 2007).

15. Money is not enough. Or, why Mr. Brown's approach cannot work.

"After all, factual truth is not the only thing that matters. It can be just as illuminating to know what people thought or pretended was true, if one can discover why they thought it, or why they had to pretend it. I do not despise a plausible legend, or totally disbelieve a miracle that everyone believed in." David Howarth.

This previously unpublished essay was completed in September 2002. Its continuing relevance under entirely different governments is itself disturbing, if unsurprising.

Statists seek to restrict change to what they believe can be predicted in advance. We have seen that this form of astrology has a poor political prognostication. It does not work well in planning or in delivering services.

Similarly, there can be no system free from unpredictable, adaptive change. Everywhere there is always something new inevitably changing the system.

The feelings of a loss of control have, however, often prompted government to try to increase central controls. This has worsened the situation. For only open markets can gather the information that successfully prompts unplanned evolutionary and emulative responses to changes. It may be no comfort to Mr. Gordon Brown, but his own refusal to move away from the fundamentals of statism is itself necessarily changing the possibilities. It is a slow process, however, especially in the absence of leadership enunciating the adaptive alternatives rooted in individual financial empowerment. Meanwhile, the door continues to creak. Massive amounts of oil have not stopped the sounds of decay in health and education services. In the short-term, however, the gravest risk – in terms of much avoidable individual pain and suffering – is that the necessity to re-model English care entirely has perhaps been put back for a decade and more by Mr. Brown's approach as Chancellor, and by what looks like its continuance from No.10.

All the money that Mr. Brown has spent along statist lines has improved salaries, and increased some capacity. But it has made insufficiently discernible difference in service. Productivity has not improved. It has declined. As has public satisfaction. Staff morale has also plummeted. These difficulties are underlined, too, by the facts that the challenge of change arises in a political environment subject to emotion, confusion, and a disabling electoral chronology. Continuing and lamentably damaging Conservative failures to enunciate fundamentals, to make the explicit argument for liberal capitalist adaptive markets – and to refer events to these options – have made a major contribution here since Mr. Blair was first elected in 1997. *[There is no evident change under Mr. David Cameron's majority government, freed of Liberal-Democratic vetoes, in 2015].*

Politics (or serendipity), probably, will ultimately decide the case in one sense. But a change of administration is not necessarily a change of mind. The electoral test will be not merely whether services have improved, but have they improved *enough*. This is an emotional measure at best. And meanwhile, politics itself disables the moral test. It disables, too, the management of services, as it seems also to disable the principled offer of an alternative view of the potentials of individuals. The likely disappointment of heightened expectations will educate for change, but only along creative lines if leadership is offered. It may be that only a further crisis in care – and thus in politics – will produce real change. When that comes what will be done next will be influenced by the ideas on offer – ready "until", in Milton Friedman's phrase, "the politically impossible becomes politically inevitable." [1]

Until surprisingly recently some people felt they might be reaching some kind of summit in health care, led there by Mr. Brown's huge new investment. But this summit proved to be a rocky outcrop without cover from the cold. The path back to mutual purchasing in a patient owned co-operative – and to a European-style social insurance system – will be tricky in the dark. However, in due time, it will be the only route to safety, both for patients and for politicians. Of course, there are many successes for individual patients in treatment. [2] But, overall, an increase in funding without systemic change worsens the difficulties – because the basic ideas upon which Mr. Brown continues to insist are fundamentally wrong. This makes the failures more dramatic. This will be so irrespective of the amount of money thrown at the system.

Thomas Jefferson urged decentralisation as one of the most important works of government. He said that power and liberty were uncomfortable together. But this is not the present government's approach. And, indeed, de-centralisation is itself not necessarily the answer. De-centralisation, to whom? If to local government – which has little legitimacy – we will be no better off, and with no more individual patient leverage. Mr. Brown's irresponsible mix of more money (from extra national debt), closer central management, intensified regulation, more inspection, and some talk of decentralisation struggles to retain Fabian ideas of 'experts' running things.

Thus, Mr. Brown has spoken of making the NHS patient-centred, but it has not empowered the individual to make this rhetoric real. The individual has not yet been given control of cash, free to make decisions for themselves about which decentralised service they prefer. We have seen that Mr. Alan Milburn took some crucial initiatives on direct cash-payment for social services. These directly contradicted Mr. Brown's own bias. But these initiatives apart, we have had a new structure of more intrusive and detailed supervision – to hit targets and produce a sustainable improvement in standards of provision at a local level, but managed from the centre. I argue that this will not help us to make advances towards the key objectives of liberty. Indeed, as a famous Peckham independent trader would say, *au contraire*. Decentralisation to local government or local health authorities of Whitehall powers over purchasing – described by Ed Balls, Mr. Brown's closest adviser as "constrained discretion," in which the Minister remains in charge of the money – merely moves central power and mentalities into a local postal district, as we have seen. [3]

This is a managerialist change, a geographical shift, but not a change in nature. And it is one that lacks the competitive imperative that must be placed on purchasers and providers, with consumers in charge of their own destiny. Although, here, two major controls will seemingly ensure that the big hospitals on the hills will continue to dominate local markets: the centralisation of A&E in major regional centres, and the Royal College approvals necessary for doctor training to be registered. Here, the contestability of management may be the only possible and practical solution. But none of the major political parties has prepared for this. No work has been done – as I know from asking leading figures in Whitehall.

Meanwhile, the move to decentralise will remain a model of technocratic governance, close regulation, central funding and thus metropolitan reporting. However, it ought to reveal the necessity of setting up a competitive market. If that emerges, competition itself must then be vigorously defended by government, this being the soil of adaptive experimentation and evolution. For the spontaneous results which can enable a system to genuinely evolve in response to users' preferences and feed-back cannot be constructed in advance by progressive planning which seeks uniform, comprehensive sufficiency in a single blueprint for all. Nor is more money enough. It is insufficient, too, to go towards decentralised management without offering a choice between decentralised services. We should each be able to move to the one of our choice. Better management through central diktat is an inconclusive method, and politically risky, too. Scrutiny of detail by regulation, without changing the architecture is, too, no magic formulae.

There is a contradiction, indeed, between Mr. Brown's left and right hands. What Mr. Brown is doing in health care policy directly contradicts his other policies. He has encouraged the re-distribution of economic power in his search for economic growth without inflation, and of redistribution through higher productivity. He has spoken of government as "enabling and empowering, not centralising and controlling". He has urged a vigorous competition policy, linked competition policy to risk-taking and to economic dynamism, and supported rapid innovation. He has been an enemy of feather-bedding. His has been a stress on macroeconomic indicators of performance, on productivity growth and rising living standards, and on the diffusion of economic (and thus of social) opportunity.

Mr. Brown, too, has encouraged the micro-economic goals of entrepreneurship, efficiency, and productivity. None of these are notably Bevanite commitments. Yet he has *exempted* health care from the search for competitive solutions to deliver macro and micro-economic changes. He insists that increased public spending to deliver an *expanded* public service is sufficient – although cultural change driven by the consumer is the real necessity. [4] And he seems to have made it difficult for Mr. Milburn to progress his 'Foundation hospitals' project to give the best hospitals some more freedoms. [5]

This seems bizarre, given Mr. Brown's realisation that competition is the enemy of class rigidities – for it is this which specifically hinder working-class health care. Competition, too, generates more favourable economic results than any other system. This deficiency, this reliance on 'public policy' rather than on competitive markets in healthcare, may be due to a predictable (and rational) mix of blind spot and ambition, and an awareness of the visceral nature of Labour's kingmakers. But the structure is exempt from the incentives Mr. Brown has otherwise deployed. And the reliance on greater inputs translating into greater (and timely) outputs seems eccentric, both in political and health care terms. For recent evidence indicates that large sums intended to improve front-line services vanish into the system. Mostly on staff pay, and on paying off old debts. The Commons Select Committee on Science and Technology recently reported that new money for cancer care has disappeared into the system without any noticeable benefit to patients – some £280 million of £570 million has been spent on paying debts. [6]

Low morale amongst doctors and nurses is a problem, too. But happier, better paid doctors will still be an *insufficient condition* for reform, as I am arguing – even if more doctors can rapidly be trained (which looks very difficult – there are inevitable time lags, and service plans require an extra 15,000 consultants and GP's, an extra 35,000 nurses, midwives and health visitors, 30,000 more therapists, and 412 new hospitals by 2008!!!). Even if the extra money can be spent effectively (which will take much better management), even if direct incentives come into use (which is not yet proposed by any major political party). [7] And costs seem likely quite inevitably to rise. [8]

Similarly, it seems that only a fraction of the £50 million reserved for palliative care in the National Cancer Plan in 2000 actually reached hospices, which are a supreme example of charitable and voluntary care in our system. They provide 80% of palliative care in the UK. In the summer of 2002 they were turning away the dying and cutting bed numbers, two years after the government said that specialist care for the terminally-ill should be provided to all patients. [9]

Here, we should increase economic incentives to individuals for donations, and for giving of their time and skills. We should build on these mostly small, charitable organisations. We should value the fact that what they do is *not* done by government, but by local people responding themselves and showing care. We do not want government to expand its role, *despite* calls from Help the Hospices for more state funding. This would be a backwards step. Instead, we should expand the voluntary role – Gordon! tax incentives! – and encourage individual commitments to individual compassion. Gordon! CBE's! But this does not invalidate the point that the new spending by Mr. Brown will not achieve what he seeks, which is a matter of political and philosophical analysis.

MONEY IS NOT ENOUGH. OR, WHY MR. BROWN'S APPROACH CAN'T WORK

Mr. Brown's health care policies (aided and abetted by Mr. Ed. Balls and Mr. Ed Milliband), it will be seen, have over more than a decade represented a principled alternative view concerning surprise, individual knowledge, and patient empowerment. The physicist Freeman Dyson called this approach "premature choice" – or betting all your money on a horse before discovering whether she is lame. The approach of the Wanless Report to funding of health care is the major example of Mr. Brown using political power deliberately to short-cut the learning that comes by trial-and-error. He insisted that public monopoly funding of the NHS is *a priori* necessary and the most advantageous approach, but without testing the alternatives. Indeed, without prices Mr. Wanless could offer Mr. Brown no useful information on which to assess the claim that NHS services are efficient – and superior to the alternatives. Insofar as he could offer external assessments – notably, by the OECD – these were discouraging to such a claim to superiority. Indeed, they showed our standards and services were in the main lamentably bad, and among the worst in Europe, including Bulgaria!

The numbers themselves at first sight may look impressively extravagant – billion spent today, and more billions to come. And Mr. Wanless and Mr. Brown have assumed success for public health initiatives, patient involvement, the uptake of new technology, innovation and its diffusion, and productivity improvements – and all on a scale that has never been seen before. This, note, against a backdrop of assumed increases in wages of 2.5% in real terms per year. Yet expenditure cannot be taken as a measure of effectiveness. And the public-sector inflation rate is nearly four times the overall inflation rate of 1.8%. [10]

The distinguished financial writer Christopher Fildes has emphasised that increased public spending does not necessarily correlate to improved public services: "One measure of this spending's efficiency, or lack of it, is the public sector's rate of inflation, now puffing along at a steady 6 per cent. In the rest of the economy competition and choice have held the inflation rate down – if it falls any further, Sir Edward George [the then Governor of the Bank of England] will have to submit an explanation in writing – but these anarchic forces are not to be let loose where the state is the supplier of services. Think what that might mean for the workload." [11] The political risk is that Ministers will be blamed for what they cannot control, since they cannot necessarily ensure that desirable personal and local outcomes actually happen. [12]

There is no clear public-sector relationship between expenditure and healthcare 'outcomes', as these substantial increases in expenditure on the NHS demonstrate. They are accompanied, too, by increasing dissatisfaction. The difference, for example, between the experience of patients in the French system and our own is commonly concerned with staff attitudes. It has less to do with money than might be thought. I had expected that Mr. Blair would go to the polls and show that the change is not coming fast enough, if at all. And that he would focus his own vigilance and vigour on real alternatives, saying "Look, I'm a pretty straight kind of guy. We've tried. It isn't working. So this is what we will all have to do instead…" [13]

This was an enormous missed opportunity. Meanwhile. Mr. Brown's approach represents at least three problems. First, the ideas on which the NHS is based are incorrect, and its results are there for all to see. These statist ideas conflict with the basic principles of voluntary exchange. Second, the numbers produced of the funding that will be available by Mr. Wanless and Mr. Brown do not add up. [14] Third, money without cultural (and managerial) change will not make the necessary differences.

The first point suggests that the system cannot work, no matter at what level it is funded by the state. It cannot achieve its hoped-for sedative effect, for the fundamental ideas are in error. Thus, the state as the compassionate director and controller of individual services; of the state taking over responsibility from the individual – and from mutual-aid organisations created by responsible individuals; of resources distributed according to "need" (which experts decide), and without awareness of cost. Each of these ideas is mistaken, and from these problems much further corrosive distortion follows.

The second point concerns the numbers offered by the Chancellor in the Wanless exercises. They mislead. Even as the economy generated the cash, this did not bring the improvements that a market-led system gives or which funding by social insurance and top-ups can give, as European (and Australian) experience shows us. But Mr. Wanless and Mr. Brown ignored this notion, as they did demand-side change. They gave no serious consideration to alternative funding mechanisms. They thus excluded the immediate benefits of the known alternatives and the unknown possibilities of invention and adaptation in the future – as well as missing the vital point that without price there is no natural limitation on the demand for services free at the point of supply. [15]

Compared to the Brown/Wanless project the alternatives offered by dynamists are rather humble. For they offer no-one total power. They make no assumptions about expert omniscience or political wisdom. They do not rely on political power to insist on a view. Instead, they wait for this to emerge instead from the interaction of free choices. Instead, a more diverse approach – to a mix of funding, to diversity in purchasing, to variety in provision – acknowledges the uncertainties of knowledge. And the potential of alternatives living alongside one another, together with the requirement to test out ideas in practice. There is an expectation of fallibility, respect for human differences, and acknowledgement of the possibility of varied preferences of how best to live. By contrast with the top-down approach there is the offer from Freeman Dyson again: "There is no way to find the best design except to try out as many designs as possible and discard the failures." [16]

The third point suggests that by the nature of the system the investment will not generate improvements of the kinds required, for these concern huge cultural changes. The problem is exemplified by developments, or lack of, in the NHS Cancer Plan, published in September 2000. This was to aim at reducing by 20% deaths from cancer in people aged under 75 within 10 years. Its effectiveness is not clear. [17]

Can we tax our way out of trouble? No. Our ability to tax our way out of trouble is also likely to be much restricted by the huge social and cultural shifts now impacting on the ability of government to tax with consent. The Maastricht rules and the continued development and wider scope of European law, limit the deficit financing of state welfare. And European-wide rationalisation on tax, health care spending, and entitlements will have an increasing impact – direct, indirect, and unintentional, from economic and social policy, and via litigation (for example, the European Court of Justice's decisions on the free movement of patients). [18] The requirements of international competition, too, cause us much concern about levels of taxation impacting on competitiveness, which is essential if we are to afford *any* public services.

Meanwhile, and despite Mr.Brown's insistence, as Alice Miles recently wrote in *The Times*, "The NHS is an odd case of reverse branding – clinging to an outdated brand which no longer reflects, if it ever did, the true identity of the organisation. It's not national, it's not free, it's not equitable, it's not the best in the world, and it's only partially public. Much of what the public has been taught to 'love' about the NHS actually works against their interests, not least the staff within it. Of course, if we understood this we wouldn't support the imminent tax increases 'for the NHS'..." [19]

However, before we can really get down to the kinds of radical reforms which I propose it seems that we may have to go through another period of learning, alas. But we should try to set out what we will do when the opportunity is there. And in terms of a modern, liberal, capitalist and entrepreneurial consumerist society a Conservative Party leader should be waving this flag. Yet here is my complaint about Conservative leaders and Shadow Secretaries of State for Health since 1997. No-one has done it. Even so, as the Swedish commentator Johan Hjertqvist has shown, that even the most retrograde welfare socialist system can be led towards market-driven change by inspired understanding and leadership (and despite opposition from vested producer interests).This has been shown by the Stockholm transition which has both deployed direct incentives and involved professionals in innovations – and in the most unpromising of environments. [20]

Mr. Brown's approach, by contrast, will not work because of many inter-linked cultural, practical and financial factors. Conservative leaders should notice this now. In summary:

a) Mr.Brown's policy. Or ten strikes against change.

It offers a managerial model of health services, which takes its priorities from bio-medicine, which it seeks to make more efficient. This approach, by disciplining professionals and directing them from the centre, offers a more intrusive and more expansionist reliance on planners. It excludes a dynamist model focussed on self-responsibility for those things which are not the fault of heredity, or of misfortune, but result from personal behaviour.

- It offers no direct incentives to doctors or to managers to change their gaze and focus on patient preference (or patient-centredness) in order to deliver good services, and thus to earn incomes from those who have choices.

- It offers no incentives to patients for self-responsible care, for responsible demand on the system, or encouragement to contribute to diversified funding.

- It does not offer more respect for the unique knowledge which only patients can bring to bear, or empower this.

- It does not shift our gaze beyond biomedicine to greater self-reliance and for non-medical changes.

- Government instead insists on top-down, politicised and managerial control. This does not help doctors build appropriate partnerships with patients in new organisations but instead politically manages Primary Care Trusts and Hospitals etc which must respond to political control, Treasury-set budgets, targets, and centralised policy. Such an approach undermines the creative therapeutic development of the doctor-patient relationship, and the impact of faith on outcome.

- Mr. Brown's approach offers more money to primary care, but on a managerial model under political controls which does not enable GP's to direct Primary Care Trusts in response to empowered patient preferences. This makes it unnecessarily difficult for patients to achieve routine access to better care, and for doctors to negotiate with autonomous patients about their hopes, and about the possible and the impossible in medicine itself.

- Government policy has still not achieved the necessary shift of power away from hospitals as the dominant cultural force, and towards general practice, to home-settings, and chronic disease-management which is central not peripheral. It over-privileges hospital-based objectives.

- The NHS still seeks the treatment of patients in bulk, whereas optimal personalised care requires a greater understanding of patients as individuals.

- Mr. Brown leaves undisturbed the hierarchical culture in which doctors continue to take control, routinely and not only in emergency situations, reinforcing the biomedical model. Misselbrook: "the more we control them, the less patients control themselves. That damages the patient's ability to continue to control themselves, which is morally undesirable, and may actually damage their health." [21]

Government is thus failing to encourage a public debate about the proper limits of medicine, and of its domain, of the responsibilities of individuals, and of the selection and training of suitable personalities (not the same thing at all as clever 'A' level gatherers) for medicine in a changing culture. The issues of the true basis of liberty and autonomy, of learning and self-knowledge, in which self-care, self-responsibility, and personal decision-making are all fundamental. They are neither considered nor addressed by the centralising focus of government, nor by its reductionist approach. [22] As a consequence preventive self-care (which is different from statist healthism) remains a marginal activity. Self-knowledge itself is marginalised. [23] And the numbers Mr. Brown offers do not add up.

Consider, too:

b). As a result of these policies...

This approach has serious results, aside from its failure to introduce a flexible, multi-sourced funding structure:

- It wholly excludes the solutions offered by pluralist competitive, market disciplines.

- It dis-empowers the individual and undermines incentives to cope with illness, and to make self-reliant choices.

- It endorses the problematisation of normality by the biomedical culture, and the expansionist definition of "health" with its intrusiveness and its alternatives to autonomy and responsibility, self-care and self-control.

- It suggests that the only definition of health which is credible and useful is achievable within a biomedical norm.

- It tightens a politicised hold on doctors and at the same time undermines their effectiveness, without achieving appropriate individual accountability.

At the same time, it worsens pressures on scarce resources.

- It increases the grip of the state on the individual and on the expectations of the individual, and this undermines the individual's ability to cope.

Alas, to borrow a phrase from Misselbrook, "To the man with a hammer, every problem is a nail." [24]

The cultural commentator Virginia Postrel unerringly helps us. She has said that the centralising, "expert" mentality "overvalues the taste of an articulate elite, compares the real world of trade-offs to fantasies of utopia, omits important details and connections, and confuses temporary growing pains with permanent catastrophes. It demoralises and devalues the creative minds on whom our future depends. And it encourages the coercive use of political power to wipe out choice, forbid experimentation, short-circuit feedback, and trammel progress." [25]

I suggest that Mr. Brown – both as Chancellor and now as Prime Minister – has stood not only against a huge accumulation of evidence, but against a philosophical perspective – that of the dynamist. And against the practical structure of social insurance which works in every other advanced country. He disregards the OECD facts that others do more (and much more successfully) than can be attained by his statist approach. Indeed, his defensive approach has worsened the position, both relatively and absolutely. By making the pain of the present system prolonged he will ultimately build support for alternative approaches, but only after unnecessary and damaging delay. Yet in the present absence of direct incentives – themselves both devices for change and the mirror of a dynamist, open society – politicians of all parties seek various sorts of market mimicry by which to achieve reform and continuing political control.

Mr. Brown's view and the market-led alternative both engage with the future. Each expects the bulk of funding to continue to come from taxation. The debate is not about being for or against tax-payer funding. It is about who will spend the money, and how, and about how to ensure both responsive provision and self responsible individuals. The difference between the two views is in part economic and in part philosophical. It is about whether or not individuals are to be permitted to make legally-enforceable choices as the best way of adaptively shaping service development and provision, and of supporting and directly incentivising *self*-responsibility in care.

The debate goes back to Colonel Rainsborough's Putney address, where he spoke of "The poorest He that is in England [who] hath a life to live as the greatest He", which is a text Mr. Brown would recognise. We have, indeed, much to correct if health care is to be promptly available to all, and if it is to be as good as is commonly met with on the continent of Europe. It is, indeed, an urgent task. Perhaps we should return to the heath at Putney?

NOTES.

1. Milton Friedman, *Capitalism and Freedom* (Chicago, Chicago University Press, 1962; revised edition, 1982), p. x.

2. J. Humphrys, "The NHS isn't dying – just ask my two-year-old boy", *Sunday Times*, 1 September 2002, news section, p.15; S. Pearson, "A day to remember" [Health & Social Care Awards, 2002], *NHS Magazine*, September 2002, pp.8-9.

MONEY IS NOT ENOUGH. OR, WHY MR. BROWN'S APPROACH CAN'T WORK

3. P. Riddell, "All fingers will be crossed at No.10 today", *The Times*, 15 July 2002.

4. In the short-term, the growth in waiting lists has not slowed. Waiting lists rose in July 2002, although the numbers waiting for more than 12 months fell sharply. "2-month limit for NHS waits", *The Times*, 7 September 2002, p.11.

5. A. Miles, "Firms to run hospitals in Milburn masterplan," *The Times*, 15 January 2002; A. Milburn, "We have to give the voters more than this", *The Times*, 7 August 2002, p.18; first leader, "Right idea". An efficacious prescription for the Labour Party", *The Times*, 7 August 2002, p.19; A. Miles, "Labour duel threatens revival of ailing NHS", *The Times*, 8 August 2002, p.18.

6. House of Commons Select Committee on Science and Technology; O. Dyer, B. Christie, "Cancer money siphoned off to pay debts", *BMJ* (324) 2002, p.755.

7. Latest figures at www.doh.gov.uk/dohreport/report

8. R. Robinson, "Gold for the NHS", *BMJ:* 324, 2002, p.987.

9. Department. of Health, *A Plan for investment, a Plan for reform* [NHS Cancer Plan] (London, Dept. of Health, September 2002); www.gov.uk.uk/cancer; A. Frean, "Funding shortfall forces hospices to refuse the dying", *The Times*, 28 August 2002, p.8.

10. D. Smith, "Public sector inflation 'out of control'", *Sunday Times*, business section, 14 July 2002, p.1.

11. C. Fildes, "How to pay more and more for less and less – ask Gordon to collect the money", *The Spectator*, 20 July 2002, p.30.

12. Labour's own 'people's panel' of 1,000 voters, to monitor its performance in office, indicated that public regard for public services had plummeted. Certainly, the pace of delivery of changes in productivity and improved services is slow. In the immediate years which were the prior context for Wanless, between 1999 and 2000 NHS spending rose by 9.2%, but the number of cases increased only by 1%. Between 1995 and 2000 there was a 20% increase in consultant numbers, but only 5% more day cases were treated. In Scotland, with spending 20% higher per person than in England, health outcomes worsened. Additional funding was used by NHS Trusts to pay off debts, raise wages, and cope with public sector inflation at some 4.9%, nearly twice the government's target of 2.5% for overall inflation in the economy. In the first quarter the position deteriorated further, with a public sector inflation rate of 6.5%. This indicator suggested that increased public spending had not been efficient, for in the rest of the economy choice and competition held down the rate of inflation to historically low levels. Perhaps two fifths of Mr. Brown's £5 billion increase in NHS funding in England in 2001 went into higher pay – very motivating in some respects, and good people must be rewarded. But the whole process did not necessarily impact on value as perceived by patients. S. Pollard, "Brown must stop throwing money at state monopolies", *The Guardian*, 16 July 2002, p.20; Melissa Kite, "People's panel blasts public service reform," *The Times*, 1 August 2002, p.4.

13. Fildes, *op. cit.*; first leader, "Beware Mr. Moneybags," *Sunday Times*, news section, 14 July 2002; D. Smith, "Public sector inflation out of control", *Sunday Times*, news section, 14 July 2002; J. Sherman, D. Charter, "Public sector workers to be offered 10% pay rise", *The Times*, 1 August 2002, p.8.

14. See my sketch of Mr. Blair's Great Health Care consultation, in this volume, chapter 17.

15. Price Waterhouse Coopers, the professional services and accounting group, warned in July 2002 that even Mr. Brown's increases in taxes would be insufficient to meet his objectives. Taxes would have to rise by £12 billion a year – the equivalent of 4p on the basic rate of income tax, if the government was to meet its NHS pledges arising from the Wanless report which it had accepted. "NHS pledge 'means more taxes", *Evening Standard*, London, 10 July 2002, p.2. In addition, the centralising King's Fund warned in April 2002 that by the time UK health spending reached 8% of GDP (in 2005-06), the rest of Europe was likely to be spending 10.7% based on a weighted average excluding the UK. This implied that the NHS would need about £30 billion in real terms by 2005-06 than currently pledged. King's Fund, *Five-year Health Check*, ibid.

16. F. Dyson, *From Eros to Gaia* (New York, Pantheon Books, 1992), p.56; D. Wanless, *Our Future Health. Taking a Long-term view. Interim Report* (London, Health Trends Team, H.M. Treasury, 2001); *Securing Our Future Health: Taking A long-term View. Review of the trends affecting the health service in the UK* (London, Health Trends Team, H. M. Treasury, April 2002).

17. The Dept. of Health said that it was starting to achieve some of its goals. There were more cancer consultants in post than in 1999, bringing the total to almost half way to the target of 1,000 new consultants for 2006, although this would still leave us significantly behind the developed world. Speed of referral had improved, too, but again we were still slow compared with developed nations. The quality of the service was still questionable for many patients. CHI reported that many patients were still treated by surgeons and physicians who were not specialists in their field, which clearly reduced the patient's chances. The fact was that for the second year running cancer specialists complained, in August 2002, that money to treat their patients was not reaching the front line. Clinicians said they had received little or none of £255 million ear-marked for cancer care last year, and feared that the £76 million allocation for 2002-3 could also "disappear." Of course, this may be part of the bidding for 'rents' by pressure group interests. But Professor Mike Richards, National Cancer Director, was reported as saying he did not know if the new £255m had reached cancer care. If *he* did not know, who did? At least half of the 34 nation-wide cancer networks set up to lead the fight against the disease and co-ordinate services had been left short of money. Health authorities who received 'ear-marked money', as this was, had the option of what to spend it in different ways. Professor Richard is now Sir Richard. And a Baron to be?]

18. F. Dyson, *op. cit.*, p.243.

19. N. Hawkes, G. Hurst, "Cancer policy on knife edge, Milburn told", 27 August 2002, p.1; F. Davern, "Death rates will be the real test for cancer plan", *The Times*, 27 August 2002, p.4.

20. E. Mossialos, M. McKee, "Health care and the European Union," *BMJ*: 324, 27 April 2002, pp.991-2; B. Duncan, "Health policy in the European Union: how it's made and how to influence it", *BMJ* (324) 2002, pp.1027-1030.

21. A. Miles, "The new me is, alas, much the same as the old one", *The Times*, 27 March 2002.

22. J. Hjertqvist, "Can the UK learn anything from the Stockholm health care transition programme?", in Vaizey (ed.), *op. cit.*

23. Self-knowledge and motivation has a remarkable therapeutic potential, too, as the recent

case of Lara Masters demonstrated. Stricken with a degenerative spinal disease (arteriovenous malformation, or AVM), confined to a wheelchair for six years she refused to accept that she would never be cured, would not accommodate to her disability, and with the power of imagination and the control of mind over matter has trained and strengthened her body and who can stand – and hopes to walk – again. See L. Masters, "Where there's a will to walk, there's a way", *Sunday Telegraph*, 14 July 2002; A. McFerran, "From wheelchair to first steps", *Sunday Times*, news review, 4 August 2002, p.8.

24. Misselbrook, *op. cit.*, p.147.

25. Virginia Postrel, *The Future and its Enemies, The Growing Conflict Over Creativity, Enterprise, and Progress* (New York, Free Press, 1998), pp. xvii-xviii.

16. Inside-out. Or, the contradictions revealed by present policies.

"...where party advantage, the condition of England, and class interest were at stake, men who dismissed clerks and put down contractors with warm conviction, rarely did more than take residence in the capacious doctrine of circumstances." John Vincent.

This previously unpublished essay was written in June 2002. It was the basis of a lecture I delivered at the University of Glamorgan. It could very easily have been written yesterday!

In the Spring of 2002 there were published three singular government documents which told us more of the irreconcilable contradictions (or tensions, depending on your point of view) which remain within health policy and practice.

These were:

- The Final Wanless Report, *Securing Our Future Health: Taking A long-term View. Review of the trends affecting the health service in the UK.* [1]

- Mr. Gordon Brown's Spring 2002 Budget presented by The Chancellor of The Exchequer on 17 April, 2002. [2]

- The announcement to the House of Commons the following day by Mr. Alan Milburn, Secretary of State for Health, of the Command Paper *Delivering the NHS Plan.* [3]

The Wanless Report has had few friends, but it is more honest about the alternatives than its Ministerial sponsor. This, despite its limited remit: "My Terms of Reference specify that I should examine the resources required for **a publicly funded**, comprehensive, and high quality health service…" [Paragraph 2.15, original emphasis].

First on funding and on health outcomes, it commenced with the perspective of *The NHS Plan*, directly contradicting what the OECD reports showed – "the systems used by other countries do not provide a route to better health care." This statement was demonstrably false, even on the level of measuring the resources that comparable nations have devoted to health care, let alone with their evidence of better outcomes.

The claims made for the NHS by comparison with the OECD material was extraordinary, even breath-taking. And neither Mr. Brown's budget nor the final Wanless report offered guidance on a better mix between mandatory and optional funding which we should seek. Indeed, Wanless did not even take a look. His terms of reference forbade it, in effect. And Mr. Brown's Budget, together with the government's headline document *Delivering the NHS Plan* – whilst offering many welcome developments – still further emphasised the contradictions between central control and user empowerment. Their intense focus paradoxically magnified the problems.

There were gains and losses from these three documents. Spending increases on the scale envisaged 7.4% more a year, [over and above the rate of inflation] could hardly fail to make some difference, although as it turned out much of the spend was dissipated. It went to squaring some old debts, on staff incomes, and with funds intended for improving cancer care "disappearing." It was, however, impossible not to welcome this increase in funding, for we are talking about urgently relieving pain and suffering in individual lives, and the funds needed to help prevent many otherwise avoidable deaths.

Even so, the increase still meant an over-reliance on one source rather than on a more mixed funding structure. And it cannot achieve within the NHS what has been routinely achieved over a long period by other comparable European countries whose systems are based on social-insurance, such as those seen in France, Germany, Belgium, Holland, or Switzerland. All of which the OECD shows, get better results than the NHS and extend many lives which, under NHS systems, are not extended. This is in part because in the NHS more cash and more managerial targets are still not directly tied to incentives, sufficient pluralist competition, and public information on individual clinicians, their teams, and their performance. The proof of the pudding is in the lack of increased productivity, efficiency, responsiveness and accountability.

And so increased UK spending significantly increased the cost to each individual, but without there being any contract for guaranteed services between the individual and providers. Secretary of State for Health Mr. Alan Milburn rightly commented that the NHS must move "beyond the 1940s monolithic, top-down, centralised NHS towards a devolved health service, offering wider choice and greater diversity." The proposal to offer service-users a wider (if, as yet strictly limited) choice of hospital or clinical team is very welcome. However, this decision will ultimately depend on the Primary Care practitioner, however much the patient is consulted. This is not the same thing as the individual actually controlling a personal fund with which to purchase a policy guaranteeing them preferred access to care. Money may follow the patient, when the patient is sent by a doctor to a hospital. But the patient will not control the funds, nor make the choices.

There thus remain at the core and kernel of government policy six pivotal contradictions:

- First, Chancellor Gordon Brown's generalised emphasis on competitiveness, but with the NHS exempted.

- Second, the explicit emphasis on creating consumer-led services, but without any devices proposed which financially empower the individual to make choices real.

- Third, the continued lack of effective direct incentives to address the issue of self-responsibility, which is fundamental to improving individual health status while also relieving some of the intensifying pressures on the already over-stretched NHS. . [4]

- Fourth, it has been consistently argued by opponents of social-insurance that the European model is a tax on competitiveness. Yet English companies may now pay four-fifths of the total tax rises in the Budget to fund increased health spending (with the corollary that tax increases depress growth in GDP, and hinder vitally necessary wealth-creation.).

- Fifth, the increase in Ministerial interventions conflicts with strengthening local management (which itself has no incentive to turn outwards to the consumer).

- Sixth, why should any one service be accorded much higher priority than other genuine public goods such as education, law and order, transport, and defence, even if a centrally-funded monopoly can be transformed without the direct-incentives of competition and user-choice?

The Budget offers some ideas which should do something to improve quality. But these are bureaucratic substitutes for the compulsions of markets and consumer choice. Thus, "improved" inspection, audit, and regulation to tackle (for example) what the government's own Commission for Health Improvement recently called "the ineffectiveness of quality control across the *entire* service." (Italics mine). [5]

However, consideration of the Budget and the final Wanless report (which says we should triple current spending levels to £184 billion a year by 2022-23) does not change the analysis of first principles and the proposals to put these into practice already set out. Indeed, they reinforce them.

One major, persistent and perennial public concern is waiting times. The Wanless projection suggests that we shall not catch up with other European countries for many years. In European social-insurance systems (once again entirely wrongly dismissed in Budget week by Gordon Brown and by Rabbi Julia Neuberger, Director of The King's Fund, as less fair than the NHS) there are no waiting times. [6] This attractive situation of no waiting – for the poor just as much as for the better-off – is currently *routine* in many European countries. This is because a different approach to funding, purchasing, and provision of health care (and to social solidarity) was taken in France, Germany, Holland, Switzerland, Belgium early in the last century.

However, realities ultimately find sea-level. I conclude from the Budget and from

Delivering the NHS Plan that there is a significant opportunity for Labour to combine public support for huge new investment in the NHS with further, incremental moves, to introduce genuine market-led change. And that what we shall gradually see will be a fundamental shift towards a market-based structure. Changes will be set in place incrementally, and by trial and error, as the contradictions of present initiatives become fully obvious to the public. They will be stoutly opposed by "Old Labour", and there will be a fight for control of the Party's soul. On the evidence so far [stretching into late 2015], post-Thatcher, there are no indications that the Conservative Party will encourage this necessarily adaptive development, become the part of the consumer, and change the structure fundamentally.

Meanwhile, the concerns remain:

There are no direct incentives for providers to be accountable to consumers.

There are no effective incentives for individuals personally to take seriously preventive care.

That new money will not achieve what is claimed for it by Ministers, in the absence of incentives. Indeed, an *official* study published in May 2002 cast new doubts on whether Mr. Brown's massive injection of cash will produce the improvements ministers are demanding. [7]

That the Budget ignores the issue of price (and value for money) as the basis for consumers to make relative choices, and for markets to evolve. Thus, it cannot bring into balance rising expectations, the diverse sources of funding, and the capacity to provide services

That government persists with a near-monopoly of funding, purchasing and provision, centrally supervised. Thus, it insists that government should and can decide on how much is spent.

That the lack of direct incentives and individual leverage – despite the potential for change which these offer – and the then likely evolution of Primary Care trusts into community insurers. This negativism restricts market development, whilst the Budget has again raised public expectations of achieving "the best health service in Europe."

It will be seen that the Budget (and *Delivering The NHS Plan*) still provides no direct user leverage for choice or financial-empowerment for the individual, which is essential to market development, higher revenues, and new provision. This is the most effective way to encourage a market in public, private, voluntary, and not-for-profit provision.

'Choice' remains an abstract notion. Enabling Primary Care Trusts – by 2004, controlling 75% of the NHS budget – to purchase services from a wider range of sources may be a step towards giving individuals exercising cost-conscious choice and mobility with money. But it is not the same thing yet, just as the 'internal market' of the early 1990s was not a genuine market for there was no systematic consumer choice or much more than very limited competition to attract GP funds.

The suspicion remains that New Labour still believes that government is good at running things, even if the supply of all tax-funded health care does not mean supply by the government. And it will be very difficult for politicians to relinquish power when the system remains predominantly tax-funded.

Meanwhile, the centralised approach – even with some decentralised flexibility – will not achieve a system in which the poorest people in society routinely receive a high standard of care because they will have no individual control of money and no legally-enforceable contract for services. Thus, the Budget does not combine individual leverage with social solidarity so that middle-income people pay for themselves and the poor.

There is still no visible link between the money an individual pays and the services an individual receives. The annual cost to the individual will rise (in one estimate, by David Smith of the *Sunday Times*) from £1,133 to more than £3,000 (in today's prices) in 20 years' time. The commentator Stephen Pollard puts the current figure at £2,387 per taxpayer, rising to £3,854 by 2007 (dividing the NHS budget of £65.4 billion a year by 27.4 million taxpayers). But whichever is right, there will be no transparency in the link between payment and services. The Budget offers no direct financial incentives for change by providers, or for greater self-responsibility from consumers. It provides no direct pressures from financial incentives for vested interests (identified by the NHS Modernisation Board as the greatest obstacle to change) to alter their working practices, and focus unremittingly (and with new attitudes) on the wishes of the empowered consumer. [8]

Even very significantly more money – a boost of 40% in real terms over the five years to April 2008 (two-thirds of which will probably go on pay) – will not necessarily improve performance and quality sufficiently to match European access and outcomes (which themselves are likely to continue to improve, and from a higher base-line). Thus, a political price will threaten, which will itself undermine progress.

The NHS persists with dependence on a single-source of funding, rather than by general taxation supplemented by voluntary extra insurance, and cash payment, and that this will not increase cash, capacity, contestability, or choice. But government continues to argue – despite World Health Organisation global evidence to the contrary – that the NHS system of funding is fairest, and that it does most to help the poor, whereas the triple monopoly of the NHS facilitates middle-class advantage through linguistic, and other kinds of cultural power.

Mr .Brown clearly does not appreciate that devolution must go beyond shifting central control from centre to locality, and that individuals must be in charge of their own lives. Otherwise, the NHS will remain a system of allocation of artificially-restricted resources, undertaken on our behalf (and for our own good) by "experts", even at higher levels of spending.

And so the required imaginative, consumer-responsive management required will not be set in place in the prevailing structure, focused on delivering central targets rather than satisfying empowered consumers.

One result is that the NHS will continue to fail Labour's own key tests of equity and efficiency, of social solidarity, help for the poorest, and optimal outcomes for all. Thus a continuing stream of reports of serious failures – for example, from the Association of Community Health Councils for England and Wales in its annual survey, *Casualty Watch*, which found that patients with serious illnesses are spending up to four days in casualty departments because of NHS shortages. [9]

What government offers instead is targeting, regulation and audit. Important as they are, they are no substitute for consumer-empowerment and market-based reform. For the most valid inspection is informed purchasing and user satisfaction. The necessary mobility of the patient's funds. In addition, in health care it is very important to buy quality, but there is little discussion or understanding of what that means, how to define it, how to purchase it by contract when all the political pressures are to buy volume and access. Further, managerialist and politicised control continues to deter recruitment, depress morale, de-motivate retention, and reduce quality. So, too, does the emphasis on the bio-medical model which undermines self-reliance, draws many non-medical issues into the ambit of medicine, and generates impossible levels of demand.

However, it seems we will have to endure more of the final fling of centralised, bureaucratised, remote control before politicians persuade themselves and vested-interests – and before the public learns by further bitter experience – that this prescription cannot work. Or will not work as effectively as a social insurance approach in which the service-user is both a policy-holder and a purchaser of care to whom insurer and provider have contractual obligations.

The three initiatives – Gordon Brown's budget, Derek Wanless's reports, and the DoH's Flagship *Delivering the NHS Plan* – make it clear that the NHS will thus remain outside the modernised, consumer-driven, service-based economy. Yet government still declares (and perhaps even expects?) to achieve this level – without direct incentives or an insurance-based structure with a broader financial base. It is thus out of the question to be able to attain *current* European standards of clean, modern, efficient, well-equipped, fully staffed facilities achieving high quality care and significantly better outcomes *within 20 years*. Mr.Brown recently told trade union leaders who were opposed to using private finance to build hospitals and schools that "ideological dogma" must not stand in the way. [12]

Physician....

INSIDE OUT. OR, THE CONTRADICTIIONS REVEALED BY PRESENT POLICIES

NOTES.

1. [Wanless Report]. *Securing Our Future Health: Taking A long-term View. Review of the trends affecting the health service in the UK* (London, Health Trends Team, H .M. Treasury, April 2002).

2. .On the Budget, see C. Hall, "Spending must double for the NHS to recover", *Daily Telegraph*, 18 April 2002; E. Crooks, B. Groom, "Brown raises taxes by £8.3bn to fund health", *Financial Times*, 18 April 2002. For a variety of perspectives see S. Pollard, "If we really do have the best possible system, why isn't everyone else trying to copy us?", *The Independent*, 18 April 2002; first leader, "Theory and Practice. Milburn's challenge is to implement flexibility and choice," *The Times*, 19 April 2002; A. Miles, T. Baldwin, "NHS not bound to cost £184bn, says cautious Wanless", *The Times*, 19 April 2002; leader, "Insurance at a premium", *Daily Telegraph*, 19 April 2002; leader, "Mr .Milburn is saying the right things about patient power. But can he deliver?", *The Independent*, 19 April 2002; D. Orr, "Now let the health service get on with its work", *The Independent*, 19 April 2002; leader, "Hey, big spender," *Sunday Times*, 21 April 2002; D. Smith, D .Cracknell, L. Rogers, "So much for prudence", *Sunday Times*, 21 April 2002; S. Pollard, "The great health gamble could backfire fatally," *Sunday Telegraph*, 21 April 2002; leader, "Worse than income tax", *Sunday Telegraph*, 21 April 2002.

Two recent commentaries on social insurance alternatives are L. Craven, *A Radical Alternative to Wanless* (London, Bow Group, March 2002) and A. Browne, M. Taylor, *NHS Reform: Towards Consensus* (London, Adam Smith Institute, April 2002). See also Lord Desai, "You're wrong, Gordon, this isn't the way to heal the NHS", *Sunday Times*, 28 April 2002.

3. Dept. of Health, *Delivering The NHS Plan. New Steps on Investment, New Steps on Reform* (London, Dept. of Health, Cm.5503, 18 April 2002). N. Timmins, "Record 7.4% growth a year for NHS comes with tough audit conditions", *Financial Times*, 18 April 2002, and "A final chance for a return to health", *Financial Times*, 18 April 2002; J. Carvel, "Watchdog with teeth to monitor how the new pot of gold is spent," *The Guardian*, 18 April 2002; D. Charter, A. Frean, "Milburn defends decision to create another new health inspectorate", *The Times*, 19 April 2002; D. Charter, "15,000 doctors and 42 new hospitals," *The Times*, 19 April 2002. The government proposes to strengthen and rationalise audit, and to enhance the role of the existing Commission for Health Improvement (CHI). However, hospital inspections by CHI are "extremely variable", "only consistent in their inconsistency" and "lack precision and authority", according to a study of its recent 25 reports. P. Day, R. Klein, "Who nose best?", *Health Service Journal*, 4 April 2002, pp.11-14. The *HSJ* said "It remains to be seen what effect CHI reports have on improving patient care."

4. Department of Health, *The NHS Plan: A Plan for Investment, a Plan for Reform*, Cm.4818 (London, HMSO Stationery Office, 2000).

5. For example, about half of all English adults are reckoned to be overweight. More than a million prescriptions for obesity were written in 2007, according to the government's Information Centre for Health and Social Care on 31 January 2008. This is an eightfold increase in seven years. Obesity drugs cost the NHS £47.5m in 2007. In 1999 the figure was £4.9m.The ICHSC said the cost of treating obesity and its consequences was between £990m and £1.2bn, or between 2.3% and 2.6% of total NHS expenditure. Some 20% of English men and women have a body mass index (BMI: dividing the weight in kilograms by the square of the height in metres) of 30 or more, which is the definition of obesity. Severe obesity is

linked to a twelve-fold increase in deaths among young adults, and women who are overweight are three times more likely to have a stroke.

Professor Mario Maranhao, President of the World Heart Federation, recently said that "The obesity epidemic is caused largely by an environment which discourages physical activity and promotes unhealthy eating. Urban populations in many countries have changed their diets, increasing their consumption of saturated fats and sugar and reducing fibre consummations. This has a direct impact on children. An estimated 22 million children under five are overweight." In Britain obesity has trebled since the 1980s. Treating it costs the NHS £500 million p.a., and reduced productivity and output costs £2 billion. As Professor Sir Charles George, medical director of the English Heart Foundation, recently stressed: "Medical research can do so much to save lives but in the long run people must take responsibility for their own actions." However, there is evidence in the Health Survey for England, published on 31 January 2008, that there is an increase in people exercising, eating fruit and vegetables, although more people are eating more fat than is recommended. S Connor, "Record fall in heart disease mortality rates despite Britons becoming more unhealthy", *The Independent*, 1 February 2002; C .Ayres, "Health warning: eating can make you fat", *The Times*, 14 June 2002; N .Hawkes, "Overfed, overweight, and over here," *The Times*, 14 June 2002; Sarah Boseley, 'Drug prescriptions for obesity soar to 1.06m', *The Guardian*, 1 February 2008, p.5.

6.Commission on Health Care Improvement, *CHI Investigation into the West of London Breast Cancer Screening Service at Hammersmith Hospitals NHS Trust* (London, CHI, 15 April 2002); H. Rumbelow, "Breast cancer inquiry a 'wake-up call for NHS'", *The Times*, 16 April 2002.

7. J. Neuberger, "General taxation remains the fairest and most efficient method of healthcare funding and the government is right to commit to it," quoted, J. Carvel, "Watchdog with teeth to monitor how the new pot of gold will be spent," *The Guardian*, 18 April 2002. [Neuberger is now a Baroness].

8. Analysis by the Office for National Statistics, in *Economic Trends. Productivity in Public Services*, 14 May 2002, suggested that NHS efficiency fell sharply between 1995 and 2000, while spending climbed by £10 billion – a 25% increase in resources, with an increase of services to patients of 15% which implies a fall in productivity for every pound spent. The concern for Ministers is that raising NHS spending to £105.6 b. by 2007-08 may not produce the hoped-for step change in performance as well as improved public perceptions. Surgeons, too, are carrying out fewer operations than they did in the 1980s, according to data from the Professor John Yates (Health Services Management Centre, Birmingham University). In the second quarter of 2001 the NHS treated only 5% more patients than in the same period in 1997, but Mr. Milburn has said that the number of operations is now increasing. See G. Duncan, "Extra cash for NHS fails to improve care", *The Times*, 15 May 2002; N .Hawkes, "Surgeons operate less despite rise in funding", *The Times*, 25 May 2002. On productivity questions see reasons offered by surgeons for why this has fallen – inadequate provision of beds; nursing and support staff shortages; increased time spent training junior doctors; more time spent on direct patient care; improvement of emergency care; banning of 'parallel' lists – letters on "NHS consultant surgeons' workload," *The Times*, 29 May 2002; G. Duncan, "Extra cash for NHS fails to improve care", *The Times*, 15 May 2002; N. Hawkes, "Surgeons operate less despite rise in funding", *The Times*, 25 May 2002.

9. NHS Modernisation Board, *The NHS Plan: A Progress Report* (London, Department of Health, January 2002).

10. H. Rumbelow, "90-year-old left in casualty for four days, check finds", *The Times*, 28 May 2002.

11. I offered a list of tests by which we can see if the rhetoric of consumer empowerment becomes reality, in my "Safe in *whose* hands? Effective consumer power in healthcare", in E. Vaizey (ed.) *The Blue Book on Health* (London, Politicos, 2002). See also chapter 12. Abolish the customer? Or, safe in *whose* hands? in this present volume, .

12. G. Brown, "We need new investment, not excessive ideology", *The Times*, 26 September, 2001, p.22

17. History as It Might Have Been. And Might Still Be. Labour's Opportunity on Health Care Reform.

"The past is not dead; it is not even past." - William Faulkner.

This essay is, of course, fiction. It was written in June 2004. It was initially intended as a think-tank publication as a pamphlet, but it grew too large for its shirt. However, I kept it, and publish it here since something very like could indeed have happened when Mr. Tony Blair as PM was determined to press forward his agenda for public service reforms as the keynote of his second term from 2001.

We now know from his memoirs that he was himself disappointed that he did not dare to be much more radical in reforming public services. Had these radical NHS reform policies been fully developed we would all be much further forward in making the choice-agenda effective. Both provision, access, and care outcomes would have been improved. At all events, some such discussion will still have to happen sooner or later. What happened to Michael Gove, shunted aside when he sought to reform education and to challenge powerful vested-interests is, however, instructive, and to the public's great loss.

Meanwhile, as an entertainment the paper sets out many fundamental issues which remain relevant in 2015.

It is early Spring 2003. The Prime Minister welcomes an invited group of colleagues to Chequers, the official country residence for successive Prime Ministers since 1921. Mr. Blair has been conferring with his closest advisers about the urgency of further change in public services. He is said to feel that his first term did not deliver enough change. The 'away' weekend at Chequers is one result. It was to be followed in a month's time with a similar meeting with individual patients, volunteers and charity workers.

It is uncommonly warm, and the renewal of the land in the cycle of the seasons has revived every spirit. The house in the Chiltern Hills of Buckinghamshire, forty miles from Downing Street, is looking especially lovely. This is the setting for a vital and extremely private meeting with Trade Union leaders and key advisers, as Tony Blair prepares to take significant new initiatives on health care. The General Election is thought to be a year at most away. For the first time, this unofficial transcript can be published. It has been provided by a contact of a key participant. The transcript – seemingly based on an illicit and now leaked recording by an unidentified participant – does not however give an exact date.

Those attending have driven down in glorious spring sunshine, through the beech woods of Berkshire, to the historic house. They have been shown into their well-furnished, elegant rooms, and welcomed with drinks in the Hawtrey Room. They are now gathered and seated in the Great Parlour, the L-shaped room on the first floor which serves as the conference room.

a). Part One: "Welcome!"

The Prime Minister – who is casually dressed in a startling mauve shirt, with an enormous floppy white collar and short-sleeves, blue jeans and a pair of very battered brown 'loafers' – conversationally welcomes the group. He is drinking tea from a 'Stars and Stripes' mug. The gathering comprises many political 'heavy-hitters', including those responsible to him for ensuring that his policies are developed in detail and then delivered.

The chief purpose of the meeting is to try to keep Trade Union leaders on board, as innovative new health care policy is being finalised. Considerable ground work in preparation has already been done, much of it quietly and privately by John Prescott [Deputy PM]. But the mood amongst unionists has been ugly for months. Those attending (save for Chancellor of Exchequer Gordon Brown, who is abroad – conveniently for him, ducking again!) include virtually everyone who matters if Mr. Blair is to secure his new health policies. He is convinced that he must come to the electorate with an optimistic presentation of a programme for a third term of government. This has often looked a very difficult part of 'The Project.' Thus, a charm offensive, in particular focussed on the trade unions.

The participants are the 'usual suspects' : John Monks (in his last months as General Secretary of The Trades Union Congress – and thought to be a 'modernizer'), John Edmonds (General Secretary, the GMB, also soon to retire), and Dave Prentis (General Secretary, Unison – the opposite of Monks). Invited, too, are those who hold or who have held major appointments in Blair's team: Alan Milburn PC, MP (Secretary of State for Health) and Charles Clarke, PC MP (Chairman of The Labour Party). Clarke – a sceptic on proposed education reforms – is seated next to Alastair Campbell (Chief Press Secretary and PM's Official Spokesman), who is seated next to the PM. On the PM's left are seated two of the other most influential figures, Jeremy Heywood (Principal Private Secretary to the PM since 1999) and Anji Hunter (Head of the PM's office, and, like Campbell, a long-term key confidant.). Next to Hunter sits Sally Morgan (Director of Political and Government Relations). Bruce Grocott MP, Blair's Parliamentary Private Secretary is in and out during the meeting.

The conference table usually only seats 14. And so also accommodated on the additional seats which have been squeezed into the space available, adjacent to the conference table, are the very influential Simon Stevens (Special Adviser on Health Care to the PM; now, in 2015, Chief Executive of the NHS), and Geoff Mulgan (Head, No.10 Performance and Innovation Unit and also of The Forward Strategy Unit, Downing Street). These two, 'though little known to the wider public, have a pivotal influence on policy. Also seated there are Professor [later

HISTORY AS IT MIGHT HAVE BEEN. AND MIGHT STILL BE

Sir] Michael Barber (Head, No.10 Delivery Unit), who gets things done. So, too, is Wendy Thomson (Head, No.10 Office of Public Service Reform), Andrew Adonis (Blair's chief education policy adviser, and Joint Head, No.10 Policy Unit – later Lord Adonis and an education minister) [1], Peter Hyman (Strategist and Speech writer), Professor Paul Corrigan, and Darren Murphy (Special Advisers to Mr. Milburn).

Professor Corrigan has been the architect of much of the detail of Mr. Milburn's policy development. Robert Hill (Policy Adviser) has also been working on healthcare, particularly on possible new changes in the NHS, and will expect to answer questions from trade unionists in particular. Ed Milliband (Special Adviser to The Chancellor of The Exchequer) is there, 'representing' Gordon Brown. The support group includes David Triesman (General Secretary of The Labour Party).They all jostle their papers and their chairs. The atmosphere is not comfortable. Indeed, it looks much cosier than it is. Alastair Campbell – glancing round him – suddenly says, by way of seeking to lighten up: "Bloody hell, let's hope nothing bloody happens somewhere today. There's hardly a soul at No.10 today 'cept some of the 'garden girls'! And the Duty Clerk. They, and the cops on the door, will have to cope!" Anything serious, I'm only a 'phone call away. The only ones not here are Presco [John Prescott], whose in Adelaide, and [Lord] Birt. They've both got the 'Get Out of Jail Free' Cards!'

The Prime Minister (laughing):

"Yes, Alastair. Quite. But Jonathan [Powell] [Chief of Staff] is on-call. So let's just hope for the best – from here and from Adelaide! Bet he gets air-miles, too!

Well, good morning. Hi! Let's make a start. Great to see you! I'm very grateful that you could all come down for the week-end. Very grateful. You are all busy, I know. Plenty to do. It's good to see you all. I appreciate your time. I asked you all here because I want to talk to the serious people. When we're finished today I hope Alastair will be able to brief our discussions as real co-operation for clearing various log-jams to change.

As you all know, I want to consult closely with you all on the next stages of improvement in public services, to which we are all wholeheartedly committed. We've invested huge new sums, and we've seen many improvements. We're doing much better on delivery. I'm not so sure we are as successful as we'd like to be on presentation. And we've still much more to do. In fact, I think we need a new mood. We need new moves. We've got to make more progress. We need new momentum, new confidence, and a more co-operative approach. We need long-term stability, of course. But first we need many more changes than have been produced by the new investment which has just about tripled NHS spending. I know there's lots of light and shade. But that's the bare bones of it. Quite frankly, we're now trying to take a more strategic approach to policy, which is – surprisingly – new territory for government. That's what John Birt is helping us

COMING, READY OR NOT!

with, as a special adviser, with the 'blue-sky thinking.' What he is telling me, by the by, about civil service skills in maintaining the status quo shakes even me. Michael [Barber] is onto that. I owe a lot to JP and to Lord Birt on all this. They have both put in the hours.

Now, I'm not going to say 'Trust me, I'm Tony!'

[Relieved laughter].

OK. OK. Enough! I do need to consult with you very privately. I need your advice. And I need your support. There wasn't enough room on the sofa, or in the den! Anyway, we're better here than in that cramped warren at No. 10.

We're here to work. But I hope you'll enjoy the weekend. Some of you, of course, are already familiar with the place. For others, welcome for the first of your visits. It *is* a wonderful place. So many historic associations. Many historic links with every PM since Lloyd George. And with that John Hampden who was an ancestor of the Civil War hero, with Oliver Cromwell's family, with the Walpole family. And many others. So you'll enjoy that, Brendan! So many important decisions have been made here. No need to stop now!

Frankly, it's no exaggeration if I say that you, too, have an important part to play in our history. When the Trust deed giving this place to the nation was drawn up, Lord Lee of Fareham spoke of "this house of peace and ancient memories". He hoped the place would have a "humanising influence." I'm sure it does, on us all!

[Some audible groans].

It's peaceful here. And it's historic. And, as I say, many important policies have been decided here over the years. Take a few moments to reflect on that history. Churchill broadcast to the nation from the Hawtrey Room, where we all met for drinks when you arrived. It's steeped in history. It's a good place to see things clearly. It's a place with a special spirit. When you're here you soon get a sense of proportion about most things. I've certainly always found it so. Particularly as in politics you have to conduct most of your education in public. And we all know what *that's* like! I think it's a good place for us all to try to consider some important questions together, in a relaxed atmosphere, amongst friends. Above all, I want to reach out to the rank and file through you, and with your help, advice, and support. I need your 'buy-in' to our new ideas.

No Rolls Royces in the car park, I see! Ha! So no-one has given into the temptation of [Lord] Hugh Thomas, the Thatcherite who hired a Rolls Royce when Mrs. T invited him here! None of that pomposity, I'm glad to see. I hope you like your rooms. Do explore the house. Make time to walk in the grounds. Feel free to wander. Do see the rose garden. That's where the famous inscription above the entrance reads "All Care Abandon Ye Who Enter Here." And do use the Long Gallery. It's comfortable. You can relax and talk there. It's not wired, is it Alastair?

HISTORY AS IT MIGHT HAVE BEEN. AND MIGHT STILL BE

And there are some wonderful books. There's the first illustrated edition of *Paradise Lost*. And many other wonderful things. Be careful, though. There's a secret door in The Long Gallery. And there's a false door there, too, but it only conceals a fire hose!

Alan, I see that you are in the Lee Room. When he was Churchill's guest during the war, the Soviet Foreign Secretary Molotov slept there with a loaded revolver under his pillow! Yeltsin had that room, too, when he visited Major here. When Molotov gave Churchill's famous 'V' sign to the Coldstream Guards that formed the Guard of Honour then he got it the wrong way round!

John, you are in the Prison Room, up the spiral staircase. Lady Jane Grey's sister Lady Mary was imprisoned there in the 1560's. But they'll let you out on Sunday evening!

I'm not sure who is in the room with the Russell family portraits – is it you, Dave? Yes? You'll be interested to know it was Carol Thatcher's room, too. No, sorry, you can't be moved into another room. We're full up.

A bloke called Sir Robert Frankland Russell invented the pop-up picture books for his children at Chequers. Just like Conference! Anyway, I trust that you are all comfortable.

This is, of course, a working week-end. We'll not be much interrupted. Mobiles don't work here. But there's good food, and good long walks. There are good books in your rooms, too. I've seen *Vanity Fair* – where someone they want to get rid of is sent to be Governor of Coventry Island! There's a vacancy there now!

The rest of Alan's Ministerial team, plus Adair Turner will be joining us for dinner this evening. Professor Julian Le Grand – *our* Old Etonian! – will come down from the LSE to help us consider key issues such as equity. He'll tell us radical things, but in soft tones. We'll hear their latest thoughts on where we've got to now, and what's next. We've a lot to do once we get down to it today. But do enjoy the time here as well! You've all got Norma Major's book on the house and the estate by your bed-side, together with the little private guide Lee himself wrote for guests. [2] They tell some good stories. I especially like the one about Lord Lee setting up a tractor training school at Chequers, to tackle the shortage of drivers in World War One. In Norma Major's book you'll see she says that on a clear day you can see seven counties, across the Berkshire Downs, the Salisbury Plain and the Cotswolds. I hope we can see clear policies, too! You've all seen the house on Prime Minister's Christmas cards, and several of you have been here before – some of you long before I was elected, some of you actually taking part in Alastair's football matches! But be careful, avoid his Marathon training runs!

Well, we'd better get down to work. You all know what this is about. You've all had the papers. It's about what to do about the NHS. Or, as Alastair says, when he reminds me of a remark made by Mario Cuomo when he was governor of New

York, "It's about who clears the drains." Who gets rid of the blockages to change.

First, let me start by saying, saying, and saying again that we are all deeply committed to the founding values of the NHS. That goes without saying, of course. But I've said it anyway! And the British people expect us to deliver on these values. Fair and fair alike, if you like. But let's all be clear about the *political* position. They gave us the benefit of the doubt last time. They won't do so again. I see your eye-brows, Dave. But they won't you know, Dave. They won't. Look at Phillip [Gould's] polling and focus-group stuff. So we really have got to sit down together and talk seriously about what's happening in health care. And we have got to do some very different things – I won't hide the point – if we are to deliver the values, and survive the changes too. This means working with you, with the staff of the NHS, and maintaining the morale of the people who actually deliver the services.

I've stressed this on several occasions. We've of course got to do that. But we've also got to empower the consumer. Yes, *the consumer*. This isn't an easy line to walk. But I think we can do it, although – as I want to say today – we have got to find real mechanisms by which to do this.

This is a whole lot tougher than any of us ever expected when we came into government in 1997. We thought it was the one issue that would never hurt us. Remember the John Maples memo. You remember? In 1994, shortly after my election as Labour leader, he circulated thata memo warning that the Conservatives could be heading for serious defeat, because of "a feeling of powerlessness and insecurity about jobs, housing, health service, business, family values, crime etc, and no vision of where we are heading." A particular problem, he believed, was the NHS. The public thought the reforms were clumsy and they believed what doctors and nurses say about them, which was almost universally hostile. So we all thought the NHS was forever a Labour issue. But it's all turning out very differently. Even though the Tories are completely clueless about policy. Even though they have completely wasted their opportunity to set out the systematic NHS faults, and to explain the alternatives. Even though they have failed to build understanding for change. Even though none of their so-called Shadow Secretaries of State for Health would get a job here as a janitor. Even so, we still face a series of hard battles, and we must face them together. So, if we may, let's look at what's happened in the NHS since we came into government. And what we can all try to do something about it and its future. We all need a reality check here.

b). First, the money.

There's always lots of excitement and fuss about the money. We're all used to that! No peace from the media – or from some of you! – about the money we spend or could spend. Well, as you all know, we've kept up our spending plans. Indeed, despite all the difficulties, we've done a lot better than we promised. We didn't slow the rate of investment after the attack on America. 9/11. We spent a lot of Gordon's war chest on the Iraq war. But we've still done all we can for the NHS, especially since the extra £2 billion in 2000-2001. There will be real increases of at least 6% every year now. Your members have done well – higher pay and shorter working hours. Bit of a smash and grab, really!

Now we've put good people into positions to help us get change. We've listened carefully to all your ideas. We've pushed all the right management buttons. We've set up all the necessary task-forces. We've done all we can to support public sector pay. We've quangoed ourselves silly. We've got regulators coming out of our ears. We've spent a lot more on improving quality, shortening waiting times, and getting the most seriously ill seen more quickly. We've raised taxes to help to do it all. We wanted to increase spending and to increase the *effectiveness* of spending. But, taking all that into honest account, crucially, I can see – and I can see that the voters and your own members can see – that *it still isn't really working*. Not, y'know. Just not.

[Some audible protests...which PM ignores.]

Or, even if it is working – and I know that some of you want to say that, but hear me out – it's working too slowly, too little, and too late. And Philip's polls tell us people don't believe it's working. A lot of the investment, of course, is in quality. But that takes a long time to show in results. Now we've got to get onto other ground, including the reform of working practices, and increasing capacity. That means getting it where we can – including more work with the private sector and with voluntary bodies.

[More interruptions...]

Give me a break Dave, I'm the one who won the bloody general elections!

You've all said to me that much more has got to be spent. Of course, you are right, more has got to be spent. We've said so long and loud. But a lot of the advice I'm getting says that taxes can't go any higher. And even if they do, unless there is a direct and obvious connection between the tax paid and the service an individual gets, we won't get the credit. We can't keep on diverting funds from investment that creates wealth and jobs, either. That's where the taxes come from, after all. That's dangerous territory. Remember, Thatcher spent much more – she did, you know – but the Tories never got the credit for that. She spent more, but was labelled for "cuts." Quite wrongly, if you look at the actual numbers.

[Guffaws...]

Grunt like that, if you like. But it's thin ice in political terms. And even if we manage to get taxes up so that we reach the European average in government spend – whatever that really is, it still isn't going to be nearly enough. There'll always be demands for more. More new technology, too. More new drugs. All that stuff.

People may or may not want the Euro, or further European integration. But they still know a lot more about what health care is like in many European countries. They travel there. A lot of them see what's on offer. Or hear about it from friends living there, in the sun. And then there's the web. All that's itself a big change in the past few years. And the media won't let up on us now. Look at the latest piece by David Smith in the *Sunday Times* this week. And look at the *Sun's* version of it. Melanie Phillips in the *Mail* hits the same targets, too. That's a lot of middle-England votes. That's a lot of opinion formers. And there'll be a lot more headlines about "Dr. Brown's bitter pill." You know and I know, too, that the more people go on holiday in Europe the more letters we get about the health care there. A lot of them are from your own members. And, we all know, more than 3.5 million of your members also get private insurance of various kinds.

[Audible grunts, and chairs being moved backwards...]

Protests? Well, you're wrong. They do. You know they do, too. Ask your own members. If you dare!

We've done a lot, of course we have. We've made a huge move forward. But meanwhile, we haven't – let's be honest about it – carried the public with us. They don't believe it's working. Everyone knows someone who used to admire the NHS, until that someone went into hospital or tried to get a GP appointment and had to wait five days. Nurses love it, until they actually get into an NHS bed as a patient. *Then* listen to them moan! Staff levels are still at dangerously low levels. We haven't managed to improve management sufficiently. Productivity remains enfeebled. Value for money is crap. Doctor morale is fucking awful, even though GP's are coining it. And even with more nurses attracted back, even with more doctors recruited, it takes a very long time to show any differences. *Real differences* that people see in their lives. And real differences that they express in political support, too. Meanwhile, recruitment, morale, doctor emigration, all give us nightmares.

c). Second, the structures.

So, we've got to look again the structure of the thing. We can't cling to abstractions. We need pragmatic solutions to specific problems. We need a lot more clarity here, too. And more precision. We've got to constantly review our ideals in terms of how they work out in practice. We should recognise that the truth of yesterday might be no more than the superstition of today. And we can't indulge in the dream that it's possible to go back, entirely unchanged, to old ideas. We really have to shift from the ideal to the real. That's actually been my message to the Party since I began. I meant it. I still mean it. I bear the scars on my back.

I'm told by the press that I'm someone who takes no risks. Well, that's not right at all. Actually, it's total balls. And I'm well aware that if we don't get real changes in our approach to the NHS the risks are huge. *Huge.* Humungeous! Not just to the Party and to the majority, though that's obvious enough. But to the people of this country, to our economy, to our place in the world community. I'm told, too, that I'm always abroad, trying to fix the new world order. Well, I'm here, too. And I'm fully focussed on the issues that matter – patients, parents, and passengers.

So we've really got to think seriously about different ways to fund the show, to purchase the care, and to have it provided. Europe is where we've had to look, as well as at Singapore and elsewhere. Alan's been there. I know it's not one system – Europe. The countries are different. Denmark is the most like us. But they've got the same intractable problems as us too. Decentralising hasn't done the job there, because it's decentralising to local authorities, not to patients or their own organisations. That is NOT the answer.

France, Germany, The Netherlands – and even Switzerland; even the Ozzies – are doing so much better. Even in bloody Bulgaria much renal care is better. Even as we move up to the average European spend from the public purse, they all still spend much more as individuals. And that remains the difference between the two systems. More, the ordinary patient has financial clout – and without the need to become political or to join a pressure group. There's more money. From more diverse sources. And they spend it more efficiently and manage the outcomes better. It's going to take years and years for us to catch up. We are decades behind. If we go on as we are we'll never do it. And actually, the gap is growing. Even with bloody Bulgaria, that Bolshevik nightmare! *Bulgaria!* I ask you!

Ed Milliband interrupts: Well, if Gordon was here...

The PM: But he's not, is he?

And you've all seen the recent reviews we did. There are copies in your folders, with Alan's annotations, and David's confidential commentary. Alastair has added an appraisal of the messages that we might expect to be welcomed and used by the media and also what we expect the opposition to say. Please read it. It's coming to a TV and radio station near you.

Now, new technology is the biggest changer, the biggest challenge we've got. The biggest change-maker of the lot. And the first Wanless Report on the NHS told us about the new demands we can expect, from technology – including innovations no-one has thought of or imagined at all. And then there's genomics, and the rising expectations of an ageing population, and masses of new drugs for cancer etc. which we can't afford and have to deny to people.

Everyone is going to want things they have not yet heard of, that they didn't know they wanted, but which they will convince themselves they can't do without. And which we can't afford. We'll have to achieve quite historic and unusually large increases in spending just to stand still. Certainly, spend 10% of GDP at least. Probably 12%. Even 14%. Much more than we'd ever thought.

Adair Turner of the CBI has looked at what we need to do. But he gives us no encouragement that the job can be done from the structure we've got, even if modernised. And what a job the modernisation project is proving to be, too!

I know that Gordon has always said it can all be done, must be done, and can only be done by higher taxes. Maybe. *Maybe.* Unfortunately, he is away at the monetary conference this week-end. But we've discussed this constantly. And we're glad to have Ed [Balls] with us today. His Master's Voice! I think Gordon's view is too optimistic. He thinks I'm wrong. But I still think he hopes for too much from taxes alone. Frankly, it won't work. People need to be more directly linked up, with money more directly related to the personal and individual services they can see they get. And if Gordon wants to go on with re-distribution – as many of you do, and as I want to do, too – then we can use changes in funding structures to get to that, too. We've got to do both – to do more for the low-paid, and to get much better care for everyone. And we've just got to face the political and the health-care realities now. Professor Le Grand recommends weighted vouchers. We've got to look at that.

Alan has done a lot of work, studying Europe, and visiting facilities. Hunting for Spanish doctors, and all that! He'll tell you more in a few moments. He's had meetings with you all separately and privately already, I know. And there will be more.

I know that we've got no marginal seats on the other side of the channel! But, still, look across the channel, and look at the gaps. Look at the beds they've got. Look at the modern equipment they've got. Look at the nurses and doctors they've got. A lot more for every 1,000 people than we have. The devil of a lot more. You've all got the figures there in your packs. Look at the health outcomes they get, too. And no waiting lists in France or in Germany. None! Bloody hell!

[Sullen silences, and then rattling coffee cups…]

That's the truth. And people know it, too. No waiting lists. None to speak of, anyway. And none for routine things, where we ask people to wait a year or more. The perishing Germans, you know, even offered to clear up all our back-list! How come they've got the capacity, if we can't do it? And at an average of £5,000 an operation that's a bill of £5 billion!

Look at the letters we're getting from people Alan has already sent abroad for their operations. They want to know why the French and the Germans can do it immediately, when they've been on the waiting list for 18 months and more. They grab me in the street at elections and shout it at me about their dying husbands and partners. That Sharon Storer in Birmingham when I went to the Queen Elizabeth Hospital there to open the new cardiac unit last May. That woman the local Post-mistress whose partner was supposed to be having cancer treatment. Who couldn't get a bed in a bone marrow unit. And that letter from that woman Mavis Skeet, that 73-year-old whose throat cancer became inoperable after her urgent operation was cancelled four times in five weeks. She was only scheduled the first time for her operation nearly a year after she was first diagnosed with cancer of the oesophagus. Poor woman! And more like her out there, as, we all know.

Just look, too, at the comparisons from the Imperial Cancer research Fund on how long people survive who do somehow manage to get an operation. Bloody ghastly figures. They kicked out that bloke at Brighton when he said so. Major and Bottomley funked it! They should have told the docs what for, and backed that Chairman. This was a pivotal moment. It was the chance to say to the BMA and the consultants, "*We* are in charge, not you. *We* appoint Chairs to Trusts, not you. *We* set policy. So *get on with it.*" Instead, what did they get? They lost a genuine advocate of patient's interests, and then had two further forced resignations as Chairs too.

And look at what happened to Robert Winston's Mother as an NHS patient. Rightly, he kicked up hell. But it's very few who can do that and get action pronto. Just try it if you fill shelves, or if you're a postman, or a fireman, or work in a shop, or rely on your job to pay the mortgage and to feed the kids. Robert's a top doc, a Labour peer, and a TV personality. He *could* raise the winds. But what of ordinary people – what of what happens to them all the time? Bloody awful. Just awful. Just appalling. And avoidable. Definitely. Surely so. Think of that, Major.

And the voters are constantly reminded of our shortages. You'll remember the Royal College of Physicians report that we need an extra 6,500 consultants to provide a safe and effective service, let alone a service like the one that's routine in Germany. *Routine*! Some disciplines in the UK need four times as many extra consultants even now just to reach a safe level. So what have services really been like for the past decades? We've had some staff expansion, of course. Some improvements. But we've a long way to go.

It's an absolutely fair point when people ask why should cancer patients be in such trouble about drugs, too – trying to get access to modern drugs. The Cancer Research Campaign continues to press the case for 'Temodal.' I'm told it's an effective drug for the most dangerous form of skin cancer. But it's denied to British patients. Awful. And why should anyone wait five days to see a GP? Why should anyone face disasters in care in old age? Why should the elderly be kept in hospital unnecessarily because there are no social beds for them to go to? Why have we taken bloody well *forever* to get the one-stop shop concept in place in outpatient departments? A lot of reasons. But including the obstructive attitudes of privileged consultants and of trade unions.

Yes, Dave, let me tell you.

Many out-patient departments *have* been chaotic from the patient's point of view for decades. I know, Alan, that you have this sorted now. But why didn't the system do the job for itself, without having to be sat on hard? The same goes for too many A&E Departments still. Half of all hospital work is done there, but it has low status and very varied performance. Not many of us would like to see our parents or our children admitted there. Not if we'd like them to have a friendly and tolerable experience. A Sussex GP I know certainly told his wife in the clearest possible terms that "If I'm ever ill or in an accident, drive me in the opposite direction from the Royal Sussex County Hospital in Brighton!"

That reforming bloke at Brighton who was driven out by doctors, he knew. He complained about the attitudes in A&E. He said that British cancer outcomes were very poor compared with overseas, too. Particularly in breast cancer treatments. He was bang on right. We are absolutely miles behind Europe in everything. STILL! Ask the OECD. But you can't dare say so. The BMA *will* do you. And so they did for him. But he was right, you know. He said we were losing a lot of lives unnecessarily from our nationally inadequate cancer services. Literally, hundreds of thousands of lives a year. They struck their knives in him for saying that. He also wanted to introduce some payment by results. Desperate heresy then. But right spot on now. He tried to sort out a lot of these issues. And to try to find out what actually went on in that place. I'm told that results are even worse since then.

As I've said, we'd be a lot further on if Major and Bottomley had backed him. They should have said that he was right. He was the local Chairman. He was in charge. Those changes were needed. Even now, we're struggling with it all, with a hardly changed culture. If they'd tackled the doctors then, we'd have had managers in charge, not doctors. What's the language docs use? 'Repel boarders!' Or try to make sure the blokes who come in from outside go native? What they needed to support then was persuasive change-agents, real leaders, and not just more of the conventional admin people they've got plenty of already. Well, I've a lot of sympathy for him. I've got the same scars on my back. But sympathy won't cook cakes, heal patients, or win elections. We've got to do more now. This is the biggest job we'll ever do.

It's not just the doctors, or the managers, or the money either. Look at our inherited, unmaintained buildings, too. Crumbling away. And then look across the channel at the attractive buildings, and the friendly, professional staff in Europe. And at the extra capacity. We're still fourth world. Look at specific areas where quick interventions really save and improve lives. Like renal care and stroke care. The last is particularly shaky. Renal care no better. Just take one European city. Berlin. Alastair tells me that there are 24 dialysis units in Berlin alone. And if you go on holiday in Germany they send you to a unit close to where you are, on your holiday! Compare the cuts to two days a week in dialysis in the NHS. Not nice. And bloody well avoidable. Kinnock was right. Don't be old. Don't be ill. Don't be poor. But, as we've seen, his solution – just bung in the dosh – wasn't enough by itself.

[Sounds of uncontrolled coughs, and of throats being cleared…]

Coffee soon! I know I'm going on a bit. But there's a lot to say.

We need to get through it. Geoff has prepared a big file on European systems. As you'd expect, there is stuff there too from Byzantium, Indian and Chinese experiences! And if you want to know what Xenothon said about healthcare, or what John Nash's puzzles tell us, Geoff will tell you! Alan has briefings from the Department. Much more prosaic. But Geoff and Alan have considered all of it, and tabulated everything. It's very revealing. It really tells you.

This includes all the usual OECD material. But they have also especially looked at it from the point of view of access, fairness, equity, and social justice here in the UK – from our own core agenda, our own founding values. You'll find the results startling. We are not only doing less well than most in clinical areas. Look at cancer – dreadful. Look at heart disease – dreadful. Look at renal care – we're doing less well in key respects than places like Bulgaria! Bulgaria! BULGARIA FOR GRACIOUS SAKE! Bloody rotten, crumbling, out-of-date, agricultural, peasant, Commie, Commissared-to-buggery Bulgaria! For heck's sake!

[Interruption: 'point of order', PM...]

No, *don't interrupt* please, you Trade Union blokes. Let me finish this.

We *are* also doing less well in the terms we all usually stress most, too. Access, equity, safety, fairness, justice, and outcomes. Now, that's a real shock. You're telling me! This isn't a difference in standards due to differences in endowments of natural resources, is it? This isn't about pragmatic, day-to-day management of problems, is it? It's about fundamentals. We've got to get them right. A hell of a lot of people die every day, in pain, unnecessarily, and too damned early too. You can see why I want power to the consumer. And more competition. How else is it all going to change? You tell me!

I've asked Geoff to take the first workshop-session at 10.00 tomorrow morning. He'll take us through all this material. Alan will Chair that. He'll give us his response, too. Please keep in mind the recent MORI poll (done for the GMB, in fact!) which showed that 53% of Labour voters said they would consider voting for another party or not voting at all if they believed that public services had not improved by the next general election. I don't want to have poisoned relations with any of the Unions. I want us to co-operate. Yet, you, John [Edmonds], pledged £1 million of your member's funds would be cut from future Labour contributions when I just *started* to talk about choice, diversity, and decentralisation, only *weeks* after we were re-elected! Pat [Hewitt] had a rough time at your conference, too.

And you, Dave, were threatening strikes throughout the NHS, led by Unison. Strikes! Good for patients? Who else thinks so? Well, I'm not old grey spineless facing the wall with my back to it! Major. I won't funk all this. But I think we'd better break for coffee on that note! Or I'll get too upset again! Let's say half an hour? OK? Fine. Back at 11.00. No time for any kick-about football, Alastair .But when we break this afternoon you can go and get the Burnley half-time score! You've already had your early morning run!

John Edmonds: "Well, Tony, We've all been scribbling notes like mad. And we've all respected your wish not to interrupt, 'though I've been sorely – *sorely* –

tempted! I know we'll all have our shot soon. But let me just say now that I'm reminded of that scene in *Butch Cassidy and the Sundance Kid*. When the Sheriff and his men leap out of the box-car, and ride towards Butch. You'll recall that he says to Sundance, "I don't know what they're selling. But I'm not buying!" And then he rides away as fast as he can!

The PM: No surprises there then, John! And remember where *they* end up!

PART TWO.

a). "You can't get personal !"

The Prime Minister (who has changed into a Denver Fire Service sweatshirt and grey-green tracksuit bottoms):

Well, let's get started again. Over coffee I've been thinking about Butch Cassidy, John. Two outsiders, looking in. They got it wrong. But they realised that power and money stand together. This is why we've got to find ways to put that power into the hands of ordinary people. You know, we've got to look really hard at all the alternative ideas we've persisted with for years. Look at the proposition that you *can* actually get a personalised service put in place through a public-sector monopoly, where your money has been taken from you, but with no legal guarantee of a service when you want it. And look at the idea that you can get good services without incentives.

Well, it ain't so, y'know. It really does look as if you can't, y'know. It really looks as if the only people who can build a consumer-focussed service are consumers, y'know! With managers locally responding pronto. Yet public-sector monopoly has set the basic rule: "First abolish the customer!"

[Some yelps of dismay…]

Yes, I know I'm being contentious. But too often the patient is a bloody nuisance. Why are they interfering with how *we* want to run things? Who do they think *they are*? Bloody lucky to get what we give them, aren't they? So shut up, and get in line. I can see that you, Dave, are having apoplexy. But I'm right. And be careful – remember what I've already said about A&E!

What clout does the ordinary customer, the voter, the patient really have? Voting? Well, they voted for me in big numbers, with landslides in seats. We even won Hove, for gracious sakes! But I haven't been able to change the NHS culture, hardly at all. And I can't deliver the individual service, nor can I (or the local MP) make sure it happens either.

And what about markets? Some of you, I know, don't want to think that markets can work. You insist we can get all the information, knowledge, sensitivity, and discipline without markets or price mechanisms. And that we can do so in advance. Well, it doesn't look like it, does it? Performance is poor, and productivity too. Lousy. Unchanging. Waiting times not much better. Attitudes bloody awful. The new money hasn't done it. Stuck with that culture still.

Apoplexy, Dave! Careful! We've got para-medics here, but bear with me, please. I see those glances and those digs, and John, why are you asking Dave "Why are you kicking me under the table?"!

And, by the by, who wrote the note we found on the floor: "He's been seeing Thatcher again!"? We don't miss much here, you know. You are being watched by Alastair's thought police!

My turn to interject a few replies. I might say here that the decision of the GMB to withhold £2 million from its donation to the Labour Party, and instead to spend it on campaigning against public service reform has back-fired. We don't want any more battles of wills with the Unions. I'm on the side of our friends here in many respects. But we've all got to recognise that the polls show a falling number saying they think taxes should rise to pay for the NHS. Falling! And the polls also show that people want much more of a public-private mix. They don't much care who does the job when they want an op., or where they go – public or private. And they'll go to Europe if it helps them. As Alan says, "Facts is facts." They just want the job done. And all the polls show that people are not convinced that NHS services are improving. You should see, too, some of the private polling stuff Philip [Gould] is sending me! It's political dynamite.

These are your members, too, John. And yours Dave. It's not only that people's willingness to pay more taxes goes on weakening. It's the individual horror stories about the NHS and their families, too. Please don't tell me that that's not the case. Ask those nurses who yell once they become patients themselves. Don't tell me that the Party itself believes you, either. They don't. I hardly need to tell you, I'm *not* that weak twit James Prior! [1] Nab Philip and he'll show you the numbers, and the focus group records. Even among all the depressing trivialities people bring up, that's the powerful overall message. And anyway John, I'll bet your own private polling is telling you the same tale! Yes? Ah!

Some of you have campaigned to get constituency parties to find candidates who take your view. Candidates who will join your campaign versus service change. Those bloody GMB ads asking if you could trust me not to privatise the NHS didn't help, either. John knows how pissed I was about all that. Well, the lists of newly selected prospective candidates we're now seeing clearly show that constituency parties are not having a lot of truck with that idea. They aren't insisting on adopting candidates who are against our reforms. This isn't a Walworth Road fix, either. They're making up their *own* minds. They have a pretty good idea of what St. Hilda's is like up on the hill, even when they campaign to save it. And so we are going to have more support for change in the next Parliament than we've had in this. Not less.

Anyway, hear me out. Please. I think we have made a basic error in our assumptions. I can see there are some grim faces when I say that. But look at Geoff's data. Everybody else seems to have achieved much more personalised services. We haven't. And we are the ones – well, Denmark, too, but no-one else, not even Sweden, which was mad enough to spend 67% of GDP in the public sector in the early '80's – that have persisted with public-sector monopoly. We've actually toughened-up on the necessity of competition in every other area of the economy, even in some areas of education. Gordon pushes this, as you know – but not in health care. I tell him he's inconsistent about enterprise. I don't think he really takes that on board. But between these four walls, the real issue underlying all our discussions is the choice between monopoly and competition. Which of these are we going to protect?

You know, we can't face the country in the old ways any longer. We can't depend and insist on the old NHS model any longer. I don't think you can still insist that your attitude to the NHS is the litmus test of how genuine you are for modernisation, reform, and constructive change. That won't wash any longer. We face a cultural crisis, if we're to redeem the service and remould it. So holding on tight to old attitudes has actually now become a destructive narcissistic pleasure, like contemplating your own image. As one of my civil servants said to me – as they still do – it's the picture of the decadent style. They read the classics, so they tell me that it's like someone called Petronius lamenting a dying civilisation, a civilised man expiring like a perfect gentleman, banqueting with his friends before slowly opening his veins. Well, I don't want that as my final epigram or epitaph! And I can tell you, nor does Peter Mandelson!

I'm not, by the by, interested in all the bloody Marxigook sociology from Sussex University and critics like that. I'm not interested in constant sniping about the social democratic state, and how it's never to be changed one iota. I know all about the class divides in health and in education. I've done more than anyone to improve access to welfare, and to widen participation. I'm interested in getting the job done. And in getting onto safer consensual grounds politically, too, if you want to know. Frankly, we'll make no progress with a lack of candour. It won't work to try to go on insisting we've got the best health service in the world. And that how we do things can't be changed. That won't work at the next election.

And it isn't even true! No-one has copied the NHS. No-one. No other country. Not anywhere. No-one.

And even for us the thing itself doesn't work any longer. If it ever did. Even with the changes with the Concordat with the private sector, which of course is still highly marginal – only some £40m in a £46 billion NHS set-up. And, actually, I think the public know it won't work any more. You just can't fall back on the old safety-net of saying things have to be done the old way, in a nationalised industry, with only trade unionists able to give public service. The public are ahead of many of us already on that. The facts are too obvious to be denied. They know we've only just about kept the rickety, ponderous show on the road. They know, too, that 'public service' is given by every private business in the country. If it isn't, they go bust. We've gone on denying these facts despite all the cyclical and the systemic pressures, despite the war, despite the economy easing. That's all true.

John E: Well, I can't buy that...we've got to protect our members...

PM: But the voters *are not interested* in that special pleading, or any such explanations – those are your problems, not theirs. They know we've just patched and made do. It still breaks down. They see it when they move from saying by heart that the NHS is the best in the world to actually going into hospital, or queuing for an appointment with a GP and having to wait days for it. Try seeing the same GP twice, too. Family doctor? They see strangers. And this despite the new money, despite all the attention we've given it as a priority.

I know that we said it could be changed if we spent a lot more public money and raised taxes. But it's still drifting. We under-estimated the state it was in, how much it would cost to get it right, how long it would take, how much political damage it would do. And we misunderstood the nature of the institution, too, and what money from the centre and more and more targets could actually achieve – without changes to direct incentives. The electoral price all this can impose is huge. I know that's my problem. And Alan's, and Alastair's. But it should be your concern, too. Just look at it. Look at it honestly. Look at with an open-mind. Look at what we all want to achieve. Good care for all. A health system renovated and renewed. A health system which genuinely gives you access when you want it. Proper equity. For a feasible cost. And with good outcomes.

But despite all this huge extra investment, despite this priority treatment, despite my own focus on it, despite all the sheer guts and drive that Alan has shown – and he has – we are still not able to guarantee and to deliver good health care for all. And in many places we can't even deliver safe, basic, rudimentary, reliable care. That's truly shocking. And the voters are shocked. They're awake and alert to it. And ready to say so. And in large numbers. And, you know, good care should be the right of the many, not just the privilege of the few. The staff – your members – want to do more for people, but they just can't get the job done. I've come to you to ask you to support me in real change. Change which will deliver all the things we believe in.

But look, I'm trying to cover a lot of ground. Maybe too much. And I can see lots of people wanting to break in. Well, let's go to lunch and let's air some of the concerns and ideas over lunch. I'll eat while you talk! Back here in 90 minutes? Fine. I'll conclude my review then. And we can discuss the issues more formally. We have got to decide how to play this with the party, the media, and the public too. That's Alastair's patch. The key message here is that to control the debate you've got to control the language. And you've got to have momentum from the start. I'm not very *au fait* with sentences like Gordon's "neo-classical endogenous growth theory." I'm a simple soul. I'm not a politician. I like it simple. Let's break now, with those thoughts in mind.

PART THREE.

The Prime Minister:

a). "It's attitudes, y'know."

Well, welcome back again. We've covered a good deal of the ground so far. As I've said, we've put in the money you always said was needed. Of course, the largest part goes directly into salaries. We really want more people, more people behaving differently too – not the same people just paid more, and without attitudes changing. We all know that.

We've done a lot to direct money to priority areas like cancer care. Heavens, it *was* needed. As I've said, we've tried to get the NHS budget increased by 35% between 1999 and 2005. But the problem isn't only money. It's attitudes. It's management. It's the inherited culture. It's the lack of self-responsibility. It's the vested interests. It's the civil servants, too. It's the attitudes where patients are looked down upon. As some doctors say, "The patient is always right, but we've got some right patients." Funny joke? Some think so. But not me.

What about incentives? People just don't make the connection between life-style and health status, not personally. And the incomes of the staff have no direct relation to public satisfactions. We've not got very far, either, with the self-responsibility of the service-users. There are those, still, who don't believe smoking makes a difference. Or that baking in the sun causes skin cancer. We've got to do something about self-responsibility. But how? I think it's linked to financial incentives again. I'm going to ask the LSE folks to report on this. That's you, Julian.

Now, I still speak to voters. Y'know I do. And they tell me that there's no clear connection between the promised big new NHS personal spend and the assurance that you'll get the personal service. They voted for us – with a huge majority – when we said we'd put the consumer, the patient first. And just look at the troubles we're having to actually get it done! I bear the scars on my back. Just like that Brighton bloke. My private office gave me an article about healthcare that he'd published as being necessarily uniquely timely, personal, individual and intimate. And that you couldn't get it without having control over money. Voting don't do it. Consulting don't do it. Citizens' whatnots don't do it. S'money that does it. As your TU members with private cover know!

Well, he's right. What's that book called, Alastair? *The Invisible Hospital and The Secret Garden*? Yes, that book. If the Brighton doctors had listened we'd be a lot better off, all of us. As I said earlier, [Virginia] Bottomley and Major should have stood up to the doctors then. Bottomley blew it. Major funked it. Cumberlege didn't help. The chief executive was an absentee in the argument. So, too, was the successor in the Chair, that dreadful Emerton woman. The NED's – the lot of them – didn't lift their fingers. And so we're all still stuck with the consequences. It was a pivotal failure to get hold of the doctors, and to tell them that it was the consumer interest which was to come first. That Brighton bloke was years ahead of his time. [2]

The Milliband boys both want us to spend more. Well, more tax ain't the answer, either. It really does look, too, as if people will spend more on their own care which they won't agree to pay in taxes for other people's care. If that's a reality, we need to face it. We've got to find a direct link between what you pay and what you get, once we guarantee that everyone gets a service at least as good as what we have now. That ain't privatisation, John [Edmonds]. That's doing what the NHS is there to do. We've got to offer them a legally-guaranteed contract, where they know that from their taxes they will actually get the care they want, where and when they want it. No more of that lark of them saying "I've paid in all me life", and then people being told "Sorry, mate, it's sold out – get on the waiting list!" Of course, we've all got to pay something towards the care for people who can't pay taxes. Everyone knows and accepts that. That's not hard to sell. It's a done deal. Andrew [Adonis] and Alan [Millburn] both agree with this. But we've still got to find the money. [3]

Now, be honest, you blokes. You know, from what your own members want, that there are better ways. Now – it's got to be said – some of you do try to have it both ways. You attack us for not spending enough, and for seeking to do more with the independent sector. You opposed the Concordat [with the private sector]. And then some of you guide your members on how to get private care if they are a Union member! Why? You want to build members! It works because individuals, in health terms, want quality and timeliness! So they sign up with you! Well, we've got to draw upon that experience to get massive support for the necessary reforms. No way round that, you know. It's obvious that the quality that many of your members see every day, taken for granted by them when they want care, has got to be guaranteed to everyone. It is in an old co-operative labour tradition, too. It's not right wing. And what's good for the union goose ought to be good for the ordinary bloke. Time, too, for him, and her not to be a gander!

What patients get routinely in France and in Germany is only visible here in a few NHS hospitals. And in my new Independent Treatment Centres. Or privately – ask your union members. You know – let me just emphasise this again – from your own members that more than 3.5 million subscribe to independent health care. That's more than half of all TUC members. More than half! You know the places they go to are clean, well-managed, and that patient satisfaction is high. Of course, you don't tell *The Guardian*. Of course, I know that the independent sector doesn't do the most complicated things. I know that when things go wrong they take people back to the NHS.

But that's not entirely their fault, is it? Governments of all parties have made their life difficult. They could build and manage better facilities, if patient cash could flow to them willingly. But we've at least begun to build a better relationship.

The hapless uneducated Major with his soapbox didn't so much as touch that option. Nor did Hague make any move on that. Nor have any of his successors in the Tory leadership. IDS gone before he'd arrived, of course. Haig. Howard. Nowt done. Even Thatcher – there a decade – only tinkered, and kept away from the demand side. She was actually much more pragmatic and craftier than anyone ever believes. She kept away from financial reform. The internal market improved value for money, but it didn't touch the fundamentals. She got away with it, partly because the left was so divided. We're now in a wholly different world.

So, come on. We all know we have a responsibility to offer good quality care to everyone. Bill Morris [who became Baron Morris of Handsworth; General Secretary of the Transport and General Workers' Union 1992- 2003; the first black leader of a British trade union] likes the European labour laws. So he ought to want their health and social care system too! And, you know, there's a lot of value in encouraging people to look after themselves and their families. That's, after all, why they join Trade Unions and Friendly Societies in the first place, isn't it? So, we have all got to think seriously about how we get change, and how we get a consensus for change. About funding, purchasing, and provision.

I'll do my bit. You have got to do yours. Of course, John, we'll protect public sector pay, pensions, and conditions. Of course we must. That, though, has got to be transitional, and not a permanent state of affairs. We are going to have to give more independence to local hospitals, and we can't forever insist on national pay rates. They need local flexibility. They need local deals. We can't be held back any longer by out-dated ideology. Or by those who mount the box on all our behalves, claiming to know our best interests better than we know them ourselves. We owe that to poor old Sidney and Beatrice Webb. Well, thanks but no thanks!

It's not that with one bound we can be free. There's no big systems answers either. However, I've learned from what we tried to do with Frank [Field] and Harriet [Harman] on welfare reform that contradictory messages are a disaster. So for starters, first clear message: we've got to change the way we finance and provide health care. Broader funding, as well as more of it. More diverse provision. Some competition. Shake up the structures. It will take a couple of generations to do it. All the more reason for making a start now! Today's losers mustn't suffer more as we do it. We've got to protect those with pre-existing conditions, and the poor – and that includes the working poor, and especially those suffering from long-term conditions and mental health troubles. Big users of services. We can do that by special individual but compulsory catastrophe insurance as part of the whole package, if we go to social insurance. But we've got to make a start. And now. You know the Tory alternative – "sell em off and tear them down." That's not what we want. We can do a lot better than that.

When you think about all this I think you'll agree: we're at the end of the road for the old ways of doing things. Now, as it is, we can't even guarantee an old lady with cataracts that she will be treated before she goes blind. We can't promise patients who are racked with hip pain that they'll get treated within a year. We can't guarantee that a cancer sufferer will see a cancer specialist. Or that they'll see a doctor who has ever seen their condition before. We can't give people choices, or provide enough revenue. What's the message, get cancer and die? Sorry, can't have drugs they get in Europe. *No way Jose.* We've got people waiting months for life-saving operations. And look at the shocking variations in outcomes that these league-tables in *The Times* are demonstrating. Morale is collapsing. Recruitment is nowhere near enough.

People are finding out where what that Brighton bloke called Dr. Deadwood works. So as to avoid. And where they can instead see Dr. Up-to-date. But they can't be certain to get the first and avoid the second. And there are still too many Dr. Deadwoods, protected by their medical colleagues. Who fear that they are next to be found out. And look at what people like Stephen Pollard – as you know, a long-time adviser to us on health care – has been saying. I've got one of his articles here. Listen to this: "On almost any measure of acceptability – from cancer survival to hospital cleanliness – the NHS forces us to accept conditions which would shame any of our neighbours." And listen to this too: "Switzerland which has a fully private system of competing insurers beats the NHS hands down in its treatment of the poor." A powerful message, and from one of us!

Quick comfort break, I think. Ten minutes?

b). New ideas.

The Prime Minister:

All seen round the house? Make the time, do. [4] And now, just to finish this off.

We've reflected deeply and honestly on many sides of these issues. My research people have done a huge amount of work. I've read mounds of stuff in red boxes. Alastair is preparing opinion. Philip is measuring it. But it's clear we've still got a lot to sort out.

Most critically, we've got to change funding. Need much broader base. To ensure adequate revenues and proper provision. But that money has got to drive cultural change, and not just volume. We've got to get more nurses, doctors, beds, operations – and much better outcomes. We've got to persuade more women nurses and doctors to come back to us after starting their families. We've got to get more money into the system so that we can pay them much better, and in more flexible working. We've got to go on setting the standards, the framework of rules, how things are done. And we've got to make it clear what the government will still pay for. But we've just got to get to a mix of tax, insurance, and co-payment.

This means something like a Medical Savings Account, compulsory insurance which we will have to phase in, tax-transfers to the poor, and all the devices which are carefully set out in your packs. David has done the work, and Paul has devilled with the detail. I've asked Alastair to plan the time-table, to see how we can best influence opinion, to work with opinion-formers, to get the context ready. To get the headlines right. Which he does so brilliantly! And all my policy people are continuing to work on the details, fine-tuning. We are doing all we can to get the context ready for change, and the change ready for the context.

So, y'know, you have to play your part. And, y'know, there's no escape from affordability. Financial affordability. And political affordability. And you've got to help me get this right. I'm appealing from and to our shared sense of values. To deliver good care for all. Free at the point of demand. With everyone covered. And no exclusions. This isn't going to be anything like in America. That's voluntary insurance, but with Federal government interference. [3] We'll make it very clear that we are not going to be like America – although, you know, there's a lot of demonology talked about American health care. The evidence actually shows they have moved towards a much better balance of co-ordinated care, and of public and private. Much more solidarity than formerly, 'though lots of us have anxieties about access and equity there. We shouldn't be put-off by American scare-stories, and the suggestion that that's what it could be like here. Switzerland's magnificent results, their system, should be our model. Should be our aim. Those results.

'Course, we are not going to have people deprived of normal health care, not covered by government or employment funding, and stuck in a health-care poverty trap. No-one left in the gutter because they haven't got a Blue Cross card. We're not going to adopt voluntary insurance. We have thought about all that. But we *can* get cover like in France and Germany, with everyone included on a 'community-rated' basis. That's the right phrase, isn't it, Simon? Yes, it is? Thanks. We want renovation, cohesion, solidarity, and higher quality. And we want it for everyone.

Ok. You've all got some more reading to do. There's a pack of summary reports we've prepared for you to see. And the outline of our policy proposals, with a tentative time-table, and some measure of the Parliamentary time it's going to take, too. I think you'll find that it's a very thorough job. We're here for the whole week-end, so we can all look at the material, and talk it through informally over the week-end. Let's get any problems out in the open and let's debate them. Then we'll confirm the work programme. The real heart of all this is that I'm appealing to your values.

This is about how we can all work *together* to truly deliver the founding values of the NHS. And that has got to be emphasised in every interview, every talk, every article, every party meeting, every trade union branch, every door-step chat. This is NOT about privatisation, sell-offs, breaking up the NHS, dumping the poor, ratting on solidarity, leaving the uninsured in the gutter, shunting the elderly who cost too much, or demanding a credit card at the ambulance door. Nor is it adopting the costly American system. [5]

HISTORY AS IT MIGHT HAVE BEEN. AND MIGHT STILL BE

And, of course, we want a third term, to complete all our other work. No-one hides from that reality. So, do you want to see much better health care here, or don't you?? Do you *want* the Tories back? Do you *want* to win the election or don't you? I do! You do, I know you do. So our Party and your sectional interests have got to take second place to the needs of your government and of the patients. You know what we're saying is right. It's a change that has got to be made. I know it's going to be hard for you to say so right away in public. But I'll value it if you can make the right noises. You know, the novelist Thomas Eidson said, "You weren't born in the woods to be scared by an owl." Keep it in mind!

Actually, you know, the more you think about it, what I'm proposing is what Nye would have wanted. I hear you Dave! "I knew he'd get *there* in the end!" Well, I'm there! He'd have wanted us to deliver the founding values in modern circumstances. And we all hold to those, like the last temple in our souls.
Cherie gave me a quote to read, too. Tennyson was right when he wrote:

> "More things are wrought by prayer
> Than this world dreams of."

No, I'm not going to go on about faith! But let's all be aware of the political requirements. Let me quote something that Matthew Parris wrote in *The Times*. I noted it down in April 1992, two years before I became Party leader. He's no friend of mine. Ex-Tory MP. Close friend of that awful Alastair Cooke. But Parris wrote then: "It is at times of retreat that an army's strengths can be observed best and in moments of triumphalism that we first see the seeds of its downfall." We have got to retreat from centralisation, if we are to go forward to deliver the founding values. We've got to learn the lessons of competition and choice. This is what government must protect against all-comers. We need much more broadly-based funding, too. That's an absolute essential.

What Parris says is really the same thing that Kipling's poem says. That fame as an impostor, too. It bears us all thinking about it when we're looking at what we've got to do to deliver optimal health care. We all have to maintain our integrity and our commitments, even in the face of public resistance.

It's going to be a big transition. And, y'know, you do only find out how something really works when you try to change it!

But it's something I'm very much behind. We've got to raise our game. This really matters. It's really important. And especially if we want to protect and help the weak. Otherwise, why win elections at all?

Of course, there's a sense in which every generation lives in an 'age of transition'. But there are also revolutionary moments, moments of major dis-continuity. We're all at one now. At the point where we're asked to stand up and be counted.

So. Who's in, and who isn't? I for one have got to make a start now, if we're to get this right by the next election. All my policy people are trying to understand the trends we're trying to shape, the cultural changes we see and sense around us. Probably, none of us have these fully within our grasp. To that extent, there's the potential for tragedy. But we've now got to do our very best, and to make some tough choices, and to offer some clear answers. What we've been able to do so far is a mere bagatelle, hard as it's been to do.

As PM, it's my job to try to do much better. To see the pattern in the carpet. To understand the larger shape of events for our country. To maintain our tradition of positive action towards social welfare. But in ways which strengthen the country and improve people's lives. And not to do the reverse. Otherwise, there's no bloody point in being in this job at all.

I've got to make all the big plans, and start the national debate. Now. Well before we go to the country in the autumn of '04. I've said that I think we have to go for different ways to fund, purchase, and provide care, if we are to deliver the founding values. That's initial capitals: Founding Values. That's the basis of Alan's new document which we hope to put the party shortly. The latest draft is in your packs. It's called *Delivering Our Founding Values: Health **and** Wealth: A Better Basis for Personal Security*. Bit long. But good stuff. Andrew [Adonis] is on side for it all.

So, the big question is "Will you back me?" And if any of you won't, just ask yourselves what are the prospects for good care, and for good government? AND for our re-election too! Bleak, I'd say. Bleak. *Bleak*. Bleak. *Really bleak*. And a really tragic waste of the opportunity we have been given these past years. We've all got to decide which side we are on. We've got to get all the issues, the doubts, the opportunities out in the open. This is a really key group of people here today. The big hitters. We've absolutely got to do this together. I don't think there's anyone here who is the least bit surprised by what I've said.

[Very loud groans!]

Ha! That again! Well, clearly it's time for some drinks! And time to get the work done together. You've all read the signs, just like me. And I'm sure you've all read your Kipling, too!

Last words: Churchill…

[More load groans…]

… Churchill made many of his most important war-time speeches on the wireless here from Chequers. I often have a lot of sympathy with him when he wrote of the situation at the peak of the Battle of Britain: "The odds were great; the margins small; the stakes infinite." But, like him, let's show resolution. Let's offer the nation a strong lead. Let's argue the case in persuasive language. Let's all keep our heads. Let's get the narrative right. Let's get it out there. Let's go out and get it done.

HISTORY AS IT MIGHT HAVE BEEN. AND MIGHT STILL BE

I hear that I don't read books, or novels. Well, let me finish by quoting the words of a great Victorian advocate for social and political reform. That old positivist Frederic Harrison wrote about striving after better things: "We are on the threshold of a great time…In science, in religion, in social organisation, we all know what great things are in the air…It is not the age of money-bags and cant, soot, hubbub, and ugliness. It is the age of great expectation and unwearied striving after better things." Or, if you prefer Sherlock Holmes, from *The Sign of Four*, "When you have eliminated the impossible, whatever remains, however improbable, must be true."

Frankly speaking, I've got used to having to span great divides, and at hammering out agreements. Look at Northern Ireland. Look at what we did in Kosovo. Heck, no one thought any of that possible. I had to make a lot of my own decisions. I had to take moral positions and stick by them. And with Peter [Mandelson's] terrific backing. Now you've all got to get behind my modernising agenda for health in our own back yard. Enough of the smoothing iron. People are fed up with the slow pace of change in public services. That means New Labour voters too. They're exasperated. And, frankly, I'm fed up with having to cajole, negotiate, defuse, mediate, and juggle on all this. It's time to get on with it. You've now got to help us deal with the details as well as the big picture. There's a third, and then a fourth, term ahead for the Party. Not for me. I'll be gone. But for the Party. For New Labour. But not if we cede the centre-ground to the Tories. Not if we try to go backwards. Not if we get to be unelectable again, as we were for far too long.

Don't have a seizure, Dave, but please remember with me that we've so often suffered from self-inflicted wounds. That's the bad old days of old Labour. We can go back to that, and lose again. And again, if you like. But I'll be long gone, thanks very much. John, I know that the GMB is the largest manufacturing union with 700,000 members. But keep in mind, too, please, too, that it was your members who voted New Labour. Keep in mind, too, that all unions together now only represent some 20% of the changing workforce, even if there are some 60% in the public sector. So we've just got to take a broader view. You, too, that means!

At all events, I reckon we can't go on having the same arguments. Unless we renew, it's the removal vans for us all. We must be more challenging, especially to ourselves. The country wants more. Even if the Party, even if parts of the government, even if the civil servants, even if the clinicians don't like it. As I keep saying, we've got to do what's right. My key message is: values, and how to make them real. We've got to take reform to a different level. We *can* go forward, and be far out of reach of the Tories on empowering the individual. On that, amazingly, they aren't even on square one. They're going backwards, cozying up to the docs again. But we can empower the patient because it's right. And, if you like because they Tories and their technocrats will have no other possible ground to stand on.

In the end I have to make the final call. That's my job. It's what I'm paid to do. I'm the one who has to step up to the mark as the leader. It's for the many, not the few. That's what gives us our edge over the Tories. So please don't go on misstating what we're trying to do. Quite frankly, that really pisses me off. A bit more use of the public sector isn't at the heart of it. The heart of it is our values. Our aspirations. The services we care about, and why. Both Bevan and Bevin would have understood this – how to deliver our values in changing times.

What was it that Andrew Rawnsley said in his book about us? [6] It's like standing on a heaving ship's deck trying to succeed at that executive puzzle where you have to manoeuvre those steel balls through the maze until they all come to rest in the holes, without one upsetting the others? Well, we have the chance this weekend to really get our heads round such a real challenge – of how to manage, reform, and progress effective public services. To make choice and diversity real. To agree not just a strategy. To agree a real programme. A working-plan for what we are all going to do. When. And why. For real care for everyone. I can't do it all by myself. You can do it. We can do it. Patients themselves can do it, crucially, too. So, let's go forward. Together.

Last of all, I'm tempted just to say, be under no illusion – it *was* New Labour wot won it. *But* it's your turn now. I'm listening! ***Begin!***

The transcript ends at this point. But a very lively formal and informal discussion surely followed.

NOTES.

NB. For the cases concerning Ruth Storer and Mavis Skeet see Andrew Rawnsley, *Servants of The People. The Inside Story of New Labour* (London, Hamish Hamilton, 2000), p.48. For Lord Winston's account of what happened to his Mother, Ruth Winston-Fox, see *New Statesman*, 14 January 2000. *Plus ca change*. Nigel Edwards, *The Challenge of Leadership in the NHS* (London, NHS Confederation, 2007), published on 21 June 2007, pointed to a culture of bullying, poor decision-making and lack of evidence of what works. It discussed the often dysfunctional relationship between managers and clinicians, and the entrenched power of clinicians.

1. James Prior (1927-), arch-'wet' Tory MP 1959-87, a Heathite leader of the anti-Thatcherite opposition inside the party, who held that the government was in no position to challenge the trade unions. He was opposition frontbench spokesman for employment 1974-79, Secretary of State for Employment 1979-81, and held other ministerial appointments. He also held many industrial and business appointments, including Chairman, The General Electric Company, 1984-98. He was by profession a farmer and land agent. Crated Baron Prior 1987. He believed that because he was on first-name terms with union leaders that there was mutual understanding. He was thought to be an appeaser and a defeatist in industrial matters, backed by the then Department of the Environment, which (like the Department of Agriculture) had long been captured by its client unions.

"The key steps to the Blair (2000) approach included a winter crisis in 1999 over admissions, a personal letter from Frank Dobson [Secretary of State for Health] spelling out the absolute requirement for more funding for the NHS, and a series of meetings with clinicians and

HISTORY AS IT MIGHT HAVE BEEN. AND MIGHT STILL BE

health professionals which raised the issues of under-funding and poor outcomes. *Among them was a meeting with key clinicians in cancer services reporting on poor outcomes and lack of availability of drug therapies particularly in breast cancer treatment."* [My italics]. Nick Bosanquet, 'The health and welfare legacy', in Anthony Seldon (ed.), *Blair's Britain 1997-2007* (Cambridge, Cambridge University Press, 2007), p.386. See also Mary Riddell, 'The New Statesman Interview – [Lord] Robert Winston', *New Statesman*, 14 January 2000, which refers to cancer services, his concerns seemingly being motivated partly by anxiety about the care of his elderly mother.

2. As Chairman at Brighton Health Care NHS Trust, responsible for 5 local hospitals, in 1993 I set-up what became a very short-lived Clinical Performance Improvement Unit, with a particular concern for Cancer services, when I asked '"Where is what we do done best in the world, and how do we compare?" My Mother had died of breast-cancer. And I had read in the OECD reports how poor were our national standards and our comparative UK results. I was anxiously concerned to check on and help improve cancer services nationally and locally if possible. I was talking about these OECD reported *national* results when I spoke of us killing people who could have lived. I did not know if services at Brighton rated better or worse than the norm. I am not sure that anyone really knew this. Certainly, comparative performance data was not published. But the docs rebelled, and voted me out. My comments on cancer services were cited to me. Apparently, too, I had not visited every possible department in the five hospitals – although I was, I think, the first Chairman there ever to visit hospitals during the night, where crucial staff were, in my view, insufficiently noticed. My suggestion, too, that clinical staff should be paid by results was particularly offensive to consultants, it seemed. To do it we would have had to learn a lot more than we then knew. They objected to Professor Eric Caines CB (The NHS Personnel Director) advising and supporting this idea. The Clinical Performance Improvement Unit was shut up shop pdq after I left, too.

When it came to a vote about me and my ideas a number of consultants even sent in proxy votes against me – without even coming to the evening meeting scheduled by consultants themselves in their own study centre to hear my ideas and my arguments in their support. One senior consultant told me that he agreed with me, but he had to vote against me. "Peer pressure, old boy", he said. Was there a three-line BMA whip? I thought so. For it takes a lot of organizing to get consultants into a herd. They must have really been alarmed by what I had tried to get done. The local BMA rep was indeed one of – if not – *the* leading consultant organizing the vote. I considered placing a large advert at my own expense in the local *Evening Argus* asking all of the staff if I should go. But there would not have been political support.

Mr. Blair is clearly right. Virginia Bottomley and John Major should have stood up to the doctors then. Bottomley blew it. Major funked it. Baroness Cumberlege didn't help. And the C/E, Stuart Welling, was as mum as a mouse. Indeed, that *parti quatre*, seems by then to have had had quite enough of the fray. You know, the old MFH's cry at the end of a good day out, "Oh, done enough! Done enough! Leave well alone – leave well alone – capital day's sport – horses done enough – hounds done enough – all done enough!"

I was away in Sydney at the time that the doctors began to organize against me, speaking at the first ever Australian conference on Clinical Outcomes organized by the New South Wales Health Board. Neither Mr. Welling, nor the Vice-Chairman, Audrey Emerton, contacted me about what was going on in my absence. It was one of my good friends at work, Mrs. Margaret Dann – one of the patient-focused and experienced Senior Secretaries – who got hold of me in Darwin. She told me. But at least I had the few days camping in Kakadu to think about it. Sleeping under the Southern Cross. Wonderful clear sky.

COMING, READY OR NOT!

Fascinating bird-song at dawn. Some of the happiest days I've ever enjoyed. And when I did get home a good chum, John Simmonds, Vice-Chairman when I was in the chair of Brighton Health Authority previously, gave me terrific support. His view of some of the others can't be printed! My friend Roy Lilley also gave me personal support, and in the press too. As did the leading national nurse Ray Rowden.

I was, however, correct to assert that British cancer outcomes were very poor compared with overseas, too. Particularly in breast cancer treatments. As has been definitively and regularly documented by the OECD. We are *still* absolutely miles behind Europe in everything concerning cancer, as my Stop Press note at the beginning of this volume shows. We are *still* losing a lot of lives unnecessarily from our nationally inadequate cancer services. If Major and Bottomley had backed me we could have made progress. They should have said that I was right. I was the local Chairman. I was put there to be in charge. And to get changes made. They should have said that "We, Ministers, appoint Chairmen, not the docs." Those changes were needed. AND Even now, we're struggling with it all, with a hardly changed culture. If they'd tackled the doctors then, we'd have had managers in charge, not doctors.

And not much has changed since, has it? *The Sunday Telegraph* [19 July 2015] reports in its lead story about cancer services, with demands for huge changes to what is a pretty desperate and disgraceful situation. The Report by the independent Cancer Taskforce – comprised of NHS England, the Royal College of Surgeons, the Royal College of GPs, and others, presents how appalling our results have been for years. We could have done much better if politicians had focused on the things I tried to get done more than 20 years ago. Or if there had been a proper liberal market! But it was not done. It is now said to be urgent and essential to radically change cancer services. Yet for years real change was obstructed by vested interests. Just think of the suffering that could have been avoided if cancer care had been much better these past 20-odd years all across the country.

We are now told that Cancer reforms are to save 30,000 lives per year. So if the changes I had urged in earlier diagnosis and swifter treatments nationally in 1992-4 had been effected, say, within five years, we might have saved 30,000 times some 20 years-worth of lives!!! Coming up towards 600,000 people!!!

The recent Report says that the planned NHS overhaul is to ensure 95% of patients are to be diagnosed within 4 weeks. This is exactly what I urged in 1992! Based in part on what the old Royal Free Hospital in Gray's Inn Road in London did to and for my Mother in 1950. Tony Blair, to his credit, began these changes. Now Cancer tests are to increase, with a definitive diagnosis to be given within a month, followed by quicker treatment. Again, this had seemed right to me in 1992. *The Sunday Telegraph* says that "Figures show that the UK has one of the lowest cancer survival rates in Europe, with around 10,000 more cancer deaths a year compared with similar countries." The determined and new NHS C/E Simon Stevens says that "One in two of us will get cancer at some point in our lives, and the good news is that survival rates are at their highest ever." BUT Stevens adds that "… two fifths of cancers are preventable, and half of patients are currently diagnosed when the cancers are advanced."

This is about better NHS doctoring by GPs and consultants. It is also about education and direct individual economic incentives: reducing smoking, drinking, and obesity and encouraging individual self-responsibility. But it is no good just proclaiming that. Where are the direct economic incentives? Stevens says that waiting times for a definitive cancer diagnosis are to be halved, from 8 weeks. During which 8 weeks, as I said in 1992 to Mr. Brian Hogbin, a senior consultant at Brighton and one of my leading critics, "Patients are very frightened once diagnosed, and waiting for treatment. We need to do much better" But I was told me that this wait made no difference to their clinical results. However, what about "the patient's experience"?

The new 2015 report says that the costs of cancer care will double by 2020 to £13 billion, but the proposed reforms will reduce costs in the long term. Let alone the very stark regional variations in early diagnosis and treatment – which is partly down to educational differences, partly to quality of doctors, of course. We shall see. Meanwhile, the NHS is clearly struggling with an enormous accumulated challenge – one which I had wanted addressed in 1992. It was a tough beat with little or no real support. Like facing great yawning briar-ridden hedges to leap, and a great deep ditch on the other side. Big enough to hold you and your horse. Set up the turnpike gates agin change, they did. And the so-called political leadership as stupid as muttons."

All these years after, I *still* do think of all those desperately frightened patients then, and all of those unnecessarily lost lives, all over the country. Frankly a lot of people should be heartily ashamed of themselves! Bad consciences, &c. But at least Simon Stevens and Jeremy Hunt are on the case now. Yet *they* have got to face their fences, take them in leaps…and enter into the spirit of the thing! Father Time will soon tell us if they are onto the scent at last, and whether they will run from scent to view…or whether their fox will get to earth or in a badger's den once again, and not even be dug out…Stevens and Hunt will need ALL the luck they can get!

Some part of the Brighton story is told here, some part of it is in my book, *The Invisible Hospital and the Secret Garden*. I plan to leave behind in my archive a much more detailed account concerning my experiences as Chairman of Brighton Health Authority and Brighton Healthcare NHS Trust 1991-94, including observations on the unhelpful actions of some non-executive directors then. Mr. Hogbin, Mr. Welling and Ms. A. Emerton [who were friends and Regional Officers together, before joining the Brighton Trust] may not enjoy the texts.

3. Note added 6 December 2007: Andrew – later, Lord – Adonis, originally a journalist, was one of the most vital movers and shakers who backed Tony Blair's instincts. He worked out policies for choice and diversity in education especially. Anthony Seldon, *Blair Unbound* (London, Simon & Schuster, 2007) says he was the prime influence on Blair's radical thinking on public services. See especially pp.221-2, pp. 419-27, pp. 505-11. Seldon offers a helpful summary of what was done. Here, I am struck by two personal thoughts. First, that a number of the ideas brought forward in education reform after the 2001 election were those I had put to the then Deputy Chairman of the Conservative Party, Peter Morrison MP, in 1989/90, when I served for a year voluntarily and unpaid at Conservative Central office as a special adviser on education, particularly on school governance and local accountability, after selling my scholarly book publishing business. These ideas were not then thought to be practical politics. I had urged on Peter and the Party universal academic independence from local authority control; radical reform for all state schools, including the employment of staff and the ownership of assets; change in their governing bodies; funding to come direct from Whitehall; popular schools to be allowed to expand; private school managers, churches and parent groups to be encouraged to open and run new schools; external sponsorship and business-community links; a sharp focus on performance and standards; the encouragement of the evolution of specialist schools.

I also urged a return to selection, too, the foundation of new grammar Schools, the end of mixed-ability teaching, and the discouragement of what I called 'discotheque' teaching in undisciplined classrooms – much of which is still unchanged. Second, Gillian Shepherd MP

(Secretary of State) and the supporting ministers, Robin Squire MP, and the Baroness Emily Blatch did not give encouragement to these ideas when in charge at Education. When I was Vice-Chairman of the Grant Maintained Schools Foundation for 8 years in the 1990s I continued to press for these policies. Alas these were many missed opportunities, under the intellectually unambitious PM John Major. Where would we be now if my proposal that all state schools become Grant Maintained, as independent charities, from an agreed vesting date, building on our experience of the effort to get schools out from under LEA control? As it was, we did no more than help just over 1,000 schools become Grant Maintained. And it was a huge, expensive effort. My friend Sir Rhodes Boyson MP, author of the educational 'Black Papers', with Professor Dennis O'Keefe and others, who chaired an advisory committee I put together, was supportive of radical change, as was Michael Trend MP, who joined the committee at my invitation. Peter Morrison, alas, was not interested. He was, of course, later blamed for his indolence in not properly organising Mrs Thatcher's campaign to remain leader in 1990, when he was her Parliamentary Private Secretary and leader of her campaign team. He died young, aged 51, in July 1995. He collected tin toys. He had a German-made dancing bear on his desk at Central Office. This held cymbals, which clapped when he wound the key. When I put my ideas to him he operated the bear. We got on well personally. But no further progress was made. In 1993 I last bumped into Peter on the seafront at Blackpool, during the party conference. He said then that he much regretted not having been more forceful on these issues.

4. See Norma Major, *Chequers, The Prime Minister's Country House and Its History* (London, HarperCollins, 1996).

5. The American system is much misunderstood. It remains a mixed rather than a properly open-market system. See J .C. Goodman and G .L. Musgrave, *Patient Power: Solving America's Health Crisis* (Washington, D.C., Cato Institute, 1992). Many of its difficulties arise from federal interventions and constraints, not from open market solutions. There is there too little open market, not too much.

6. Blair is referring to Andrew Rawnsley, *Servants of the People. The Inside Story of New Labour* (London, Hamish Hamilton, 2000; London, Penguin Books, revised edition 2001), p.133.

18. Illustrating liberty. The cases of Miss B., & of MMR.

"O me, the word 'choose'!", William Shake-speare.

This previously unpublished piece was written in September 2002. I have not updated it since.

I have argued that both to improve health and social care and to live in a free society where we decide for ourselves we should emphasise and enhance individual liberty and self-responsibility, in tune with the underlying Kantian principle that *individuals* are ends and not merely means.

The issues here were dramatically illuminated in the case of Miss B in 2002. She challenged doctors and said that she wished to decide her own treatment. She insisted that she had the capacity to exercise that right. A similar set of questions were highlighted for public consideration – very controversially – by debate about the MMR – the combined measles, mumps, and rubella jab. Each offered an opportunity to consider issues in recent practice. These have not, I think, been changed in any way by more recent clinical study which makes it quite clear that there is no link between the MMR jab and autism in children. There is no evidence that the MMR vaccine damages the intestine and in turn causes autism. [1] My concern, however, is with the issues of liberty and personal responsibility, not with the clinical evidence about a specific disease which are judgements beyond my competence.

Kant's principle implies that the minimal state should amplify decision-making by the autonomous individual. For people have a right – indeed, the moral responsibility – to control their own bodies, to live their own self-chosen lives, and (by the by) to hope for a good death as an essential of a good life. Indeed, this is a significant factor in defining the wholeness of that good life. Value in life does not arise from 'case history' (interpreted by others on our behalf and for our good), or from 'systems.' It derives from the individual's values within themselves. As Robert Nozick suggests, the individual may not be sacrificed or used for the achieving of other ends without their consent. For each individual has their *own* life to lead. All policy should be founded in this insight. This is the significance of the case of Miss B, and of the MMR debate too. [2]

The important case of Miss B enabled one of our most senior judges to make this point in March 2002. It concerned whether one individual had the right to make decisions about her treatment (including its withdrawal). And whether she had the capacity to exercise this right. Dame Elizabeth Butler-Sloss, President of the Family Division of The High Court of Justice in Britain [constitutionally the fourth highest judge in the land], considered the position of a woman paralysed after suffering a haemorrhage in her spine. The woman, a 43-year-old Jamaican-born former social worker was named only as Miss B for legal reasons. She had lived in England since she was 8 years old. She asked to be allowed to die.

In considering the complexities of the case, Dame Butler-Sloss attacked the "doctor knows best" attitude of the medical profession. Of course, there is no one "medical profession" view. However, in this case, despite a series of meetings, the NHS Trust in London concerned in the case had refused to take adequate notice of the patient's views, Miss B's counsel said.

The Judge stated that she could fully understand the woman's frustration at not having her wish to die (or her refusal to accept treatment, the absence of which would thus lead to her death) respected: "She is getting very annoyed because they won't listen to her. To suggest that her anger and its effect on her relationships should be treated as a loss of capacity is to under-estimate the feelings of patients in hospitals. She is angry with them for treating her in a paternalistic way, as though she isn't fit to make a decision. If you are lying there and not being listened to, I'm not sure this goes to lack of capacity. A lot of patients would absolutely object to that. Serious frustration and anger are natural emotions. You have to go a long way to say that distorts capacity."

The Judge said to Robert Francis QC, representing the patient's doctors, "You seem to be saying that if you want something and the doctors don't think it is a good idea because they want you to do something else, the more you disagree the more you will be regarded as unable to make a decision. That is a dangerous concept. There is a very paternalistic element. It's a very 'doctor knows best' concept. I really bridle at that as a member of the public as well as a Judge."

The Judge subsequently ruled that doctors were wrong not to comply with Miss B's desire to refuse treatment, although she recognised that it was wrong to force the individuals who have cared for her to end her life. She ruled that Miss B was mentally competent when she refused her consent to life-sustaining medical treatment, and that her ventilator may be switched off. Her doctors, in refusing to switch off her ventilator, had misunderstood the patient's wish to die as evidence of mental incapacity. On 30 April 2002 it was reported that Miss B had died in peace after treatment ended. And in August 2002 the General Medical Council issued new guidance that patients should be allowed to refuse care, "even where refusal may result in harm to themselves" – in the doctors or someone else's view – "or in their own death and doctors are legally bound to respect their decision." Clearly, this case has been of the most profound importance. It has many ramifications concerning choice, autonomy, and the doctor-patient relationship in a society which should value liberty – both of patients and of doctors, in appropriate situations – as an end in itself. And it matters in the continuing debate about voluntary euthanasia. [3]

In considering the case, Tom Sensky (Reader in Psychological Medicine, Imperial

College, London) made a number of points about future practice. [4] He recognised the legal principle of "the right of the competent patient to request cessation of treatment must prevail over the natural desire of the medical and nursing professions to try to keep her alive." This principle was contained in a 1999 British Medical Association report, included in new guidelines subsequently issued by the General Medical Council. [5] He then stated: "When a patient makes a decision, especially one with serious consequences, which so clearly goes against professional advice, this alone might lead a clinician to doubt his or her competence. However, this view of clinicians is clearly tautological and goes against the legal principle above. Competence must be established instead on the basis that the patient is capable of assimilating and understanding information about her condition, appreciates the personal relevance of this information, is capable of discussing it with others, and is able to form judgements by weighing up the information she has acquired."

As Tom Sensky stressed, doctors must recognise the difference between values and knowledge. This is the distinction between learning – from books, from practice, from experience – and the essence of the individual. Yet the values of patients – as the case of Miss B, and the issues concerning MMR make clear – have often been set aside in considerations of their competence. [6] However, these values cannot be accommodated merely by insisting on providing more information. Instead, the challenge is to recognise that the *world picture* the patient brings is the compelling factor, both in their own understanding of what is happening to them, and to their response to their own unique possibilities. The experience of illness and the experience of life are at one. And even if values are not static but changeable, it is those values and preferences which the patient expresses at the time which guide them and which should guide the clinical encounter.

This, indeed, is the message of this entire book, and it is one which Dr. David Misselbrook's important study, *Thinking About Patients,* emphasises. I will cite this book in several places here. [7] Clearly, too, a patient might change their mind. This choice should be accommodated, although we just have to accept that if a competent patient insists on the withdrawal of treatment which leads to death then the possibility of what they might have decided later if still alive is no longer part of the picture. This is a necessary consequence of autonomy.

Doctors are, of course, moral agents, too. They have their own autonomy. They must each exercise their own liberty and autonomy, to choose a course of action. But if they are unready to carry out a patient's wishes the judgement concerning Miss B implies a responsibility to find another practitioner prepared to support the autonomy of the individual. A doctor must not insist on his/her own view to the exclusion of other views. Again, mutual agreement should be negotiated. Indeed, this is often met with in palliative care, when patients and clinicians evolve a negotiated approach together in the management of the process of dying. We need clarity on this issue, not least because of the increasing complexity of technologies capable of sustaining "life." And the ambiguities about what constitutes "death."

There are, of course, growing numbers of the very elderly, many wishing to exercise autonomous choices. Sensky helps us with the right note and tone: "When a patient chooses to withdraw from life sustaining treatment, helping that person achieve a 'good' death is a legitimate goal for healthcare professionals. From the patient's perspective, key considerations are adequate pain and symptom management, avoiding inappropriate prolongation of dying, achieving a sense of control, relieving burden, and strengthening relationships with loved ones." [8] This is a superb statement of the intentions of the present book, across the whole range of interventions and responsibilities. We are fortunate, indeed, that Sensky was himself instructed as an independent expert in the case concerning Miss B by the official solicitor, that he was able to make personal assessments of Miss B, and that he received her permission to write up the case.

The debate has crystallised many of the dilemmas concerning choices facing government, the medical profession, the courts, and the individual. It highlighted, too, the risk of reducing the capacity of the individual to learn to choose and to make lay decisions, both within and outside a medical setting. It is vital not to undermine the ability of the ordinary person to seek to cope for themselves. We should tread carefully if we tend towards controls. For this is not an approach which will build the ability to cope with minor illness, or to take preventive care, or to consider the results of one's own actions, or to augment self-responsible liberty, or to make ultimate decisions about one's own life and death. – in advance, or in the latest days.

Then there is MMR, and the issues that the debate about it raised. MMR – the combined measles, mumps, and rubella jab – and the alleged (false) autism link has again dramatised many public policy and ethical issues concerning patient autonomy, personal and state power. [9] It is complex because it concerns parents acting as agents on behalf of minors. However, it raised the issue of whether single individuals, or large numbers of individuals making individual decisions, have the right to behave in a way that "the authorities" think is misguided. Should government's role be restricted to informing the consumer of the research-guidance, except for epidemic situations where there are notable population-benefits? Or compelling people to get their children the MMR jab?

The public outcry concerning MMR raised more than this – it highlighted the importance of popular belief, of popular culture, of the patient's own explanatory models which function in people's lives, and identified a territory which Misselbrook dubs as a folk-map signposted "Here be dragons." [10] This territory contains "some sort of norms about social interaction, childcare, daily living, work, relationships, shopping and hundreds of other mundane life skills." These are complex, and they matter, for they give "a common accepted structure to shared life needs." [11] People prioritise their learning to create a picture of the real world with which they can cope, and which reflects their hopes.

Misselbrook believes that "suspicion is an appropriate adaptive reaction to novelty", although this is the opposite of what dynamists hope to see. However, these apparently "irrational" beliefs – Misselbrook calls them "other-rational" – must be included in the full picture and valued, for they enable people to navigate their world. The values they bring to the negotiation, too, are central to the possibility of their participation in treatments.

It is a very big issue, of how is the balance to be struck between informed consent and the "right" of the state, if there is one, to control an infectious disease? Is there a public interest which the state can determine, and on what grounds? For example, where there are neighbourhood-effects (as economists call them) – such as a problem which will affect many, but which no one single person can prevent. Or for which many consequentially pay a price. How must the doctor or nurse behave, when they are both the agent of the patient and of government? In addition, some doctors insist on there being "The need for a power differential between experts and clients and for an implicit contract between the parties in terms of who delivers the expertise [which] is currently out of vogue." [12]

But evidence suggests that when doctors help patients to understand and to handle uncertainty this is an important part of enablement, both in deciding and in coping. [13] In addition, there is the recognition that patients occupy other 'space' than the clinical encounter. This is important. For the clinical consultation, whilst a key element, is not definitive of the space occupied by the patient. And negotiations about decisions, treatments, and outcomes must occur in a framework of the whole life of the individual, and in a framework of self-care. [14]

The problem is complicated when a minor is involved, and may be thought to be incapable of an informed and responsible decision – either in terms of the individual, or in terms of the impact on the wider community, especially concerning the protection of the pool of all other children, living now and coming in the future. There are numbers of people worried that the MMR vaccine may cause bowel disease and autism. But medical authorities and government want to insist on "compliance", instead of enabling individuals to be adequately informed and to make reasonable adult choices. Of course, MMR is complicated by the fact that adults must make choices for children (their own and those of others) and if population effects are included.

There is the context here, too, that the jab itself can be seen as part of the medicalisation of society. This itself may lead to a pathological society with less good health and more sick people. But the argument of 'public' benefits is that government has the right to insist on something like the triple vaccine, on the basis both of the maintenance of 'herd immunity' but also on the statist basis that it and its experts know best. The argument is that if immunisation rates drop to, say, 60% then herd immunity will be lost, and nearly all of the vulnerable 40% will get measles. This is a very serious concern. There are over 600,000 births per year in the UK, so about 240,000 children would get measles each year. On conservative figures, some 240 would die. Many may think that this in itself may justify and require coercive action. But case law now says that a pregnant woman can, for rational or irrational reasons, refuse treatment even if that fatally jeopardises her unborn child. [15]

Many people insist on making a decision, too, in other areas where others might make a different decision, and where doctors, traditionally, have sought to compel "compliance." Cultural change, too, is running with this wave, and it will be healthy if it reduces the insistence that we should spend 100% of GDP (and more!) on "health" care, on guarding against risk, and on medicalising our lives. However, I think that most people will agree that it is reasonable and prudent to control preventable diseases.

The alternative to coercive direction is both to value the world-picture of the individual patient, and to let the individual decide. Certainly, in non-epidemic situations or situations where 'herd immunity' is not an issue, informed refusal should remain an acceptable choice. The Children Act 1999 highlights parental responsibility, but for adults there should be freedom to choose. And parents still insist that the child is theirs, and it is their choice. Here, persuasion is the best course for government and the profession, not coercion. Then, incentives could be deployed to encourage doctors to offer the patient *the choice*, rather than for giving the jab itself for whatever condition. For example, in 2002/3 GPs were to receive an administration fee of £1.75 and £6.80 for each 'flu immunisation they gave to people aged over 65.

The BMA's GP's committee called for this to be extended to younger, at-risk patients, but was only permitted in Wales and the UK province of Northern Ireland. The question then arose as to why not pay at least a proportion of the fee to a GP who shows that s/he has given the patient the option, who has been provided with literature and given time to choose, rather than pay just for completion of the task. Some GP's wanted an incentive on MMR scrapped as they said it damaged doctor-patient relationships. However, when the recipient of a jab is a child there is a difficult ethical issue. And the state may be thought to intervene reasonably and with reason on behalf of a minor, when the "objective" evidence is said to strongly favour a specific course of treatment. And/or, on behalf of the 'public interest.' But what are the limits of this view?

These two cases exemplify the problem of people being allowed and enabled to make a choice of action when the consequences are both serious and/or hard to predict. They again raise the issue of incentives. And, to generalise the issue, the truth of many conditions is that *no-one* really knows the ultimate consequences of treatment, or the course of a disease for the specific individual. However, in terms of sustainable 'public health status' (which we expect government to address in the wider interests of us all) it is a matter of percentages, and of judgements too about outcomes. And about expected and unexpected side-effects, or what a community and the individuals which comprise it, can accept and live with in the management of the course of any virulent and life threatening disease. Is it the case that here, the individual is the only one who can ultimately know, whatever the advice? Or is there an overriding 'general good'? Most of us would, I think, say so. The complication of MMR, of course, is that the patient is a child. Whose child is it? What are the limits of parenting to be?

Another difficulty is that decisions have a cumulative effect, which is one reason why some fear other people being allowed to make the "wrong" choices. Ultimately, however, I think the only resolution of this difficulty lies not in the individual, but in the wider society. Here, decision-making should be aided and supported by a mix of education and advice, and of access to shared experiences between patients ("like me"), which is being much facilitated by the net. We do want people supported in making independent judgements about the claims of marketing. Essential, is the registration of legal treatments amongst which the individual can choose. But if your child's lack of an MMR jab kills or disables my child, where are we?

We should, of course, recognise that life is intrinsically a risky business. Clearly, the child is taking a risk appraised and decided by others. Yet I do not see how we can avoid the position that we must allow and accept the risk of people making many choices, even if we decide to make some exceptions such as the MMR jab? Thus, homeopathy not chemotherapy, for example, a decision which we might not make for ourselves.

What is a legitimate individual choice is culturally determined, and will change over time, as the shift in attitudes to homeopathy suggests. With all these questions in view, I urge that learning to choose, being supported to choose, having access to genuine and available choices are all fundamentals. Services must be there for everyone who can benefit from them. But in the majority of situations the individual must make the judgement about what counts as a 'risk' what counts as a 'trade-off', what counts as a 'benefit.' Liberty, as ever, is the touch-stone. An issue like the MMR jab affects the liberty of us all, of course. Your liberty may very well significantly hinder the health and liberty of others, many of whom are too young to know this or do anything about it for themselves. And irresponsible Mothers may do harm through ignorance, or unconcern. So we may have to vaccinate the herd? Being aware that all compulsions cost more than the drugs.

NOTES.

1. See Gillian Baird, Andrew Pickles, Emily Simonoff, Tony Chapman, Peter Sullivan, Susie Chandler, Tom Loucas, David Meldrum, Muhammed Afzal, Brenda Thomas, Li Jin and David Brown, 'Measles vaccination and antibody response in autism spectrum disorders', *Archives of Diseases in Childhood*, published on-line 5 February 2008; *Daily Telegraph* reporter, 'MMR vaccine "not linked to rise in autism" ', Daily Telegraph, 18 March 2008, p.17; Chris Ayres, 'Measles cases rise as parents snub MMR jab because of autism fears', *The Times*, 10 June 2008, p.31; Jeremy Laurence, 'Parents warned over measles epidemic', *The Independent*, 7 August 2008, pp.1-2. See also National Autistic Society at www.nas.org.uk.

2. Robert Nozick, *Anarchy, State and Utopia* (Oxford, Basil Blackwell, 1974). See also Ronald Dworkin, *Life's Dominion: an argument about abortion and euthanasia* (New York, Alfred A. Knopf, 1993), and discussion in my *Who Owns Our Bodies? Making Moral Choices in Health Care* (Oxford, Radcliffe Medical Press/Southampton, Institute for Health Policy Studies, 1997).

3. H. Studd, "Woman 'capable of deciding her right to die'", *The Times*, 8 March 2002; M. Hornell, S. Lister, "Right to die case judge attacks medical conceit", *The Times*, 9 March 2002; J. Rozenberg, "'Right to die' woman must wait for ruling", *Daily Telegraph*, 9 March 2002; R. Mendick, "To switch off a life or not. It's up to her", Profile of Dame Butler-Sloss, *Independent on Sunday*, 10 March 2002; J. Rozenberg, "Battling on behalf of the right to die", *Daily Telegraph*, 14 March 2002; V. Grove, "Miss B smiles as judge rules she has the right to die," *The Times*, 23 March 2002; H. Studd, "Keeping Miss B alive was an unlawful act", *The Times*, 23 March 2002; L. Rogers, "Miss B prepares for calm end to her tortured life", *Sunday Times*, news section, 24 March 2002; Law report, "Injury does not remove capacity to consent", *The Times*, 26 March 2002; C. Dyer, "Miss B to move to unit willing to end her life", *The Guardian*, 26 March 2002; J. Bale, "Miss B dies in peace after treatment ends," *The Times*, 30 April 2002; C. Hall, "Doctors told when to stop care", *Daily Telegraph*, 1 May 2002. See also, on the case of Mrs Diane Pretty which raised similar issues, P. Havers, J. Keown, "Two views on the Diane Pretty case", *The Times*, 7 May 2002; S. Aville, "Diane Pretty dies in the way she always feared", *Daily Telegraph*, 13 May 2002; C. Dyer, "Woman makes legal history in right to die case", *BMJ* (324) 2002, p.629; Z. Kmietowicz, "Woman who won right to refuse treatment dies," *BMJ* (324) 2002, p.629.; C. Dyer, "GMC to send out new guidelines on end of life decisions", *BMJ* (324), 4 May 2002; C .Johnston, "Patients win the right to refuse treatment, *The Times*, 20 August 2002, p.2; General Medical Council, *Withholding and withdrawing life-prolonging treatments: good practice in decision-making* (London, GMC, 2002).

4. Tom Sensky, "Withdrawal of life sustaining treatment. Patients' autonomy and values conflict with the responsibilities of clinicians", *BMJ* (325) 2002, pp.175-6.

5. British Medical Association, *Withholding and withdrawing life-prolonging treatment: guidance for decision making* (London, BMJ Books, 1999); GMC, *ibid.*

6. L .C. Charland, "Appreciation and emotion: theoretical reflections on the MacArthur treatment competence study, *Kennedy Inst. Ethics Journal*, 1999 (8), pp.359-76. I owe the reference to Sensky.

7. David Misselbrook, *Thinking About Patients* (Newbury, Petroc Press, 2001).

8. Sensky, *op. cit*. See also P. A. Singer, D .K. Martin, M. Kelner, "Quality end-of-life care: patients' perspectives, *JAMA* (281), 1999, pp.163-8.

9. See "Doctors angry at flu jab limit", *The Times*, 13 August 2002, p.4; B. Taylor, E. Miller, R. Lingam, N. Andrews, A .Simmons, J. Stowe, "Measles, mumps, and rubella vaccination and bowel problems or developmental regression in children with autism: population study", *BMJ*(324) 2002, pp.393-395; R Dobson, "Patient's champion or loose cannon?", *BMJ* (324) 2002, p.386; Z. Kmietowicz, "Government launches intensive media campaign on MMR", *BMJ* (324) 2002, p.383; N. Hawkes, "Questions and answers on the injection debate", *The Times*, 28 June 2002; N. Hawkes, "GPs want to end pay incentives for MMR targets", *The Times*, 3 July 2002; R. Vautrey, "Money and MMR jabs don't mix", *Sunday Times*, news section, 7 July 2002; "Parents put off other vaccines by MMR fear", *The Times*, 20 September

2002, p.8. The debate. Of course, continues. See e.g. Nigel Hawkes, 'Doctors want to combine vaccine for chickenpox with the MMR jab', The Times, 8 November 2007, p.3, which deals with a report in the *Archives of Disease in Childhood*, the journal of the Royal College of Padeiatrics and Child Health.

10. Misselbrook, *op. cit.*, p.93.

11. Misselbrook, *ibid*, p.93.

12. R. Fry, "MMR vaccine debate", letter, *BMJ* (324), 2002, pp.733-4.

13. P. Little, H. Everitt, J. Williamson, G Warner, M. Moore, C. Gould et al, "Observational study of effect of patient centredness and positive approach to outcomes of general practice consolations," *BMJ* (323), 2001, pp.908-11.

14. M. Hurley, M. Pitts, J. Grierson, "Partnership of patient and doctor may provide key to patient satisfaction," *BMJ* (324), letter, 2002, pp.543-4.

15. T. Heller, D. Heller, S. Pattison, T. Heller, "Ethical debate: vaccination against mumps, measles and rubella: is there a case for deepening the debate?", *BMJ* (323), 2001, pp.838-40; P. M .B .English, "General practitioners' two roles are not in conflict with MMR immunisation"; M. Jarmulowicz, "Single measles vaccine should be allowed"; Nick Barnes and Elizabeth James, "There is no room for lingering doubt"; all in *BMJ* (324), 2002, p.734.

19. Is choice disempowering?

'I can only say that while my own opinions as to ethics do not satisfy me, other people's satisfy me still less.' Bertrand, Earl Russell.

Is choice itself disempowering? *More* so than having none? The left would have you think so! This issue is pivotal. It concerns what we believe of one another, and of our potentials to learn and to discriminate.

I have already identified subjectivity as being an important bias for choice, with the individual making any necessary trade-offs in terms of their own values and wishes. Yet some may still query that people are capable of making choices. There is, however, good evidence that patients do make important subjective decisions. And that those with least choice in life welcome more choices. I relate in detail some of the individual stories of the recipients of personal budgets. These demonstrate their empowerment. We know, too, from the work of R. G. Evans, M. L. Barer, R Marmot, Adam Darkins, and others that participation in active decision making improves outcomes. [1]

Do people want to exercise more choice? The success of direct payments and of personal budgets suggests that they do. And that they want information, too, and use it when it is available. So, too, do recent research surveys. Professor Julian Le Grand of the London School of Economics has reviewed the evidence of recent UK research surveys on whether people want choice. The British Social Attitudes Survey, Audit Commission, and YouGov and Ipsos MORI polling evidence suggest that people do want choice. One *Which?* survey contradicts this. But I find Le Grand persuasive. Unsurprisingly, the Social Attitudes Survey and others found that the less well off, usually without choices in their lives, wanted *more* choice in health and education. There were larger majorities in favour of choice among the less well off than among the middle classes – who are the generally least frustrated by the existing system and who can always resort to their cheque books and draw on their social and professional networks.

Dr. Angela Coulter of the Picker Institute and others who studied NHS pilots – have also shown not only that when actually given choice, people take it up. And, again, that the poor and disadvantaged want *more* choices. Dr. Coulter is a left-winger, too, so must have been surprised by her results. But at least she frankly and honourably reported them. The clinical evidence, unsurprisingly, shows that choice *is* indeed good for you. A sense of control has a powerful effect on the ability to respond to treatment and on speed of recovery. In my local super*market* [my italics] my Bengali or Somali contemporary is treated the same as I am at the check-out. But this is not true in the NHS.

Our recent experience of direct social care payments and individual tax-based personal budgets for the disabled and the elderly suggest that people are indeed capable of exercising choices, and that those who have had least choice want more of it. Another recent study by the Picker Institute, suggested that people do want choice, and that the poor want it more than the middle class, who have many ways by which to benefit from public services – and to side-step them if necessary [2]

We have already seen the very serious deficits concerning information in the NHS, and the systemic reasons for this. A rationed system has not wanted to encourage demand. Professionals have preferred to make decisions. Only the well-organised and the articulate have sought to influence outcomes. In a revised structure of choice and of competing purchasers and providers those many intermediary bodies which help overcome patients' ignorance (professionals, such as doctors, the press and Internet, and charities) will still exist.

And they will continue to play an important role. Anybody who wishes not to be informed will be no worse off than today. However, with individuals holding a health savings account a charitable body (such as the RNIB or the Macular Society) can have a direct influence on the individual who wishes to listen, to consider, and to negotiate a choice via their Patient Guaranteed Care Association [PGCA]. At the moment, all these organisations can do is campaign and inform consumers of their rights (which are granted or refused by NICE). But their role will be more important in a choice-based system. And they can certainly rise to the challenge.

A crucial limitation on choice at present is that in the absence of a market *you* have to understand your doctor's job and language (and the choices of treatments and possible outcomes) to know whether he is doing a good job, or to persuade him to pursue another course. With a market, the doctor would be obliged to explain. Already, however, the digital revolution has had an enormous impact here. And the PGCA would help you too. For it would ensure this. Reputation and outcomes would be more important than processes in determining where somebody spent their money. Reputations and outcomes are easier to judge than processes, too. In addition, an important consequence of the competing PGCA will be that the existence of competition and pressure from those who do know will raise the performance of all so that even the ignorant who choose services *at random* will be better off. Notably, Professor Dan Klein has shown in a series of important studies of reputation that markets generate trust and institutions to deal with lack of knowledge in such subjective areas. [3]

In considering whether choice is empowering or dis-empowering we can begin by seeing that ignorance is at least as great a problem in the NHS as it is in a customer-driven service. It would be an optimist who tried to make the case that it is less so. Greater choice seems likely to achieve efficiencies in production, and to find different ways of treating the same problem that are appropriate for different people. Better information, more responsive care, better coordinated care, and individual choice seems likely to be more effective in a savings-driven system than in the NHS. Choice will then be much more empowering.

IS CHOICE DISEMPOWERING?

More evidence in favour of my case is emerging from the pilots in social care and personal budgets. I have urged a bold 'big-bang' (to cover all NHS, welfare, and social services) based on these pilots in social care and in mental healthcare. Policies should be set in a stable framework of economic, social and psychological understanding about how and why we can change the entire NHS too.

Analysis of the pilot projects can help us to address a series of 'standard' objections, including the idea that choice can be experienced as disempowering. Is this true in practice? Does choice generate 'confusion and uncertainty' which could be experienced as disempowering'? It has been suggested that there are circumstances where this is so. But what we know of the results of personal budgets does not echo this complaint. Nor does the study I have earlier discussed undertaken by Professor Julian Le Grand. Dr Marian Barnes and David Prior, however, openly prefer 'voice' to 'choice.' The points to which they draw attention are, however, typically the persistent deficits of the existing NHS.

Thus:

- If there is no information, or poor information, on which to base decisions.

- If people have no influence over the options available from which they are invited to choose and their possible actions are restricted to the range of options presented to them.

- If they have no grounds for confidence that what is offered will meet their needs [sic].

- If people are inexperienced or unskilled in making choices.

- In crisis situations where a speedy response is necessary to avoid or minimise harm.

- When choice creates a dilemma with which people feel inadequate to deal with.

- In situations in which public services are required to intervene in people's lives against their will. [4]

The limits of information that are a requirement of a rationed system hinder the test of predictability, of the user being able to find out about the likely effects of the service in advance. This matters even if we accept the distinction between 'search goods' (which can be tested before purchase, like cars) and 'experience goods' (such as holidays, or medical treatments, on which a judgement about satisfaction is necessarily retrospective). For many of us do want to know what happened to other patients 'like me.' And which doctors did best. Who does the procedure most often? What do other patients say about their experiences and results? Here, fortunately, many user groups are expert patients who have gathered much valuable information on experiences, performance and outcomes.

Here, the internet has dramatically changed the situation. For example, those with long-term chronic illnesses offer much information to one another about treatments, outcomes, risks and benefits. They have developed detailed knowledge which individuals can use to consider alternatives, challenge medical judgements, choose interventions which they know from experience produce effective outcomes. Expert-patient organisations challenge the 'framing' of choices, too, or how these are described and put to patients. For example, choices about when and where a service is provided and by whom are often fundamental factors in their effective delivery, and in the satisfactions of the user. And via Google, advisory patient groups also help people form good and informed mutually constructive relationships with purchasers and with providers.

Such mutual negotiations will be more balanced and more fruitful if the user of a service is informed in these complex and shifting processes, and if they control an Health Savings Accountant [HSA] by which to make their choices effective.

Such a self-organised, voluntary and ever-evolving structure already begins to empower many who would otherwise be dependent on providers, and whose services consumers may otherwise want to question. Groups give help to those who otherwise would have had no previous opportunity or need to investigate possible alternatives. These groups do much to help people develop skills in choosing. Their support and advocacy can be of great help to those who have been used to having no say, or who have – quite rationally, in busy lives – never considered healthcare policy. That is, they have just been getting on with their lives rather than being consumed by political 'activism', or who have been excluded by various kinds of disablement.

As Barnes and Prior say, access to any service depends on knowing that it exists, that it is relevant, and that one is entitled to use it. Choice between services depends on having such information about different options, and on having additional information about significant differences between services in terms of their essential characteristics, and/or the effectiveness and the acceptability of their performance.

As to available options, these are enlarged by competition, and by more effective purchasing. Similarly, alternatives which people feel will meet their case are also stimulated. As to experience in choosing, this is in part about learning to choose, in part about the evolution of assistance and advocacy. Barnes and Prior recognise this in 'the world confronted by impermanence, ambivalence and diversity.' As they say, 'Individuals are faced with the need to choose all the time: it is a condition of being in the contemporary world. And Giddens says "we have no choice but to choose"'. [5]

As to crisis situations, we may have no choice instantly, but once the individual's condition is stabilised we could have many choices. For example, if in a road accident and head-injured, recourse to the nearest A&E is vital. But effective choice thereafter concerns the most appropriate rehabilitation services. The members of a PGCA would know what to do next.

As to dilemmas, this is the land of incommensurables. We all have to choose between alternatives all the time. We expect to make judgements, even if some will have recourse to the statement, "I don't know, doctor. You tell me."' This is in itself a sort of choice, although confidence in the technical and 'expert' knowledge of professionals has declined. As we have seen, too, random decision makers benefit from the decisions others make in the market. And even a patient disinterested in choice must decide, for example, when to see a doctor, and/or whether to purchase non-prescription drugs with advice of a local Pharmacist, or (less reliably?) via the internet.

The point made by Barnes and Prior concerning interventions – such as for the mentally ill – made on our behalf concerns a public policy definition on which there is a body of law, albeit potentially fluid in some respects.

It is a 'cop-out' for Dowding to argue that people do not want choice as such, but that "What we value is getting what we *want*." [6]

How is that to be specified save by the consumer? How is it to be accessed, secured, and delivered, save by 'choice'? How is it to be known in advance, by planners?

It may be right to argue that the creation of alternative options – including choice – do not automatically add value. But here the context, the conditions and the experience of consumers all introduce new elements which can indeed add value. Hayek recognised, too, that value in choice – and in our responsibility for it as adults – attaches *both* to the activity of choosing as well as to the satisfactions in the good chosen. Barnes and Prior are right to recognise that choice is also experienced as risk, and that uncertainty cannot be avoided. And, indeed, the discussion of risk (for example in general medical practice meetings between doctors and patients) is one of the complex problems on which we need reflection. Few of us, doctors included, can estimate it well. But none of us can avoid it, even if we refuse to make choices or regard them as disempowering. [7]

Even so, it is surely false for critics like Barnes and Prior to claim that 'increasing choice cannot in itself be a means of empowerment.' This assertion by them is to use a sledgehammer without a nail. For we have to ensure that the *conditions* for effective empowerment are one of the celebrated characteristics of a democracy. Under the existing NHS this has not been achieved. Indeed, it has not even been attempted.

NOTES.

1. See Harry Telser and Peter Zweifel, 'A new role for consumer's preferences in the provision of healthcare', *Economic Affairs*, **26**(3), September 2006, pp. 4–9. R. G. Evans, M. L. Barer, and R. Marmot, *Why Are Some People Healthy and Others Not?* (New York, Aldine de Gruyter, 1994). Also, R Marmot *et al.*, 'Contribution of job control and other risk factors to social variations in coronary heart disease incidence, *The Lancet*, 350, 1997, pp. 235–9; Michael Marmot, *Status Syndrome* (London, Bloomsbury, 2004); Bruno S. Frey and Alois Sutzer, 'Happiness, Economy

and Institutions', *Economic Journal*, Royal Economic Society, **110** (127), October, 2000, pp. 128–38. I owe the last two references to Geoff Mulgan, *Good and Bad Power*, op. cit., p. 71. See also Adam Darkins, 'Shared decision-making in Health Care Systems', in *Proceedings from the Annual Research Conference 1994, Profession, Business or Trade: do the professions have a future?* (London, The Law Society Research and Policy Planning Unit, 1994); 'Introducing and evaluating an interactive video system designed to give patients detailed information about the likely outcomes of medical care they receive', *Abstract International Soc. Technol. Assess. Health Care Meeting*, **93**(9), p. 61. A recent study of shared decision-making showed that the process of *involvement* delivered benefits for patients, not the action of making the decision alone. See Adrian Edwards and Glyn Elwyn, 'Inside the black box of shared decision making: distinguishing between the process of involvement and who makes the decision', *Health Expectations*, December 2006, **9**(4), pp. 307–20.

2. Julian Le Grand, *The Other Invisible Hand*, op. cit.; Angela Coulter et al., *Is the NHS Becoming More Patient-Centred?* (Oxford, The Picker Institute), 2007. Also, J. Le Grand, *Motivation, Agency and Public Policy: of knights and knaves, pawns and queens* (Oxford, Oxford University Press, 2003); J Le Grand and W. Bartlett, *Quasi-Markets and Social Policy* (London, Macmillan, 1993); J. Le Grand, 'Quasi-markets and social policy', *Economic Journal*, 101, 1991, pp. 1256–67; J. Dixon, J. Le Grand and P. Smith, *Shaping the New NHS: can market forces be used for good?* (London, King's Fund, 2003); J. Le Grand, 'The Blair Legacy? Choice and competition in public services', Public lecture, London School of Economics, 21 February 2006, www.lse.ac.uk; Anna Dixon and J. Le Grand, 'Is greater patient choice consistent with equity? The case of the English NHS', *Journal of Health Services Research and Policy*, **11**(3), July 2006, pp. 162–6; J. Le Grand, 'Competition and collaboration in the English health reforms', Seminar, Nuffield Trust, 6 June 2007, www.wokdock.com

3. D. B. Klein, 'Knowledge, Reputation and Trust by Voluntary Means', in D. B. Klein (ed.), *Reputation: studies in the voluntary elicitation of good conduct* (Ann Arbor, Michigan, University of Michigan Press, 1997); *Assurance and Trust in a Great Society* (New York, Foundation for Economic Education, 2000); 'The demand and supply of assurance', in T. Cowan and E. Rampton (eds.), *Market Failure or Success: The New Debate* (Cheltenham, 2002).

4. Marian Barnes and David Prior, 'Spoilt for Choice? How Consumerism can Disempower Public Service Users', *Public Money and Management*, July–September 1995, 15 (3), July–September 1995, pp. 53–8. See also Anthony Giddens, *Modernity and Self-Identity* (Cambridge, Polity Press, 1991), p. 81. The classic statement is, of course, Isaiah Berlin, *Four Essays on Liberty* (London, Oxford University Press, 1969).

5. Barnes and Prior 'Spoilt for Choice?', op. cit. See also George Jones and Catherine Needham, 'Debate: Consumerism in Public Services – For and Against', *Public Money and Management*, April 2008, **28**(2), pp. 67–77.

6. K. Dowding, 'Choice: its increase and its value', *British Journal of Political Science*, 1992, pp. 301–14.

7. On risk, optimism, personal judgements and what he calls "a necessary consequence of informed, rational decision making" see Steven E. Landsburg, *The Armchair Economist. Economics and Everyday Life* (New York, Simon & Schuster, 1995)., chapter 18, 'Cursed Winners and Glum Losers. Why Life is Full of Disappointments.'

20. The 'My Daughter' test. Championing the patient.

"Every person has two educations, one which he receives from others, and one, more important, which he gives to himself. Edmund Gibbon.

*This material was written as a private advisory paper for Chris Williams and Martin Clarke of the 'Daily Mail' London features department in October 1994. It was also the basis for an introduction I gave to an NHS conference at the NHS Management School at, Swansea, and for a lecture I gave to trainee doctors at the University of Glamorgan.

The job of the NHS bosses is easily stated – champion the patient. Here is the test of how they are doing. *When someone you love has to go into hospital for an operation, does the hospital doctor pass the 'my daughter' test. That is, would your GP send his or her daughter to that surgeon? Would other surgeons and physicians send their daughter there?*

All doctors know the answer to this question, but nearly 57 million of the rest of us don't.

Yet since 1987 in-patient mortality survival rates (which vary widely) have been collected in Britain, but kept secret? Why? It is questions like these that are now being asked about the health service – prompted in good part by the success of the Patient's and other Citizen's Charters in getting the system under scrutiny. For the Charters are not only about making the clinics, or the trains, run on time – though it's a bonus when they do. They are about asking the question or how the Patient's Charter can improve health services. The answer is that we have to get to real quality issues that bite.

The Patient's Charter and the Citizen's Charter are ultimately about the biggest challenge of all in the struggle to modernise Britain. Is the social revolution of the past 15 years to apply to doctors, to teachers, to lawyers, and to accountants? Or are they remain a law unto themselves? The rest of us are accountable to the customer. We have to prove that what we do works. We have to prove value for money. We have to do a good job, and our performance has to be open to comparison and assessment. The laggards have to change, or go.

If this is important about train times, isn't it vital when we are talking life or death? Isn't it right to focus on the customer, and to ask what they want and value? Isn't it bizarre that we can't answer the 'my daughter' question openly, and for all? The NHS is a service where most users have no choice, can't afford to go elsewhere, and can't hit back. We have to find ways to open out the system to information and to choice.

The Patient's charter is a revolution based on information for the customer. To doctors – the great majority of whom work hard and are deeply committed – we have to say that medical accountability is complex. But let's do it. It's not so complex that we can get away with not doing it.

Look at the hard issues, like getting early and accurate diagnoses, appropriate referrals to the right specialist, better, prompt, informed, kindly expert breast cancer care. One in 12 women will develop breast cancer. Some 12,000 women and 98 men will die of breast cancer in the UK this year. Early diagnosis increases the chances of better care and survival, as do appropriate treatments. This is a *real* choice between Dr. Up-To-Date – the specialist who will keep more people alive – and Dr. Deadwood – the occasional meddler – who won't.

Professor John Yates, Director of the NHS's own inter-authority comparisons and consultancy until at the University of Birmingham, told the Royal Society of Medicine on 11 April this year [address, *Variety is the Price of Death*] that deaths of breast cancer patients after surgery **are six times higher for some surgeons than for others**. The reasons are not being investigated because hospital managers fear confrontation with doctors. And local Trust boards, many of whom are too weak, still believe that ignorance is bliss. Yet we know that those surgeons that operate on at least 50 breast cancer patients a year have better skills and lower complication rates than those who operate on only a few.

The Patient's Charter now has to bite here – for GPs and Health Authorities – and prospective patients! – *still* cannot find out how many operations surgeons perform. It should be a Charter standard for this figure to be published. Surgical information enabling the performance of hospitals and surgeons to be compared has been available for 30 years but has never been used. The Patient's Charter should tackle this. There will be an almighty fuss, for a raw nerve will be touched. But who owns the service, and why? Why shouldn't we know how well they do it? We spend 100 million pounds a day on it.

Outcome indicators – the jargon of what works and what doesn't – should be a Charter focus and a requirement for all those providing health services. Those who don't publish the details should not be given any business. Otherwise, a knowledge-based, science-based, best-practice and individualised health service will be a myth.

In other areas the same questions need to be asked. Did the new hip work? Did the pain stop? Was your eyesight improved? Did you need the job done? Did the doctor know what he/she was doing? What were attitudes and your experiences like?

We want clinicians, patients and carers together to share decision-making and to identify best practice. We want management and the contract culture of the health service reforms to enforce it. The objective is clear and simple: if you can deliver the best quality of care in some places, then we must make sure that everyone can

THE 'MY DAUGHTER' TEST. CHAMPIONING THE PATIENT

do it, and everyone can get it. That is the objective. We want it right. We want to know what patients think is right. We want it now. And with the costs right, too.

It's of course important for the Citizen's Charter to drive down waiting times, but we have to tell the truth about a focus on activity, with merely doing more not being sufficient. If much of what we do to people has no clear benefit, doing more is probably doing worse.

There's a second area for the Patient's Charter to examine. That's patient power and patient audit. It means asking do we truly believe that patients and users are the owners of the NHS? Do we truly believe that *it's a requirement* to satisfy them, rather than merely a purpose? Can what patients want really drive the system? This means asking them what they would like the Charter to tackle next. And surely it isn't bizarre to ask users what they want – they pay for, own, and use the services. It's more bizarre to ask the professionals alone to run it as they wish. They are there to do a job for which they are paid. If every individual held a healthcare fund, in a Health Savings Account, it would all come out.

The Prime Minister led the way on the Patient's and the Citizen's Charter. They both came down from above – as if from a Seagull, some said – but this was probably the only way we could have kicked started the process of cultural change. Now we need to be really challenging, dig deep, ask tough questions, and ensure that the Patient's Charter *is* for the patients, not for the NHS management to marginalise.

There are three shots at the target. We have to get to the real quality issues – who lives and who dies, with which doctors and why. We have to get patients to tell us what they want and involve them in personalising decisions about their care. We must get people to do much more to limit damage to themselves from their lifestyle. And we must get staff knowledge into play, so that they really get down to delivering the changes.

The Patient's Charter has developed in parallel with other major changes. The Charters help the public to start to judge us. The new performance league tables enable us to start to see who is performing and who isn't. First by provider on aggregate. Next we have to go to each speciality, then to clinical teams, and to individuals. The Patient's charter has improved services for everyone – not merely for a select few. Mind-sets have started to change. But we are still at Square One.

Here are the seven *initial* questions you should put to your GP when you are ill:

1. What's wrong with me?

2. What might happen to me?

3. Where are you sending me?

4. Who will I see? Why?

5. What are the treatment choices?

6. What results do the people get to whom you are sending me? How do these compare with the best?

7. Would you send *your* daughter there?

All this would supplement the questions about why SIX times as many people die from breast cancer treatment in, for example, The Bow-Tie NHS Trust than in the Consumer-Care NHS Trust, and why. And – publicly and systematically – ask what the Chief Executive and the Trust board are doing about it. Does the local Trust Board know, or ask? For we want to know what to do about it, what we need to target for change, what improvement measures are being set, and how these are being measured.

The Charter is just starting to get us to Action Stations, and to proper follow through. No more of the "It's not my job, mate" culture. No more putting changes on the end of a long list of urgent tasks, and forgetting about them. No more being treated in a slum and un-maintained building just because it's the NHS. We are *starting* to get to continuous improvement, and to stretch the organisation to surprise the customer. The key for management is to face the staff and ask to be partners. And to face the customer, and to ask to be judged. These partnerships are new ones – not the old socialist one of all joining hands all together to cross the finishing line equal, but joint last.

This means finding measures that are meaningful and proper to publish for a broad audience – for Joe and Josephine Public. There is a genuine opportunity for the health professions to lead this work. It is happening elsewhere. For example, since 1987 the US Federal Government has been publishing in-patient mortality data for hospitals in the Medicare Scheme. Why not here? The NHS collects that data, but refuses to publish it. If we are to set improvement goals for the service, and for individuals, we need to publish data, define professional improvement targets, and set up rigorous follow-up processes.

The professions need to ask themselves at least these three questions:

1. What interventions by doctors are cost effective and proven to work, and do we do them?

2. How can clinical behaviour be changed to respond to research data promptly?

3. How can we make sure that patient and carer opinion punches its weight and helps to improve services, including the total patient experience?

The Conservative Party reforms are supposed to be saying that trade unions no longer run this country. The BMA and other professional bodes need to join hands with us to be partners in change. This mean's educating and re-educating peer leaders, learning from patients, and putting direct incentives in place for change. Doctors have to help us to lead change, to build a performance organisation which faces the customers and delivers what they want. Doctors and other professionals have to take explicit personal responsibility for standards of performance, and for after-care scrutiny, to track patients after they have been treated. It's no longer good enough to breathe a sigh of relief when they don't drop dead in the car-park. We need to take the patient's experience seriously, scrutinising it in detail as an experience, and not just asking patients on their way to the operating theatre if they were happy with the food.

For the prestige of the system shouldn't be built on numbers treated, but on whether the treatment worked, whether the patient liked it, and whether it made a difference to their lives.

The development of the Charter is vital to all this. For we know that outcomes are better when we involve the patient. Patient audit and involvement in shared decision-making should go into the Charter. For example, all hospitals should be accredited by the Royal College of Surgeon's Patient-Satisfaction Audit. Why not require that as a Charter standard? It costs £2,000 per consultant per year. Why not require all consultants to take part, and give their hospital no business if they don't? This would help put the patient at the centre of clinical decision-making about their own care.

The Patient's Charter must be developed around these key issues. This isn't about who's in charge, but what's in charge. What is in charge should be better *personalised* outcomes. They should be everyone's target. The key is how to manage professionals, how to manage *with* professionals, and how to implement change. For we need to manage change with doctors. And let's be honest about the difficulties. No-one ever went broke by over-estimating changing the behaviour of decision-makers or professionals. Early in their training doctors learn the truth of the old Russian proverb, "The best way to protect your frontier is to be on both sides of it."

We need to re-emphasise that championing the patient is the aim. The "My Daughter" test will be a good start.

"Doc, where would you send yours?"

21. Uncurling the rope: dilemmas and duties.

'A composer is unable to hide anything – by his music you shall know him.' Yehudi Menuhin

This book is all about service. But it necessarily asks sceptical questions about great overarching systems. It is also about the state as servant, and about several others issues, both fiscal and moral, including our duty of care. In this territory – where questions of access to services, of equity, of allocation and distribution are concerned – moral principles are often difficult to address. But they are more than vital. The issues are classical and perennial. We have seen these open out, uncurled like a rope on deck. They include:

- How to finance a system effectively and efficiently, deploying incentives.

- How to balance individual freedom with the 'public good.'

- How to balance public and private obligations.

- How to exercise regulatory responsibilities lightly in a system of healthcare whose legitimacy is founded in good outcomes and which is governed by consumer preference and competition.

- How to move beyond general statements about enabling, about 'empowered citizens', about consumer 'influence and consultation' in 'choice' to real instruments of individual power.

- How to protect the weak and prevent the system being captured by the strong.

- How to increase the leverage of the poor and disadvantaged so that they have reliable access to good healthcare.

- How to exercise such protection without subduing liberty.

- How to avoid disincentives which undermine the informal, charitable, voluntary and loving giving of people to one another as friends and neighbours and within families.

And so:

- How is the 'will of the people' to be known in a mutually dependent relationship between government and governed?

- How can the possible will of an individual faced with a health crisis be known in advance by 'expert' planners?

- If that is impossible, how is knowledge best gathered to good effect when care is wanted?

- How are the strategic requirements of planning and strategy – for example, in building new hospitals or in locating A&E services – to be linked to consumer decision making?

- How do necessary investments relate to the ethical and moral claims of being able to live our lives as free from state interference as possible, and in control of our own trade-offs in private decisions about our own healthcare?

- How far and in which ways should the reach of the arm of the state be extended, to secure the conditions of social and economic life which 'experts' decide upon (our 'needs'!) and to support a structure of health and welfare (or 'wants')?

- How can we be left free to decide upon our own good life, understanding unavoidable risks, and making our own personal trade-offs?

- Which social and economic mechanisms do most to achieve these key objectives?

This book suggests that we can handle appropriate answers and their risks, both individually and in mutuality – in local and loyal, member-owned, democratic, co-operative, collective action – but without an imposed collectiv*ism*. And at the same time free people to make personal choices, tolerant of those other choices that others might make for themselves but which we would not make for ourselves. For example, if diagnosed with breast cancer, will the individual accept chemotherapy, or not?

I suggest, too, that we can manage with a system in which we can share in decisions that affect us very broadly – 'strategy' – while also ensuring that we can secure a service which will be specific to our wants. The one, indeed, should imply the other and not exclude it. For having influence on the choices that others may make – in discussion, negotiation, party politics, voting and so on – should not mean that when push comes to shove we are forbidden to make our own individual decisions about our own health treatments and social care.

We are here talking of two aspects of democracy in a free society. We can indeed be mutual and cooperative. And almost all of us can also learn to choose and evolve the competencies to be self-sufficient in the appropriate circumstances. We should be able to address our own optional and financial approaches to a purchasing fund if we wish.

I believe in moral goals. In 'common benefits' being generalised for the wider good. And in such specific moral instruments as mutuality and cooperation for their achievement. I believe in the potential of a historic movement towards change which will make such inclusive instruments real for all. And thus replace the misleadingly easy but unreliable 'certainties' of state monopoly health and social care. For creative and adaptive markets embedded in a culture of social values, financially empowered individual choice, competition and pluralism, and adaptive rather than tightly designed institutions (or 'master-plans') are much more likely to deliver the best services to the poor and to the working classes. Indeed, these social and economic mechanisms together can do much to achieve an ideal of one people in one market for one service.

Legitimacy matters. But what are its sources? Choice and the satisfaction of individual preferences should be the source of the knowledge which gives legitimacy to the system, and the authority *for* authority. This legitimacy is conditional on performance. I hope and believe that changes in the control of money will make the difference. This is coming for a number of reasons:

- as experience teaches, notably by current innovations in personal budgets in social care.

- as the 'cognitive coherence' of the otherwise prevailing present state system of funding (or un-funding) and of provision continues to unravel and lose legitimacy.

- as people struggle with the tensions between demanding better services but being afraid of losing what they've got.

- as people further lose trust in an observably failing NHS and social care structure which performs poorly and has grave but inevitable difficulties rectifying 'mistakes', despite unprecedented new investment.

- as beliefs in society and the communications between people continue to change.

- as the digitally-connected customer mobilises and informs *everyone*.

Government should respond by introducing direct economic incentives for new ways for individuals to use their own savings, as added funds, to purchase preferred health and social care beyond the rationed minimum offered by the state.

All the pressures are helping to change the way people think. And they are changing the ways that government must think if it is to retain legitimacy. It is not only children who know the story of the Emperor's new clothes.

It is time, too, to finally move beyond the memories of the 1930s and 1940s and into the modern world. Samuel Johnson once wrote that "The chains of habit are too small to be felt until they are too strong to be broken." This has been the case for a long time with regard to the NHS and elderly social care.

The reason it has proved so difficult to shift away from the NHS monopoly and failing local government structures in social care significantly concerns how our national identity has been defined for us since the Second World War. This is a core of identity which has substantially survived unaltered despite Mrs Thatcher's decade in power and despite multi-cultural changes since.

We have already seen, in the case made by the Marxist Professor Buck-Morss how the ideas of the 'expert' knowing our interests better than we know them ourselves go back to the French Revolution, and forward to 20th century totalitarianism. An influential British cultural exemplar was John Reith of the BBC, with what Winston Churchill called its non-political but "pontifical anonymous mugwumpery." The definitions which the NHS has represented reflect this 'know best' attitude of What We *Ought To Want, or Be Grateful for Being Given*. And also a deeply embedded suspicion of 'abroad' and of European methods. Thus, disinterest in health savings accounts, insurance models and much better outcomes abroad. The introduction of the NHS reflected a genuine anxiety about the inter-war slump and its sufferings. As my own uncle, Alfred John Root, in his forthcoming memoirs *Land of Promise* shows, my own North London working-class family asked for an answer to the most fearsome question they faced in the late 1940s: 'Will mass unemployment come back?' [1]

The NHS was introduced in 1948 at a time when society had apparently come much closer together to repel Hitler, and which was now apparently investing in national revival. This new hope was signified for many by the NHS itself, and by the great Festival of Britain of 1951 with its emphasis on modernist design and a new optimism about the possible quality of ordinary life. There was, too, the accent on reconstruction, social progress, slum clearance, New Town development and green belt conservation. [2] The NHS was one explicitly socialist face of this official revival. Yet it was actually a denial of much of our mutuality and our history. It was also disastrous in terms of opportunity cost – of investment and economic growth, as Correlli Barnett has demonstrated. [3] And of what we could instead have built based on existing mutual organisation. We have a responsibility as historians, too, to understand the power of myth and invention.

As another leading Marxist, Professor Eric J. Hobsbawm *[CH!]* has emphasized, these factors are essential to the politics of identity by which people define themselves. As Hobsbawm says, these myths and inventions were produced by educated professional people. It is important for independent critics to stand aside from what Hobsbawm contentedly calls '"the passion of identity politics."

But the past *is* inevitably a permanent dimension of our consciousness and an inevitable component in our institutions, vales and patterns of life. This 'sense of the past' still influences how we consider the NHS. [4] Yet, in terms of long-term elderly care it was recognised very accurately in 1949 by the Royal Commission of Population and by the 1954 *Report of the Committee on the Economic and Financial Problems of the Provision for Old Age* that there would be large numbers of older people in the next few decades. This was the precise and prescient moment to encourage incentives to save for that eventuality, but the opportunity was disastrously missed. [5]

The war had, indeed, been a physically, morally and emotionally demanding struggle to hold onto our threatened identity. The NHS was presented as a reward and as a corrective to the inter-war slump, and by all political parties. Despite the Thatcher years – which now look, increasingly divergent from the usual attitudes of Conservative governments – the Conservative Party has never escaped from this shadow. Indeed, under David Cameron it has further embraced it – becoming 'the party of the NHS.' [6]

The debate about the NHS and the alternatives has a moral dimension, of course. In 1948 many recognised the price paid by ordinary people in terms of fighting, being bombed, and by the sufferings occasioned by mass inter-war unemployment. National identity was a mobilising force in this planned social transformation. It was once the case that the NHS seemed to define Britain, together with the Shakespeare plays, the white cliffs of Dover, and Winston Churchill's wartime rhetoric. But as we now struggle to change cultures the difficulties in doing so recognise the importance of what are by now deeply embedded symbolic relationships. These allow us to grasp material realities. Their representation by symbolic forms coheres cultures but also makes them very hard to change.

Ebenezer Howard put community institutions at the centre of his projected garden cities. One of the reasons why local people struggle to save St Hilda's on the Hill is that (whatever its quality or outcomes, which can be very dodgy) it represents 'the community' – just as local churches, railway stations, local sports clubs, sports grounds, and local cenotaphs all symbolise community emotions and attachments. Indeed, many buildings and institutions *are* iconic, especially at a time when many local identities have been diluted by insensitive building developments, by the replacement of local shopping parades with malls – welcomed by the young; distressing to many of the old – and by changes in shopping itself. The anonymity of malls, supermarkets and drive-ins has removed many forms of local identity.

The local DGH, whatever its (usually unaudited and unknown) results is something that people somehow regard as definitive of their community. They try to hold onto it, as the regular 'Save Our St. Hilda's' marches demonstrate.

In the new digital world, where my mother and grandmother always stopped to talk in every shop, we stand alone now and listen to electronic beeps at check-outs. We have much greater choice, much more variety and better value in our wider lives. But every price has a price. Every opportunity has a cost.

The initial validation of the NHS in 1948 was proclaimed as an entry into the world of popular sovereignty. Yet it has never delivered this. Indeed, it has subtracted from it. However, it is now being required to perform and deliver in a very different modern world. The argument that the NHS is the best possible system and is the only rational way to give meaning to caring for others in mutual commitment in civil society is much less persuasive than it was in these concrete post--war terms. On the basis of performance the 'narrative' of the NHS is thin. And its moral anchors are much looser when set alongside valid international comparisons like those of the OECD, the standard international audit of healthcare performance. [7]

All such processes – in both 'public services' and private – must be judged by how well they increase investment, access, equity, choice, value for money, and good outcomes for real flesh-and-blood human beings. My sense is that there is a huge shift happening between wanting still to believe in the NHS and realising the truth all around us. That there is much less patience than formerly with the argument that because the ends or intentions are good we must accept the often threadbare results of a state monopoly means of funding and delivery. Power has significantly drained away from that older consensus and those moral claims, not least because a system founded in the principles of equality seems instead to magnify inequalities.

It was these arguments, indeed, which underpinned what Mr. Tony Blair as Prime Minister (1997–2007) and Mr. Alan Milburn as Secretary of State for Health (1999–2003) tried to do as they challenged the NHS to change. They then discovered that those opposed to reform were well organised and those in favour of reform less so since they were just getting on with their lives. They nevertheless drew on a growing realisation that the claims made by the NHS were not being fulfilled, that effectiveness and competence were not reliably delivered, and that there were good and moral alternatives worth trying. As my analysis of the difference between the dynamist and the statist shows, they were on the side of the dynamists.

It is adaptive trial and error which will now surely uncurl the rope. Events over 65 years show that we should share a scepticism about grand abstractions. That we do better without 'the transforming state' on the Leninist model. Provisional, adaptive, inventive, open societies reveal the unexpected, discover the unknown, and release the new potentials of us all. They and only they do so. We do unnecessary damage, too, when we think of people as categories or classes: 'the masses'; 'the proletariat'; 'the patients.' Here, I have observed the practice of bureaucratic state hierarchies up close, to my dismay.

Isaiah Berlin made the case for 'negative liberty' – or being let alone to live our lives – as against a concept of 'positive liberty' imposed ideologically and 'for our own good.' [8] The state should be servant, not master. We can bring the realities of British health and social care much closer to the ideal of equal access to good services.

Here, individual choice is crucial to self-awareness, to self-responsibility and to individual health. So, too, is the individual deciding for themselves what their preferred outcomes will be, what they can best live with, which trade-offs they can make. All this can make a huge difference if people can govern their own actions and choose their own paths, as the middle classes know. They, too, have used social and cultural power to secure advantages within the system of state-allocated welfare. Wider, financially empowered choice is the necessary corrective to such elite capture. It is time the see-saw tipped decisively in favour of the individual, irrespective of class or cultural clout.

As the greatest of all writers, Francis Bacon, said, 'Time will reveal the hidden truth.'

NOTES.

1. See Susan Buck-Morss, *Dreamworld and Catastrophe ? The Passing of Mass Utopia in East and West* (Cambridge, Mass., MIT Press, 2002). Also, Paul Rennie, *Festival of Britain Design 1951* (Woodbridge, Suffolk, Antique Collectors' Club, 2007), which offers a left-wing perspective, even for a Club whose members are investing in valuable antiques!

2. Ebenezer Howard, *Gardens Cities of To-Morrow* (London, 1902), reprinted with Preface by F.J. Osborn and Introductory Essay by Lewis Mumford (London, Faber & Faber, 1946).

3. See the Correlli Barnett trilogy: *The Audit of War: the illusion and reality of Britain as a great nation* (London, Macmillan, 1986); *The Lost Victory: British dreams, British realities 1945-50* (London, Macmillan, 1995), and *Verdict of Peace: Britain between her yesterday and the future* (London, Macmillan, 2001). He regards the NHS and the welfare state as a mythic diversion which had a disastrous effect on the British economy, on economic development and on our international competitiveness. Steven Landsburg has said, too, that 'Vanished opportunities are costs in any reckoning. In the economist's reckoning they are the *only* costs.' Steven E. Landsburg, *The Armchair Economist. Economics and Everyday Life* (New York, Simon & Schuster, 1995), p.66.

4. On tradition and the power of myth, see Hobsbawm (ed.), *The Invention of Tradition* (Cambridge, Cambridge University Press. 1984), pp. 7-8.

5. *Report of the Royal Commission on Population* (London, HMSO, June, 1949); Phillips Report, *Report of the Committee on the Economic and Financial Problems of the Provision for Old Age* (London, HMSO, 1949), Cmd. 9334. See also Pat Thane, *Old Age in English History: past experience, present issues* (Oxford, Oxford University Press, 2000).

6. David Cameron, speech 'The NHS at 60', after visit to Trafford General Hospital, Manchester [where Aneurin Bevan launched the NHS in 1948], 2 January 2008.

7. OECD, *Health at a Glance: OECD indicators* (Paris, OECD, 2007).

8. Isaiah Berlin, *Four Essays on Liberty* (London, Oxford University Press, 1969).

22. Right Place, Right time. The relevance of NHS Estate management to advancing the Reforms.

Or, how many beans make five?

"There will be more loose ends. But it is out of loose ends that freedom and progress are made." D.S. Lees.

This invited keynote talk was given at the launch of the NHS Management Executive Estates Report, Environments for Quality Care, at the King's Fund Centre, London, on 4 February 1993. I am asked for copies of this more than for any other recent talk I have given. But, alas, estates managers have not seen their status improve. What did this tell us about the importance of the patient's experience in the NHS still? A friend of mine's husband was recently [July 2015] treated for cancer at the Royal Sussex County Hospital. in Brighton. "What was the estate like?" "It was grim."

One of the most authentic and resonant questions at the core of the contract culture, in the new value-for-money, responsive, chartered-to-patients NHS is this question, which every school boy and school girl knows: how many beans make five? And the answer: two beans, a bean, a bean and a half, and half a bean.

The NHS Estate has been under-valued for too long as the half a bean in the management equation. But it's clear from the projects in this superb report that some very fine, 5-star work is being done. The lead it gives us offers a major opportunity to advance the Reforms, enhance patient choice and quality experience, and generate staff inspiration. Especially so if purchasers want to succeed in delivering quality. And if providers want to earn the other four and a half beans in the five!

The estate is pivotal to the patient's experience – what it's actually like to be on our sites. It's got to be vital in detail to the purchasers demands in contracts and so, too – it had better be – to the economic performance of the provider Trusts. We need, too, not only better refurbished and new buildings but good attitudes from our staff. A new building with rude staff and you are not winning.

The estate proclaims the values of the organization. It speaks your values. Every detail speaks. It has an inspirational role in motivating men and women to deliver responsive, thoughtful, kind, quality services in the detailed interests of *individuals* as patients. In terms, too, of the patient's own values and not those of the over-powerful professional groups, or the bureaucracy, or of out-moded practices in management, medicine, and personnel. It's in the balance sheet now, too, so it costs. But, of course, it's not more (or less!) cash alone that will change our *culture* (though it will buy a bit more performance). It's the individual patient's choice and the personalized focus on patients, driven by the Patient's Charter *and* by competing purchasers *in the market*, which will change the culture.

We all need to work together to find out what works environmentally, clinically, and socially – and then to specify it, deliver it, audit it. Auditing both the systems, the clinical events, and individual experiences. Auditing the estate. Critically, auditing the individual experiences as reported by patients.

The internal managed-market focuses us on categorical promises to patients and, inevitably through the contract to supply, on the beans. How many make five? What do we spend them on? What do we get for the money? What do *patients* get?

The new market has set two collaborative enabling agendas: for the purchasers. The model is to identify the wants – bureaucrats still talk of the 'needs' – of the local population. And ensure their delivery. Which is very hard to do without proper, individually financially-empowered consumers in an open market. But purchasers are buying *what* and *when* and *where*; choice, volume, quality and price; and the patient's experience, to which the state of the estate makes a fundamental contribution. And, coming, I hope, to a Trust near you soon (with all necessary extreme care) clinical performance and productivity, outcome and effectiveness, analyzed consultant-by-consultant. *Published*. For the purchaser must be the big cat in the NHS jungle – a 'sophisticat', too – calling the shots in detail.

In the Estate, in non-clinical areas, specifying standards to improve the patient's experience. In clinical areas, insisting on surgical specialization, for example, to reduce mortality in areas such as cancer and vascular surgery. Capital has also got to be available for the estate development. Contracts offer the essential new and necessary sense of organizational jeopardy. The customers – the purchasing authority – can hit back, and *require* change, and which we need to advance the Reforms. In clinical and non-clinical areas where urging, counselling, encouraging, hectoring (and even medical merit awards) haven't done it.

As my good friend and colleague John Greetham CBE, the NHS Chairman in Leeds, put it to me: "The power is where the revenue is." And purchasers are now working hard to shift from budget management to quality buying. Clinical evaluation is the next big card to play. All this is about results for individuals, quality controls, and outputs in a culture that is much less obsessed with inputs separated from provable results. Much more transparent and open. Focused on the fundamental question of what in fact works in actual medical practice and in the environment, too.

Of course, to test price and quality we need a significant priority investment in standard definitions with a methodology to get us to cost-per-case. The contract culture is the key to deliver the *Health of the Nation* project, the *Patient's Charter*, community care, mental health care waiting-list gains, *Opportunity 2000*, and health promotion itself. It's a big agenda. To deliver all this providers who value their estates in the scales at half a bean will make a fundamental strategic error. The patient's experience on NHS sites is pivotal. And those who get this wrong will find the supply of beans (or cash) ebbs instead of flows.

For the provider, life is simpler than for the purchaser, some say. *All* we have to do is to respond to contracts. Big smiles. Business development. Income protection. Staying afloat. Actually *managing* plans and meeting targets. Entrepreneurial, but without going over the competitive edge. For the purchaser's writ to run – and all of this is about whose writ runs and with whom, for whom – provider management must *really* manage the professionals, really change clinical behavior, really work with issues of power, analyze appropriate treatment and outcome. And all the while purchaser and provider must both live within their means, and both help to manage activity. Purchasers will have to agree to pay for estates upgrading and quality advance, *if* all this to happen successfully in contributing to the much better patient's experience of being on our premises.

The internal-market will endorse what works, and that practice will spread. Whatever fails will go into the margin, and receive a knockout blow. And providers should, I think, expect that purchasers will start to look carefully at what private providers can supply, too. The shrewd and wide-awake Trust provider will follow the commercial model of leading innovation, protecting market share, controlling costs, and being creative. We need to take our skills and our quality to the market – not wait for purchasers to come to us.

And if we are to deliver the logic of the Reforms and the results they require, Trusts need the maximum freedom we can negotiate for provider opportunities to respond. The *obviousness* of this will not, *in itself*, deliver change. Direct financial incentives are vital. We need to behave for change, believe in its benefits, and work hard to manage for controlled results. Boards of Directors have to back you in doing so in Estate's. And we need to do far more to learn what patients think of clinical and non-clinical care, and judge ourselves by what we are told.

You have a special inheritance – the Estate. In many places, it is however still one of the most important, unfixed, NHS problems. Yet good estate management, fitness for purpose, continuous improvement, is a basic discipline of the service. For a paramount issue for the NHS is how do we manage the assets (*all* the assets). And, indeed, sweat them.

This new report gives us both a *philosophy* of the Estate and its management – a guide to its role in quality and improving the patient's experience – and a *method*. It offers both purchaser and provider a genuine developmental opportunity to press at the boundaries for real change. It offers optimism and a belief in personal action. The culture of apathy needs this shock. The idea that nothing can be done, or that it isn't the individual's responsibility, has got to go. It is a strikingly practical report. It is clearly rooted in the experience of the people running your organizations. It tackles recognizable problems, and captures the imagination. It makes us all want to be involved – a real policy, vision in action, helping us to fulfill our values in locating what is quality, and how we describe it, recognize its components, price it, purchase it, verify it, and spread it to make the Reforms real operationally.

And to achieve this we need not only quality assurance but quality control. Quality assurance is the strategy. *Control* is the management of it.

Here, real, in-focus, purchaser (and patient defined) indicators are essential, so that we can understand what doing the job really means. Maybe we need providers to give money-back guarantees, too? Then those who do well will be paid properly for quality, and those who do poorly may not be paid at all.

All of us – from *the* most lowly Chairman to the most powerful of Royal College leaders – need, too, to really believe and accept that effective choice is a customer saying: "That's not what I want. Change, or I'll walk away." And acting to really try to satisfy that individual customer. The imperative is not only to make certain that nothing goes wrong clinically (vital though that is, as Dr. William Pickering has persistently shown in his innovative and persuasive proposals for an Independent Medical Inspectorate) but stretching to genuine, detailed, visible concern about the patient's experience and wishes. For purchasing reform is not only about public health definitions. It is also about asking what kind of an organization am I dealing with here? What does it deliver? What is it like to go through this place? What's the estate – and what are people's attitudes – like?

As purchasers bear down on what kind of an organization they are buying from, big battles will be fought on your territory and on your ramparts. You are not a support service. Yours is a strategic role. And the advent of the patient-focused hospital will make it more so, based as it is on the fundamental assumption that everything a hospital does (including the physical layout) should be centred on the wants and experiences of the individual patient.

Bill Murray's report gives us both an intellectual understanding of what we need to achieve, and examples of how new approaches to the estate have made a difference. With *practical* guidance on how to do it. It prompts chief executives on both sides of the contracting line to ask 'What can I invest in to make a difference here?' And it shows patients and staff consulted and involved in the changes. I believe that to achieve these gains we – all of us – must maintain a sense of outrage. Don't go native. Don't believe that poor buildings and bashed-up old seats look and feel 'all right.' (I have seen, on the Brighton hospital estate, terrible and disregarded things like this in A&E, which I have tried to get fixed).

Especially directors of quality and of estates are faced with the question: What is *your* vision? Don't be happy with humourless service. Deliver the broad vision, too. But get it specified in detail. Audit it. Yell when it's wrong. Someone's 'phone has to ring. Remember the Marks and Spencer branches round the corner. If they looked like some of our estates, we would walk on by. We wouldn't feed their food to our children. Nor wear their clothes. Why should hospitals be worse?

The public may not be able to judge clinical outcomes – yet. But they can and do judge the environment, hotel services, and staff attitudes. Ask a GP Fund-holder. Look at the financial consequences if you don't. And from the staff and the patient point of view, look at such critical factors (and the costs) of failure-to-attend rates, which are surely influenced by the feeling of 'wellness' in the estate. For example, patient's being answered on telephones is about this feeling. So, too, are receptionists. "'ello, Brighton General." Or, "Hello, Brighton General Hospital, can I help you? Just putting you through" And after only a very few rings. At reception, "Hello, Mrs. Smith, how nice to see you again." Or, a surly and disinterested *"Yes?"*

Clearly, as we change the environment, we must change attitudes, behaviour, and the delivery systems (the 'culture') within. Look at positive examples, such as the Ante-Natal Clinic at Fazakerley Hospital in Liverpool. After the 1989 demonstration project, patients were reassured that they would always see the same midwife on each visit – an issue for purchasers elsewhere.

As, indeed, is the general problem of matriarchical attitudes among obstetricians to midwives, and the waste those attitudes generate. The report picks out in detail some service areas like this which we need to change for quality. It's for you, for managers and for clinicians, to look in the mirror. A purchaser wishing to prompt the re-design of services from the patient's point of view could learn from the maternity services at Hillingdon hospital, featured in this report. Or from Bart's, where patients are only asked to remove their clothing, their teeth, or their hearing-aids when there is a good medical reason for doing so. Both *visualize* and *support* the patient in his/her experience of the service.

The logic and relevance of the Reforms is that purchasers must move from hopeful generalities and volume to targets, specifying tolerances, auditing them, and narrowing them. For example, insist on good lavatories. As Ken Clarke once told me, when I was an adviser on education policy – *the* test of an organization! Set standards that can be measured. Insist on a specific number of lavatories; on a cleaning programme, and on inspection. And what about penalty clauses, too? Fix it. To improve, we shouldn't rely only on punitive contracts, of course. We need to engage and reward staff too. Why not *ask* staff 'Is this standard acceptable? What do *you* think?' Auxiliary and domestic staff can show real solidarity and we should appeal to pride (even hurt pride). If they block us, they may agree to change and then carry on as before when we aren't there. We've got to engage them. And check-up later, too.

Collect, analyze, and act upon patient's opinions too, as they have done at Queen Elizabeth II Hospital at Gateshead. As a provider, prove what they want. Insist on what they say they want. Ask them about clinic times, notice-boards, reception areas, car-parking, lighting, patient-held records, hospital information, changing areas, staff areas (often much worse than motorway cafes), landscaping, food, cleaning, bereavement rooms, and counselling. And, in clinical areas, what about patient-led control of pain relief through informed drug choice? Or multidisciplinary out-patient sessions, with immediate referral from one discipline to another to save patient's time (and re-visits). Or informed choice of patient treatment, as in breast cancer?

In all these areas, purchasers should *insist* on change. Don't touch providers who won't respond. Set up informed decisions by patients. On it goes. Fix it. Ensure that the provider personalizes the experience by engaging staff in it. For example, the pediatric purchasing and delivery at Hull Royal Infirmary, in this report, which is a genuinely child-centred environment.

We know that one vital area is signs, mapping and routes: the journey to and through the hospital. If this is done well it genuinely places the patient's needs at the core. What a difference it can make! But how many signs are mere professional ego, have only an internal function, or are just unobserved and forgotten clutter, tatty, old, out-dated, illicitly fly-posted, or even indecipherable abbreviations in jargon. Or are merely bossy? 'Don't do it!'

My friend Malcolm Míles (who is here today) has been a pioneer in the inclusion of art in capital schemes, and the integration of art and craft works, which he rightly says creates a 'cultural bridge' between the hospital and its community. But our signs and maps can pull up the drawbridge and leave us surrounded by a muddy, cloying, indecipherable, unnavigable moat.

At Brighton, our Patient's Advocate, Bec Hanley, is taking this area very seriously. We have had surprises. We found that some people do a trial run to the hospital from 30 miles away, days before their appointment, in their anxiety about finding the specific department, or *even* the hospital! We need to see how easy it is to get lost. We need to be able to reassure prospective patients that they will be able to get around without getting lost, especially as many people will need to be seen in several different departments during their visit. We want them to feel good about coming to us, reassured even in their clinical anxiety. And better signposting is not enough. We need to look, too, at volunteer welcomers (as successfully pioneered at Ipswich), guidance at cross-roads on key routes, colour coding and shape coding in the hospital itself, taking the system from a coloured appointment to a coloured sign system. Tower Block appointment: Green card, Green route. Or follow the Kangaroo picture-signs, if colour blind?

In Brighton we have launched two other initiatives following on from the refurbishment of our Out-Patients' department, which was itself a catalyst to demonstrate that estates change can lead patient care. My 'Search for Quality' and my 'Search for Choice' initiatives seek to put in place two dozen practical changes before Easter. Ideas such as providing today's daily newspapers every day in out-patients.' Or providing attractive bags for the effects of the deceased – not black bin-liners. Large notice-boards outside our sites with information about how we're doing. Carpet which prompts people to say, "Sorry, I must be in the wrong place"! As many internal and external details as possible, seen from the patient's point of view, very ably guided by Malcolm Miles of the British Arts Care Health Centre.

In Brighton, our nurse team on Home ward (a rehabilitation unit for elderly people) set up a patient's forum. They discovered ways to build patients' self-esteem, a sense of personal space, and gave them less of a sense of helplessness. They found that to the patient small things mattered. And they involved the estates department. Patients asked for notices to be put at wheelchair level. They met with the maintenance and catering manager to discuss heating, food, a trolley service. And patient involvement produced environmental change, better relationships between patients, and with staff. People were-activated, re-socialised, re-integrated – estates and nurses found practical solutions to patients' wants. And they made discoveries by asking patients what they *really* wanted.

A society should be judged by its public buildings – they speak its values. Sadly, the NHS has contributed its share to alienation and neglect in society as part of the concrete shopping-centre culture. Look at what we built in the 1950s, 60's and '70's. The Turner Art Prize, rightly derided, is won by piles of bricks and blocks of concrete, on the floor of the Tate Gallery. In the 1950's we put them together and called them hospitals. We could have won the Turner Prize annually! I am not the first to ask – and, indeed, this is an area in which the Minister, The Hon. Tom Sackville, MP has himself made a major personal commitment – 'Where is the soul, the romance, the imagination, the quality, in big, boring, sterile, style-less boxes – these seemingly designed in a megalomaniac antiseptic delirium, and then left to fall apart?' The Minister mentioned a possible prize for the best estates work, and I am sure we all welcome this. For those who don't, could we have a separate prize? It could be called the 'Plastic – or concrete? – Dodo Prize.'

Four final short points:

If the District General Hospital didn't exist, we wouldn't now invent it. Changes in medical practice have major revenue consequences. What could Estates management do to reduce costs and innovate flexibly and adaptably?

Works departments. Are they there to prevent things happening, or to encourage innovation and change?

Are we re-designing our estate to deliver the specific requirements of the Patient's charter – for example, in Accident and Emergency Departments? If not, why not?

The bell of Trust freedom must ring clearly, with as little restriction as we can negotiate in a tax-funded, cash-limited system, if we are to achieve the objectives of the Reforms. As purchasers drive we need the freedom to deliver.

Which brings me finally to the Intermediate Regional tier. If it is to have a big blackboard, if we are still to hear the chalk squeak, let's have less top-slicing, less back-pocket financial secrecy, let's have more funds circulating, with quality driven down the purchaser chain and with the purchaser-provider split maintained right up to the Secretary of state's door. Don't merge it at Region. It's too low down the chain. For, with the Reforms, we haven't come this far just to draw. Let the Reforms win. Let's settle a management form onto the organization which enables us to perform effectively as Trusts and as purchasers. Experience costs. But let's keep our nerve.

The NHS is a village. We learn quickly from each other *(or we should!)*. I am convinced that the propositions and purposes of the Estates Report are hand in glove with the imperatives of the Reforms. The message to chairmen and chairwomen, to chief executives, to directors of quality and to directors of estates might be this: Buy A Rail Rover ticket! See what others are doing. Learn for yourself. See how many beans make five. Talk to patients about their experiences. Don't settle for half a bean. Remember, you can count beans. And they also grow. Jack went up one to slay the giant!

I am deeply grateful to Bill Murray, to the NHS Estates Department and to its leadership – to Chief Executive John Locke, to David Batten, to Malcolm Miles, and to the Minister – and I am proud to be involved in this work for patients and for staff.

PART THREE:
23. No More Soviet 'Akademgorok.' Or Stop Taking the Medicine from Dr. Marx.

"Demolishing a Bastille with seven prisoners in it is one thing: demolishing one with fourteen million prisoners is quite another." G. B. Shaw.

This piece was written in 2006, and sent to a friend, much mentioned. It has not previously been published. But its analysis seems undisturbed by the passing years. And this despite the collapse of the Soviet empire in Eastern Europe.

The Soviet Union is gone. Unlamented. But the NHS – and some of its attendant and client 'think tanks' – is one of the few places where those with anti-competitive attitudes and quasi-Marxist convictions can still hide and flourish. As indeed they do, together with their Comrades in the BBC.

Those who hold such anti-democratic views privilege many assumptions. This is so even though the OECD evidence of international health care performance often entirely contradicts their arguments about the benefits (particularly to the poor) of state control and the deficits created by the triple British paternalist monopoly of funding, purchasing and providing.

Much that these monopolists accept is clearly falsified by the daily realities we see around us. As it was, indeed, by the truth about the USSR. And this long before Mr. Gorbachev told us that many Soviet hospitals had only cold running water, when indeed they had any water at all. No-one believed me when I said the same thing after returning from a book publishing 'trade mission' visit to Moscow in 1980. However, these closed eyes and minds and these anti-competitive attitudes remain surprisingly influential – in leading charities, in academic life, in the BBC, and amongst many managers in health and social care in Britain today.

The challenge to these Marxist assumptions has, too, been seriously inadequate in terms of Conservative political leadership. And the Department of Health does its best to control 'academic' opinion by the short-term (but renewable!) funding of several University Centres and some think-tanks concerned with healthcare as a topic.

There has, too, and on all sides, been insufficient persistent and principled argument in favour of an open society, an adaptive free market economy, and all that it contributes morally and practically to millions of lives. There has been inadequate and half-hearted challenge by Conservative politicians to much of the work done by some allegedly independent charities and several of the state-funded University Institutes which are so often quoted in media debates on health care. It remains a cultural curiosity that the Leninist under-pinnings of these ideas are still unquestioned, *and even accepted as normal*. Many of these allegedly independent commentators continue to offer one-sided commentary. They are uncritical in privileging state power, and in excluding the evidence of alternatives. Apparently on principle. Too often they use debates about health care to advance political and proselytising ideas about "inequalities" and "unmet need." This is fundamentally damaging to patients.

The real research and scholarly task is (or ought to be) independent and objective enquiry with an unbiased assessment of evidence, as the world wears away. The task is not one of privileging "historical materialism", or of "building socialism", or of using state medicine as a means towards an imposed but artificial and politicised "equality." It is false to assert that these ideas have a worthwhile eternal presence, rather than being a nostalgic illusion for some and a threat to the fundamentals of free lives for many. And especially for those who have suffered under it, including many whose early deaths were avoidable. Nor is the task to defend the alleged virtues of rationing, which we hear from many academic commentators, who seek the role of helping to make this "fair.""

We need less ideological and more open-eyed discussion if we are to make progress in this fundamental area of human endeavour. This imperative places special responsibilities on those in positions of leadership. This is so of those specialist health-care commentators who should know better. It is true, too, of all three major political parties. Yet, like Marley's ghost, these still drag with them the steel-wrought chains forged by living men, the glum inheritance of more than half a century of recalcitrant error concerning the state and services, the attempt to use state power to "improve" our lives.

Powerful and well-resourced organisations offering comment and guidance have the opportunity to do much more to insist upon independent, open debate about the various alternative approaches to funding, purchasing and providing care. They are accorded a pivotal (indeed, a privileged) role in these debates. Even a non-Marxist outfit like Reform, which made an impressive and encouraging start and continues to produce good information, still does not tackle fundamentals like the necessity to create levers for financially-empowered individual choice.

Some of the other most powerful commenting bodies such as the King's Fund still function as an 'institute of one idea.' Much of its 'expert' commentary is a monologue on the bigger State, and with little rigorous regard to free market alternatives which we need when considering the actual consequences of the impact of the all-intrusive State on health and social care services. There is very limited questioning. The role of independent and voluntary care or of alternative funding, purchasing and provision is generally ignored. This will not do, if we are to have an objective and carefully-costed assessment of those alternatives which deserve consideration and debate. Not least because they are *the norm* elsewhere rather than the *exception*. Not least because the OECD health data shows that these alternatives generally work much better than our own statist approaches. [1]

These think tanks and charitable bodies have a responsibility – if they are to remain credible, useful, and respected – to ask and answer the truly significant questions. To do so without quasi-Marxist prejudice. Without adherence to sentimental lies. And with a more historically-informed and economically-literate approach (like that of the Institute of Economic Affairs, the Adam Smith Institute, the Centre for Policy Studies, Politeia, and the promising newcomer, Progressive Vision – to name five who honourably demonstrate this professional skill). They help us as sources of disinterested and independent enquiry.

However, the value of much that is written and said by the policy establishment is limited by being written for, by, and about a specialised group, itself imprisoned in one sociological view (or one view of sociology), and the distortions of their mirror. Unlike these Comrades, Professor David Marsland is one of the commentators with the clearest and most honest approaches. The Blairite London School of Economics Professor Julian Le Grand is also unusual in citing people with whom he disagrees, and for confronting their arguments. More widely, we have to recover a balance to objectively assess the evidence, and the choices. And to get away from the shamanistic and cloistered elucidation of scripture in a tight, self-contained system of canonical instruction. We have to abandon allegiance to an unchangeable doctrine concerning the importance of the state. These ideas otherwise represent a deep cultural impediment to alternative ideas receiving a fair hearing. They are a direct challenge to liberty.

It is not the function of academic research and comment to be a matter of collusive harmony with a pre-determined result. Nor to look at everything except what is before it's very eyes. That, indeed, is the inheritance of the excruciating but now-vanished world of Soviet 'Akademgorodok', which is described by Colin Thubron in his philosophic travelogue *In Siberia*. [2] As Dickens said (of the now forgotten early 19th century religious organisation at Exeter Hall in The Strand) "It might be laid down as a very good general rule of social and political guidance that whatever Exeter Hall champions" – replace this with one of the captive think-tanks you can think of – "is the thing by no means to be done." [3]

There is one pivotal academic point which is fundamental for all such organisations to recognise. It is this. It is not sufficient to *know*. Nor is it appropriate or intellectually respectable to resist on principle any objective appraisal of independent approaches to health care, and the contribution of choice, competition, and markets. It is indeed, disabling, disadvantageous and destructive to insist upon the old, seemingly unappeasable desire to believe. This "desire to believe", irrespective of the evidence, has much harmed open debate about the alternative approaches to health care, which evidence shows are often more successful than the state monopoly approach of the NHS with its narrow financial base. Too often policy is approved from the point of view of a wished-for political future, and which is Marxist in structure. These political attitudes and their focus on imposed political "equality" are no satisfactory substitute for asking hard questions, for genuinely appraising the evidence, for using a respectable and testable methodology, and for awaiting the answers which the evidence offers and reveals. Questions like genuinely comparing alternative overseas experiences, and considering the unity, complexity and persuasive insight of the evidence. And not ignoring the OECD evidence.

It would indeed, be an attractive innovation if all such institutes concerned with health care should insist that commentators and researchers they employ should never decide upon their conclusions before appraising the evidence – including that evidence which they assume to be of no consequence. The King's Fund could and should give a lead! For no serious scholarly study dismisses the inconvenient as an illusory alphabet or ignores different perspectives because they do not suit politically. If commentators in such think-tanks really do want what patients want, why do they persist in denying the possibility of discovering surprising things as services are allowed to evolve under creative, dynamist competition? In *Sketches by Boz* Dickens writes: "We pause for a reply; – and, having no chance of getting one, begin a fresh paragraph."

What is required instead of ideology – and if we are to make genuine progress – is an evanescent loyalty to the open appraisal of alternative ideas. Not special favours to ideology. Nor the self-hypnosis which sustains illusions. We need independent intellectual scepticism. We need to subdue pre-conceptions, and, indeed, to value innocence if we are to think our way forwards. The job of academic enquiry is to appraise the evidence objectively. Not to campaign to privilege a particular (and a political) view. Not to treat competing ideas as if they were an unknown alphabet. But I will be accused of having an ideology in opposing ideology, by those who only think in terms of ideologies! For these see ideology everywhere, save in themselves!

Department of Health funding of think tank work is one of the sources of menace. Some University study centres specialising in health care accept the drip-feed of Department of Health money for special projects and for training budgets. A big risk is that they can be kept on a short leash, dependant on the next set of funding decisions. This is an inexpensive way for the DoH to discipline them, to limit them to the framework of unchallenged assumptions and thus to bland commentary on current processes. There is too much description of systems, half a pace behind the frontier, and insufficient independence of mind.

One could name some very prominent 'talking-heads' who stay just half a raindrop ahead of the wave, and describe the current weather. By this means they have somehow established reputations for expertise. They are certainly very convenient for the DoH.

One academic commentator is Professor Alan Maynard – like another adventurous figure, Robinson Crusoe, associated with York – is indeed an exception. He is an unusual, independent, and constructively dissident figure in the world of British academic comment. [4] So, too, as I have mentioned, is the outstanding figure Professor David Marsland of Brunel University, a courageous independent scholar whose ideas, words, and publications ring true in every respect. [5] Dr. Heinz Redwood, the author and independent industry consultant, is another whose work demonstrates the exemplary objectivity, the necessarily cautious and careful appraisal of a the fullest range of questions, enquiry, theses, and evidence.[6] It would be a surprise to see either on the BBC. For too many other much-quoted "experts" G. B. Shaw coined a useful word: "buffleheaded."

Will we may now see a sea-change, forced upon academe by much greater public and media awareness of the realities of health care here and overseas, and the world wide web? We hope so, indeed. And many patient groups are now and by this means helping one another to make up their own minds. Yet the rear-guard action continues (and is documented week by week in the parish magazine of the true-church, the *Health Service Journal*). Some organisations of which I am critical may seem like granite obelisks, forever durable. I do not name them, because of the laws of libel. However, some are named by being unnamed. They will, however, erode in the changing world unless they open up to a wider and more legitimate debate. Otherwise, what we mean by independent scholarly enquiry, what we mean by rigorous methodology, what we mean by evidence and its objective appraisal is itself betrayed.

Circularity remains a difficulty. It does not help us if debate is controlled by a restricted circle which only cites others within the circle. For this offers the reader or listener – by a process of indoor map-reading – only what is to be viewed within its own world. It would be most unusual, even unique, to see a commentator who regularly publishes in the *HSJ* cite Professor David Marsland, for example, or the late Arthur Seldon, or myself. Or, indeed, Facey Romford, Jr. And the invaluable Roy Lilley website nhsManagers.net

Too often this leaves us in a nest-like world of Russian dolls, one in which dreams shroud facts. The debate on the NHS, indeed, does need to draw on a much wider literature than NHS publications and NHS-minded "experts" commonly regard as appropriate and relevant. For the wider cultural and economic literature offers important insights and frameworks for thinking, but which NHS commentators generally ignore.

However, one seeks unavailingly in NHS debate for *any* reference to the highly-relevant works of Nobel Prize winning economists James Buchanan and Milton Friedman, to the pioneering work of Gordon Tullock, a founder of the "public choice school". [7] And, indeed, to the writings of Isaiah Berlin, as well as the works of Friedrich Hayek. [8] More recent work by such scholarly lamp-lighters as Professor David Marsland, Dr. Arthur Seldon, Lord Ralph Harris, Dr. Heinz Redwood, and Professor Nick Bosanquet [9], or the important American cultural critic Virginia Postrel, whose superb work strikes at the heart of the issues. [10] So, too, does – itself in a surprising place – the excellent (but grossly over-priced)

Fabian Society pamphlet by the visiting American commentator Steven Henning Sieverts. [11]

All these offer intellectually significant, rigorously argued, carefully documented, stylishly presented counter-veiling argument to that of the centraliser and the seeker after politicised "equality." Yet one still searches for a very long time to see the ideas of alternative but serious scholars considered and understood by NHS pundits. They remain outside the Pale of Settlement. Instead, there is an insistence on the voices of the failed future. It is particularly surprising that they should ignore Isaiah Berlin, whose philosophical work has been universally valued for more than a quarter of a century, who is one of Britain's most celebrated intellectuals, and whose biographer and defender, the novelist Michael Ignatieff, is himself a self-declared 'authority' on human rights, and also an icon of the left. [12]

Crucially, however, in an intellectually respectable approach which is also going to be practically of use in responding to evidence we need to value counter-argument, which is as important as argument. It is the responsibility of independent charities and University institutes to point these out, and to insist on their appraisal. There are, they may notice, magisterial precedents. Darwin, for example, said in his *Origins* (of one discovery), "The case at present must remain inexplicable; and may be urged as a valid argument against the view here entertained." How often do we see such modesty and self-reflection in the work of authors from the King's Fund, for example, trumpeting centralised health care? Instead, we need horizontal thinking and not merely vertical and internal reference. We need much wider and tougher questioning to achieve a new synthesis which combines available information – notably from the OECD, from the internet, and from an increasingly sceptical media. And we need understanding from several perspectives and from all fields.

We are certainly approaching major changes in funding, purchasing and provision. The new arrangements will no doubt be complex, and transitional. But change is inevitable. And there are important reminders for those who stand in last ditches, or insist on the NHS as a model of eternal civilisation – the sole meridian – or who require precise clockwork and a planner's model to answer every query prior to any change.

First, that it is unhistorical to insist that one model can persist forever. Umberto Eco's words in his *Reflections on The Name of The Rose* are more persuasive, when he speaks of "the usual topos (the great of yesteryear, the one-famous cities, the lovely princesses: everything disappears into the void) all these departed things leave (only, or at least) pure names behind them." [13]

Second, that evolution and surprise is in the nature – indeed, *is* the nature – of *all* things.

Third, that you cannot buy a ticket to paradise, with all the conditions and every niche precisely forecast and pre-printed on the back. Trial and error is, indeed, the very best policy. Testing what works, adjusting as we go, improving by experience, surprise, and successes.

The defenders of centralised systems now huddle their wagons in a circle. Yet modern health care is increasingly marked by new technology, the genomic revolution, longer life, the global information revolution and radically altered consumer expectations. Nothing is constant except mobility itself. The value of Hayek's evolving spontaneity, of the providential logic of the market, and of organic evolution is more than obvious.

The evidence is all around us. And those centralising charities, think tanks, and the politicians in all parties who have insisted on a state-monopoly solution should ask for our forgiveness, as we seek to heal the health system they have helped to wound. For they have lived in a world of their own. And, indeed, they have encouraged us – with their emphasis on political values and a social laboratory – to vote ourselves much poorer health care than we could have had if we had instead sought the advantages and persistent vitality of competition and choice in 1948. We could have done so by beefing up purchasing power (especially of the poor, who have done least well from the NHS) in a regulated market.

The great cultural historian G. M. Young once noted that the natural end of every dogma need not be another dogma. He told us, too, that "we go out into the Waste Land of Experts, each knowing so much about so little that he can neither be contradicted nor be worth contradicting." [14]

But if he were alive today, however, I suspect he would urge us to continue to try to halt the continuing NHS advisory world of Soviet 'Akademgorodok.'

NOTES.

1. *OECD Electronic Publications*, Paris, *OECD Health Data 1998: A Comparative Analysis of 29 Countries*, and in *OECD Health Data 2001: A Comparative Analysis of 30 Countries* (10th edition).

2. Colin Thubron, *In Siberia* (London, Chatto & Windus, 1999).

3. Charles Dickens, "The Niger Expedition", *Examiner*, 19 August 848, reprinted in B. W. Malz (ed.), *Miscellaneous Papers* (London, Chapman & Hall, 1914), p. 108.

4. For example, see Alan Maynard, *The Public/Private Mix for Health* (London, Nuffield Provincial Hospitals Trust, 1983), and many research papers and pamphlets. I often disagreed with him, but admired his independence of mind.

5. David Marsland, *Welfare or Welfare State Contradictions and Dilemmas in Social Policy* (London, Macmillan Press, 1996); *Seeds of Bankruptcy* (London, Claridge, 1988); "Methodological inadequacies in British Social Science", in S .Cang (ed.), *Feschrift for Elliott Jaques* (Washington, D.C., Cason-Hall, 1992); "Not Cancelled – Postponed: A Revolution in Healthcare", *Health*

Business Summary, Vol.13, pp. 4-9, 1994; "Public Service Plus: The Role of the Independent Sector in Health Care", *Health Summary*, Vol.13, pp.8-132, 1996. All essential reading.

6. Heinz Redwood, *Why Ration Health Care? An international study of the United Kingdom, France, Germany and public sector health care in the USA* (London, Civitas, 2000). Again, an essential contribution.

7. James M. Buchanan and Gordon Tullock, *The Calculus of Consent* (Ann Arbor, Michigan, University of Michigan Press, 1962); J. M. Buchanan and R .D. Tollison (eds.), *Theory of Public Choice* (Ann Arbor, Michigan, University of Michigan Press, 1972); J. M. Buchanan, *The Limits of Liberty. Between Anarchy and Leviathan* (Chicago, Chicago University Press, 1975); J. M .Buchanan &c. (eds.), *Towards a Theory of Rent-Seeking Society* (Austin, Texas, Texas A&M Press, 1980); Gordon Tullock, *The Vote Motive* (London, Institute of Economic Affairs, 1976) and his *Private Wants, Public Means* (New York, Basic Books, 1970). See also Arthur Seldon, *Capitalism* (Oxford, Basil Blackwell, 1990); Peter Self, *Government by the Market? The Politics of Public Choice* (London, Macmillan, 1993), and Brian Griffiths, Robert A. Siroco, Norman Barry & Frank Field, *Capitalism, Morality and Markets* (London, Institute of Economic Affairs, 2000); Milton Friedman, *Capitalism and Freedom* (Chicago, Chicago University Press, 1962; revised edition, 1982); Milton and Rose Friedman, *Free To Choose, A Personal Statement* (New York, Harcourt Brace, 1980); their *Tyranny of The Status Quo* (San Diego, Calif., Harcourt Brace, 1983).

In 2015 one could very safely offer a very considerable cash prize to anyone who could discover a senior NHS manager or "leader" who had read Edmund Phelps, *Mass Flourishing. How Grassroots Innovation Created Jobs, Challenge, and Change* (Princeton, N.J., Princeton University Press, 2013).

8. For example, Isaiah Berlin, *Four Essays on Liberty* (London, Oxford University Press, 1969). For example, F. A. Hayek, *Individualism and Economic Order* (Chicago, Chicago University Press, 1948); *The Constitution of Liberty* (Chicago, Chicago University Press, 1960); *Studies in Philosophy, Politics and Economics* (London, Routledge, 1967), and *New Studies in Politics, Economics and the History of Ideas* (London, Routledge, 1978).

9. David Marsland, *Welfare or Welfare State Contradictions and Dilemmas in Social Policy* (London, Macmillan Press, 1996); *Seeds of Bankruptcy* (London, Claridge, 1988); 'Methodological inadequacies in British Social Science', in S. Cang (ed.), *Feschrift for Elliott Jaques* (Washington, DC, Cason-Hall, 1992); 'Not Cancelled – Postponed: a revolution in healthcare', *Health Business Summary*, **13**, pp. 4–9, 1994; 'Public Service Plus: the role of the independent sector in health care', *Health Summary*, **13**, pp. 8–132, 1996; Nicholas Bosanquet's work includes a series of reports written for the think-tank, Reform [www.reform.co.uk], including *The NHS in 2010* (London, 2004), and his *A Successful NHS* (London, Adam Smith Institute, 1999). Arthur Seldon's masterpiece is *Capitalism* (Oxford, Basil Blackwell, 1990). See also, e.g., A. Seldon (ed.), *The Long Debate on Poverty: Essays on Industrialisation and the 'Condition of England'*, (London, IEA, 1972; 2dn. ed., 1974); A. Seldon (ed.), *Re-privatising Welfare: After the Lost Century* (London, IEA, 1996); Ralph Harris, A. Seldon, *Choice in Welfare* (London, IEA, series 1963, 1965, 1970, 1978, 1987).

10. Virginia.Postrel, *The Future and its Enemies, The Growing Conflict Over Creativity, Enterprise, and Progress* (New York, Free Press, 1998).

11. Steven Henning Sieverts, *No Pain, No Gain. Lessons from US Healthcare* (London, Fabian Society, 1996). Alas, its circulation was not helped by its outrageous price – one of the most expensive pamphlets ever published. The author (a visiting American) was not to blame,

although he was ill-served by this publisher. Was the price set so deliberately high – and beyond all reason compared with contemporary prices – to restrict circulation?

12. See Michael Ignatieff, in addition to his fiction, *The Russian Album* (New York, Viking, 1987); *The Warrior's Honour. Ethnic War and the Modern Conscience* (London, Chatto & Windus, 1998), and *Virtual War: Kosovo and Beyond* (New York, Picador, 2001). Also, his *Isaiah Berlin* (London, Chatto & Windus, 1998).

13. Umberto Eco, *The Name of The Rose* (New York, Harcourt Brace Jovanovich, 1893), translated by William Weaver.

14. G. M. Young, *Victorian England. Portrait of An Age* (Oxford, Oxford University Press), p.160.

24. Sidney Webb, 'self-deadness', & the NHS.

"In our own time the division between the high-born and the base-born has become a fiction, transparent to every eye. But the distinction between the lowly manual world and the lofty intellectual one continues – no longer as lord and serf, but as officer and subaltern, party cadre and party member, expert and everyone else. Even after the rights of property have been unmasked, those of intellectual labour remain." R. L. Heilbroner.

This essay was written in 2007, and remains relevant to an understanding of public-sector Trade union predominance and of 'experts' in the NHS. Consider, too, Trade Union declarations of support for the ultra-left Mr. Jeremy Corbyn MP as Leader of the Labour Party in the summer of 2015. And with Mr. Blair's successes in winning three general elections (which no other Labour leader has even ever approached) but he was referred to by a trade union leader as a "virus."

Where did these ideas of the 'expert' who knows our interests best come from? Who encouraged the notion that *they* could know our interests better than *we* can know them for ourselves?

One culturally and political overwhelming source was the French Revolution. Another, the anti-democratic (and, indeed, totalitarian terrorist) Leninist coup in Russia in 1917 – the result of the social collapse due to the First World War, and not to any popular belief in what the Bolsheviks wanted to do to Russia.

More recently, one important figure in British history who can represent the culprits is Sidney Webb. He is a peculiarly chilling figure, even amongst such a very frosty phalanx.

The Fabian leader and Labour Cabinet Minister Sidney Webb (later, Lord Passfield) spoke of programming himself to 'self-deadness.' This is a chilling phrase. What he meant by it was to subordinate the individual self to the collectivist social whole. He, like later communists, sought to create his own reality and to subject others to this. Indeed, the ideas of his monotheist faith had much in common with the realities of the Communist state indelibly shown in George Orwell's *1984*. Here state power so shaped categories of thought and narrowed the language to 'newspeak' so that there were no alternatives that could be imagined and thus exist because the words did not exist by which to express them.

Webb started work as an office clerk at 16, but raised himself by his own efforts and married Beatrice, the famous eighth of nine daughters of the railway magnate Richard Potter. Together their books famously included *Soviet Communism: A New*

Civilisation, itself reflecting a centralising view of the intransigent facts of human diversity and conflict. [1]

For Webb, the individual life would have no meaning save as an element in a 'movement'. Social policy and the people for whom it was intended were both means to ends. The focus was on force as the basis of the holistic and authoritarian state, rather than on the ethics of an organic, self-organising spiritual whole. Thus, the project of perfect justice and the ideal state. Webb lived for this life and perception. It was one of governmental 'blue books', committees, and unrelenting officialdom in the pursuit of certainties. He lived and breathed bureaucratic public institutions. His was the perspective of the rationalising, modernising, professional centraliser. He lived on behalf of others. Yet Webb, husband to Beatrice, said he could never write his autobiography because he had "no inside." And that "the desire to lead an individual life is the survival of the brute in man." [2]

Orwell's representative victim, Winston Smith – although ultimately subdued by overwhelming state power and psychological terror – at least tried to dissent. He held onto other half-remembered truths, images, and hopes. But Webb, like O'Brien of the Inner Party, was committed to re-design reality, seemingly for the benefit of men like Smith. Webb was one of those who wrote the constitution of the old Labour Party, with its commitment to nationalise the commanding heights of the economy and to neutralise alternative sources of power. He helped lead Britain forward to the introduction of uniform, centralised, bureaucratic and unrelenting state monopoly institutions.

Indeed, the NHS and its practices of mass production and complex bureaucratic controls were intended to prefigure a wholly socialist society. It was but a preliminary or prefigurative and seemingly benign change in what was to transform the life of the individual and the state. This approach was in fact, driven by then contemporary industrial models of cost-control and low-cost sourcing for highly standardised services, rather than a responsive, an individual, or a quality focus. It was meant with historical inevitability to reach every nook and cranny of existence. And its welfare structures have sought to do so. For our own good.

One major – and, for working people, calamitous – consequence has been the suffocation of independent, self-organised working-class organisations of mutual help. Another was the removal of the disciplines of open markets, including the loss of elementary rights of ownership. This state action undermined individual autonomy and self-respect. It proved to be a disastrous denial of our history, by an illusory and distorting appeal to what socialists like Webb and pro-Soviet British Marxists like Harold Laski, E. H. Carr and E. P. Thompson claimed to be the inexorable laws of history. Instead of resolving inequalities of power and worth it worsened these, whereas markets otherwise lifted all boats. [3] However, by insisting on the historic mission of the proletariat, on revelation rather than experience, on pyramids of control topped by officials, it assumed and encouraged individual helplessness in the face of a high command of hierarchical bureaucracies.

It denied, too, what the Cambridge-based literary critic K. K. Ruthven recognised, that "Most working-class people would rather become middle-class than classless." [4] The hopes of what proved to be a hallucinatory future suffocated the creative, living, and successful alternative of self-organised working-class mutuality – as Frank Prokashka and David Green have shown. [5] The reason why this still matters in debate is that many in 'public service' (and in British Universities, the last hiding places of unreconstructed Marxists) retain an affection for such ideas. And that even such apparently new ventures such as 'social enterprise' initiatives carry within them the same hierarchical assumptions since the individual receiving services has no power over the money.

For Webb, the 'self-dead' man, there were to be no irresponsible individual freedoms. Instead, there was to be expert machinery, or the machinery of experts. There was one heaven, and one road to it. There was one vehicle: the interests of the state and the individual were identical. Here, the lower orders, despite their history of collaborating in mutual organisation, were not to be permitted to run their own affairs. Instead, these would be run in their interests, but by others. Thus, working-class health-care, education, and housing were engulfed gradually in the suffocations of Webb's Utopian 'self-deadness.' They were captured in Webb's own images of a world of industrial production, its possibilities and its limits, all of which were historically determined as a prelude to the revelation of a socialist (or communist) nirvana.

This allegedly rationalist, 'progressive', systemic vision posing as the inevitable wave of the future was the basis of social consequences suffered by the many. And it was offered without reference to what those who actually tried to get access to care, or to seek the education of their children, or who wanted to live in one kind of housing and not another, actually preferred. And which they would otherwise have striven to provide for themselves. But what would *they* know? We were all 'Sidney Webbed' and 'T. Dan Smith-ed', for our own good. Ultimately, the processes and the machinery "encouraged the queuers to show their wounds and to think of themselves as victims with entitlements rather than as agents with challenges." The demoralisation of the working-classes then proceeded apace. [5]

Sidney Webb's approach to the inner-self of the individual and to the older organisations of working-class self-help thus represented a loss of faith in individual self-reflective and self-responsible power, and in working-class association and self-organisation. Instead, collectivist policy had to be the guide. 'Ordinary' people became patients (needing patience), where they had previously been thoughtful agents of their own lives. Life would be lived vicariously through the collective. And the only source of policy, in planned production, was its shaping by experts who were professionally trained for this work, and who saw us not as individuals but as masses. Even in a democracy "experts" would recognise a wider "consciousness of consent." Instead of reflecting an optimism for working-class potentials all this offered a disdain, even a loathing of working-class life and mutuality. It introduced instead compulsory standardisation, and central administration. [6]

Something very remarkable was lost, something vibrant and very special in English life. And yet it remains in the main unknown now. As Ferdinand Mount has written, "It is not too much to say that the lower classes in Britain between 1800 and 1940 had created a remarkable civilisation of their own, and which it is hard to parallel in human history: narrow-minded perhaps, prudish certainly, occasionally pharisaic, but steadfast, industrious, honourable, idealistic, peaceable and purposeful." History and the State has suffocated the memory and the reality. "As a result, for most of us today the civilisation of the working classes is largely hidden from view, buried under the ideology of social progress which is our orthodoxy and which has been drummed into us by schoolteachers, historians and self-congratulatory politicians ever since." [7]

The losses in terms of opportunity-cost, in terms of individual access to personal services, and in terms of the collapse of working-class self-organisation, were enormous. Webb was not the only sufferer, in terms of 'self-deadness'. The argument he presented is that of the post-war welfare "settlement." This established the institutional and intellectual conditions and the ascendancy of this viewpoint. Men like F.A. Hayek and Arthur Seldon have long challenged it. But it is only now being much more widely assessed, not least by its inheritors. Even so, and despite the removal by Mr. Tony Blair of Clause 4 in the Labour constitution (which Webb helped to write in 1917-18), many such incantatory Webbian attitudes prevail. In terms of its 'scientific' analysis, Tony Benn remains a prime example. Gordon Brown is not innocent of the charge.

Matthew Arnold, too, had outlined a vision similar to Webb's, in the dogmas of his *Culture and Anarchy* (1872). But some of Webb's own contemporaries were wiser. They were alert to what Webb stood for, and many did not like the look, sound, and smell of it. William Morris – himself a romantic socialist, of course – thought that Webb's ideas concerning the role of the individual and of the "expert" distanced him from the people's cultural traditions.

The co-operative historian Percy Redfern spoke for the skilled workman, the artisan, and the self-improver when he put it like this: "Everything which I loved personally called to me as a free person; but on another side I was being moulded in spirit to a complete dependence on collectivist aims and plans, especially as to be authorised by the state. The two attitudes could not continue to coexist." [8] Morris warned of "the danger of the community fall into bureaucracy, the multiplication of boards and offices, and all the paraphernalia of official authority, which is, after all, a burden even when it is exercised by the delegation of the whole people and in accordance with their wishes." [9] His welfarist admirers do not seem to notice or to quote this statement very often.

We should undertake a brief historical diversion, to bring these realities fully into focus. For they help us to see why we are in such difficulties in seeking to implement patient empowerment, and to cope with some of the questions outlined in my Introduction to the present book. These, as we have seen, concern the perennial issues – they seem everlasting enigmas – of how to combine equity and economy; how to integrate local autonomy and accessibility, how to change controls. All this, preferably, from what is known (contentiously) as "below", with much more personal responsibility for behaviour and consequences, for decisions and results. How to combine, too, the contradictory imperatives of local autonomy/accessibility with central financial and political strength; how to universalise services, whilst maintaining local sensitivities and control; how to maintain the morale/skills of professionals in medicine, yet with transparency and accountability; how to combine fairness, markets, the discipline of pluralist competition, social solidarity and consent without imposed 'equality.' None of which has followed from Sidney Webb's "deadness" blueprint.

The Webb view is irretrievably statist. The dynamist view offers very different models of how to bring together large numbers of financially empowered subscribers in a co-operative health care purchasing organisation – and without the individual being submerged in the mass. We hear about information asymmetries. Yet it is Fabian solutions which, we can see, have brought about the existence of a 'deskilled' patient community. Patients are then blamed for a present (but not necessarily permanent) inability to choose. We have become reliant on "consultation" and "representation" by an agent. Dynamism and co-operation instead offer us an alternative approach to how to delegate authority upwards, whilst enabling the subscribing members of mutual-aid organisations both to mandate and to recall powers – as well as how, too, to control costs but achieve quality and equity.

As we have seen, Sidney Webb and the development of socialist elitism within the Labour Party led to the NHS run by a professional managerial class from 1948, serving our 'expert-defined' "needs." We should look closer at the hand of history. For it is necessary to discover where this emphasis on "needs" comes from, to see what was suppressed by its victory, to appreciate the unfulfilled potentials of another model.

The challenge here is that between the idea of individual and adaptive change and the idea of structural change, or better care through central controls. The two have been seen as antithetical. But they can be synthesised if we can combine self-ownership with self-responsibility in a society which continues to produce the wealth to fund improvements. The identification of self-ownership and equality of opportunity is not difficult. What is incompatible is self-ownership and enforced economic equality, or social control by an elite deciding upon our "needs."

The antithesis between individual development and social control has, however, been the basis of the NHS. And, as the Marxist philosopher Professor G. A. Cohen noticed (of nationalisation), "joint ownership of the external world rendered the self-ownership of its inhabitants merely formal. They could not use their rights of self-ownership to achieve substantial control over their own lives, since anything that they might want to do would be subject to the veto of others." [10] Just like the railways, no-one owns the NHS that we all theoretically 'own.' Thus ownership – expressed as occasional voting – does not secure a personal, intimate, separable, timely service. Instead, the system responds to vested interests. Meanwhile, this putative joint-ownership degrades self-ownership, and removes incentives both for service and for self-care.

Disastrous as was Sidney Webb, he and his wife Beatrice were not the sole originator of the troubles they sponsored. In fact, the roots of these difficulties go back well beyond 1948. They lie embedded in Marxist theory, in the so-called inevitable and hidden hand working towards fruitful revolution, and of the *Communist Manifesto:* 'From each according to his ability, to each according to his needs' (1848). Its roots, too, lie in the interpretation of these ideas by the founders of the Labour Party itself, as Professor Stephen Yeo has shown in his important studies of this shift from self-organisation to state supervision. It is a shift of mentalities with far-reaching consequences. Yeo (a socialist; former Labour candidate for Westminster; Principal of Ruskin College, Oxford from 1989-97, and a leading cooperative figure now) has analysed this as a choice of leadership which adhered to statism, collectivism, and expertise from above. This set aside working-class mutual-aid and direct organisation – which Yeo calls 'associationism.' [11]

Webb advanced a statist alternative from the 1880s, right through into the year of his death in 1947. The philosophical foundations of these claims are now in irreversible decline. But for many years his voice echoed through a long career as a prolific and influential author, as the Labour Party constitution-maker (1918), as husband and partner of Beatrice, as lecturer, then as founder of the London School of Economics (1895) where he was a Professor of Public Administration from 1912-27. It was heard in his platform of the *New Statesman* (which he founded in 1912), and as Cabinet Minister (1924-31). And then as a peer from 1929, as Baron Passfield. William Morris and other contemporaries identified his approach and they had no illusions. They saw it as a tension *within* socialism. To others, like Yeo, it is analysed as an *alternative* to socialism.

Morris said in 1895 in conversation with Webb." The world is going your way at present, Webb, but it is not the right way in the end." [12] Morris saw Webb's new class of 'experts' as "the creation of a new middle class to act as a buffer between the proletariat and their direct and obvious masters." [13] The tension – with Webb's voice still in the ascendant amongst many working in 'public services' – still resonates today. Aneurin Bevan built on what Webb had riven. He is thus not the sole guilty author of the NHS, but he might have known better. He should have noticed that Webb was a founder of the idea of the substitution of working-class choice and direct working-class organisation by policy which would be "slowly and cautiously worked out by experts in administration." [14]

Webb's project of social elitism – which essentially promoted a lack of individual freedom – led to the dominant NHS "needs" analysis – which, to borrow from Marxist philosopher G. A. Cohen, may be seen as "the hard factual carapace surrounding their values." [15]

This social elitism was early caricatured by H. G. Wells in *The New Machiavelli*

(1911), but it led to "The development of a larger state dispensing social politics from above" – as "both a cause and a consequence of electoral labour politics." [16]

These policies, this goal-displacement, became a bureaucratic substitute for ideals of co-operative commonwealth which had a rich life prior to the welfare state in working-class self-organisation and across a wide front. People were organised in trade unionism in co-operation, in Friendly Societies, "and other vehicles through which working-class aspiration was capable of being expressed, such as School Boards and Working Men's Clubs."

As Stephen Yeo has shown, "academic social-engineering elitism" took over 20th century Labour politics. It provided State-enlarging 'social politics', "to be understood as social control rather than the benign development of a welfare state." And, through a Marxist analysis, it emphasised economic equality both as historically inevitable and morally right. It relied, too, on the concept of the 'dictatorship of the proletariat' – but expressed through the agency of experts (or "the Party"). The predictions of Marxism have, in Cohen's words, been "shredded" by history. But the associationist approach, of co-operative self-organisation, remains an option. I see this again evolving, in an open market (but without Yeo's approving Marxistant prescription of class struggle and revolution). [17]

The losers were the working-classes, as they would be further from a violent revolution if it came about. We can see, too, that the Webbian approach is elitist. It suppressed a powerful and competing *working-class* tradition concerned with *re-making life from within*. It was "antagonistic to the belief in working class will and collective self-activity which distinguished the socialism of the 1880s and 1890s."

Yeo's analysis of the growth of the Labour Party and the ideas it encapsulated suggests that the Party captured the expression of demand for fellowship, unity, participation, egalitarian fraternity now, but it only partially embodied those demands in actual associations. The Party itself enabled people to ignore the contradiction between the ideals of self-organisation and the national practice of the Party itself, which had annexed their associations. This tension remains visible on the fragmented sectarian British left.

It is, then, powerfully represented in the prevalent "needs" analysis and planning of the NHS compared with what the socialist (and gay) Sheffield pioneer and poet Edward Carpenter wanted: "the State, qua State, and all efficient government are superseded by the voluntary and instinctive consent and mutual helpfulness of the people..." The early Labour leader J. Keir Hardie also once proclaimed: "Socialism is not help from the outside in the form of state help. It is the people themselves acting through their organisations, regulating their own affairs." [18]

There was a fascinating and revealing exchange between Keir Hardie (representing the Ayrshire Miners) and D. O. Burt, at the Royal Commission on Labour on 11 February 1892:

D. O. Burt: *Would you not say that it is rather a natural result that if you teach men to look to the state or to an outside power for their salvation it will happen that the spirit of self-help and of self-reliance will be weakened?*

Keir Hardie: *I think not. Socialism is not help from the outside in the form of state help, it is the people themselves acting through their organisation, regulating their own affairs industrially as well as otherwise...Socialism properly understood tends to organisation as a necessity rather than to the opposite."* [19]

A Labour reformer of the calibre and vision of an Alan Milburn, MP (in his youth a Troskyist book-seller in Newcastle!) could lead change, echoing older Labour co-operative, non-Webbian traditions. For, as Yeo says: "Stress on self-produced change was also part of working-class anti-statist ideology, which, because it was anti-state, was not thereby anti-socialist". This collective action without collecti*vism*, this mutual-aid, this moral concern for others – but shedding the now clearly failed models of Marx-derived authoritarian and centralising politics – can be and should be re-captured in my proposed democratic, voluntary, co-operative, member-controlled purchasing bodies, the Patient Guaranteed Care Associations.

It is, indeed, a royal route now for Mr. Alan Johnson and for Mr. Alan Milburn. It can re-capture submerged national and working-class traditions. It can actually deliver the aspirations of the NHS, without continuing with its statist ideas. This approach is entirely compatible with mutual-aid organisations of the kind which working people organised for themselves on a large scale, and which would again synthesise self-help and organisation in co-operative Patient Guaranteed Care Associations. This does not require class-war, nor, indeed representative agents automatically expecting to make decisions for people.

Indeed, the Labour Party leader and MP Keir Hardie's own biographer said: "It is because the class war dogma led the workers to look outside themselves for the causes which perpetuated their misery that he opposed it as being made a leading feature in socialist propaganda." He expected people to look to themselves, to their self-reliance and mutual-aid, for solutions. [20]

However, these ideas of self-discipline, self-discovery and self-ownership lost the day to the competing ideas of Sidney and Beatrice Webb, Bernard Shaw, and others with what Yeo calls "Fabian diagrams." This offered what the socialist historian A.D.Agostino calls "intelligentsia socialism", and which Yeo calls a "mis-shaping process" in which socialism was replaced by 'political science.' Thus, there was "a distorted reflection of itself in the mirror of 'social politics' and welfare legislation, and a rapidly enlarging State." Bureaucratic machinery captured idealism. Socialism became "the ideology of administrative and academic social engineers: socialism [became] confused with superior understanding by experts of what the working class 'needed." [21]

Here are the roots of anti-democratic "needs analysis," and the Napoleonic expansionist project of planners to be forever discovering "unmet needs." This fever is strategically placed within the capitalist process itself – pursuing the discovery of new clients, characterised both by their exploitation and by their neediness (as defined by managers). Knowing best, deciding on our behalf, making our decisions for us, being more aware, as they believe, of our "true interests" than we are ourselves. The clear historical alternative is for people to be (as they were in large numbers, voluntarily) committed to self-organisation, voluntary association, and mutual-aid in leisure, education, politics, welfare, social and religious life. Lord Beveridge himself stressed the permanent value and significance of a huge self-organised, voluntary movement in health insurance.

Meanwhile, can we escape the long and dark shadow of Sidney Webb and "self-deadness"? I believe we can return to the people we were prior to the advent of Sidney Webb, to a nation of resolve, of energy and imagination, eager to experiment, impatient for progress and yet ready and able to consider where we should be wary and where willing to take risks. [22]

As we have seen, we are so smothered by the rhetoric of welfare and the "official" history of the NHS that we can easily forget our own history. However, our major institutions, indeed, do not originate with the state. Schools, universities, hospitals, police forces, charities, emergency services, local initiatives of all kinds including the organisation of churches, clubs and institutes, mutual-aid fellowship, private foundations, libraries, the post-industrial response to urbanisation and the evolution of national societies rooted in local action, even the county identity and ties of regiments – these were all sponsored initally, evolved, and administered locally, often on the basis of voluntary organisation. The centralised state is a relatively recent growth. [23]

The re-deployment of financial power will re-develop this historical co-operation and mutual-aid. The establishment of Patient Guaranteed Care Associations itself chimes with our national traditions.

At the heart of these issues, too, is the development of competition policy, of regulatory – and de-regulatory – actions. These are difficult tasks. However, I have much sympathy for the formulation offered by the economist and expert on regulation, Dr. Irwin Stelzer, who says that "markets are a more efficient instrument for allocating resources than even the wisest of regulators or legislators. But for markets to function efficiently they must be effectively competitive. "

"That is why – but not only why – the most important of all policies is competition policy."

"We should aim to root out barriers to competition among existing competitors, and halt practices that deter new entrants. These are functions that take on added importance in so-called 'high-tech industries', in which companies have a great incentive to erect shelters from the gale of creative destruction that is the key to better products and lower prices. Where competition is effective the chore of deciding which businesses shall succeed and which shall fail, and how society's resources are deployed to satisfy consumer wants, can be left to Adam Smith's invisible hand." [24]

The question of balancing national identity with local ties (and the legitimacy of our institutions) is an important part of the debate. The role of individuals in *their own lives* – and not merely as local 'activists' – is critical, too. The last century taught us plenty about the dangers of the concentration of power. This concentration has not produced routine, effective and sufficient health care for all. The lesson is that governmental power must be dispersed, to promote both the evolution of 'voluntary communities' in localities, and to make a reality of choices.

This turns on the dispersal of economic power, if it is to signify. This will mean tax transfers to the poor, to enable them to be meaningful purchasers of care in common with everyone else. This is a 'public interest' argument, and to some it will be controversial. But I suggest that this re-distributive step is moral as well as being practical politics. It is a comfort that the economist Sir Samuel Brittan endorses this view, and says that "There is nothing sacrosanct about the distribution of wealth and incomes produced by the combination of luck of inheritance and the market. Nobody was more insistent that these did not and could not represent a just pattern than the great champion of free markets, F. A. Hayek." [25]

It is not as if Mr. Gordon Brown as Chancellor of the Exchequer [and then as PM] ever feared using the tax system to promote policies. The tax system has been used by this government to gradually take over as the means of delivering income support. It could be similarly used to strengthen ordinary purchasing power in health care, and this step would underline the government's strategy of targeting the poor. These are arguments which should appeal to those on the left who have always identified economic power as essential, but who make an exception for the NHS.

Nobel economics prize-winner Milton Friedman put the point concerning economic devolution as follows: "Viewed as a means to the end of political freedom, economic arrangements are important because of their effect on the concentration or dispersion of power. The kind of economic organisation that provides economic freedom directly, namely competitive capitalism, also promotes political freedom because it separates economic power from political power and in this way enables the one to offset the other." [26]

Does this truth explain the reluctance to make the case for free liberal capitalist markets not only by such a figure as Mr. Brown, but also by the leading Tories of this generation – Mr. Iain Duncan Smith, Mr. William Haig, Mr. Michael Howard and now Mr. David Cameron [*Mr. George Osborne and Mr. Boris Johnson excepted?*]

One good judge, the former leading Thatcherite Minister and Tory MP, Michael Portillo, recently wrote that "The differences between the parties on health and education are academic." And Mr. Cameron declared that he would make the Conservatives "the party of the National Health Service." [27]

However, they should be reminded that defensive operations settle nothing. History is silent when you seek for examples of a society in which there has been a large measure of political freedom that has not also used a free market to organise the bulk of economic activity. Communist China is a contemporary experiment on the largest scale, whose outcome as a one-party state remains in doubt. As a leading commentator of the left, Mr. Geoff Mulgan, commenting on the failure of revolutionary ideas since the French Revolution has put it, "Buffeted by ideological excess, the twentieth century has not been kind to such stories. The grander the story, it seems, the grander have been the unintended consequences." [28]

Economic freedom is a major part of political freedom. This is an idea which does not corrode the essence of virtue or the essence of culture, despite the claims of the intending builders of utopian systems. On the contrary. And, indeed, Western leaders remind the present Communist Chinese leadership of this truth, if *sotto voce*. The attempt to avoid this truth is like having a horse with its front legs over a fence, and its back legs on the other side. To persuade others that this particular horse can jump requires the persuasive powers of a Belzebub in discussion with Dr. Faustus. *[Or of a Facey Romford, Jr!]* [29]

Instead, what we want is an intensity of aspiration and an explicit commitment to the great motive power of adaptive change. We want a convincing moral and practical analysis of what has gone before; a morally impeccable challenge to this; and an organised argument to capture attention and convert opinion about personal, social and medical possibilities. This calls for the confident presentation of an explicit theory about human life, including a distinctive approach to ethics and duty, self-responsibility and conduct, about which those on the left have never been shy. It calls, too, for us to step away from the mythic idea or state religion that somehow we can depend on the state to achieve alignment and harmony with a cosmic order known only to 'experts.'

Those on the left should consider what Sidney Webb's "self-deadness" has done to others. Those who wish for self-responsible mutuality, for collective action without collectiv*ism*, should do so, too. They should look beneath the centralised erasure of our working-class history, to recover the now shadowy history of independent initiatives and institutions. These gave way, under Webb's tutelage, to his "incurable partiality for elites and for bureaucratic organisation" in Andrew Vincent's words. [30]

Sidney Webb's ultimately uncompromising ideas – which mingled scientific hope and millenarianism dream of a world without scarcities and with no problems of allocation – were indeed, to re-phrase the title of William Morris's own fantasy of utopia, news from nowhere. Those on the left should appreciate this lesson, and act upon it. Those on the right should recognise when they are tempted to genuflect to these ideas, and cure themselves of the temptation. Statism or dynamism? *Axis mundi*?

NOTES.

1. Sidney and Beatrice Webb, *Soviet Communism: A New Civilisation* (London, Longmans; New York, Charles Scribner's Sons, 1936). The Webbs travelled to Soviet Russia in 1932, the year in which Stalin directed his campaign against the Kulaks, which resulted in 6 to 10 million deaths. The Webbs added a question mark to later editions of their two-volume panegyric. Beatrice Webb was wiser in her much earlier book *The Co-operative Movement in Great Britain* (London, Swan Sonnenschein, 1891; third edition, 1895). There she praised working-class self-organisation, wrote in favour of Robert Owen's moral vision of reform and against "the Socialism of foreign manufacture which cries for an Utopia of anarchy of foreign manufacture to be brought about by a murderous revolution.", p.16. Sidney, too, offered a much more moderate and less elitist survey of social reform in Britain in his own *Socialism in England* (London, Swan Sonnenschein, 1899; second edition, 1893). The ill-conceived book on the USSR did much to harm the reputations of the austere and dutiful duo.

2. Sidney Webb, *St. Martin's Review*, no.452, October 1928, p.478; Royden Harrison, "Sidney and Beatrice Webb" in Carl Levy (ed.), *Socialism and the Intelligentsia 1880-1914* (London, Routledge & Kegan Paul, 1987), p.57. See also my discussion of the intellectual roots of the NHS in the Introduction to my *Patients, Power and Responsibility*.

3. On the delivery and results of democratic welfare capitalism, see Robert Goodin et al, *The Real World of Welfare Capitalism* (Cambridge, Cambridge University Press, 1999), and Virginia Postrel, *The Future and its Enemies, The Growing Conflict Over Creativity, Enterprise, and Progress* (New York, Free Press, 1998). Also, W. Fraser, *The Coming of the Mass Market, 1850-1914* (London & Basingstoke, Macmillan, 1981). I have also discussed the issues in my essay, 'Why does Gissing matter?' in John Spiers (ed.), *Gissing and the City. Cultural Crisis and the Making of Books in Late Victorian England* (Houndmills, Basingstoke, Palgrave Macmillan, 2006).

4. K.K. Ruthven, *Feminist Literary Studies. An Introduction* (Cambridge, Cambridge University Press, 1984), p.27.

5. Frank Prochashka, *The Voluntary Impulse, Philanthropy in Modern Britain* (London, Faber & Faber, 1988; *Philanthropy and the Hospitals of London, The King's Fund, 1897-1900* (Oxford, Clarendon Press, 1992), and *Royal Bounty* (London, Yale University Press, 1995). See also D. G. Green, *Working-Class Patients and the Medical Establishment* (London, Maurice Temple Smith, 1995); the magisterial Bentley B. Gilbert, *The Evolution of National Insurance in Great Britain, The Origins of the Welfare State* (London, Michael Joseph, 1966); Helen Bosanquet, *Social Work in London, 1869-1912* (London, John Murray, 1914; new edition, introduction by C. S. Yeo, Brighton, The Harvester Press, 1973); Robert Whelan with Berendina Smedley, *Helping the Poor. Friendly visiting, dole charities, and dole queues* (London, Civitas, 2001). See also, John Jewkes and Sylvia Jewkes, *The Genesis of the British National Health Service* (Oxford, Blackwell, 1961); John Vincent. *Disraeli* (Oxford, Oxford University Press, 1990), especially pp.115-116.

5. Ferdinand Mount, *Mind The Gap. The New Class Divide in Britain* (London, Short Books, 2004), p.221.

6. Royden Harrison, in Levy (ed.), *Socialism and the Intelligentsia 1880-1914*, p.76.

7. See F. Mount, *Mind the Gap, ibid.*, pp.198-225. See also my *Patients, Power and Responsibility*; also, David G. Green, *Working Class Patients and The Medical Establishment. Self-Help in Britain from the Mid-19th Century to 1948* (London, Maurice Temple Smith, 1985);

David Gladstone (ed.), *Before Beveridge* (London, Institute of Economic Affairs, 1999). Also E. G. West, *Education and the Industrial Revolution* (London, B. T .Batsford, 1975). *The Labour Year Book*, published in the 1890s and after – in particular the early volumes – give a full picture of the 'life of labour' and the distinct culture, which was replaced in part by state compulsory education, in part by the ideas of the Fabian Society. The Harvester Press of Brighton reprinted the volumes for 1895-1948 inclusive [including *The Reformer's Year Book*] between 1970 and 1974.

A key paper is C.S. Yeo, "A New Life: The Religion of Socialism in Britain, 1883-1896", *History Workshop*, 1978, pp.5-56; see also Royden Harrison, "The Young Webb: 1859-1892", duplicated paper for Society for the Study of Labour History, Anglo-American Colloquium, 1968;. Yeo, "Notes on Three Socialisms – Collectivism, Statism and Associationism – Mainly in Late-Nineteenth and Early-Twentieth-Century Britain", in Levy (ed.), *op. cit.*, and his *Religion and Voluntary Organisations in Crisis* (London, Croom Helm, 1976). Also, S .Webb, *Socialism in England* (London, Swan Sonnenschein, 1893); S. Pierson, *Marxism and the Origins of British Socialism. The Search for a New Consciousness* (Ithaca, N.Y., Cornell University Press, 1973).

8. P. Redfern, *Journey to Understanding* (London, Allen & Unwin, 1946), pp.100-03.

9. Quoted by S. Yeo, in C. Levy (ed.), *Socialism and The Intelligentsia, 1880-1914* (London, Routledge & Kegan Paul, 1987) , from W. Morris, 'True and False Society' (1886), in *The Collected Works* (London, Longmans, 1910-15), Vol. XXIII, p.230.

10. G. A. Cohen, *Self-ownership, Freedom, and Equality* (Cambridge, Cambridge University Press, 1955), p.14. The book otherwise offers an elegant course of unrealism, posed in a dream-like world.

11. S. Yeo, "A New Life: The Religion of Socialism in Britain, 1883-1896", *History Workshop*, 1978, pp.5-56, quoting Royden Harrison, "The Young Webb: 1859-1892", duplicated paper for Society for the Study of Labour History, Anglo-American Colloquium, 1968. See also S. Yeo, "Notes on Three Socialisms – Collectivism, Statism and Associationism – Mainly in Late-Nineteenth and Early-Twentieth-Century Britain", in C. Levy (ed.), *Socialism and The Intelligentsia, 1880-1914* (London, Routledge & Kegan Paul, 1987. See also Yeo's *Religion and Voluntary Organisations in Crisis* (London, Croom Helm, 1976); S .Webb, *Socialism in England* (London, Swan Sonnenschein, 1893); S. Pierson, *Marxism and the Origins of British Socialism. The Search for a New Consciousness* (Ithaca, N.Y., Cornell University Press, 1973).

12. Yeo, in Levy (ed.), *op .cit.*, p.220, citing R. Page Arnot, *William Morris: The Man and the Myth* (London, Lawrence & Wishart, 1964).

13. Yeo, *A New Life, ibid.*, p.220.

14. Yeo, *A New Lfie, ibid.*, p.44.

15. G. A. Cohen, *Self-ownership, Freedom, and Equality* (Cambridge, Cambridge University Press, 1955), p.7,

16. Yeo, *A New Life, ibid.*, p.43.

17. Yeo, *A New Life, ibid.*, p.37, p.46. Yeo identifies statism as one aspect of many new developments: "They included: new developments in the scale and nature of business

organisation, new areas of penetration from those business modes such as leisure and the means of communication, increasing domination across the whole culture of models based upon the consumption and distribution of goods, and State-enlarging 'social politics' to be understood as social control rather than the benign development of a welfare state." Yeo, *A New Life, ibid.,* p.46; Cohen, *Self-Ownership, op. cit.,* p.7.

18. Yeo, *A New Life, ibid.,* p.47, Edward Carpenter, *My Days and Dreams* (London, G. Allen & Unwin, 1916). See *Royal Commission on Labour, Minutes of Evidence,* Group A, 11 February 1892, q.13172; Yeo, *A New Life, op. cit.,* p.15.

19. W. Stewart, *J. Keir Hardie,* (London, Cassell, 1921), pp.212-4. Trade union leader Tom Mann, too, spoke of being "in favour of the highest possible development of the individual", within "good machinery." Robert Blatchford, founder and editor of wide-circulation working-class newspaper *The Clarion,* made the point, too, about 'agency' that "If the people are not strong enough and wise enough to regulate their own affairs and keep their agents and officers in their place Democracy is impossible and socialism undesirable." Tom Mann, "Preachers and the churches", in A. Reid (ed.), *Vox Clamantium* (London, 1894), p.303; Yeo, *A New Life, op. cit.,* p.15,, p.36; *The Clarion,* 3 November 1894.

20. Yeo, *A New Life, op. cit.,* p.31; A. D. Agostino, "Intelligentsia socialism and the 'Workers Revolution'", *International Review of Social History* (xiv), 1969, pp.54-89; G. B. Shaw, "The Illusions of Socialism", in E. Carpenter (ed.), *Forecasts of the Coming Century* (Manchester,, 1897), pp.141-73.

21. Lord Beveridge and A. F. Wells (eds.), *The Evidence for Voluntary Action* (London, G. Allen & Unwin, 1949); A. Kidd, *State, Society and the Poor in Nineteenth-Century England* (Basingstoke, Macmillan, 1999), p.53, pp.92-7, pp.109-160 esp. D. Gladstone (ed.), *Before Beveridge. Welfare Before the Welfare State* (London, IEA Health & Welfare Unit, 1999) ; H. Pelling, "The working class and the origins of the welfare state", in his *Popular Politics and Society in Late Victorian Britain* (London, Macmillan, 1968); A. Seldon (ed.), *The Long Debate on Poverty: Essays on Industrialisation and the 'Condition of England'* (London, IEA, 1972; 2dn. ed., 1974); D .Green, *Working Class Patients and the Medical Establishment* (London, Temple Smith/Gower, 1984); F. Prokashka, *The Voluntary Impulse: Philanthropy in Modern Britain* (London, Faber & Faber, 1988); C. Hanson, "Self-help: The Instinct to Advance", in A. Seldon (ed.), *Re-privatising Welfare: After the Lost Century* (London, IEA, 1996). See also, on self-help and education, E .G. West, *Education and the State* (London, IEA, 1965; 2nd.ed. 1971; 3rd.ed, Indianapolis, Ind., Liberty Fund, 1994). Hardie, evidence to Royal Commission on Trade Unions, 1885, cited in Alan Milburn, speech 'New Labour: the ten year agenda', London, 14 September 2005. Milburn was an effective Blairite.

22. See the detailed discussion offered by Roger Scruton, *England, An Elegy* (London, Chatto & Windus, 2000), especially his chapter on "English government," pp.174-198.

23. I. M. Stelzer, *Lectures on Regulatory and Competition Policy* (London, IEA, 2001), p.184. pp. 13-14.

24. S. Brittan, "Comment," in Seldon, *The Dilemma of Democracy, op. cit.,* p.128; *Essays: Moral, Political and Economic* (Edinburgh University Press, for the David Hume Institute, Edinburgh, 1998), and chapter on "Redistribution – Yes, Equality – No", in *Capitalism with a Human Face* (London, Fontana Books, 1996).

25. M. Friedman, R. D. Friedman, *Capitalism and Freedom, op. cit.,* p.9; also Sean Williams,

Alternative Prescriptions. A Survey of International Healthcare Systems (London, Conservative Policy Unit, Conservative Party, April 2002).

26. What can be achieved, too, is necessarily limited, and one of the disadvantages of the medicalisation of our culture is to disguise this truth. For example, we have the capacity to decide for ourselves, in how we choose to live. We can often benefit by avoiding treatments. We should not persuade ourselves, either, that death is ultimately optional, or that nature gives us no messages when we age, are infertile, &c. But an extreme dynamist notion would suggest that there should be no boundary to genetic engineering – itself surely *the* science of the 21st century – and technological intervention, no 'natural' boundary; that trial and error should prevail. And that we should support individual self-fashioning and not impose resolvable suffering on anyone. See Misselbrook, *op. cit.*, and Postrel, *op. cit.*, chapter "Creating Nature".

27. Michael Portillo, 'Long and wrong – Brown's big weakness is experience', *Sunday Times*, 6 January 2008, comment section, p.19.

In November 2007 David Cameron, Conservative leader, announced the Conservative Co-operative Movement. This is to be chaired by Jesse Norman, Executive Director of the think-tank Policy Exchange and Conservative candidate for Hereford and South Herefordshire, co-author of a pamphlet with Kitty Ussher MP [Economic Secretary to The Treasury] and Danny Alexander MP [Liberal Democrat Shadow Secretary of State for Work and Pensions], *From Here to Fraternity. Perspectives on Social Responsibility* (London, CentreForum, 2007). This urged a radical programme of change away from the centralised state and towards the individual and constitutional reform. Alas, Norman urges those old panaceas "devolving more power from Whitehall to local government and a delocalisation of public services" without reference to individual financial empowerment. However, he does want new life to be breathed into co-operative organisations, and promised that he and his colleagues "will be looking at how shared ownership can be extended into the public services, in key areas such as education, social services and the welfare system which rely so much on personal engagement and the human touch." We shall see if the Conservatives apply these ideas to health care and to education. Norman's Conservative Co-operative Movement planned to publish a new book by Amy Coyle, *Nuts and Bolts – Or, How to Start a Food Co-op*, in 2008. See Jesse Norman, 'Buy into Cameron's co-op', *Sunday Times*, 11 November 2007, p.23, comment.

28. Geoff Mulgan, *Politics in an Antipolitical Age* (Cambridge, Polity Press, 1994), p.23. Bright guy, but lacks the common (or uncommon?) courtesies of answering letters.

29. See Facey Romford, Jr, *The Facey Romford Papers. An Everyday Story of NHS Folk* (Brighton, Edward Everett Root, 2015}, preface by Roy Lilley.

30. A.W. Vincent, 'The Poor Law Reports of 1909 and the Social Theory of the Charity Organisation Society', p.85, in David Gladstone (ed.), *Before Beveridge* (London, Institute of Economic Affairs, 1999).

25. Open Sesame! Derek Wanless and the *official* revelation of crisis in health care.

"Things and actions are what they are, and the consequences of them will be what they will be: why then should we desire to be deceived?" Bishop Butler.

Mr. Derek Wanless (1947-2012), a banker and adviser to the Labour Party, was commissioned by the Gordon Brown British government to write two reports on the future of healthcare. These were: Securing Our Future Health: Taking a Long-Term View *(published in April 2002), and* Securing Good Health for The Whole Population *(published in February 2004). This present (but unpublished) essay was written in March 2002, just after Derek Wanless issued his first report. This assessed the challenges and long-term resource requirements; the second up-dated the challenges faced in implementing the first report. Subsequently, Wanless also wrote* Securing Good Care for Older People: Taking a Long-Term View, *commissioned and published by the King's Fund in March 2006.*

Wanless was Group Chief Executive of Natwest Bank 1990-92 and later a director of the ill-fated building society Northern Rock. He was knighted in 2005 for his "services" to the NHS. He was a Non-Executive Director of Northern Rock between 2000-07, where he was Chairman of its Audit and Risk committees. His position became highly contentious, following the incipient collapse of Northern Rock in September 2007, due to inadequate risk provision, and a 'run on the Bank'. This was only halted with promises of unlimited UK government support. Sir Derek was heavily criticised regarding his role in the Northern Rock affair by a committee of MPs sitting on the Commons Treasury Select Committee on 16 October 2007. His resignation was accepted by Northern Rock's newly appointed Chairman on 17 November 2007. He died of pancreatic cancer at the age of 64 in 2012.

The two Wanless reports on the long-term future for British health care warrant re-examination – particularly the first of these. Unexpected consequences are often the most interesting. And in political life it is consequences that matter (rather than preconceptions, however powerfully sponsored). Derek Wanless let the NHS genie out of the bottle. Crisis is *official*. [1] Ali Baba is out of the cave. Wanless opened sesame, not least in unexpectedly helping us to see that a number of arguments offered in the debate by Mr. Brown as Chancellor of The Exchequer need to be examined with great care, and a suspicious eye.

Notably, the almost exclusively tax-based approach to funding, purchasing, and provision. The reports assumed as true those things which are normally to be proven by evidence. For example, that a public state monopoly with the NHS funded by taxation is the best thing for Britain. The OECD evidence, indeed, at the time showed that the opposite was the case. Wanless – and Mr. Gordon Brown – also assumed that public service can only be given by a unionised labour force in a state monopoly institution. This is a prevailing attitude in the NHS itself. Often, indeed, this implicit case is argued by a vested interest posing as the national interest, a state within a state. We see this in the traditional histrionics of the British Medical Association and the Royal College of Nursing. In fact, much highly-valued public service is consistently given by voluntary, charitable, and independent sector endeavour – notably in the hospice movement and in mental health and elderly care. And, indeed, by millions of private businesses. The truth is that we would be in the gravest difficulties without these other large services being routinely provided by the private sector. It is a fact which is neither denied nor avoided by seeking to double-lock the door against change. And, just as Scrooge discovered on Christmas Eve, this will not secure us against surprise.

Even so, the Wanless Report has been friend-less. But it is an important event in uncovering the nature, meaning, and reasons for health-care crisis in the UK, and the alternatives. And even Wanless says many things which the rules Mr. Brown set were supposed to exclude. The second report, on funding – expected in March 2002 – will certainly provoke further keen questioning. The interim report was, of course intended by Mr. Brown to call a halt to the hunt for broader-based alternatives for funding. Wanless was invited to wear the hunt-button of a *static* system. But the job has not proved an easy horse to ride.

And Derek Wanless himself has proved honest and open to further discussion – both in his report and in his comment to the media on publication. Indeed, the discussion of his interim report has taught some hard lessons of what now happens when a politician seeks to muffle discussion by limiting the terms of reference of a wider cultural debate. That fox has not been shot. Instead, it has capered away for a long run on another day. No one now believes that as a consequence of the Chancellor's statement on the Wanless Report that the NHS as it is now – even with very significant additional tax-funding – will come jog-jog-jogging home.

The place of the individual and of self-responsibility has come centre-stage in the discussion about what happens next. We have the media – and its independent sound music – to thank for this. The NHS and the absorption of personal obligations by the state has served as a power to disable the very idea of the transcendent individual, however honestly and efficiently health care staff have grappled with a huge and complex social issue. There is something very seriously awry here, for health-care is particularly and unavoidably specific to the individual. It concerns intimate, personal, inseparable and timely individual services. And we live in a service society where personal choice is increasingly pivotal. Yet in the most important area of all we maintain culturally powerful institutions which deny this.

There is a sense, too, in which the absorption of all functions by the state has itself favoured the development of narrow-minded selfishness, in that it has reduced mutual obligations and seemingly relieved people from their obligations towards one another. Kropotkin made this central moral point in his *Mutual Aid*, when discussing the collapse of the medieval guild's: "in the guild – and in medieval times every man belonged to some guild or fraternity – two ' brothers' were bound to watch in turns a brother who had fallen ill. It would be sufficient now to give one's neighbour the address of the next pauper's hospital." [2]

We see today, as he did, that the state's response to crisis is to increase subservience and control. The friendly societies, the unities of odd-fellows, the village and town clubs organised locally, all focussed association and mutual-support in an extremely wide-world of voluntary and charitable endeavour. They encouraged and supported socially-cohesive habits and customs of great ethical and practical value. They gathered independent men like C .S. Forester's fine creation, Rifleman Matthew Dodd, in his Peninsula-war novel *Death to the French*. They still offer a moral and a constructive alternative direction of travel.

However, the NHS remains – despite talk of a "personalised, modernised, 21st century service" – an old-style nationalised industry. It persists outside the modernisation of the British economy in key respects. True, it talks increasingly about becoming more of a service and less of a nationalised structure. But the NHS fundamentally – in its heart, structures, and assumptions – firmly resists the idea that to be a service means satisfying a customer who has a choice. One who may choose to remain loyal to a purchaser or to a provider, not because of compulsion or because of lack of choices but because they have considered the open and well-informed offer of effective alternatives. In the NHS – despite many recent (and courageous) shifts by Mr. Milburn which are of crucial psychological importance – there is, still, no competition, no choice, and insufficient capacity which would enable a service to test itself against this truth. The debate about the meaning of the Wanless report needs to concentrate on considering these issues. And we need to be mindful of what Dickens showed us, that what is *nobody's* fault is *everybody's* fault.

The NHS insists that it is "cost-effective." It does so as if this is the chief justification for a structure. This is itself very debatable. But even if the concept itself were not open to challenge – and it is – the governmental language of 'cost-effective' is not a patient-focussed measure. It is, instead, a Treasury gauge. If I am a cancer patient who is refused effective drugs this does not seem cost-effective to me, especially if I would like to pay for the effective drugs (on offer in Europe in an insured system) as an extra co-payment within the NHS. But I am forbidden to do so. And GP's (themselves officially protected from competition by the licensing of who may practice where) is forbidden from prescribing these drugs privately to an NHS patient who would pay for them. That must change. For we remain captured by the idea that government should judge these points, rather than the individual. This idea is increasingly less obvious than it seemed.

Each political party is in difficulties over health care. And we are all in difficulties because of the politicisation of health services. However, the New Tony Blair Labour Party has moved a long way in a short time. [3] And I believe it will move much further in setting out first principles by which the public can learn about the real choices. If this had been done sooner – by New Labour or by the Conservative opposition – daily events concerning health care could have been explained and understood as they occurred. The discussion itself would have educated for change. There has been a genuine opportunity for the Conservatives. It has been missed. It was possible, in a long period in opposition, to sort out the meanings of different styles, voices, and purposes, and to open out the choices and their meanings. To set out systemic problems, to set out alternatives, to lead public understanding, to be ready for change in office. But this opportunity has been wasted, save for the initial introduction of a European term of reference in healthcare debate by Iain Duncan Smith very recently. The Wanless report in its final form will surely take account of this new emphasis, which offers the opportunity for a practical and constructive consensus.

If, however, consensus does not come about, the winner in the debate about health care will still be the Party who shows it knows how to deliver the values of the NHS, to ensure much better patient experience, to empower consumer bargaining power, and to sustain higher professional morale. This will require huge cultural changes, including very significantly increased funding. This should be tied to individual contracts between mutual-aid purchasing organisations and individual consumers of these separable, personal, intimate care services. A legally-enforceable contract is fundamental. It will comprise voluntary mutual obligations and the encouragement through economic and life-chance incentives and of self-responsibility. Cash, capacity, choice, competition, and wide cultural change are all fundamental elements in sociable and personal improvement. Crucial here is the financial empowerment of the individual patient.

We can, I think, still envisage a much-changed context by the time the final Wanless report appears. However, one consequence of the previous failure of Conservative Party leadership (and, it seems, of comprehension) has been that much of the context within which the Wanless report was able to be discussed remained controlled by "old Labour" assumptions. This has hindered the opportunity for careful, detailed, serious study – and for the growth of wider public understandings. The opportunity for development of this necessary basis of understanding has been frittered away. Commentary from the Liberal Democrat Party, too, has offered little but the authentic tax-and-spend voice of the past. Debate over much of the past decade, too, has been on the level of "the figures are fiddled."

This is Westminster talking to Westminster, not to the people. Instead, the responsibility is to offer genuine leadership, and to help explain realities, if these are to change. It is, too, the responsibility of leadership to stress the fundamental point that it is the user of services whose satisfactions matter most. Not those of providers. Not those of special-interests, including the special-interests of politicians themselves which the "public choice" (or "economics of politics") school has highlighted as one of the disadvantages of substituting a reliance on political activism for price and markets. [4]

The lesson is to have less reliance on politics and more reliance on ourselves. We need to face our own selves – to appreciate, for example, that 50% of premature deaths result from smoking, alcohol consumption, and obesity – but also to learn to make choices, as we each learn to cope with the exogenous factors (technological advances, &c.) which set the context of our care. [5]

There remain many difficulties, not all of which are openly discussed. For example, the very word "European" is a difficult currency. It is an emotive word, as we seek to appraise overseas systems which deliver much better outcomes. It is not only that there is no such thing as a European system, but that we as a nation are recidivist about Germany and the Germans, as our football culture demonstrates regularly. We remain, too, suspicious of the cultural obliqueness – as we see it – of the "fang-de-seeaycle" French. This is to wilfully ignore the achievement of the German and French (and, indeed, the Dutch, and Swiss systems) in *consistently* and *routinely* offering everyone irrespective if income or social class much better care than the NHS normally achieves. Legally-guaranteed and contractually-enforceable care, too. The discussion of the Euro in 'little England' terms itself hinders popular discussion of continental health systems.

And what of 'price'? We need open discussion about the truths about price, without which we shall never be able to try to match demand with possible supply. We need financially-empowered demand. And we shall achieve nothing without incentives that work. Here, we need to be realistic about the incentives which we see deliver better services in every other area of our lives.

Access for all is crucial in a civilised society. We like to think of ourselves as a "fair" nation. But we need more discussion about what we mean by "fair." Too often the word is cited as a mantra to curtail thinking, as the reason to seek to impose "equality," and to side-line the objective and impartial consideration of uncomfortable evidence from sources such as the OECD which contradicts NHS claims about its own superiority as a service.

Fairness, indeed, is very different from pushing everything down to the lowest common denominator. Yet this has been the reality of fairness in the NHS. We have all "enjoyed" uniformly low standards, in the interests of a political wish to suppress competition and choice in case someone does better. This, even when we know that somewhere someone doing better can be emulated so that all do better. We need to re-consider what being "fair" means, and how what it means can be achieved. For example, giving everyone the same information would be "fair". Giving everyone consistent quality would be "fair." *Giving everyone individual financial leverage would be fair. What could be more so?*

Enabling much better survival rates to all, including the poor, would be "fair." Giving the poor a tax-transfer into a personal health-care fund, which enabled them to join a mutual-aid organisation to buy care on their behalf and on the same terms as the middle-class would be "fair."

It is difficult to see why the prevailing system that encourages huge waste, irresponsible consumption, and a lack of self-responsibility and self-discipline is "fair." Equally, if a person has saved, exercised self-control, made an effort to take care of themselves and from a poor start, why is it "fair" that their money should go in taxes to those who can't be bothered, as at present? We need less ideological debate about what is "fair" and what isn't. We need to get to the heart of what it means to effectively enable the system to be "fair". We need to do so, too, with regard to words like "profit" and "investment." Again, this is an issue to be presented positively by a vibrant Conservative leadership

The issue concerning profit is not that it must not exist. It is essential if we are to see investment, and the survival of the best services. The issue concerning profit is not that we do not want it, but who gets it, and why. In health care it should go to reward good management, encourage investment, lower costs, and improve services for users. Without profit what would be the incentive for huge investments over 20-year cycles, from idea to market-place for pharmaceutical companies to explore and discover new drugs, which have a huge impact on health status? Who would deny profit (or, the potential for future investments) to the company which solves conundrums such as HIV/AIDS, or another huge killer like lung-cancer? What would be truly fair would be to have a mature adult understanding of such issues, as well as to guarantee social solidarity and access for all, including the poorest, to high quality care. As they do in France, Switzerland, Germany – and in Australia too.

We should grow out of these primitive, deep-rooted, but economically-illiterate prejudices about profit. The only alternative to state care, too, is not necessarily 'for-profit care.' Indeed, much voluntary, charitable and not-for-profit care is typical throughout Europe (and more so in the USA then is commonly credited). Of course, even not for profit organisations need to achieve a surplus to survive. The word "profit" itself remains a difficult one for many English people. We need a more mature discussion of this issue, too, if we are to encourage appropriate investment, and the great benefits investment and good management can bring.

The crisis of capacity, too, concerns patient self-responsibility, professional recruitment and morale. We need real debate about self-responsibility from many respects. First, of course, in terms of individual behaviour and consequences – notably in the prevention of costly but avoidable disease. But also if we are to help make professional lives become less stressful and more liveable, and to address the serious problems of low-morale, high levels of early retirement, and falling applications to medical schools.

However, I believe that appropriate incentives can achieve what is wanted. Indeed, if we can increase and diversify funding and introduce direct incentives for self-care we can build upon the remaining good-will and commitment of staffs which can be released to enable much better care to be achieved by individuals. The key to effective purchasing and provision is the contract between the user and the provider. We need, above all, an individual and legally-enforceable contract between the consumer and the provider of services, if we are to shift from seeking occasionally (and unreliably) to try to discipline a system by voting to securing a personal service by contract.

Is mutuality a solution? I have already urged mutual purchasing. However, we need to be careful, too, not to be lured without thought onto the ground of "localism." We need to look carefully at the benefits that can be delivered by the new emphasis on localism and on de-centralisation, especially since the socialised, politicised, and under-funded Danish model of health care is being held up as a model. For Danish health care has many of the grave difficulties of capacity and outcome with which the NHS itself wrestles. Localism without consumer bargaining power will not do enough to help us. Certainly, more management responsibility in localities is necessary, and less political direction and micro-management from above. But local management will not be worth its name unless it has to respond to the discipline of the consumer who can shift a personal health-fund to preferred alternative suppliers of insurance and of care (through joining a competing mutual-aid purchaser).

Here, the conception of a common territory – the necessary cohesion of thought and action appropriated or protected by common efforts – should be defined as personal initiative and the self-responsibility of the individual. This, together with a shared concern for the disadvantaged who should be helped in many ways, including by financial empowerment. Centralisation easily marches under the banner of regional or local power. But without consumer command the re-location does not change the realities.

In addition, Andrew Adonis's struggles on education reform were based on removing as much power as possible from local authorities. He sought radical school reform for all state secondary schools, including the employment of staff and the ownership of assets. He wanted change in their governing bodies. He wanted to make schools independent of local authorities. Funding was to come direct from Whitehall, and popular schools were to be allowed to expand. Private school managers, churches and parents groups were to be encouraged to open and run new schools. This was an ambitious and necessary list of changes. But if the case was right to take away powers from local authorities, removing their dead-hand in control of schools, why do the opposite with hospitals? Why propose to give local authorities *more* control over health when it was wrong to do so over local education? Why undermine mutuality in this way? The objectives Andrew Adonis set out for schools could be achieved by my proposed Patient Guaranteed Care Associations. [6]

Mutual-aid in purchasing does offer great latitude for individual initiative, while it responds to the need for mutual support. This shows the principles of federation and free association at work, with the variety, the self-reliance and the force of initiative which are the best pledges for freedom. They stand in place of what Kropotkin, in *Mutual Aid*, calls "the dominative tendencies of the minorities of wizards, priests, and professional or distinguished warriors" in the "strongly-centralised State." Here, "by too much trusting to government [people] had ceased to trust to themselves." As Kropotkin wisely said, "Communal cultivation does not, however, imply by necessity communal consumption." [7]

What future for the NHS as a provider? The NHS provider should become a local free-standing charitable body, with local Trustees, and function within the framework of rules set by government. But it is essential that consumer purchasing power guides its investment, management, and required outcomes. It must be an absolute first rule of existence, success, and survival that the NHS body (indeed, any provider) must need to actively seek revenues by satisfying purchasers who have a choice. Yet the NHS, under any of the models so far offered for reform by the present government, will continue to receive its funds from above, as if this were a free good. This is 'the Brown effect.' And this would remain true under a system of a hypothecated health-care tax – unless the individual consumer owns an individual fund which the consumer can shift, and with which the consumer can bargain in exchange for a legally-enforceable contract of service (and which itself is one of mutual-obligations).

However, the political history of the NHS and of its major vested-interests is that of an institution dedicated to fighting against change. Such a reformed contract structure is the only one which ultimately can overcome the decades of resistance to change, the political culture of antipathy to change, and resistance to public encroachment on traditional jurisdictions held by privileged and well-connected bodies which persists within the NHS.

As my lecture to the National Association of Primary Care in Birmingham made clear [printed as chapter 1 of this book], I had expected the Prime Minister to lead the necessary changes in funding, provision, and self-responsibility, to be ahead of history, to ride the wave and actually deliver the founding commitments of the NHS. Suddenly, in the aftermath of the Wanless Report, this looks a more fragile assumption. But the report itself has opened up an un-stoppable discussion. It is the Barnes Wallis bomb which has in fact breached the dam. Its authoritative rehearsal of the systemic failures of the NHS is full of unimpeachable critical evidence. Wanless has said, too, that he welcomes diverse comment and that he is open to the discussion of alternative financial structures, and of ways to achieve required outcomes. I believe that the electoral facts and the continuing media discussion both set a new context, and this will renew the validity of my arguments.

One of the oddities of our culture concerns our attitude to the individual. We hear much derision concerning the word "individualism" (with its implication of private judgement, and of a personal assessment of the claims of 'absolute truths' of various kinds). We hear it called "unbridled". Yet we warmly and proudly value a national literature in which the picaresque individual is the most admired. Dickens – who provided the most striking examples – remains our national saint, and rightly so. His characters are a national benefit (and he keeps all our child-hoods alive and ever-green). His inventions transcend fiction itself, in their richly realised *individuality*. Each is with us all, as Dickens says, as "fellow-passengers to the grave," yet they have remained fully alive as we each make what he calls the journey towards "that sombre caravan in which we must one day make our last earthly journey." [8]

Such individuals as Copperfield, Pip, Joe Gargery, Madgwick, Sam Weller, Tiny Tim, Gradgrind, Dombey – each established a unique relationship between Dickens and his public, past, present, and future. In Walter Bagehot's words, Dickens was "like a special correspondent for posterity." [9]

An artist so much admired as Oscar Wilde put the case, too, advancing the idea that the artist's individualism – for which we should all reach – is the highest good. As he wrote in his *The Soul of Man Under Socialism*, first published in *The Fortnightly Review* in February 1891: "...the Renaissance was great...because it sought to solve no social problem, and busies itself not about such things, but suffered the individual to develop freely, beautifully, and naturally, and so had great and individual arts, and great and individual men." [10]

It is very odd that we value individuality and individual choice in fiction and the other arts, but we have done so much less in fact itself. Yet this is where the shoe pinches. It's odd, too, that the left insists on "free union" of many diverse kinds in personal relationships, but limits this thinking when it comes to health care. Single-sex marriages, and so on, are central to this topic. But free union in relation to the state and its institutions, when there are clearly non-state alternatives – such as independent, voluntary, and charitable care – are not commonly admitted into the debate.

And so we should 'listen to the reed', and to the tale it tells. We must, at all events, take an active view of these questions. If we do not do so we will find, as Picasso said, that "There are so many realities that, in trying to encompass them all, one ends in darkness." [11]

NOTES.

1. [Wanless Report], *Securing Our Future Health. Taking a Long-term View*. Interim Report. (Health Trends Team. London, H. M. Treasury, 2001); *Securing Good Health for The Whole Population* (Health Trends Team. London, H. M. Treasury, 2004) Subsequently, Wanless also wrote *Securing Good Care for Older People: Taking a Long-Term View*, commissioned and published by the King's Fund in March 2006. See also interview with John Carvel, *The Guardian*, 12 September 2007.

2. Peter Kropotkin, *Mutual Aid, A Factor of Evolution* (London, William Heinemann, revised edition, 1904), p.227.

3. And it has gone a very long back since his resignation on 27 June 2007.

4. James M. Buchanan and Gordon Tullock, *The Calculus of Consent* (Ann Arbor, Michigan, University of Michigan Press, 1962); J. M. Buchanan and R. D. Tollison (eds.), *Theory of Public Choice* (Ann Arbor, Michigan, University of Michigan Press, 1972); J. M.Buchanan, *The Limits of Liberty. Between Anarchy and Leviathan* (Chicago, Chicago University Press, 1975; J. M. Buchanan &c. (eds.), *Towards a Theory of Rent-Seeking Society* (Austin, Texas, Texas A&M Press, 1980; Harcourt Brace, 1983); Gordon Tullock, *The Vote Motive* (London, Institute of Economic Affairs, 1976) and his *Private Wants, Public Means* (New York, Basic Books, 1970); W. A. Niskanen, *Bureaucracy and the Representative* (Chicago, Aldine-Atherton, 1971). See also Arthur Seldon, *Capitalism* (Oxford, Basil Blackwell, 1990) – his masterpiece. The IEA has recently published *Capitalism: A Condensed Version* (London, IEA, 2007), with introductions by John Blundell and Philip Booth. See also Peter Self, *Government by the Market? The Politics of Public Choice* (London, Macmillan, 1993), and Brian Griffiths, Robert A. Siroco, Norman Barry & Frank Field, *Capitalism, Morality and Markets* (London, Institute of Economic Affairs, 2000); Milton Friedman, *Capitalism and Freedom* (Chicago, Chicago University Press, 1962; revised edition, 1982); Milton and Rose Friedman, *Free To Choose, A Personal Statement* (New York, Harcourt Brace, 1980); their *Tyranny of The Status Quo* (San Diego, Calif., Harcourt Brace, 1983);

David Marsland, *Welfare or Welfare State Contradictions and Dilemmas in Social Policy* (London, Macmillan Press, 1996); *Seeds of Bankruptcy* (London, Claridge, 1988); "Methodological inadequacies in British Social Science", in S. Cang (ed.), *Feschrift for Elliott Jaques* (Washington, D.C., Cason-Hall, 1992); "Not Cancelled – Postponed: A Revolution in Healthcare", *Health Business Summary*, Vol.13, pp. 4-9, 1994; "Public Service Plus: The Role of the Independent Sector in Health Care", *Health Summary*, Vol.13, pp.8-132, 1996.

In addition, two publications by the Libertarian Alliance by Professor Marsland, *Real-Welfare. Self-Reliance or State Dependency* (London, 2003), and *An End to Paternalism in Healthcare* (London, 2004). Also valuable are the publications by Nicholas Bosanquet, including a series of reports written for the think-tank, Reform [www.reform.co.uk], including *The NHS in 2010* (London, Reform, 2004), and his *A Successful NHS* (London, Adam Smith Institute, 1999). Philip Booth, *Getting Back Your Health* (London, Adam Smith Institute, 2002) remains exactly to the point and is a valuable and masterly commentary.

5. On Adonis's proposals, see Anthony Seldon, *Blair Unbound*, pp.289-93.

6. Kropotkin, *Mutual Aid, ibid.*

7. Sir Derek has subsequently offered his own critique of his reports. He found that the NHS has made lacklustre progress, and that a number of key opportunities had been missed or not fully exploited. Appropriate data to show what is happening had not been collected, for example, with regard to productivity, and which needs to measure both quantity and quality. There has been very little evaluation of policy, except by external agencies. He argued that funding would have to increase substantially, too, to deliver the aspirations of the original review. There is "very little robust evidence" to demonstrate "significant benefits" from new pay contracts, which accounted for £18.9bn of the extra £43.2bn given to the NHS since 2002. There have, however, been some clear and notable improvements with staff, equipment, infrastructure, waiting times, and in coronary heart disease, cancer, stroke and mental health care. Mortality has fallen and life expectancy increased, but relatively low priority has been given to public health. Derek Wanless, *Our Future Health Secured. A Review of NHS Funding and Performance* (London, King's Fund, 2007). See also Daniel Martin, 'Five years and billions of pounds later, has anything changed?', *Health Service Journal*, 19 October 2006, pp.16-17; Oliver Evans, 'Potential return to huge debt in three years' time', *Health Service Journal*, 13 September 2007, p.14; Nigel Edwards, 'The NHS wasted its big chance: will it learn from its mistakes? *Health Service Journal*, 20 September 2007, pp.14-15. Sir Derek has also published *Securing Good Care for Older People. Taking a long-term view* (London, King's Fund, 2006).

8. From Charles Dickens, *A Christmas Carol* (1843).

9. Walter Bagehot, 'Charles Dickens' [1858], in *The Life and Works of Walter Bagehot*, edited by Mrs. Russell Barrington (London, Longmans Green, 1905), Vol. III, p.85.

10. Oscar Wilde, 'The Soul of Man Under Socialism' first appeared in The *Fortnightly Review*, (February 1891, No. CCXC, New Series: No. CCCXXVII.

11. Karen L. Kleinfelde, *The Artist, His Model, Her Image, His Gaze: Picasso's Pursuit of the Model* (Chicago, University of Chicago Press, 1993), p.89.

26. Working practises in the medical profession.

The *Health Service Journal*/Glaxo Debate, 23 May 1995.

"Neither the naked hand, nor the understanding, left to itself, can do much; the work is accomplished by the instruments and helps, of which the need is not less for the understanding than the hand." Francis Bacon

*This is the address I delivered at the Botanical Gardens, Edgbaston, Birmingham, in successfully proposing the motion that "This house believes that doctors have had too much unchallenged power in the NHS for too long, and that the new authority of managers presents an opportunity to abolish inefficient and outdated working practices in the medical profession to the benefit of patients." I was then in post as Health Policy Adviser to The Social Market Foundation in London.

We can well imagine that, the way that public bodies function, that Sir Humphrey in his retirement is now an NHS Trust Chairman. Lord Bernard Woolley and Viscount Hacker still meet and reminiscence. They remember Jim's rehearsal for his first TV broadcast as Prime Minister – his 'Grand Design.' He begins, you will recall, by practising the speech. It is dreadful, vacuous. "This says absolutely nothing, Bernard," Jim says in shock. "Oh, thank you Prime Minister. You are most kind," is Bernard's reply.

The debate about doctors and managers is one in which lots of people desperately try to say nothing. But the compelling questions include "How do doctors work, and how well do they work?" "What witness does the empirical and cultural evidence offer?" "What could reconciliation mean between doctors and managers, and how could it be achieved?"

I will not say anything controversial tonight. For we all know that the existing system has done and still does untold damage to everyone – *everyone* – involved in it. Doctors. Managers. Patients

How is change to come?

Doctors wish to be left alone to manage themselves.

Trust and other Executive managers – understandably – have got their heads down below the parapet, and they stress survival. They need the jobs.

Politicians are anxious to avoid any conflict that might arise from exerting control and requiring development, and thus risking paying a political price at elections.

The issues are indeed widely understood. But no-one wants to tell the truth. Unless we start with the truth we will get nowhere, and the reforms will slowly go down to defeat. We will certainly not get to the reconciliation between doctors and managers that patient care needs. Nor sort out the terms on which that must happen.

This is 1995, not 1945. What do we need now?

Frist, we need a 'Contract With Patients.' It must say "We guarantee to do what works." What works – that must be the source of reconciliation. If we collaborate to get that done we can build mutual understanding. But, at the moment, where is the absolute right to services for the individual? There is no such right. We need a legally enforceable contract, to back up the promises of services made by the NHS.

Second, we must make sure that doctors and managers together run the system on the basis of knowledge. But do we?

Third, we need to think really hard about cultures. Look at the system we have constructed. Test its results. You then see – it is daunting – that neither policy (either nationally or locally) is evidence-based nor properly evaluated.

We *know* that we know little about the cost-effectiveness of diagnostic and therapeutic interventions. We know too little of the work of individual doctors and of clinical teams. The majority of medical practices are unevaluated. But alarming variations in practice are observable everywhere. We know little of outcomes. [1]

We wilfully waste scarce money to no effect – even when doctors determine best practice and publish it, it can take 30 years before practice changes.

Our lack of focus, too, on prevention is lethal. And the direct incentives for the individual are absent from the system. The lack of self-responsibility is lethal.

Our coordination and management of breast cancer – to take just one area of large-scale preventable deaths – remains lamentable. **Witness:** see the writings of Professor Karol Sikora, Professor Ian Fentiman, OECD foreign comparisons – and a cemetery in every town. [2]

Look at the people who study this dispassionately and see what they say. **Witness:** reports of the government's own Audit Commission. Or look at junior doctors. No job descriptions. Inappropriate tasks. Poor supervision. No continuity of care. Operating beyond competence. Inadequate subsequent review. Subjective career assessment. Failures in top leadership from the Royal Colleges. **Witness:** See Audit Commission publications and Professor Trisha Greenhalgh et al, *How to Spread Good Ideas*. (London, NCCSDO, April 2004). [3]

Satisfactory working practices? *Satisfactory?*

Our opponents do not have to rebut *our* arguments. They face a rockier proposition.

Rebut the Audit Commission and the OECD. Good luck!

This is not only about the occasional missed session by a consultant. The existing system has done untold and wider cultural damage to everyone involved in it.

Witness: we take clever, sparky, optimistic young people and turn them into 'doctors', who then have to work in the over-burdened un-priced NHS, when they could be leaders of positive change. But few are.

Witness: there is a drop-out rate of 25% among students beginning medical courses. [4] Gender bias is rampant. Compare those women, who don't make it to consultant. For example, 87% of consultants in Obs. & Gynae. are men.

Witness: The Patient's Association asked Junior doctors if they were trained to give bad news. They found a lack of training and empathy, on doing things like telling a patient that they are going to die. There was no systematic education or help to aid junior doctors to deal with the pain of dealing with the situation. This is not a healthy kingdom. This needs to come into touch with reality. This is *not* OK in doctors' hands. It is not OK in *anyone's* hands. [5]

This is not about scapegoats. It is a search for understanding. It is a search for truth as the basis of change. The scapegoat theory has the convenient effect of only blaming doctors, thus exonerating politicians, managers, Non-Executive Directors, and irresponsible patients. Whereas we *all* share the responsibility.

This is about seeking to understand and to change two deeply embedded and conflicting cultures, each set up to go in different directions. First, the management culture that does not include Trust management. All the key levers of socialisation and success are in doctors' hands. Selection, training, promotion and reward. They function in a culture of their own alongside, but hardly within, the NHS. Psychologically, they are outside it. Doctors work for other doctors. Their careers depend on other doctors, to find a key top job. Indeed, to find any job. No wonder they don't believe they should be managed by a Trust chief executive. It is a subjective, private system. **Witness:** consultants' contracts are still held by the NHS Regional offices, and not by the Hospital Trusts where they work. **Witness:** your own observations of the world you work in. We haven't found a way to involve all doctors as stakeholders in reforms. But we have to help them, disentangle from the undergrowth in which they are trapped.

We cannot manage, however, by going around doctors. They have to be brought into management, into accountability, into a psychological bonding which willingly delivers both clinical effectiveness and accountability. The difficulty is the present duality of cultures and of psychological states. The problem is graphically expressed in a provider Trust Board and a separate Doctor's board or 'Medical Advisory Committee.' This dramatizes our lack of progress. The centre, the politicians, and the service has to decide where it wants to be and how to shape the organisation to get there. [6]

Where are the opportunities for change? Rome was not unbuilt in a day. But the key focus is on understanding cost-effective outcomes and their improvement. This is the route to collaboration, understanding, and communication. With this focus, train doctors and managers *together* as managers. Redesign medical education to make medicine fit for patients. The best change is often doctor led. Work with the young generation for change. Get change from those who believe in it – especially those who understand what management is about. Doctors need to accept its disciplines, to embrace its psychology, to be followers.

We do not just want white coat approval. We want white coat participation and compliance within and in management. Not merely doctors as managers, but doctors who *are* managers.

Evaluate. Measure. Liberate staff knowledge down below, where they know what needs doing but are not freed to act. Prove the pudding. Move away from controlling patients to evaluating outcomes.

The future is not about control of the hermetically-sealed patient. It is about the open and honest management of uncertainty and of choice. We need, too, a frame of mind that empathises with the user's values, which changes services to accommodate these, which changes the expectations we have of ourselves. This would be a system newly practised and passionate at involving patients – and at avoiding insensitivity and even the degradation of patients. "We do it." *Do we?* *Witness*: visited a Mixed Ward lately?

Jim Hacker was right to demand a speech that said something. This motion says something that matters.

The NHS is like Poland – in Simon Schama's words – "a country whose frontiers march back and forth to the command of history." [7] Do not be marched backwards tonight. Send a message to the service. Send a message to the centre. Think effectiveness. Reconcile to deliver it. *Be it* for patients. I beg to move.

NOTES.

NB. In July 2015 I have added some more up-to-date notes, taking account of later reports and publications.

1. See Dr. William G. Pickering, 'Systematic clinical accountability is required', *BMJ*, November 2003, 327: 1109; Pickering, 'An independent medical inspectorate', in: D. Gladstone (ed.), *Regulating doctors* (London: Institute for the Study of Civil Society, 2000), and Pickering, 'Clinical accountability: check it out', exclusive http://bmj.com/cgi/eletters/338/jan15_3/b157#207651, 25 January 2009.

2. See the writings of Professor Karol Sikora, Professor Ian S. Fentiman, OECD foreign comparisons, and a cemetery in every town. See www.karolsikora..com; https://kclpure.kcl.ac.uk/.../ian-fentiman(60415187.../publications.html; www.oecd.org/

unitedkingdom/ and, www.oecd.org/unitedkingdom/.

3. See Audit Commission, www.nao.org.uk/pubsarchive/publications-archive-1984-1998; also, Professor Trisha Greenhalgh et al, *How to Spread Good Ideas. A systematic review of the literature on diffusion, dissemination and sustainability of innovations in health service delivery and organisation Report for the National Co-ordinating Centre for NHS Service Delivery and Organisation R & D* (London, NCCSDO, April 2004).

4. For later figures see B.M. Maher et al, *Medical School Attrition-Beyond the Statistics* A Ten Year Retrospective Study (London, BMC Medical Education, 20103) www.biomedcentral.com/content/pdf/1472-6920-13-13.pdf.

5. See later reports, bma.org.uk/news-views.../juniors-workload-threatens-patient-care6 Aug 2014; www.patients-association.org.uk/wp.../Themes-Report-February-2015, and BMA, "Memorandum of evidence to the Review Body on Doctors' and Dentists' Remuneration, September 2007."

6.When I was Chairman of Brighton Health Authority and then of Brighton Healthcare NHS Trust in 1991-94 it was rumoured that the senior consultants met regularly in caucus prior to official Trust Board Meetings (which were all held in public), to decide their own attitudes towards proposed policies, who and how they would speak to issues, etc.. I was also informed that there were active Masonic Lodges in our hospitals. I do not know if there were, or what these were, or who belonged, but some suspected that this private system, if it existed, was part of a separate career management structure as well as an opportunity to caucus and organise concerning local proposals for NHS change.

7. Simon Schama, cited, Michael Barone, *The New Americans: How the Melting Pot Can Work Again* (New York, Regnery Publishing, 2012), p.202.

AN ENTERTAINMENT [?]:
27. Whatever Can We Do With The Kids Today? The 'Heritage Hospital' Experience. A Bank Holiday Treat.

By Edward 'Ted' Llewellyn, as told to John Spiers.

"Rich are the diligent, who can command Time, nature's stock! And could his hour-glass fall, Would, as for seed of stars, stoop for the sand, And by incessant labour, gather all." WIlliam Davenant.

Dateline *'Bank' Holiday Monday, August, Brighthelmstone, S.E. England.*

It was the best Bank Holiday we have ever had. If yours wasn't a good one, we can recommend 'The Heritage Hospital Experience.' It's a winner!!!

We visited 'The NHS Past,' thanks to the Countess of Wight, the former Mrs. Bottomley. We spent a day in one of the 'Heritage Hospitals', which she saved for the nation. So that we can always see again what the NHS was like before the genuinely market-led reforms changed it all. It was just like a day at Madam Tussaud's! Or like what happens to Scrooge in *A Christmas Carol*!

Funny, really, as our favourite NHS 'Grand Dame' once said that she was not in the business of preserving hospitals in ancient buildings for their own sake. But there they are, giant beacons to 'caring', concrete and glass behemoths, passionately preserved alongside the Gothic churches, the Georgian terraces, the splendid country houses, and Denys Lasdun's National Theatre. The Mirror of the Big State.

Our day-out started badly, but ended well. Every parent dreads, bank holidays. Glumly wet again. Long-range forecasters triumphantly accurate. Ozone depletion. Gulf-stream diversion. Volcanic eruptions. Meteor near-misses. Only ice-prancing on the tele. And a second decade of wet Mondays in August. So...what to do with the kids – with our ever-questioning Mensa-quality Ophelia (seven), and our lovable rugger-playing Toby (nine). They've already done the lot. Euronetdisney. GatesWorldNet Flip. Parent-Steward Voucherday at Tebbit-talk Radio. Howard-prison-shackle-Half-Marathon. The Silent Knight Sir Nickelodeon Pass-the-Pension Chauffeur Big Car & Expenses Game. And *still* they're chasing us for action.

What to do? We don't want to be 'fail-jailed' by the Parent-Surveillance Agency. Nor are we keen on being 'net-nabbed.' So, family fun it must be! Poryphia (the wife) tells our Gopher to search the pages of the *Net-Times* for likely escapes. Not too far. Not too dear. And no picnicking.

White-Water-World-Mars-dome? Nope, too far. William Morris Icelandic Poetry and Cave Day? Nope, done that twice with your Mother. Zoo? Nope? Still un-PC, though I'd love to see a Coelacanth. *[Now available in the Emerton-Welling Twin Building at Whipsnade. June 2015.].* And *nothing* like the real thing, as I remember when I was seven at Brighton. But what about this one – THE HERITAGE HOSPITAL EXPERIENCE." ??? Looks possible??? Yes???

It's about those places preserved by the Countess of Wight when she was Minister for Fun. You know, like that one with the slogan 'Unchanging Care in an Hostile World.' Good old Ginny – not like this present lot – a *real* politician who genuinely cared. We could do with her now. And she did show how incredible those places still were in the early 1990s, before the Milburn Reforms. And before this new lot came in. I remember that *Today* interview from her *Land Rover* on the M25. Stunning! Very quotable. Give her credit when it's due – it was an idea of genius, preserving these Hospitals like this. Keeping a dozen old hospitals open just as they were before the Milburn reforms. Stuck in mid-90s aspic (and *Dettol*). Staffed by actors, like those American villages with '17th century settlers', people trained to pretend. Learned the jargon, and all that.

Just imagine! Oh, how easily people forget!!! Still, it is hard to believe, really, that it used to be possible to be called into such a hospital without knowing in advance who was to do your operation (or when). Or whether the doc was any good at it. Or what other results had been. Or what it really cost. Hospitals were not even PA approved. No Lilley/*Which* Manager Mark. No 'My Daughter' Test – of where top docs would send their own kids. Remember, too, when there wasn't even a Virtual Reality Health Council, like the one we now use in Boots the Chemists? *[On the net, now, of course].*

Kids ill? You couldn't check with patients like you in advance. Terrible lottery. Of course, took one Lottery Queen to spot another though. You have got to admire what she did, that Ginny. But then she always did have flair, and she *did* care about patients. A wonder, really, that they ever let her near the NHS! Like letting a Christian be an Archbishop! Or a socialist lead the Labour Party [*pre-Marxist Corbyn!*]

So we bought a family ticket, and became 'Day Cases.' We had no idea what to expect!

First, we had to apply to the local NHS out-patient's by post for the ticket. A real old-style ticket, too. Small piece of white card, with duplicated text, in what we later learned was deliberate preserved 'Heritage Experience' language: "Dear Sir/Madam. Best Heritage Experience in The World. Best health service in the world. Envied by every other nation. We meet all Patient Charter Standards (Chartermark, 1998). Your appointment is at 10. a.m., Bank. Hol. Monday. Out-pats. Heritage Hosp., Brighthelmst. Signed, Lord 'Owzat. [Illegible]." No map attached. *[This is long before satnavs, and WristWhiozers].*

WHATEVER CAN WE DO WITH THE KIDS TODAY?

The card [NHS Ref.No. %64892000762/*] had boxes to tick on the reverse side. We found out why later when we did 'The Charter Experience' on site, and were moved from one waiting area to another. We then were told we had 'Been Seen', and now please wait here another hour. Had to stand. "All this realism is a bit much", said Toby.

Our shocks began right at the very start. Heritage Hospital – where *is* the place? First, we found that we would have to drive *into* town. Get that! Unbelievable. But in those days people went there all the time. We locked all doors. Then we realised that Heritage Hospitals are *supposed* to be hard to find. This one took some finding. Porfie remembered that her father, old Brigadier Gunby-Noles, once drove over the day before his op. to see if he could find the hospital. And he couldn't.

But we get to the town centre. Bent black-and-white sign (old metal; no interactive screen): "To Hospital (No A&E)." Toby and Ophelia start to giggle – '*Are we There Yet?*' Toby asks, 'So what do you do if symptoms persist?' '*Ring Dalrymple!*' the wife says. We both shout to the grumbling kids – who would have preferred to go to Rubic'sCubeVille – 'Shut up you two! We're *Nearly* There....'

But here has really begun the Heritage Hospital Experience. Five hospitals in the town. But which one do we want? Ticket is no help at all. It's a patient initiative test, just like the old days. We aren't told which one of the five we 'need.' Only one has an Out-Patients department, where all Heritage visitors have to begin. But which one?

Inducted! Welcome to NHS [or N£sd?] Snakes & Ladders! Off we go! In for a penny, in for a pounding!

No net–map provided. Back when, pre-WWW, you didn't even get a zoning-beam, or even a printed map. When we do find the place, it's in the back-end of town. Mostly painted magnolia. Big tower block but no name sign up high so can that it can be seen from afar. Reminiscent of those old Adams-family films on the fibre-optic. Like W.H. Auden's famous face, it looks very lived-in. Golly, there used to be *hundreds* of these places! *[Taxpayer's Ahoy!" – Facey Romford, Jr.]*.

At the entrance there's a kiosk. With no sign except 'Hospital Management Committee.' A man sits there, smoking. He ignores us. An actor, of course. But good. Very good. After a couple of minutes he puts down his picture 'paper (*The Somefink*). "Yeah, wot?" he greets us. Traditional greeting, it seems. So charming, and so realistic. They really do try, these Heritage people. Actors, of course. Only pretending. But very realistic. Well-rehearsed, evidently. Then we get another surprise. Yes, we *have* got a ticket. But no, we *can't* come in. "You're in the wrong place mate." Apparently, "They all do it."

We discover that we can't just park, walk in and ask to see a generic health-worker or a doctor of our own choice, as based on the conventional *Lilley Mediprompt Netsearch* and *Dr. Foster's Good Doctor Guide*. Not likely, chumee! We have to go back a lot more than three spaces. We have got first to go to 'a GP.' Porfie remembers those from when she was a teenager. They were some sort of specialist-generalist, who rationed care for the government. Open 5 days a week, but for short hours. Shut at weekends. You had to be referred by them to a Hospital and to a consultant. Like being packed up in a parcel and posted off to someone they had been in college with. Or a golf-partner. They were a sort of predecessor of Individual Patient Fundholding. But they controlled "your" [sic] budget.

So we go back the required several steps. When we do manage to 'Pass Go', we are told to pretend that three months have passed. All this takes until mid-day, in our Heritage Experience Day Out.

Kids by now already very tetchy. But even then we get back to the kiosk we can't get in. The original bloke has gone. No note like 'Back in 10 minutes.' No guidance to anyone else. And there's no scanner-entry, no Digi-Gene PRC, and this is years before the now usual Digital and Generic Patient Record Card with all our medical records, held by us like our credit cards. None of that. So we have to be "processed" somehow. But where, and how? A porter ambles by, and lets us in past a wooden barrier. Another actor. And we then park our own car and pay to park it. If this is what it was really like, small wonder that the Ray Rowden Patient Courts were always in session!

We arrive, *eventualement*. At what we are told is Square One. Main entrance Hall. But most prominent notice is 'The Board', with photos, and a small shop full of crisps and Coca-Coker. Whackered by now. Tearful, fed-up kids. But at the postponed start of our day. We see lots of people – actors, of course – wandering about. Some smoking, in their pyjamas. Some with a leg strapped up behind, to look like amputees. Smoking heavily still. And this place created work on a big scale! There are several hundred people, hired to queue silently [*"Queue"*, obsolete term since the Lord Lilley reforms, but previously a clever BMA-gadget which enabled people to stand in-line and receive offers of private treatment. – Ed.].

People wait in corridors, lie on trolleys, sit in the A&E department [chairs there especially worn and a shambles, top doc-actors particularly rude]. Patient-actors spend hours wandering about, pretending to be lost, and clutching X-Ray images in big envelopes. Actor-Porters trained to complain to patients about management. Actor-Nurses trained to roster to suit themselves. Actor-Consultants absent in private rooms at other end of town. 'Cept a few in another large Study Centre, voting against everything and everybody. Operating rooms lying idle. And much unutilised capital equipment. Chief Executive "at lunch." It *is* very well done.

Indeed, it *is* a clever time-warp. No uniformed greeters, with 'Ask Me" buttons. No change-machines for parking [all stolen]. No Victorian post-box [stolen; sold on the net]. But we stop and ask a flustered looking man where we need to be to start with. His badge declares him to be 'Dr. Bogstandard Meddler.' A Senior Doc. Top Man. Royal College delegate. An actor, of course. On his way to visit the Female cancer unit, which is apparently named after a man, can you believe! The

WHATEVER CAN WE DO WITH THE KIDS TODAY?

Dr. Nigel Hogbinbottle Clinic. Named by unanimous local consultants after one of their retired colleagues. What kind of message is that? But we are directed by this nice old duffer, standing under an entrance arch, to get 'kitted-up.' We stand by a machine dispensing 'Trust-Fed Cola', and are given little white coats to wear. He also gives us little leather boxes *[called wallets – Ed.]* with old-style metal coins, which we will need if we want to replenish our drinks later. If the machine is in working-order.

Now our guide arrives, puffed out. His badge says he is 'Cllr. Alfie Peardrop, B.Com, Chairman.' Another figure from the old days. Something like a doorman or cinema Commissionaire. But appointed by central government, and paid £25,000 a year for working two days a week. We learn that he also ran 'The Strategy' locally. Apparently, every pre-reformed hospital had one. They even paid him (usually a him). But the job was really a reward for other political work done. OBE usually added later. Each Heritage Hospital now keeps one, together with a suite of half a dozen 'Non-Executive Directors.' *[Work done by these never ascertained, but paid £5,000+ pa. – Ed.]* There was also a Medical Director on the hospital board. *[Doctor's shop steward. Usually not a very high-flier doctor otherwise – Ed.].*

We asked one of the actor's labelled on his yellow and blue badge 'NED' what he did. "We do management work by wandering about. This is what they did before the Consumer-led New Health Service came in." Here, at our Heritage site, they still do it, and are much-photographed. We get to take a nice pic with the Chairman and the kids *[Taken by an actor – pre-selfie. Ed.].*

We got the children to play "I Spy Oddities." We've already noticed many oddities. No valet parking. No kimono-style welcomers in an attractively planted Arrival Atrium. No customer-relations interactive consoles. No art. No soft music. No smiles [discouraged]. No aromatherapy. No obvious notices to the loos. But plenty of paper-covered, peeling and neglected sellotaped notice-boards. Apparently, a *real* sign of an NHS facility in the old days. Remember, these *were* the old days. Before the David Green Act for Cost-Conscious Choice. Before the Finkelstein Public NHS Information Act. Before the Roy Lilley Digital Commission on Clinical Improvement and Patient Access. Before Advance Accreditation of procedures, doctors, costs and expected outcomes introduced by Lord Lilley. Before the Facey Romford Young Manager of the Year Awards. Instead, we confront the old Load Your Trolley and Fight Your Way There system. Just as it was before Advance Accreditation of Procedures, doctors, costs and expected outcomes. Just as it was before the Dr. William Pickering Independent Clinical Inspection Board. It's still the world of those old supermarkets and these old NHS medical centres. It is *indeed* a Heritage Experience!

As we walk around we see the roadways and corridors named after old managers and managerial obsessions: 'The Welling Building'; 'Re-engineering Avenue', 'Radical Re-appraisal Terrace', 'PFC Square', and 'Clinical Improvement Unit [Closed]', the Emertonks Sitting Bull 'Be Personally Ambitious' Garden Sheds; the Klingfilm Fund Cats & Dogs crèche, sponsored by Bugginsturn PLC. All now hopelessly obsolete, of course. But evidently, this big place, which had beds and carried out virtually everything on a single site, apparently was the first deserved winner of the 'Plastic Dodo Award' for special architectural achievements in the 1990s. We see it won the award 9 years in a row. No wonder its Chief Executive, a Mr. S. Bludgeon, went on to such great things!

Cllr. Peardrop, our pretend-Chairman, then takes us through our choices for the day. As he talks he tells us that we have to *stretch our imaginations*, to get the best from our day out, to get *into* the box!" Imagine a happy and relaxed time," he says, "when you could smoke and drink and do the drugs all you liked, refuse to exercise, eat junk food galore, cook no vegetables, ignore fruits, and still expect other people to pay the healthcare bills!" *[Taxpayers Ahoy! –Facey Romford, Jr.].*

Imagine a time when no-one asked you about your preferred outcomes in advance. Oh Lord! I do *try hard*! But it's not easy! I ponder while he prattles on, with his *Health Service Jungle* magazine blather. But just think of not being asked about quality of life at all! Or of not being spoken to as a person! Or being spoken *about* as if you were not sitting there in the room! Or not knowing whether the doctor was trained, and when retrained. Or having no say in what happens to you next. "Really," he adds, "I know this is a tremendous challenge for you, and especially for children. But it stretches their minds."

We walk with him. A bit befuddled by now. It's all *too much!* But we just about manage to keep the children with us by regular supplies of Maltesers, and promises of ice-creams "Soon!" Past the 'Consultants only' car-park (empty today – they are busy helping with the Private Practice Heritage Experience in Hove, where no actors are trusted to do it properly).

The 'Chairman' tells us we should not miss the Waiting-list experience. Here, a medical secretary is put in charge of us. But this is not recommended. Usually, this is cancelled at least once, after you have travelled, and then twice if you come in the middle of the night. We could usually have done the 'Unnecessary X-Ray by Junior Docs Experience', but this one is presently suspended as a service. It is in process of being re-considered by the Heritage Improvement & Endorsement Commission *[Chair, Baroness G. .A. Emerplonkii – Ed.].*

It is reported as too chillingly realistic, and still quite current. But, hesitantly, we enrol for the 'Unsupervised Junior Doc' and the 'Junior Doc Working Beyond Knowledge and Capacity' events. Two similar experiences, in which some volunteers are anaesthetised. Some visitors choose the 'Medical Training Experience', to try to become "good clinical material" for the future. To do that course properly, you need to book yourself in on a Saturday or a Sunday evening, when there are no senior docs in the place. Then a lot of people – especially if pensioners – are asked to lie still on trolleys, and 'Play Dead.'

Meanwhile, some visitors today visit the jargon side-shop. Some go off to the Purchasing Experience – where, to win a soft-toy you have to try to guess within 50% of the costs you spend when compared with 75 other then current NHS hospitals, all of whose spending varies by several hundred percent, it seems. Not many Teddy Bears are won.

But that Purchasing Experience seems to be a long car ride to the hospital HQ, in the middle of the area where nobody lives. Everyone is getting tired by now. Some go to the disabled lavs. where once sat down you can't get up again. No grab rails. No red cord to pull to signal help needed. Door won't lock properly, or, if jammed, won't unlock.

Some go to inspect the old Mixed wards, with the two in one-loos – & no doors on the loos – and plastic curtains separating the men's beds from the women's. Fancy that? No, thanks!

We *can* go to the 'A&E Experience', but it is very crowded and noisy. We don't like the look of this at all. It looks very uncomfortable. There are a lot of unattended trolleys, which look wobbly. They also often lead you to an anaesthetist's attentions. And apparently in the mid-90's they didn't – amazingly I know – publish the records of A&E teams, death rates on different days and at weekends, and the records of doctors including anaesthetists. So you don't know if you'll come round, or what might occur, and which bit they'll cut. You have to be 'half-cut', too, to be admitted at all. But it seems most people are. We meet another family, jostling along the corridors, who are on the way out from the A&E Experience. One seems rather drunk and shouts in violent language. They have had something called 'Triage.' We discover that this means they cannot be seen immediately, and are left instead to sit with old magazines lent by a local dentist.

The Chairman advises us that we should take the by now traditional wheel-chair tour. He recommends this. Wheelchair Tours began here in the mid-1990s. Apparently, he started it, in 1993, to demonstrate the difficulties of the hospital from the patient's point of view. And as a consequence he had to leave for a while. Chair probably trod on a few doctor's toes?

This is clearly a very special and totally unchanged Heritage site. Chosen, we suppose for truly encapsulating everything we would otherwise have all forgotten. Toby tries this wheelchair tour. He tells us later that it begins when he can't get in the entry door to the hospital unaided. There is no slope up. The automatic door isn't. The revolving door is too small.

Then there are the porters. Good actors these! They are very believably rude. Uncouth, even. Surly, resentful, not glad to be in the job, even though paid for it as well. No badges, so you can't check names. Not likely! Must be realistic, after all. The lift the porter takes us into stops six inches below, or above, floor levels. I can't reach the floor choice buttons from the wheelchair. Stuck!

Eventually, a nurse-actor releases me. And then my son comes back with one of those souvenir mock newspapers – you know, "Manchester United Defender Drinks Ballarat Pubs Dry, or "Battling Gran KO's' Tyson." Toby comes back with the *Righthelmstone Bulletin* headlined "Toby Takes Invisible Hosp. Tour – Returns Alive!"

Meanwhile, we've taken our daughter – who likes cheap thrills – on another ride. We decide to stick together. We hold on tight, a bit like taking the Ghost Train ride at the fair. We eventually do select the new 'Day-Case Experience." Unexpectedly, we are whisked away on three different trolleys – separated from our daughter, just like in the old Workhouses [which part of this hospital once was]. We are trundled up what a leaflet calls "The Longest Corridor in The NHS." Apparently every hospital had one. Exposed pipes, partly rusted. Rubber-flap doors. Cracked khaki linoleum. No art displayed. Cold wind blowing in. Thin aertex blanket. Musty dressing-gown. Teeth out (if fitted). A bit too "Very Realistic" says our actor-porter. *"But never mind, eh? And I'm on double-time, too"*

So, The Heritage Hospital Experience! We all did it. *You* should try it, too. It will make you grateful for the NHS reforms, which have finally – after half a century no less! – actually *begun* to focus on *the actual patient's experience* as well as clinical quality and personal choice. That all down to the work of the Institute of Economic Affairs in Westminster. And on that, too, patients are setting out and insisting upon their own preferences. Values. Beliefs. Quality of life. Stuff I used to hear about vaguely from my Dad, when I was still a schoolboy at Muffles Primary. Grateful now!

Of course, I know that if all this had *really* been real I would have had to book two and a half years in advance. But we benefitted from another kind of reality which we contributed ourselves to the truth of the experience. Porfie's Uncle Perceval is head of something or other in Medicine in Cambridge. And on the national executive of the Royal College of Vested Interests which I read about in that *Facey Romford Papers* book. [1] Still, you probably know someone like it, too? Goes to Great British Whitewash PLC meetings, too, when in 5-star hotels in good resorts.

Anyway, to our surprise the kids actually loved it. I would not have thought so. Not with all that messing about in cubicles, being fitted up in funny nylon shirts loosely and partly tied at the back, being shuttled about between departments, lost and found, asking people the way, nobody answering, or knowing, no-one communicating, time no object, no sense of pace. And then trying to decipher mysterious signs, all initials, signs all meant for staff but not for patients, odd words. AND nothing priced of course. So everything available except what you really want, which is to be treated as an individual and to be sure of a personalised, timely and effective service.

As we leave, we are confronted by a very plum bloke. "AND where are the bloody antibiotics?" he demands. As if *we* knew!

Toby, bless his inventive little soul, took it upon himself to help him by breaking the computer code and getting into the superplush management suite via his WristwhizzTop.. Coo, Just like a display room at Harrod's, it was! And once in there Ophelia couldn't resist all those chances to stick up her own out-of-date hand-written notices with blue tack and sellotape. But I told her she would have to do better than that. I didn't think anyone would notice. Next time she said she would put on a white coat, stick her fingers in the pockets, and stomp about. No better, alas. Must have a word with her teachers.

For myself, I spent days afterwards worried about Porfie. Apparently, her actor-consultant had bed-blocked her. So she couldn't come home. She couldn't be discharged for five days! In Heritage Hospitals, apparently, consultants own the beds. And social services locally had no money, and no staff to help her. So she had to stay bed-blocked.' Porfie says that a consultant's own name was above her bed. Instead of her own name. Decidely odd, but realistic apparently. And there was no one allocated to look after her at home, if discharged. So *not* discharged.

Credit where it's due, though. They *do* go to every length to re-capture every little detail of past NHS reality, all that the reforms have swept away. So we're grateful to the Countess of Wight. We know how lucky we are. But we're keeping up our Top-ups, and Catastrophe Insurance cover, and our 'Singapore voucher' payments. Just in case that Josef Corbyn wins an election!!!

Still, you've got to admit it. Ginny did succeed as Minister of Fun. She got the previously unmanaged Heritage Business into consumer-focussed shape. National Trussified. English Heritedged. She directed National Lottery funds where they did the best job. She involved everyone. She did that, too, of course, with these Saved Hospitals, backed up later by Lord Havant of the Banks. So, if you seek her monument, look around you.

But for me, just one dose of a Heritage Hospital will last me, thank you. Next Bank Holiday I might manage to get to the zoo, after all. And the children can try the Gillian Sheppard Heritage Comprehensive School Experience next!

As if....

NOTES.

1. Facey Romford, Jr., *The Facey Romford Papers. Days in The Life of the NHS. An Everyday Story of N£sd Folk*. With a Preface by Roy Lilley, and an Afterword & Commentary by Soapey Sponge VII (Brighton, Edward Everett Root, Publishers. 2015).

NB. *21st Century OED*. "Consultant", obsolete term. Medical professional. Part-time. Usually male. Retired examples still employed, tenured, in Heritage Hospitals. Can be booked in advance. As historically accurate, will not listen to you, and then give their "expert" opinion. Recognition signs include bow-ties, golf clubs, and special handshakes. NB. Patient's entitlement to second opinion a legally enforceable right under Millburn Rules, 1992, following Robinson Report on the NHS Complaints System and Patient Redress, 1998.

THE KEY MESSAGE:
28. Changing the rules, to achieve change...

"As the circumstances change, institutions need to adapt. What matters therefore is for institutions to have the agility to change as circumstances change. It needs not only rules that determine how the economic game is played, it needs rules to change the rules if necessary in a way that is as costless as possible. In other words, it needs meta-institutions that change the institutions, and whose changes will be accepted even by those who stand to lose by these changes. Institutions [in the past] did not change just because it was efficient for them to do so. They changed because key people's ideas and beliefs that supported them changed." Joel Mokyr.

It is politicians who need genuinely to believe in the power of ideas. For the real challenge now – given all that we know about the dangerous train that is coming so fast down the track – is how can we achieve the necessary transformational change, given the short-termism and electoral fears of politicians, the entrenched positions of medical professionals, the predominance of 'public-service' trade unions, and the deliberately imposed ignorance of a population long infantilised by the NHS?

The function of knowledge should be economic and social improvement. It is ideas which open doors. Here the leading modern economist and historian Joel Mokyr has said that the rationalist Baconian Enlightenment programme was built on two unshakeable axioms. First, that the expansion of useful knowledge would solve social and economic problems. Second, that the dissemination of existing knowledge to more and more people would lead to substantial efficiency gains.

Adam Smith, too, suggested that radical breakthroughs often required an outsider, or someone from a different background. But outsider change-makers (and even insider-outsiders) are discouraged. And where has the NHS's inwards-looking information about itself led us? Until now, into cul-de-sacs in healthcare. However, the internet – which now counts as an 'informed institution' which is changing power relations – is radically amending the cultural and political situation rapidly. It, too, is The Necessary Outsider in the game. And with the regular and respected independent OECD international comparisons, too, we know much about how other nations do much better in health and social care. The OECD exemplifies what Francis Bacon called "ordered experience", the systematic and objective observation of what is really going on in health systems across the globe. This is the context in which new ideas can flourish.

The OECD and the vibrant internet – comprising many knowledgeable expert patient-bodies as well as some eccentric quacks – addresses the old problem of asymmetric information. That is, that doctors have known more than the patient. And so it has been difficult for the patient to assess the doctor, the diagnosis, the quality of care offered, and the effectiveness of clinical self-regulation as well. The alternatives of treatments that the patient might undergo have been problematic for the patient to judge. Here middle-class people have enjoyed better health for many reasons, including their ability to listen and to be listened to, the confidence to wield some cultural clout within effective networks, and being accustomed to make their own judgements about information provided or researched. Now the internet is adjusting the situation in the new knowledge-economy. This is supplying useful knowledge at ever increasing levels of sophistication and detail, and for everyone. It is changing the starting-place for everyone.

As to the existing and inherited institutional framework, it is not only that the NHS is not good enough – 'though it isn't. The problem is that what has been provided could have been much better, as other countries with broader funding and different approaches to purchasing and to provision demonstrate clearly. Yet this level of care still can be achieved in the UK if we pursue radical changes now. But this will require political leadership which takes on persuasion as *the* major task. It will require conviction, and determination.

The OECD provides the material on which to base reforming arguments and new policies. As does the internet. It is essential to deploy the new information we now have persuasively, and with conviction about what else might now be introduced to create a modern structure of broader and more sustainable funding, purchasing, and provision of health and social care.

This is all about in what a good and efficient society should consist. It is about the role of the state in the economy. It pivots on the necessary self-responsible role of every individual in their own lives. And, root-and-branch, it concerns the evolution of cultural beliefs and norms about the NHS. Here the new knowledge which we are gaining from the OECD and the internet focusses us on persuading people that what exists is not the best that can be provided. Fortunately, we have this explicit and cumulative evidence – not only in the persistent revelatory scandals of the NHS itself but with the international comparisons published by the OECD. Here the UK generally scores very badly. Many of our citizens still die too early, and unnecessarily so – notably in cancer care.

These independent international reports are very telling, if we use the information to tell the truth. And then to lead the nation towards broader funding and competitive-purchasing and competitive-supply solutions. We also have our own recent experience of the efficiency and effectiveness of individual social-care and mental-care budgets, and the public support for these by those who have experienced them. Thus far, this lesson has been wasted by politicians. And so the concept needs to be rigorously extended and much more fully funded for all acute and also routine community care.

The location of the boundary between what government should do and what the free market can do is, of course, a matter of dispute, and there is no consensus. I suggest that a key role for government in effecting real changes is to gather, organize, and publish systematic and reliable information that can be used by the public – both as individuals and in democratic and competing Patient Guaranteed Care Associations purchasing care on behalf of the individual holding a Health Savings account. Government has a strategic and co-ordinating role, and we should discuss its functions here, and its limits. But the critical mover and shaker must be individual tax-based funds.

It is essential, too, that the changes proposed achieve legitimacy, in an area of our society where myth is in charge and where politics is in the way of change. As Mokryl shows, in the past Britain has always been fortunate in that its institutions have always been flexible, and have changed as circumstances demanded. This agile capacity to dismantle failing, wasteful and costly structures and to adapt to radically changing circumstances has over time led to many improvements. These have previously allowed the growth of useful knowledge, technological and economic advance, and sustained social developments. Indeed, new technology has often been the prompt. The role of the market has been pivotal, too, in generating this modern economy. We need again to free the creative forces it encapsulates. We need to give positive signals to innovators, as the whistling train – *Ready or Not!* – comes so swiftly down the track. If we do not do so the existing NHS structure will fail further than at present, and we shall have nothing to put in its place. Major change now will be less disruptive than doing nothing. And many lives can be saved.

Reform will not be easy. However, as a society we have long been fortunate in having the kinds of open and flexible institutions which have been suitable both for growth and for change when it was required. Here, as the economist Joel Mokryl says, the existence of the *meta*-institution of Parliament enables us to change the rules of formal encounters. In a parliamentary democracy the government has the power to lead change, or to reflect changing public opinion. And so we can achieve reforms without revolutionary violence. This political structure thus enables us to make changes which are adaptive, and at relatively low-cost (compared with violent revolutions elsewhere) when the need arises. A basic part of achieving a new structure of change is that a continuous process of persuasion is necessary now.

Opposition to major structural change to the NHS is usually focused on the argument that the poor will do least well. But as I have argued, it is properly functioning markets with economically-empowered individuals which have given us all better lives *in every area of our post-1945 existence*. Markets are the *only* means by which to empower the poor. If we make this change and make available tax-based personal care funds there will be genuine equality. It is markets too, which will enable us to tackle the many provider and purchaser deficits of the NHS.

I have argued against substituting one Master Plan for another, and in favour of adaptive and cumulative change over time. The distribution of individual funds to everyone is the key here, if we do indeed seek the fundamental transformations which will address the threat-points represented by the oncoming train. If we want to put the poor on the same basis as the middle-class we need to act. The challenge is made urgent by us all living longer, wanting more, knowing more about new drugs and treatments, and deploring their denial.

Most cultures have been anxious about innovations, until they have actually happened and proved beneficial. This is the tale of the 1980s. Without leadership none of these essential changes could have happened.

In addition, for more than two centuries, Enlightenment thinkers have struggled with the ever-present dilemma of how to offer poor relief, and how to combine compassion for the unfortunate with what economists have called 'incentive compatibility.' We need to maintain compassion towards the deserving poor, while using direct economic incentives to encourage everyone to do as much for themselves as possible. Health Savings Accounts, with the poor supported by tax-transfers (but with an 'excess' or deduction for consciously wasteful behaviour) is surely a large part of the answer. This is morally right, and it also helps to cope with the political environment.

Competition is essential, in a wasteful and costly 'public service' where barriers to entry have always been set up quite deliberately – by government, and by trade unions – to reduce competitiveness, and to curb demand. This has generated price-fixing, untested transaction-costs, poor productivity, inadequate weekend and evening cover by hospital consultants and GPs, and a permanently low level of competitive pressure which has deliberately protected the 'rents' of vested interests and the political fees for collaborative 'experts' who have been highly-educated, politically-aware, dexterous and clever (and almost always) men.

The power of these guilds (locally and nationally reinforced by the networking of localised mutual associations, including Free Masonry?) has been a dominant paradigm of the mal-functioning NHS. That approach implies forbidding moral overtones, and it has had far-reaching consequences. However, to address these serious deficits we need *effective* competition to improve the efficiencies of existing services, to speed up the diffusion of new techniques (on which the NHS is notoriously and shockingly bad), and to act as a signalling device both to present and to potential providers (including those for whom doctors currently do their private work). If ideas and knowledge – essential to a modern economy – can flow more easily this will favourably affect access costs, management, productivity, and outcomes. It is under competiveness that organisations necessarily re-invent themselves. Without it they do not do so. They see no need.

We know that the leading medical organisations have been skilled at extracting rents, or privileges and economic resources, by using their political and cultural power. This has enabled them to redistribute income and wealth by using their market power, and excluding that of others. And this at the expense of the consumer. Latterly, these clinical professional organisations have found themselves on the defensive, but they are still in charge. The leading medical organisations still successfully disguise their own interests as the national interest. From their viewpoint this is rational, if selfish, behaviour. But it has led to an inefficient allocation of scarce resources, and erected artificial barriers to competitive provider entry and other encumbrances which have benefited the elite provider few to the losses of the consumer-many.

What the Nobel economics laureate Professor Milton Friedman called the 'iron-triangle' of collaboration between political elites, bureaucracies, and special interests has sustained this structure, to the detriment of the consumers of services. Medical elites have thus long captured the system, achieving redistributive gains by well-organised, well-funded, and continuous lobbying. This has suited the fiscal needs of the state, with special interests granted special privileges at the expense of possible competitors and the consuming public. It has also been convenient for politicians. Thus state power has established what economists call exclusionary rents, in exchange for relative peace for politicians – until very recently, that is, with the rise of the new knowledge e-economy.

This is now having immense (and often traumatic) cultural consequences. For the NHS the whistling train is indeed fast coming down the track. This is the great global event and change-maker of our time. It has the potential to improve the clinical lot of us all. And politicians and doctors seem very unlikely to be able to evade its implications and its consequences. Instead, they should recognise that we need medical professionals and politicians to argue for a much broader base for NHS funding, for liberal market change, for competition, and to live in a new world where patients lose their fears. They and we will then live better lives. They will be able to do what they came into medicine to do. We must hope that they will be persuaded, and that they will persuade others, helping to create a willing public.

We know from economics that people respond to incentives, and we have to determine what they should be. I have urged direct individual economic controls. And if cultural and political evolution needs focussing devices, the information internet is surely it. So, too, the OECD reports. This is all providing consumers with the information necessary to be able to judge services and outcomes, as well as for us all to ask again 'who shall guard us from the guardians'?

The impact of the internet and its global information is surely the prompt for politicians at last to deviate from the accepted inherited 'wisdom' of the past, too, and to innovate anew. It is necessary for politicians to respond now, to give incentives for new investment, to enable economic exchange, to make markets work, to help determine clinical successes, and to marginalise or outlaw the anti-democratic functioning of 'private-order' institutions. Politicians need to help generate the kinds of innovation that can spur economic growth, too, for this pays for all welfare and will more fully and more broadly fund healthcare. We can take what is best from the past, and add what has missing. It is time.

The economist Joel Mokyr, in his superb study, *The Enlightened Economy. An*

COMING, READY OR NOT!

Economic History of Britain 1700-1850, cited Lord Shelburne, an avowed disciple of Adam Smith.

Shelburne told the House of Commons in 1783 that "Monopolies, some way or other, are ever justly punished. They forbid rivalry, and rivalry is of the very essence of the well-being of trade…I avow that monopoly is always unwise, but if there is any nation under heaven, who ought to be the first to reject monopoly, it is the English. Situated as we are between the old world and the new, and between the southern and northern Europe, all that we ought to covert upon earth is free trade, and fair equality."

Alas, since 1945 the medical organisations have been permitted to run distributional coalitions, 'rent-seeking', and evading market processes. They have relied on political clout and on well-funded and well-focussed noisy propaganda activities to halt or limit the adoption of different ways of purchasing and providing care. Governments have until recently decided how much to spend on the NHS, and let doctors decide everything else. Governments have here collaborated with vested-interests, to the detriment of individual consumer interests and to the possibility of much better services. Now, the lives of medical professionals, their social status and their independence are being challenged, as we all live longer, want more, know more about new drugs and treatments (which we are often still denied as "unaffordable"), and are less likely to defer. The dismantling of these ideological and vested-interest aspects of the NHS structure should be a prime target for enlightened reformers, together with the broad funding issues.

Negotiating cumulative change (and some necessary compromises?) with the doctors' trade union the BMA and the oligarchical Royal Colleges is a skill which the present Secretary of State, Jeremy Hunt MP, seems to have. There is no one-line answer to all of the inherited problems, and we are unlikely to be able to deliver a linear solution. But to enable Mr. Hunt to make progress, the existing rules within which these discussions have to occur have to be changed. The long lasting and fixed tolerance of vested-interests has to change. And new rules in the genuine public-interest of individual consumers need to be made explicit now. We do need, of course, always need the knowledge and expertise of doctors and other medical professionals. But these new parameters need to reflect the major social, technological, informational and cultural changes which the internet reflects for us all.

We need incentives and practices in production to reflect and to cope with these new realities. The existing rules which permit such industrial lobbies to function ideologically and in their own interests are increasingly dis-functional. The NHS, public-sector trade unions, and medical institutions have to change, and deeply too. The rules within which medical interests and trade unions negotiate, bargain and compromise need to be explicitly altered, and with the public educated as to why so as to assure legitimacy for changes.

Crucially, too, we need dynamist competition, with the purchaser and the provider facing the cash (voucher/Health Savings Account) consumer, to whom strong management must respond. The users of services must have the power to move their money, to abandon a current purchaser or provider and to cast their lot in with another. And we know that for a modern economy to function well purchaser and providers must exist in a motivating economic culture and themselves as organisations respond to direct incentives. This is a major deficit of the NHS at present. But if we ask for dynamism in the system we must have it in *all* its parts. However, the new knowledge which can be gained in the market will then be communicated to society through the market mechanisms. And the discovery processes of markets, the right prices and services will lead others to compete anew in the knowledge-economy – which the great Friedrich Hayek wrote of in several works between 1933 and 1948.

Of course, some regulatory interventions and oversights will be required, but we need to discuss what these should be. Certainly the proposed Independent Medical Inspectorate which the late Dr. William G. Pickering long advocated should be an essential part of the new structure. And *every* branch of NHS and social care activity (including the management of A&E departments) should be contestable. As in the wider economy, genuine and consumer-focused progress will be the progeny of such contestability. We need easier entry for providers and purchasers, in a genuine and stringent competitive market. We need improving institutions which can be instrumental to better outcomes, with the correct personal and institutional economic incentives in the system. And where the most resourceful individuals devote themselves, their time and energies to achieving the best possible care. Rather than, at present, being at least in part occupied in defending privileges, excluding competitors, and lobbying government for incumbent gains. We want health workers to face outward to consumers, not upwards to politicians.

The challenge in the autumn of 2015 by the Secretary of State for Health Jeremy Hunt concerning consultant opt-outs from so called "after hours" work crystallises this issue. The proposed contracts for 24/7, 365-day A&E hospital cover dramatizes this. This problem – revealing what economists call a serious 'supply-shock' – represents the urgent need for major change. It highlights, quite properly, the need for broader-based funding, for Health Savings Accounts, and for tax-incentives for top-up funding by individuals. Its effective resolution requires a much broader funding base for the NHS in a realistic economic model. The doctors are right here to say that this should be a fundamental element in the argument. Services should be appropriately funded. Doctors and others should be properly rewarded. But they should not be in charge. Instead, we should let the market decide.

If , indeed, we are to redeem the initial NHS promissory note of the certainty of access, equity, choice, and improved care for all then politicians need to persuade people that things *can* be made better, and that personal advantages *will* be available to every party in the reformed structure. And that improvements can indeed turn out to be successes. Again, doctors' voices will be fundamental. So, too, will be the factual debate. And the counter-factual debate, contrasting the ossified NHS monopoly experience with healthcare achievements elsewhere.

The Cameron government has already tackled some of the most long-standing difficulties in other services. Michael Gove began to deal with educational reforms, as he is now doing with the justice system. Iain Duncan Smith confronted the absurdities and vast waste of the welfare structure. George Osborne addressed public-sector pensions, as well more broadly insisting upon necessary institutional reforms, aiding the economy to adapt to new circumstances and to sustain economic growth. But the NHS, the biggest bee in the hive, remains undisturbed – and under-funded. It remains, in the main, closed to free markets. It discourages innovation and entrepreneurship. It pays managers (and Trust Chairs) large sums, but their individual accountability in a risk-free environment is slight. The function of useful knowledge is much less than it could be. This despite modern history demonstrating that the evolution of competitive and open economies have always unleashed unparalleled wealth and progress, outside the 'public sector' services.

In every policy change there are, of course, winners and losers. There are inevitably those who will fight tooth and nail to resist changes. Pivotal here is the global information of what happens elsewhere in medical services. A key to the power of doctors – together with them being able to do what we cannot do for ourselves – has been their claim to special knowledge. But this is explicitly challenged by the international facts which the OECD provides and which shows the much better clinical outcomes – in cancer care and in many other areas – which are *routinely* achieved elsewhere. It is here that government can successfully focus its arguments in favour of change. Information from every local parliamentary constituency should be published, too, with MPs actively and locally making the case. If muck is like money, most effective if spread around, then so for information, too.

The NHS, and all care services, must be brought into the genuine dynamist modern economy. The Nobel economist laureate Professor Edmund Phelps has here emphasised what he has called "mass flourishing." But this recognition of this liberal capitalist success is entirely denied by closed minds – noisily and currently represented by the proto-Marxist Jeremy Corbyn MP. He is a back-ward looking, culturally and economically damaging reactionary unaware of how wealth is created. He is oblivious to the mind-sets and mechanisms on which innovation depends. He is an out-of-date statist. However, it is the creation of wealth on which the prosperity of a people depends. We need others in public life to make the point that our modern prosperity pivots on the breadth and depth of innovative activity.

That is, on 'making a difference' creatively rather than merely taxing and spending, and angrily demanding punitive re-distribution. The emphasis here is therefore on creating rather than re-distributing. On exploring, innovating, experiencing personal growth for its own sake, as a human being. And sharing this with others in a market.

Thus, in Phelps words, "Flourishing is the heart of prospering – engagement, meeting challenges, self-expression, and personal growth...A person's flourishing comes from the experience of the new: new situations, new problems, new insights, and new ideas to develop and share. Similarly, prosperity on a national scale – mass flourishing -comes from broad involvement of people in the processes of innovation: the conception, development and spread of new methods and products – indigenous innovation down to the grassroots. This dynamism may be narrowed or weakened by institutions arising from imperfect understanding or competing objectives. But institutions alone cannot create it. Broad dynamism must be fuelled by the right values and not too diluted by other values."

The philosopher John Rawls has also emphasised the pivotal importance of self-realization. We are, after all, talking about the scarcest resource in the world – the days of our lives. We are very fortunate, too, to enjoy the economic freedoms of modernity, which have supported dynamism, innovation, and the necessary commercial and financial institutions. This is a culture which has inspired and which protects individuality, imagination, self-expression, mutual understanding, innovations, and the rule of law. We need to find solutions to health and social care within this vital and democratic framework.

We might remember, too, that – as Keynes wrote in 1936 in his *General Theory* – that in the space of one generation an economy can take a shape that was unimaginable to the previous generation. Just look at the internet. As he said, too, "the world is ruled by ideas and little else." And expediency is no longer a safe guide.

NOTES.

1. For this discussion I have drawn on my reading of essential relevant works. See Friedrich Hayek, *The Road to Serfdom*, (London, Routledge, 1944); *Individualism and Economic Order* (Chicago, University of Chicago Press, 1948); *The Constitution of Liberty* (Chicago, University of Chicago Press, 1960; new edition, 2011); *Law, Legislation and Liberty (Chicago, University of Chicago Press*, 3 volumes): Volume I. *Rules and Order*, 1973; Volume II. *The Mirage of Social Justice*, 1976; Volume III. *The Political Order of a Free People*, 1979. His volume, *Individualism and the Economic Order* (Chicago, University of Chicago Press, 1948), includes the important paper 'The Use of Knowledge in Societ.' *See also Economics and knowledge. A presidential address to the London Economic Club, 10 November 1936.* First published in *Economica* (February 1937). Hayek's *Collected Works* are being produced, under the editorship of Bruce Caldwell, in 19 volumes, by the University of Chicago Press.

2. See Arthur Seldon, *Capitalism* (Oxford, Basil Blackwell, 1990) – his masterpiece. The IEA has recently published *Capitalism: A Condensed Version* (London, IEA, 2007), with introductions by John Blundell and Philip Booth. On 'rent seeking' see James Buchanan, *The*

Limits of Liberty (Chicago, University of Chicago Press, 1975); James Buchanan and Gordon Tullock, *The Calculus of Consent* (Ann Arbor, University of Michigan Press, 1962); Douglass North, *Structure and Change in Economic History* (New York, W. W. Norton, 1981), and *Understanding the Process of Economic Change* (London, Institute of Economic Affairs, 1999).

3. Also, Joel Mokyr, *The Enlightened Economy. An Economic History of Britain 1700-1850* (New Haven and London, Yale University Press, 2009; London, Penguin Books, 2011); Edmund Phelps, *Mass Flourishing. How Grassroots Innovation Created Jobs, Challenge, and Change* (Princeton, N.J., Princeton University Press, 2013); John Rawls, *A Theory of Justice* (Cambridge, Mass., Harvard University Press, 1971); *Justice as Fairness: A Restatement*, edited by Erin Kelly (Cambridge, Mass., Harvard University Press, 2001); Milton Friedman,. *Capitalism and Freedom* (Chicago, University of Chicago Press, 1962) and Milton and Rose Friedman, *Free to Choose: A personal statement*, with Rose Friedman (New York, Harcourt, Brace, Jovanovich, 1980).

IN CONCLUSION:

29. Caveat emptor. Choice in healthcare. What does it mean? How can it be made real?

"We must get behind words, and consider the things themselves." Bishop George Berkeley.

"Chalk is easily rubbed out and put in again; ink is a permanent nuisance." D. Morier Evans.

1. The barometer of change.

The barometer of the NHS is usually set to the narrative of "stormy," and some think too often to "change." It seems now firmly set to the new reading of "choice." But to *announce* a policy is not to *deliver* it. So, as I have stressed before we need to ask "What does 'choice' mean?" This is by no means clear. We need to clarify its instrumental meaning.

We should ask, too, what are the catalysts to make it real? How can it be given a critical, *instrumental* and practical cutting edge, in a realistic framework? How can it increase the patient's sense of control – which we know has a powerful effect on the ability to respond to treatment, and which aids the speed of recovery? How can it help to reduce health inequalities? How can it impact on self-responsibility? How can it help to improve positive relationships and reconciliation with professionals and service-users? How, too, can 'choice' re-pivot NHS organisations so that they all focus on the value, convenience, and customer experience of services? And how can 'choice' help to improve productivity, outcomes, costs, cultures, and the necessary competitiveness?

There are many policy problems which choice may and could help resolve. Certainly, the *idea* of more choices poses these starkly. If choice is to be *the* choice, or one of the chief priorities by which reforms are to be lead, how can this be linked to ways to increase funding? And, with popular legitimacy, help to meet inexorable new demands such as the high-costs of end of life care? And provide such needed things such as innovative cancer drugs? AND prompt very much more self-care, self-responsibility, life-style changes and the avoidance of such threats as obesity and its consequences which includes diabetes, which itself threatens to bankrupt the NHS? Cases in England and Wales have risen by 60% in the past decade. An additional 1.2 million people have thus been added to those living with the condition. More than 3,300,000 of our citizens have been diagnosed with the disease. Diabetes alone costs the NHS nearly £10 billion a year.

Can choice – together with an insurance excess to encourage life-style changes –

be politically practical, and be provided in an evolutionary manner – for example, by building on the successes of personal budgets in social care?

These issues all concern authority. Whose, over what, and how this is to be made effective.

They engage us particularly with incentives, too, both to deliver better self-care and to deter demands which can be avoided – such as damaging demands for antibiotics. Notably, if people start from the assumption that their body is their own primary responsibility.

And if more NHS rationing is inevitable then these issues ask us, too, who is to ration care, and how?

Every system rations: by price, or by delay, denial and dilution, or by regulation and bureaucratic judgements, or by longer or shorter waiting lists. These are *political and cultural issues*. The problem of choice – and, indeed, of self-responsibility – is concerned with the fundamentals of ongoing historical and political processes. It is concerned with power and who holds it. With decisions and who decides. With structures and how you change things. With cultures and their resistance. With supply, demand, incentives, and distribution. With how institutions of control (and of vested-interests) were formed and operate. With equality of access. With how the state negotiates with supervisors, agencies, and service users.

Can we solve the problems with more money? With more money, alone? Clearly, a further effort to spend our way to safety looks unlikely. And affordability cannot be escaped. If we are to 'make do' – with no future large increases in investments as a proportion of GDP, whether stable or declining – we must also mend. We must do this, in any case, whatever the level of investment. For we need a new economic and cultural understanding of how best to ensure good personal services.

These are all key issues for policy-makers as we think about resources and scarcities, values and emphases, and we confront inexorably increasing costs and demand. These are cultural, personal, and political issues concerning the definition of democratic institutions and their workings, too. And, indeed, *of how we see ourselves*, how we view the capacities of one another, how we want to live our lives, and what we think should be the role of government.

Here, we ask, too, whether the state has become more or less accessible to working people. And what are the class, regional, racial, ethnic, and gender differences and influences, too, which influence access to NHS services?

None of these are one-dimensional problems. They are factors in strategic planning and social legitimacy, as well as concerning individual personal experience in accessing services.

I appreciate of course that these issues look different depending on where you sit.

CAVEAT EMPTOR. CHOICE IN HEALTHCARE. WHAT DOES IT MEAN?

My experience as chairman of one of the largest health authorities in England, then as chairman of one of the largest NHS hospital trusts, of the South East England NHS Management College, of The Patients Association, and as an adviser at Prime Ministerial and Ministerial level, all informs my thinking, as does my personal and recent experience as an NHS patient.

Meanwhile, healthcare costs (and new opportunities) increase inexorably. In an unpriced system these can be covered either by higher taxes, direct and individual personal economic incentives – such as an 'excess' on a tax-based health savings account to deter some demand. And/or by tax-incentives to encourage more personal savings by which the individual adds to care income (which itself is a cost to the Treasury), and/or by additional insurance by the individual to supplement state cover – notably, for long-term elderly care. We probably need all of these.

You may think that much increased spending is not cost-effective, of course. But the survival evidence for cancer, for example – see *The Lancet* recently on survival rates in 31 countries, and see regular OECD reports – suggests otherwise. More money can give improved testing and diagnosis, higher clinical morale, access to new cancer drugs, significantly better survival rates. We know that an American woman with breast cancer is 88% more likely to survive 5 years in the USA than in the UK – and the American show better results too for prostate cancer, and various colon and rectal cancers.

I thus venture out onto thin ice, but with some awareness of the tensions.

In four academic books since 1995 I have consistently put the case for a tax-based system of universal coverage, to emphasise and improve equal access, especially for the poor and disadvantaged. Others have helped us, too. Professor Julian Le Grand of the LSE has shown recently in his book *The Other Invisible Hand* that people do want more choice, especially those who have little. The left-leaning Picker Institute, too, showed not only that people take up choices where they exist, but that the poor and disadvantaged want more choices. Yougov, Ipsos MORI, the British Social Attitudes Survey and the Audit Commission have each said the same.

We are thus concerned with power and who holds it. With decisions and who decides. With structures and how you change things. With cultures, and their resistance. With supply, demand and distribution. With direct and powerful incentives for renovations in institutions and in our own behaviour. With the structures of control and the processes by which these institutions were formed and how they now operate.

All these issues and factors mean that we have to think about many resources, and scarcities, values and emphases. Including, fundamentally, the resources *within ourselves*. We have to think about cultural, human, family, personal, social and political resources that allow or forbid people to exercise choices within the social and cultural system. All this poses questions about the definition of democratic institutions and their workings, and of how organisations do or do not change. Of course, we recognise that these are not one-dimensional problems.

'Choice' is concerned with what we think of ourselves, of the capacities of others, of who can do what for themselves, and what we consider to be the appropriate role of government. Inevitably, these questions pose assumptions about personality, human desires and responses, and people's insights into their motives. They involve how – by which instruments and in which situations – individuals can choose specific services, making personal decisions about treatments and preferred outcomes. They ask us to think about broad strategies as well. For example, where to build or close a hospital, and how to legitimise decisions.

The relationships between the individual and decentralised organisations, with effective *economic democracy* alongside the provision of services, and the great power of professionals remain very difficult problems concerning the relations of personal experience and social legitimacy. Here specifics of several kinds engage us with the necessity of humanity and respect for the inwardness of individual experience. And with the possibilities of individuals translating their own often tacit knowledge into leverage when, vulnerably, they face a personal crisis and want a service. It may be romanticism, but I have often been moved and carried along by the shrewdness, understanding and wisdom people have about themselves and others in healthcare situations. The successful take-up of personal budgets in social care reinforces this view.

2. Two propositions concerning how choice can work.

There are thus two chief propositions concerning how choice can work.

First, more 'citizen engagement' – whatever that can mean.

Second, to equip the individual with direct control over tax-based funds, with a health savings account, and with tax-transfers to the poor to sustain equity.

Let us look at these.

Potentially, choice is like water. It can dilute stone. It can change entire cultures. Power is the key. Money is a significant summation of power. For the service-user, or customer, there are many other factors, and these too are often summed up in the issue of who controls the money. Thus, an interest in making a choice; access to good and understandable information; advice which can build understanding; and specific economic instruments which can make self-responsible and personal preferences effective. In healthcare this mean being able to command other people's time, attention, skills, and respect. Again, personal control over money is a major lever. This is why I have urged patient fund-holding for all, with tax-based funds and tax-transfers to the poor.

Two policy alternatives pose the key quandaries. Broadly regulated 'liberal markets' or 'planning' by 'experts.' This duality is summarised in the 'problem of knowledge', and the challenges to planners to achieve both strategic investment, responsiveness to individuals, and local legitimacy. Planners are required now to undertake various consultations, but many of these seem entirely artificial, and intellectually false. Here, too, organised groups press the planners hard. In addition, the organised, politicised individual is atypical and unrepresentative of the scattered and the silent. Quite rationally, few of us wish to spend our time sitting in draughty halls and in consultations about service formulation and configuration. But we each want a personal, individual, separable service when we want it.

Politics, or local consultations with the engaged citizen only empowers the organised, the noisy, the vocal, the pressure-group and the vested interest. Whereas markets empower the silent, the dispersed, the unorganised, those without 'cultural' or class clout. If, that is, the individual has control of tax-based funds which ensure fairness, equal access, and one people in one market – demonstrated clearly with the recent revolution (and equalities!) in eye-care in the High Street.

And so it should not be a necessity to be an activist in order to impact on the provision of services. In a struggle between pressure-groups this is in any case itself a beggar-my-neighbour structure. My lung operation is your lost prostrate operation.

So if individual choice and empowerment is to be real then it must surely be about effective transfers of economic power by which to enable effective individual choice, to discover demand, to redistribute scarce resources, and to achieve supply. The argument here is that in financially- empowered markets there is a daily incremental referendum to which providers *must adjust*. In the absence of this structure planners struggle with the problem of knowledge, of how to gather information about preferences and to re-shape services.

As I have suggested earlier, much of the necessary individual knowledge is itself tacit, and genuinely unfathomable until the individual is presented with a personal crisis. The individual often only then discovers this significant tacit knowledge of themselves and their preferences. They then have to try to make their own trade-offs about their own preferred outcomes. Often, too, making choices we might not make for ourselves, as research on the choices actually made by real patients concerning possible treatments for breast cancer and prostate disease, as research at the King's Fund by the pioneering Dr. Adam Darkins and others has shown.

This kind of specific, individual and urgent personal choice is very different from the diffuse, infrequent and elusive possibilities of being able to occasionally to try to discipline a system once in a while by processes of 'citizen engagement' [beloved of The King's Fund language, but whatever that means!] or by infrequent voting. By controlling funds – as the middle classes know well – you really do control a personal choice. Or at least the chance of choosing. Money talks and preference walks. To achieve individual leverage about a specific treatment or possible outcome control of an individual fund is the genuine lever. It is the most effective prompt to managements too.

Consider language, and the values and assumptions it encapsulates. We need to be much clearer about what politicians of all parties mean by effective choice, and the propositions underpinning their declarations about 'choice.' And how it is to function *instrumentally* in terms of improving access to better public services, as well as achieving other necessary ambitions concerning the much needed improvements in productivity, lower costs and better outcomes.

As the Cambridge philosopher G. E. Moore warned, "Before you begin building these great systems, let us make sure what the bricks are made of." Or, more colloquially, what does it say on the tin? And we should ask if health services deliver this? Here, language itself presents many barriers, evasions and diversions, as Professor George Jones of the LSE distinguished in his paper in *Public Management* in April 2008. He considered the words and meanings of citizen, client, consumer, and customer – the last of which he noticed as being the only genuinely empowering instrument for individual choice.

We need to take the strictures of a great Welshman, Raymond Williams in his book *Keywords*, very seriously and examine the 'keywords' used in the choice-debate, and their cultures. Words and attitudes to them are not merely descriptive. They are indicative of forms of thought and of assumptions, whether statist or dynamist. The issues are 'who decides who decides'? Who is to take responsibility, and for what?

What, for example, does "passing power as close as possible to the people" *actually mean*? Something, or nothing? Functional, but for whom? What is meant by "people"? Is power to pass back to the individual, or to another collectivist summation of "the people"? What does "as close as possible" mean? Is it that there is nothing closer than an individual's own hands in wallet or pocket? Does it mean this? Or something else entirely?

Who decides what is possible? Is choice a proxy for something called "the new localism" – with powers delegated to local bodies? Thus choice as "community," as minorities voting, as vocal pressure groups grabbing more resources in a continued beggar-my-neighbour process? What does having "a say", even "a greater say", amount to in practice? Returning financial power to the individual is *not* the same as passing powers to local government, itself typically elected in low and apathetic polls, nor to other such bodies, nor to local 'experts,' nor to other "representative" agencies or gate-keepers such as Primary Care Trusts and their Commissioning Group replacements (which function as cartels and as rationing bodies.)

'Citizen-engagement' is the established and officially preferred consensus, which in opposition David Cameron said he would endorse if in government. Contenders for the Labour Party leadership in September 2015 have made similar assertions. Critics of this view, however, see this kind of consultation and engagement as actually *disempowering* for the individual. And the language used is often meaningless at worst, or very limited in its ambitions at best. It encapsulates the Webbian tradition of "expert" leadership and control, of others knowing our interests better than we know them for ourselves. It offers *any* wheeze that politicians (of all parties) can think of *except* giving individuals power over money. It also reflects dangerous and discredited notions of vanguard Leninist leadership and its disastrous and brutalising historical experience. Consultation with patient expert groups, and in local meetings, may contribute something. But local managers may or may not react to this. And it certainly does *not* empower the individual.

The second proposition is to equip the individual with direct control over tax-based funds, with a health savings account, and with tax-transfers to the poor to sustain equity. Here, our recent experience of personal budgets in social care has been revolutionary. Its pilots and demonstration effects are dramatic. If the elderly, the disabled, the house-bound, the chronically ill can control their budgets, then why not all, for *all* health and care services? This offers, too, I believe a positive and constructive practical way forward. If the NHS adopts Nobel prize-winning economist Professor Kenneth Arrow's recommendation that the key to successful reforms is to adjust the starting position, this is what we should do. These funds do just that. This shift gives the service-user – irrespective of income or class – the financial power and free choice which has otherwise and for more than half a century been denied to the individual in a system which has deliberately and systematically suppressed price, choice, information, and competition.

Personal budgets have seen successes for the disabled and the elderly in social care at home, who some might have thought less able to manage the innovation for themselves and their families. Such budgets have placed the poor in the same position enjoyed by the middle-classes. Indeed, there is no greater reality check than a cheque. Or its absence. Cash-ebb, not cash-flow. This changes attitudes, managements and services.

Lord Darzi's year-long review of the NHS urged an incremental shift, with users of acute services to be similarly empowered. The West Midlands RHA has a pilot project concerning acute care and personal budgets. The PM has said that 15 million patients with chronic or long-term conditions should have access to care at home, and a budget they control.

I have suggested that the mobility of money is the key, with tax-based individual funds as the guardian of the market.

First, the individual must have control over a personal, mobile, tax-based individual Health Savings Account.

Second, this could only be spent by taking the fund to one of a number of competing, member-controlled mutual and cooperative purchasers of care. Not spent on lottery tickets. Spent only on a health fund. I have called these purchasers Patient Guaranteed Care Associations.

Competing purchasers – democratic, mutual, and member-owned – would attract willing members and wiling revenues. Suppliers would be obliged to seek (and retain) these willing revenues.

The well-known Rand Corporation study showed as long ago as 1986 that when cash comes into the picture, provider behaviours change. GP Fund-holding in the 1990s, and now personal social care budgets, have shown the same. They also increase the flow of information, advice and advocacy. These new purchasing bodies could encourage more imaginative provision. They would give every individual a personal stake in the organisation. They would, too, negotiate more self-responsibility, encourage a local sense of belonging, and a genuine sense of mutuality as effective institutions of local democracy.

Where large DGH's are protected as monopolies – by geography, as in much of Wales; by the clustering of specialists in A&E; by the exclusive validation of doctor training – we need the contestability of management.

Health Savings Accounts held by every individual irrespective of income or class and with competing purchasers and competing providers can enable us to recover the mutual, cooperative, self-responsible, cost-aware ground of what were very significant working-class organisations lost with the growth of the centralised state.

The revival of such mutual institutions can genuinely empower the individual, and achieve other elusive policy objectives: to sustain more competition, greater productivity, more sensitivity to individual users of services, greater innovation, control costs, encourage additional investment by tax-incentives, and offer much more flexible services. The consciousness of members of such competing cooperatives would, too, be made or enhanced by the functioning of the organisation in their interests. But without really powerful incentives none of this can be achieved, and the culture itself cannot be changed.

3. Cultural change:

Even though personal budgets show successes – for service-users, their families, and for staff – many within the NHS still resist its wider applications in acute services. This is our old perennial policy friend the problem of cultural change. It is cultures which shape who we are. It is cultures which form how we give service. It is culture which exercises the most significant roles in structuring, sponsoring or obstructing long-term changes. And if we are to have effective individual choice then there must be permission to change, and people have to believe that this is real. There must be powerful messages, including direct incentives and rewards, which are not only financial.

Culture is, of course, always being formed and re-formed. Culture and society, in Raymond Williams' and E. P. Thompson's terms, is central to our "social being", with its emphasis on consciousness as active thought. And so NHS staff ask themselves what is ominous and what opportune, for the individual citizen and for themselves? Are the likely changes in culture positive, or not? What will happen to my job, my income, my family? Can I cope with new and major change? If you like, in the vernacular, "What's in it for me?"

Financially-empowered individual choice is not an easy option. It asks people to adopt new practices. To share new understandings. To adjust to new relationships. To endorse new realities. To believe in them. To work with them. Or to deny them. To resist them. To decry them. The most necessary cultural change is to involve people willingly in new engagements. This is one of the hardest things to achieve. For cultures serve as repositories of memories and of assumptions. To take part in change people need a different sense of 'me' before they can fit into a new sense of 'them.' Just as an organisation's culture flows directly from its values and ethos – representing the guiding beliefs which define it – so a new cultural and personal identity must be found in a very new context as the expectations of patients/service-users/customers are themselves changing radically and rapidly.

All this points to the need to deploy powerful and direct incentives which can both require individuals and organisations to learn and to institute and to sustain positive change. We have too, to manage the 'interim' territory of change. In the public sector, unlike with private firms, services cannot be shut down overnight. But very large numbers of staff have to be linked up to changes whilst continuing to work. It is a very difficult task to introduce dynamism and the capacity to learn anew amongst those habituated to very different ways of doing things. And to manage reluctance, or even bloody-minded resistance.

Significantly, this all concerns *permission to change*, and the political and social acceptance of service variety and local variation. It is a major policy challenge to support the belief that change *can* happen, and that it will be permitted and approved. Long-term. Yet we need to support a well-rewarded and well-motivated workforce with permission to change, in a responsive system of enterprise and innovation, purchaser and provider pluralism and individual choice. These are a key part of the changed ethos we expect from providers and what consumers can expect from them – and from themselves. We need to open out prevailing assumptions, as we seek to support changes and to discuss them. But they are often like very old folded linen maps, with deep creases.

You cannot change a culture by a new law. Some change may be achieved by demonstrable benefits seen in pilot projects as in individual budget holding in social care. Some by persuasion. Some by powerful employee incentives. Some by contestability of services, and the replacement of managements. Some by much fuller publication of information, including reports from consumers

The key to successful change is to take people with us. People cannot be ordered to change. They have to be carried along by leadership, persuasion, and by economic incentives. The cost-benefit principle suggests that individuals will indeed take actions when they perceive that the personal benefits exceed the personal costs. In all this the NHS staff are essential partners in change. Many, of course, joined a public service, probably in part because they are in favour of socialist and imposed "equality", and against capitalist competition. They still often are very good people who do their best to give a good service, despite the often inadequate resources, and despite the deficits of their ideology.

And so all this concerns reconciliation as well as compulsion in legislation. I believe that choice can be part of a new reconciliation – replacing targets set by Whitehall from above, detailed direction, and political management. In terms of conciliation, and reconciliation we have already started to see some of the very fruitful impacts of personal budgets in social care on work-force development and on the working satisfactions of employees. There are reports by staff that direct budgets enable them to do the jobs they came into the service to do.

My proposed Health Savings Account would supply the direct mechanisms which can reliably require, enable and support competing health purchasers and providers to respond to these messages. The result can be more flexibility at work, freedom from politicised supervision, and a stimulating and creative environment. As well as significant and urgently needed improvements in preventive care – that is, if the Health Savings Account is linked directly to self-responsibility. The results can include the immediate satisfaction of the customer's wishes, and the prestige which that will bring to the provider and the purchaser. The talents of creative, thoughtful, sensitive staff in every role can, indeed, be the essential and willing complements to the technical or engineering skills of clinical specialists.

Political leaders can talk big from the centre about cultural change. But this needs to be expressed in local initiatives. These are best led, as I have argued, by direct economic incentives. It can otherwise be difficult for people to take local initiatives when there is so much politicised central direction with targets and block contracts and so much inertia or just plain political objection and fear of the electoral consequences of innovation and entrepreneurship. These attitudes conflict with necessary local variation. If we expect to enable free choice we have to have permission for variety. This will itself produce more unexpected results, new experiences in social being, and adaptive new ways in which people handle these culturally in a changed consciousness.

We have to expect, welcome, and approve such developments. Otherwise, it is problematic for people to give up power. Especially when they have always been closely accountable to those above. They are now being asked to let go, and to let things happen for which they are not entirely accountable, or to blame. Including the consequences of individual, legal, clinical decisions taken by patients. If we expect cultural change we have to give people permission to allow local differences, individual preferences, and free choices for service users. And then to survive it. Permission to be different and to adapt, in order to meet the wishes of real people living their lives, rather than "services" defined in terms of volume, block contracts, and centralised pre-conceptions.

To actually achieve these cultural changes the key is to try to show those who resist that demand-led management, greater public information and choice can achieve more for all. But for everyone to be persuaded of this will require a key cultural shift. Each group will need to give up some of its conviction that its approach – and *only* its approach – is appropriate for solving certain problems.

In such a politicised structure as the NHS and social care it is especially difficult for people to take local initiatives when there is so much central direction with targets and block contracts. And it is problematic for people to give up power. And here service users may wish to make "the wrong choices." If, however, as I have suggested earlier, we expect cultural change we have to give people permission to allow it. And to survive it.

The necessity for the NHS is to move towards such a cultural recognition of the values and value of pluralist competition, choice, wider knowledge and independent validation, checks and exposures. This will require many changes in habits, attitude, and beliefs, both in government and amongst purchasers and providers. This calls for a minute examination of every task and for the work of every staff member (including consultants – indeed, especially them) by the staff themselves to ensure that they all focus on customer care and 'customer value' or the fulfilment of legitimate choice. A debate here, of course, about legitimacy.

But I believe that this requires that customer care is *defined by customers*, and by their purchasing representatives, their formal or informal carers, their family or friends. This involves careful and aware staff selection and training or re-training. Selecting and training people with appropriate qualities. Those who know how to speak to another human being without condescension. We need the scientific skills, too. But very preferably combined with humanity. The challenge, too, involves properly maintaining the care environment – including faultless cleanliness – as I have argued in my earlier chapter, 'How Many Beans Make Five?'

It is in the culture of the NHS and in social care that the greatest and most difficult challenges lie. We have seen, crucially, how the services cannot possibly solve 'the problem of knowledge' without putting market mechanisms in place. And that without understanding this, the services invest enormous sums of money and time trying to re-organise and manage [really, to administer] a "new" but essentially unchanging structure. They invent, discuss, assess, consult, plan, counsel, forecast, confer, re-graph, re-consult, re-view, re-vise, audit, and seek to interest the un-interested and scattered public in strategic consultations, re-configurations. And in those selective 'choices' set up by officials. 'Choices' often, in my experience, set out so that managers can explain to the public how difficult the lives and choices of managers actually are.

As we have seen in practice, this does not and cannot work. The distributed knowledge necessary for adaptive reforms cannot be gathered save in dynamic and priced markets. The individual cannot be empowered by the false market-substitutes, the 'consultative' processes. And meanwhile the staff remain unrelenting in struggling to cope with unreasonable pressures – as the growing numbers of early GP retirements indicate.

And so...

IF we want to deliver the promises made by then NHS of personal access, equity, quality, constantly improved performance, guaranteed care, and individual choice.

IF we want to catch up with the many European and other countries who generate much better clinical-outcomes now.

IF we want to be absolutely sure that every individual will receive a good outcome.

COMING, READY OR NOT!

IF we want access to be legally guaranteed and legally enforceable.

IF we want this to be part of better services as well as self-responsible citizenship.

IF we want to impact on health inequalities.

IF we want to do much better than we have done by regulation or targets or bureaucratic interventions, 'participation' initiatives and 'citizen engagement.'

IF we want to improve work-force commitment, and engage staff positively and in willing change.

IF we want to achieve significant system-wide clinical-improvement and outcomes while controlling costs.

IF we want to much improve the patient experience, alter the attitudes of staff and enhance all communications and public information.

IF we want to improve what it's like to actually go through these NHS places.

IF we want to significantly improve productivity- which speeds access.

IF we all want to see Dr. Up-to-Date.

IF... IF... IF...

Then I suggest that we need to ensure that every individual has individual financial power, and that all NHS organisations need to turn outwards to earn willing incomes and to secure patients' choices.

I suggest all this can *only* reliably be achieved if individuals control money, and if there are competing purchasers and providers.

As the economist Steven Landsburg put it, "People respond to incentives. The rest is commentary."

Lastly, let me suggest that it is a great mistake to seek another 'master-plan.' Or to impose some rigid dogmatic alternative 'good' tradition. We need the surprises of adaptive, creative evolution and the power of choice and experimentation in open liberal markets from which new treatments and unexpected advances can always arise. We need also to value local differences in our engagement with the material world, as we hold too to what the historian Marc Bloch called "collective sensitivities" and fair play for all.

In conclusion, let me end with a quotation from the classicist William Hepworth Thompson, who when Master of Trinity College, Cambridge, once said, "We are none of us infallible. Not even the youngest."

30. Finale...

"A free system can adapt itself to almost any set of data, almost any general prohibition or regulation, so long as the adjusting mechanism itself is kept functioning. And it is mainly changes in prices that bring about the necessary adjustment." Friedrich Von Hayek.

*"The power of the night, the press of the storm,
The post of the foe;
Where he stands, the Arch Fear in a visible form,
Yet, the strong man must go."* Robert Browning.

*"As we surpass our father's skill, Our sons will shame our own;
A thousand things are hidden still
And not a hundred known...."* Alfred, Lord Tennyson.

Acclaim for other works by Professor John Spiers

Who Decides Who Decides? Enabling choice, equity, access, improved performance and patient guaranteed care.

"Wonderful read. As John Spiers shows, in this sprightly, erudite, concise book, when you ask the right questions, you get the right answers. He asks what a patient-centred health care system would look like and comes up with novel and pragmatic answers." – Professor Regina E. Herzlinger, Harvard Business School.

"John Spiers detailed yet fluent book demonstrates how we can achieve better healthcare for all." – Professor Philip Booth, Institute of Economic Affairs.

"[he] has the gift of presenting complex ideas clearly. This makes this book a challenging offering to current public policy debates." ProfessorMichael Connolly, University of Glamorgan.

ISBN-13: 978 184619 276 0

Patients, Power and Responsibility. The first principles of consumer-driven reform.

"If we are to get out of the current rut in healthcare delivery we need visionaries to point the way. This book is an inspirational guide to a potential way forward." Professor Karol Sikora, University of Buckingham.

ISBN: 1 85775 924 9

Both of these titles are published by Radcliffe Medical Press, Oxford.

EER

Edward Everett Root Publishers, Co. Ltd.,
30 New Road, Brighton, Sussex, BN1 1BN, England.

Web: www.eerpublishing.com
Email: edwardeverettroot@yahoo.com or jr.spiers@btinternet.com
Tel: 01825-740448.

Scholarly & relevant books by leading international authors.

We will be pleased to consider proposals for books. This is a new high-quality British academic book publisher, founded in 2015 by John Spiers.

Some initial history…
The founder of this new firm, Dr. John Spiers, was for 20 years the founder/owner of The Harvester Press of Brighton, the distinguished academic publisher of some 2,000 titles in history, economics, international affairs, politics, philosophy, psychology and literature. His firm won The Queen's Award for Export Achievement.

As with his previous company, he again stresses academic distinction, quality in production, and effective sales. His books already have international distribution and sales representation with NBN International and Compass Academic [UK/Europe/USA/Canada], and with Maruzen [Japan].

In addition to his work as a professional publisher John has held academic appointments at The School of Advanced Study in the University of London; at the University of Glamorgan, the University of Lancaster, and London Metropolitan University in the Global Policy Institute.

The new firm is already building a significant list.

John built The Harvester Press from scratch over 20 years. It then formed a group of companies sold to Simon & Schuster.

The Harvester Press published J.L. Carr's Booker-prize runner-up novel *A Month in the Country*, and the international bestsellers by Douglas Hofstadter: *Godel, Escher, Bach. The Eternal Golden Braid,* and then his *The Mind's Eye.* John's imprint Wheatsheaf Books published successful text-books. His associated imprint Harvester Microform worked with major archival libraries including the Public Record Office, The British Library, The Bodleian Library, Cambridge University Library, Harvard University Library, &c.

Harvester co-published many titles with major overseas houses, including Basic Books, Pantheon, Barnes & Noble, Rowman & Littlefield, St. Martin's Press and Westview Press. Its American academic partners also included the University Presses of California, Chicago, Harvard, Indiana, Johns Hopkins, M.I.T., Rutgers, Stanford, and Yale. Its European partners included Editions du Seuil, Flammarion, Gallimard, Sukrkamp, and Feltrinelli.

An eye for talent...
John has an eye for talent. He published J.L. Carr's Booker-prize runner-up the now modern-classic novel *A Month in The Country*. He discovered and published for the first time the now leading historians Roy Foster, John Guy, Patrick Joyce and C.J. Wrigley. He first published the initial work by Penny Boumelha and Sue Roe. He edited and published the first novel by Maggie Gee, *Dying, In Other Words*.

Details of our first titles follow...

TO BE PUBLISHED ON 28 APRIL 2016

The Complete Poems of Asa Briggs. Far Beyond The Pennine Way.

Asa Briggs.

ISBN: 978-0-9542075-5-7. Hardback.
ISBN: 978-0-9542075-6-4. e-book.

234 x 156mm. 172pp.

This is a book of 100 poems of great richness and variety. Indeed, it is genuinely a landmark book. It is an important literary and academic event in itself.

Professor Lord Asa Briggs is one of the most important historians of Britain. He is world-renowned for his work in social history, culture, and communications. He has also been a national and international leader in education, and in life-long learning.

Now in his nineties, he has been writing poetry since he was 13. But this is the first publication of this body of his literary work.

The book is an important cultural event. It will take its place amongst Lord Briggs' other classic works, his five-volume history of the BBC, his trail-blazing *The Age of Improvement 1783-1867,* and his famous historical trilogy *Victorian*

People, Victorian Cities, and Victorian Things.

The author, a vivid writer, also provides a "strictly necessary Introduction" in which he discusses his ideas about poetry and how and why he has written poetry over the years.

Asa Briggs has a very strong visual sense and an intuitive sense of place. In his work, too, he has always related literature to history. He is widely known as an effective and entertaining serious broadcaster, and his feeling for language is special.

The volume demonstrates Asa Briggs' taste, intellectual discipline, technique and literary responses to the events and people he has known during his long life, and the challenges in his life. His style is his own, although he acknowledges his interest in the works of other poets including Matthew Arnold, John Betjeman, Robert Frost, Seamus Heaney, and Dylan Thomas.

He grew up, in a working-class family, in the West Riding town of Keighley, and at age 16 he won a scholarship to Sidney Sussex College, Cambridge.

In his long career the author was a major influence on the development of new universities in Britain, and of education abroad too. He has been Vice-Chancellor of the University of Sussex, Master of Worcester College Oxford, and Chancellor of The Open University, of which he was one of the originators. He served as an intelligence officer at Bletchley Park during World War Two.

The poems particularly illustrate the significance of locality, of boundaries, of oral history, of the world of labour, and of the importance of language and of class. They also contemplate the particular in terms of the general. And the relationships between public and private events.

All of these elements have been an important focus for Asa Briggs and for his democratic approaches. His works, indeed, have implied the case for optimism in social progress. His life and works have greatly delineated and enriched democratic culture, together with his studies of the dynamics of economic and social change.

Advance comment on this book:
"'The traveller is me' declares Asa Briggs in the opening poem, signalling the poet's movement through time, space, perspective and language – a poetic odyssey until now kept secret. The concerns of politics and place, love, life and memory combine to make a very memorable collection, and the necessity of poetic expression for the artist is brought home most poignantly in a closing line: 'I need so much to write.'"
Hannah Lowe, named by The Poetry Book Society as one of the 20 Next Generation Poets, and short-listed for the Forward, Aldeburgh First Collection Prize, and the Seamus Heaney First Collection Prize.

"Asa Briggs, most distinguished historian of our time, for the first time lays bare the most treasured emotions of his youth and later life, in carefully wrought poems that lace together universal concerns with some poignant reminders of an earlier age. From Keighley Grammar School onwards (where his school exercize book bore the marks of his first poems) the life of a remarkable man is here recounted with diligence and grace in this unexpected, heartfelt collection. His poetic world encompasses Cambridge, Bletchley Park, Abyssinia, Guernica, Santa Barbara, Beijing, Shanghai ... before returning poet and reader to the North of England, the land of hope, expectation and memory, where he reflects anew on the great, underlying themes of time, identity and love – not only a collector's item but truly 'both a literary and a historic event'. – *Dr. Sue Roe, poet and biographer of Gwen John, of the Impressionists in Paris, &c.*

"Dreams, gardens, imagistic clarity of a Chinese kind, an optimsitic faith, close and loving partnership, connections of the kind that have long characterised his abundant historical work." – *Stephen Yeo, social historian and former Principal of Ruskin College, Oxford.*

"The many-sided historian and public intellectual Asa Briggs turns out to have yet another side, secret until now: he is a poet!" – *Professor Peter Burke, Emmanuel College, Cambridge.*

The Facey Romford Papers. Days in The Life of the NHS.
An Everyday Story of N£sd Folk.

Facey Romford, Jr.

With a Preface by Roy Lilley, leading NHS commentator, founder of the website nhsManagers.net eletter and of the NHS Confederation. Formerly Vice-Chairman, West Surrey and North East Hampshire Health Authority; Chairman of the Homewood NHS Trust, Chertsey Surrey; Visiting Fellow at the Management School, Imperial College London, and at the Centre for Health Services Management, University of Nottingham.

The author is an experienced NHS non-executive director.

ISBN: 978-1-911204-02-2. Hardback £65.00
ISBN: 978-0-9542075-2-6. Paperback £29.99.
ISBN: 978-0-9542075-8-8. e-book £25.00.

234 x 156mm. 352pp. Public Policy Series, no.2.

TO BE PUBLISHED ON 12 MAY 2016

The Turf. A Social and Economic History of Horse Racing.

Wray Vamplew

Second edition, with new introduction, epilogue, and added photographs.

ISBN: 978-1-911204-04-6. Hardback £65.00.
ISBN: 978-0-9542075-7-1. Paperback £29.99.
ISBN: 978-1-911204-00-80. e-book £24.99.

320 pp. Classics in Social History series, No.1.

The author is Emeritus Professor of Sports History, University of Stirling; Visiting Professor, Manchester Metropolitan University; Special Projects Editor, International Journal of the History of Sport.

TO BE PUBLISHED IN SEPTEMBER 2016

This Will Only Hurt A Little!
Achieving Patient Benefit and the Reform of Clinical Practice.

Dr. William G. Pickering

Cloth ISBN: 978-0-9542075-4-0
e-book ISBN: 978-1-911204-01-5

320pp.

Foreword by Dr. Phil Hammond, author of *What Doctors Really Think*, &c., and the star of TV series *Trust Me, I'm a Doctor*.

This trenchant and expert book by an experienced doctor – who has worked both in hospitals and in general practice – advances the urgent case for an independent medical inspectorate to stop a host of avoidable errors which damage patients.

Dr. Pickering draws on his many years of practice and on his later career as an expert witness on behalf of plaintiffs, to marshal both arguments and detailed evidence which support the need for major changes.

To prevent many avoidable clinical errors and to enhance clinical practice we urgently need a local and independent body in every region, free from the NHS 'brotherhood' of vested-interests yet staffed by clinicians. These local inspectors would all investigate *all* clinical practices. They would do so on a regular, normal, week-by-week basis. And thus help to prevent very many everyday errors which do so much damage to patients, and which are usually both costly and unremarked, and often disastrous to patients.

As Dr. Hammond says: "It was a brilliant idea. It was strongly resisted by the medical establishment.

"Dr Bill Pickering was a huge influence on my thinking over 15 years, and along with the Bristol whistleblower Steve Bolsin and Bristol parent Maria Shortis (now Maria Von Hilldebrand), he was the most lucid thinker about patient safety that I was privileged to meet.

"Steve demonstrated the urgent need for NHS staff to be able to speak up about NHS failings without fear of persecution, and the duty of managers and regulators to act on this. Maria lost her baby at Bristol and yet started a wonderful charity called Constructive Dialogue for Clinical Accountability, whose focus was on culture change in the NHS towards an honest, open and trusting relationship between users and staff that was truly accountable. But it was Bill who had the best idea on how to achieve this.

"Although elements of it appear in the CCQ hospital inspectors and the new whistleblowing guardians. Bill's idea was much simpler, leaner and quicker – and in my view would've been more effective. Instead of sending 80 inspectors to hospital at huge expense to invade a hospital periodically, have a lean team locally placed and charged with continuously monitoring the concerns and experiences of patients, carers and staff. This would use the frontline of the NHS as a smoke alarm to nip problems in the bad and prevent them becoming disasters. It would also dismiss vexatious complaints quickly."

ALSO FORTHCOMING

Wray Vamplew, Emeritus Professor of Sports History, University of Stirling; Visiting Professor, Manchester Metropolitan University; Special Projects Editor, International Journal of the History of Sport.
How the game was played. Essays in Sports history.

Asa Briggs, Formerly Master, Worcester College Oxford; Vice-Chancellor, Sussex University; Chancellor, The Open University.
First and Last. Reflections on Time, Place, and History.

John Sutherland and Johanna Marie Melnyk. John Sutherland is Lord Northcliffe Professor Emeritus of Modern English Literature at University College, London. Dr. Melynk is an independent scholar.
The 'Prince of Puffers'. The Life and Works of the Publisher Henry Colburn (d.1855).

C. Stephen Yeo, Formerly Principal, Ruskin College, Oxford.
Alternatives to State Socialism, The History of Cooperation. A 3 volume set.
Volume 1. *Victorian Agitator, George Jacob Holyoake (1817-1906): Co-operation as 'This New Order of Life.'*
Volume 2. *A New Life, The Religion of Socialism in Britain,1883-1896 : Alternatives to State Socialism.*
Volume 3. *Class Conflict and Co-operation in Nineteenth and Twentieth Century Britain.*

Peter Burke, Emeritus Professor of Cultural History, Emanuel College, Cambridge.
Secret History, from Renaissance to Romanticism.

F.M. L. Thompson, Formerly Reader in Economic History at University College London; Professor of Modern History at Bedford College; Director of the Institute of Historical Research, University of London, and President of the Royal Historical Society.
English Landed Society Revisited

NOW AVAILABLE

Serious About Series. American Cheap 'Libraries', 'Railway' Libraries, And Some literary Series of The 1890s.

John Spiers

Senior Research Fellow, Institute of English Studies, School of Advanced Study, University of London; Professorial Fellow, London Metropolitan University.

ISBN: 978-0-9542075-3-3.

Second edition. Published 5 November 2015. Includes illustrations of 25 series, 16 in colour.

Paperback, £30.00.

x + 1-107pp. 211 x 148mm

The History of The Book series, No.1.
This is the innovative, trail-blazing enquiry into the importance, range, and history of the publishers' series in America and in Britain, by the leading expert in this field.

From the introduction: "Wherever you look, wherever you live, whichever publishers' catalogue you open, whichever integral advertisement in a book you consider, whatever your interests, there is the series. There seems to be no issue, no concern, no topic, no theme, no adult, juvenile or specialist subject, no way of seeing, thinking about or commenting upon the world which does not have its 'series.' Every series carried its 'messages' and implied advice, targeting specific readers and market segments....It is fundamental to publishing in every continent."